HANG-UPS

Dress, Body, Culture

Series Editor: **Joanne B. Eicher**, *Regents' Professor*, **University of Minnesota**

Advisory Board:
Pamela Church-Gibson, *London College of Fashion, University of the Arts*
James Hall, *University of Illinois at Chicago*
Vicki Karaminas, *Massey University, New Zealand*
Gwen O'Neal, *University of North Carolina at Greensboro*
Ted Polhemus, *Curator, "Street Style" Exhibition, Victoria and Albert Museum*
Valerie Steele, *The Museum at the Fashion Institute of Technology*
Lou Taylor, *University of Brighton*
Karen Tranberg Hansen, *Northwestern University*
Ruth Barnes, *Yale Art Gallery, Yale University*

Books in this provocative series seek to articulate the connections between culture and dress which is defined here in its broadest possible sense as any modification or supplement to the body. Interdisciplinary in approach, the series highlights the dialogue between identity and dress, cosmetics, coiffure and body alternations as manifested in practices as varied as plastic surgery, tattooing, and ritual scarification. The series aims, in particular, to analyze the meaning of dress in relation to popular culture and gender issues and will include works grounded in anthropology, sociology, history, art history, literature, and folklore.

ISSN: 1360-466X

Previously published in the Series

Helen Bradley Foster, *"New Raiments of Self": African American Clothing in the Antebellum South*
Claudine Griggs, *S/he: Changing Sex and Changing Clothes*
Michaele Thurgood Haynes, *Dressing Up Debutantes: Pageantry and Glitz in Texas*
Anne Brydon and Sandra Niessen, *Consuming Fashion: Adorning the Transnational Body*
Dani Cavallaro and Alexandra Warwick, *Fashioning the Frame: Boundaries, Dress and the Body*
Judith Perani and Norma H. Wolff, *Cloth, Dress and Art Patronage in Africa*
Linda B. Arthur, *Religion, Dress and the Body*
Paul Jobling, *Fashion Spreads: Word and Image in Fashion Photography*
Fadwa El Guindi, *Veil: Modesty, Privacy and Resistance*
Thomas S. Abler, *Hinterland Warriors and Military Dress: European Empires and Exotic Uniforms*
Linda Welters, *Folk Dress in Europe and Anatolia: Beliefs about Protection and Fertility*
Kim K. P. Johnson and Sharron J. Lennon, *Appearance and Power*
Barbara Burman, *The Culture of Sewing: Gender, Consumption and Home Dressmaking*
Annette Lynch, *Dress, Gender and Cultural Change: Asian American and African American Rites of Passage*
Antonia Young, *Women Who Become Men: Albanian Sworn Virgins*
David Muggleton, *Inside Subculture: The Postmodern Meaning of Style*
Nicola White, *Reconstructing Italian Fashion: America and the Development of the Italian Fashion Industry*
Brian J. McVeigh, *Wearing Ideology: The Uniformity of Self-Presentation in Japan*
Shaun Cole, *Don We Now Our Gay Apparel: Gay Men's Dress in the Twentieth Century*
Kate Ince, *Orlan: Millennial Female*
Ali Guy, Eileen Green and Maura Banim, *Through the Wardrobe: Women's Relationships with their Clothes*
Linda B. Arthur, *Undressing Religion: Commitment and Conversion from a Cross-Cultural Perspective*
William J. F. Keenan, *Dressed to Impress: Looking the Part*
Joanne Entwistle and Elizabeth Wilson, *Body Dressing*
Leigh Summers, *Bound to Please: A History of the Victorian Corset*
Paul Hodkinson, *Goth: Identity, Style and Subculture*
Leslie W. Rabine, *The Global Circulation of African Fashion*
Michael Carter, *Fashion Classics from Carlyle to Barthes*
Sandra Niessen, **Ann Marie Leshkowich and Carla Jones**, *Re-Orienting Fashion: The Globalization of Asian Dress*
Kim K. P. Johnson, Susan J. Torntore and Joanne B. Eicher, *Fashion Foundations: Early Writings on Fashion and Dress*
Helen Bradley Foster and Donald Clay Johnson, *Wedding Dress Across Cultures*
Eugenia Paulicelli, *Fashion under Fascism: Beyond the Black Shirt*
Charlotte Suthrell, *Unzipping Gender: Sex, Cross-Dressing and Culture*
Irene Guenther, *Nazi Chic? Fashioning Women in the Third Reich*
Yuniya Kawamura, *The Japanese Revolution in Paris Fashion*
Patricia Calefato, *The Clothed Body*
Ruth Barcan, *Nudity: A Cultural Anatomy*
Samantha Holland, *Alternative Femininities: Body, Age and Identity*
Alexandra Palmer and Hazel Clark, *Old Clothes, New Looks: Second Hand Fashion*
Yuniya Kawamura, *Fashion-ology: An Introduction to Fashion Studies*

Regina A. Root, *The Latin American Fashion Reader*
Linda Welters and Patricia A. Cunningham, *Twentieth-Century American Fashion*
Jennifer Craik, *Uniforms Exposed: From Conformity to Transgression*
Alison L. Goodrum, *The National Fabric: Fashion, Britishness, Globalization*
Annette Lynch and Mitchell D. Strauss, *Changing Fashion: A Critical Introduction to Trend Analysis and Meaning*
Catherine M. Roach, *Stripping, Sex and Popular Culture*
Marybeth C. Stalp, *Quilting: The Fabric of Everyday Life*
Jonathan S. Marion, *Ballroom: Culture and Costume in Competitive Dance*
Dunja Brill, *Goth Culture: Gender, Sexuality and Style*
Joanne Entwistle, *The Aesthetic Economy of Fashion: Markets and Value in Clothing and Modelling*
Juanjuan Wu, *Chinese Fashion: From Mao to Now*
Annette Lynch, *Porn Chic: Exploring the Contours of Raunch Eroticism*
Brent Luvaas, *DIY Style: Fashion, Music and Global Cultures*
Jianhua Zhao, *The Chinese Fashion Industry: An Ethnographic Approach*
Eric Silverman, *A Cultural History of Jewish Dress*
Karen Hansen and D. Soyini Madison, *African Dress: Fashion, Agency, Performance*
Maria Mellins, *Vampire Culture*
Lynne Hume, *The Religious Life of Dress*
Marie Riegels Melchior and Birgitta Svensson, *Fashion and Museums: Theory and Practice*
Masafumi Monden, *Japanese Fashion Cultures: Dress and Gender in Contemporary Japan*
Alfonso McClendon, *Fashion and Jazz: Dress, Identity and Subcultural Improvisation*
Phyllis G. Tortora, *Dress, Fashion and Technology: From Prehistory to the Present*
Barbara Brownie and Danny Graydon, *The Superhero Costume: Identity and Disguise in Fact and Fiction*
Adam Geczy and Vicki Karaminas, *Fashion's Double: Representations of Fashion in Painting, Photography and Film*
Yuniya Kawamura, *Sneakers: Fashion, Gender, and Subculture*
Heike Jenss, *Fashion Studies: Research Methods, Sites and Practices*
Brent Luvaas, *Street Style: An Ethnography of Fashion Blogging*
Jenny Lantz, *The Trendmakers: Behind the Scenes of the Global Fashion Industry*
Barbara Brownie, *Acts of Undressing: Politics, Eroticism, and Discarded Clothing*
Louise Crewe, *The Geographies of Fashion: Consumption, Space, and Value*
Sheila Cliffe, *The Social Life of Kimono: Japanese Fashion Past and Present*
Linda Welters and Abby Lillethun, *Fashion History: A Global View*
Therèsa M. Winge, *Costuming Cosplay: Dressing the Imagination*
Jenny Hall, *Japan Beyond the Kimono: Innovation and Tradition in the Kyoto Textile Industry*
Adam Geczy and Vicki Karaminas, *Gastrofashion from Haute Cuisine to Haute Couture*
Margaret Maynard, *Dressed in Time: A World View*

Dress, Body, Culture: Critical Sourcebooks

Rebecca Mitchell, *Fashioning the Victorians: A Critical Sourcebook*

HANG-UPS

Reflections on the Causes and Consequences of Fashion's 'Western'-Centrism

BENJAMIN LINLEY WILD

BLOOMSBURY VISUAL ARTS
LONDON · NEW YORK · OXFORD · NEW DELHI · SYDNEY

BLOOMSBURY VISUAL ARTS
Bloomsbury Publishing Plc
50 Bedford Square, London, WC1B 3DP, UK
1385 Broadway, New York, NY 10018, USA
29 Earlsfort Terrace, Dublin 2, Ireland

BLOOMSBURY, BLOOMSBURY VISUAL ARTS and the Diana logo are trademarks of
Bloomsbury Publishing Plc

First published in Great Britain 2024

Copyright © Benjamin Linley Wild, 2024

Benjamin Linley Wild has asserted his right under the Copyright, Designs and
Patents Act, 1988, to be identified as Author of this work.

For legal purposes the Acknowledgements on p. x constitute an extension
of this copyright page.

Cover design by Charlotte Daniels

All rights reserved. No part of this publication may be reproduced or transmitted
in any form or by any means, electronic or mechanical, including photocopying,
recording, or any information storage or retrieval system, without prior permission
in writing from the publishers.

Bloomsbury Publishing Plc does not have any control over, or responsibility for, any third-
party websites referred to or in this book. All internet addresses given in this book were
correct at the time of going to press. The author and publisher regret any inconvenience
caused if addresses have changed or sites have ceased to exist, but can accept no
responsibility for any such changes.

A catalogue record for this book is available from the British Library.

A catalog record for this book is available from the Library of Congress.

ISBN: HB: 978-1-3501-9724-4
PB: 978-1-3501-9723-7
ePDF: 978-1-3501-9725-1
eBook: 978-1-3501-9726-8

Typeset by Deanta Global Publishing Services, Chennai, India
Printed and bound in India

To find out more about our authors and books visit www.bloomsbury.com and sign up for
our newsletters.

For Mr Kite

This book considers the past's influence on our present and advocates a return to first principles. It is appropriate that I dedicate it to my former history teacher, Ralph Kite. Ralph scoffed when I told him that I intended to study A-Level History. He queried why I wanted to learn 'more and more about less and less' when I told him of my plans to undertake postgraduate study. I hope the writing that follows makes my motives plain, and that he approves.

CONTENTS

Acknowledgements x

Introduction 1

1 Undress 21

2 Gender 39

3 Race 57

4 Sexuality 75

5 Age 95

6 Religion 111

7 Wealth 129

8 Violence 147

9 Shape 163

Conclusion 183

Notes 191
Bibliography 249
Index 277

ACKNOWLEDGEMENTS

Writing this book has been invigorating, challenging, upsetting, uplifting. I am grateful to very many people for helping me to persevere. I would like to thank my students, past and present, within Manchester Fashion Institute. Ideas pursued within this book have developed through the Fashion Cultures and Fashion and Society units I have convened since joining Manchester Metropolitan University in 2019: students' curiosity and willingness to embrace contentious and sensitive ideas has made teaching a joy and, I hope, the arguments of this book more robust.

Limited space prevents me from mentioning all whom I should, but I must single out Sophie Thérèse Ambler, Ben Barry, Sara Bernat, Liz Barnes, Tom Brimelow, Richard Cassidy, Georgina Chappell, Kyle Chong, Doris Domoszlai-Lantner, Joanne Eicher, Michael Elliott, Rosie Findlay, Hilde Heim, Reemé Idris, Jo Jenkinson, Susan Kaiser, Helen McCormick, Steve Miles, Barbara Nigro, Philip Sykas, Amy Ward – providing suggestions, sources, sustained scrutiny; enduring snatched conversations; stoking my self-confidence when I had (frequent) doubts; saving me from embarrassments of my own making: I am very grateful to you all for your contributions. Special and particular thanks are due to Paddy Lonergan for reading part of the book in draft from. I am also grateful to the anonymous reviewers for their supportive suggestions on the complete manuscript. Omissions and faults that remain are down to me alone.

At Bloomsbury, I have continued to benefit from the support and very great patience of Frances Arnold. My questionable efficiency has been much improved by the kind assistance of Rebecca Hamilton. During the typesetting and proof reading the diligence of Mohammed Raffi has spared me, and leaders, from many mistakes.

INTRODUCTION

Re-setting the fashion industry

'At a time of crisis, we have to think about a radical reset'.[1] So claimed Anna Wintour, global chief content officer for Condé Nast, global editorial director of *Vogue*, and editor-in-chief of American *Vogue*, at the beginning of March 2020. As the Covid-19 pandemic spread, government-imposed restrictions on people's liberties increased, and estimates on the social and economic recovery lengthened, Wintour was one of many fashion leaders to insist upon immediate and decisive change across the industry. Two weeks after she made her clarion call, Alessandro Michele, then creative director of Gucci, shared his thoughts about the state of the fashion industry and the society it clothed in a series of excoriating messages on Instagram. He lamented people's 'reckless actions' that had 'burned the house we live in'. Fixated on '[s]o much outrageous greed', he asserted that humankind had lost 'the harmony and the care, the connection and the belonging'.[2] More poetic than Wintour's rallying cry, Michele was hardly less pugnacious in claiming people, the fashion industry specifically, had gone 'way too far'.[3] In May and June 2020, open letters that summarized embryonic plans for 're-wiring' the fashion industry were published in *The Financial Times* by *Business of Fashion* and Ellen MacArthur Foundation, respectively.[4] Differing in degree, but similar in kind, the people and the proposals they proffered envisioned a fashion industry that would be more responsive to and reflective of its consumers' values, needs and circumstances. In a word: decentralized. Decentralized because the conception of garments would mirror rather than make consumer expectations; decentralized because the creation and consumption of garments would strengthen local economies and avoid unethical and unwieldy supply-chains; decentralized because the fashion industry would cease to be 'western'-oriented.

Noble and necessary, the framing of these changes was nonetheless problematic. Proposing help, the plans exposed the cultural myopia of the fashion industry. Conceived and conveyed by 'western' people embedded within the 'western' fashion industry who were conversing primarily with 'western', anglophone audiences, the statements and strategies for action appeared to treat the pandemic as cause rather than catalyst for problems that many people, especially those living beyond the 'west', had been enduring for years. Consequently, as the pandemic escalated, the credibility of 'western' fashion leaders to implement change appeared to decline in direct correlation. Three reasons stood out. First, the pandemic emphasized systemic inequalities that maintained the privileged position of people, typically white, from within the 'west' and the peripheral – sometimes persecuted – status of people, typically other than white, who lived beyond the 'west' or resided uncomfortably at its physical and figurative borders. Second, fault lines were exposed within 'western' countries, the United Kingdom and the United States particularly, as exponents with divergent values clashed over the re-configuration of their societies through 'culture wars'.[5] Fundamental beliefs about people's faith, gender, sex, their histories and memories became sites of violent exchange, conceptual and corporeal, as social structures typically taken for granted were interrogated with a passion that frequently occluded pragmatism. On the one hand, people longed for safety and psychological salve in a world turned upside down. On the other hand, people, at once vilified and valued as 'woke', wanted to catalyze change. Third, and specific to the fashion industry, the calls of people advocating most loudly for change seemed hollow, even hypocritical, because they had been among the more heavily criticized for their perceived 'western'-centrism before the pandemic.

Anna Wintour apologized to employees of American *Vogue* for not doing enough to acknowledge and 'elevate' the contributions of black people in an internal memo of June 2020.[6] Her regret was questioned because it underscored how she had not previously used her authority so explicitly to effect change. To the contrary, it was suggested that she had presided over an environment that had 'sidelined and tokenized' the place of women of colour, 'especially Black women'.[7] Quoting from André Leon Talley, a former creative director of American *Vogue*, who described Wintour as a 'colonial broad', journalist Edmund Lee averred that she had 'helped set a standard that has favoured white, Eurocentric notions of beauty' in an article for *The New York Times*.[8]

Alessandro Michele had previously described his aesthetic and design process in bombastic terms. He appeared to have little regard for the world's global cultures. In an interview with Italian *Vogue* in 2017 he asserted:

> I am brazen. For me, creating means regurgitating, distorting and assembling everything that has passed through me and continues to do so . . . For me, reworking the past over and over again is a way not to trivialise the garments and not to obsess over hem lengths. What I am interested in, as a matter of fact, is telling a story and, if someone sees fragments of other stories in it, be my guest. I don't have to justify myself. What is urgent for me is what I want to say.[9]

The construction of self-referential narratives from different global cultures is encapsulated in the strategy of Guccification that had been pursued under Michele's creative directorship. The term, coined by the brand and featuring prominently on its products, explains how Gucci seeks to become a 'cultural industry firm' and 'icon' through the expression of a coherent artistic style.[10] The brand's emphasis on art and cultural production is not unique, even if its resulting aesthetics and commercial success are striking, but part of a broader shift within the luxury industry, articulated by marketing scholar Jean-Noël Kapferer, in which 'western' brands seek to manage growth and maintain their distinction through artification, a process by which non-art is re-constituted as art.[11]

The pre-pandemic attitudes and actions of Wintour and Michele jar with their subsequent moralizing. Harbingers of change, their careers remain allegories of the fashion industry's perceived ills. The bind facing the contemporary fashion industry appears intractable because the discomfiture evinced by the doublespeak of its 'western' leaders reflects deep-rooted problems. Three issues are acute. First, as fashion scholars Paul Jobling, Philippa Nesbitt and Angelene Wong observe, attempts to conceptualize the fashion industry as a vehicle for social change remain difficult because 'clothing bears the weight of its own exploitative commercialisation'.[12] Designers and brands use fashionable garments to convey and critique social values, but this rarely occludes their pursuit of promotion and profit. Second, the persistence of a 'western' belief that clothing shapes its wearer's character means the conception and consumption of dress is deeply imbricated with socialized assumptions about people's public behaviours. As sociologist Joanne Finkelstein avers of the 'west', 'in our strong interest in appearance and our deliberate attempts to fashion and shape the body, we have tacitly endorsed the essential idea of the physiognomic perspective that the image and appearance of the individual is somehow representative of character and sensibility'.[13] The corollary is that the (fashionable) clothing people wear can be considered to reflect the unselfconscious values of the designers and brands who produce them. The structure of the contemporary fashion industry means 'western' perspectives are privileged. The consumption of dress, from purchase to styling, is equally shaped by the subconscious values of consumers. This point can be linked to a third factor that confounds the contemporary fashion industry. Anthropologist Daniel Miller, following philosopher Jürgen Habermas, observes that a condition of modernity, at least within the 'west', is that people are increasingly inclined to question strictures on how they should act and behave.[14] The repudiation of traditional values and the institutions that uphold them might seem to create an ideal space in which to critique 'western' attitudes, but the acknowledgement that we are individuals 'burdened with the task of creating normativity for ourselves' has a paradoxical effect. Miller argues that 'pressure to create our own normativity . . . produces a tremendous desire for self-reassurance'.¹⁵ I suggest this is more likely to lead to the reification of 'western' ideas, rather than their revocation.

The resulting situation is circuitous, even vicious. Whilst the contemporary fashion industry reaches globally, its geographic and cultural focus remains 'western'. Problems and possibilities that affect the industry are consequently interpreted through a 'western' perspective and become urgent only when they impede 'western' modes of living. So framed, strategies that are conceived to minimize obstacles or maximize opportunities will likely perpetuate 'western' priorities.

At least three interrelated implications follow from these points. First, critical discussions about the state of the fashion industry need to be cognizant of wider social issues, contemporary and non-recent, that frame the formation and performance of human identities. Second, the pursuit of decentralization so far as it pertains to expanding the oculus of the fashion industry beyond the 'west' is fundamental if lasting and effective change in line with pandemic-era proposals is to be achieved. Third, and caveating the previous point, attempts to shift and expand the oculus of the fashion industry will be fraught and protracted because 'western'-centrism is so engrained within it. Informed by these arguments, the chief premise of this book is that any reset within the fashion industry, and fashion education – from where my engagement with the industry stems – is more likely to be purposeful and permanent if it is understood how the contemporary industry became 'western'-centric. Consequently, it is important to go back to first principles and to reflect critically on why the fashion industry developed into its twenty-first-century form. Two closely related concepts frame my approach: history and culture. History is a form of culture. In making a distinction between the two, I seek to emphasize the importance of understanding the relevance of the past in the framing of people's attitudes and actions in the present. I also advocate the use of analytic and interdisciplinary methods associated with the discipline of history to facilitate this process. Influenced by literature scholar Edward Said's remarks about humanistic critique, my intention in this book is to 'introduce a longer sequence of thought and analysis' and, in so doing, 'to use [my] mind historically and rationally for the purposes of reflective understanding and genuine disclosure'.¹⁶

Thinking historically

The pursuit of first principles is motivated by a remark of Virgil Abloh in February 2021. Then artistic director of Louis Vuitton, Abloh was in conversation with *Business of Fashion* editor-at-large Tim Blanks. He argued that fashion needs a 're-contextualisation' every decade.¹⁷ Abloh did not elaborate on what this exercise might involve. For me, contextualization is the interpretation of any output of the fashion industry, from garment to campaign, that is informed by recent and non-recent attitudes, behaviours and events from across the world's global cultures. The adoption of a diachronic perspective and, with this, an acute historical awareness, are particularly important components of a contextual critique, as Abloh and Blanks acknowledged in their discussion. Summarizing attitudinal shifts within the industry over the past three decades, Blanks underscored the importance of contextualization to ensure fashion designers and brands could face up to the 'fierce reckoning' that he perceived to be at hand:

> But I think what happened was as fashion, as the world found out about fashion through the nineties, and then into the noughties, it started to become part of something else. It started to become a mass entertainment. And I think what we're seeing it doing now is becoming socially responsive in a way it's never been before. It's responding to current events. It always did. Fashion was always a mirror, but now it's been called on to contribute in a much more substantial way. And I think that is a very, very fierce reckoning for the industry. I mean, it's stand up and be counted time.[18]

A substantial challenge for the industry, which connects my observations, is the freighted relationship it has with history; its own and that of the people it clothes. The reason for this is at least twofold. First, fashion as it is conceived within the 'west' is conflated with modernity and a linear chronology that associates the future with progress and prosperity. If the present is a prelude to the future, the past is the abnegation of it. Second, dominant fashion narratives are typically authored by 'western' anglophones. These accounts valorize the role of 'western' designers and brands, lauding specific garments for their perceived epochal significance that encapsulate contemporary conceptions of modernity. Consequently, recourse to the past is typically partial, involving comparisons of clothing designs along simple chronologies, often with the explicit intention of establishing the precursors for trending styles.[19] Nonetheless, the creations and campaigns of the fashion industry, and commentaries upon both, emphasize the important role that divergent global histories and their telling have in shaping how, what and why fashions form, fascinate, frustrate and fade.

The paradox of history being simultaneously present and absent within the fashion industry is apparent from ambivalent remarks made by Abloh in his *Business of Fashion* discussion. At one point he claims to 'love history', but asserts at another, 'I never look back. Like, it's distinctly not in my frame of mind, to sort of look back at projects and dwell on it.'[20] Talley, a history graduate, explained the ambiguous place of history within the fashion industry by invoking the analogy of a shadow: 'fashion is not an industry that lives in the past, but rather carries its past along. Like a shadow, wherever it goes.'[21] An inability, perhaps unwillingness, to engage with the past can be understood as another consequence of the fashion industry's 'western'-centrism. Fashion is not unique, and not necessarily any worse than other global industries for its 'western' focus, but the ubiquity of its presence through the economic, social and political influence it exerts acutely emphasizes the narrowness of its priorities and privileges.

The alacrity with which people around the world adorn and dress their bodies because they have come to accept a 'western' belief that clothing determines character has contributed to the establishment of histories that entrench attitudes and beliefs that were formed during the eighteenth and nineteenth centuries when European economics, empiricism and empires became globally established.[22] The increased growth of the fashion industry, particularly from the 1980s, means the fantasies – and phantoms – informed by these complex histories have become ossified, rather than overturned. This is especially the case at this moment in the twenty-first century because the differential impact of the Covid-19 pandemic, which has followed the global economic downturn between 2008 and 2010 that saw the largest redistribution of wealth since before the Second World War, has led people to question the concepts of fashion, history and culture and to suggest they are reaching their nadir.[23]

A professional caveat is necessary here. I am a historian and teach contextualization units within a UK higher education fashion institute. My educational background, my nature, not least my current teaching role, inclines me to respond to contemporary happenings within the fashion industry from a historically informed perspective. More than this, I agree with the judgement of philosopher Fredric Jameson who opined, some three decades ago, that we are living in 'an age that has forgotten how to think historically'.[24] This is a bold, potentially divisive, statement that requires explanation. Jameson makes this remark at the beginning of a study of 'western' postmodernism. He suggests that a sense of detachment from the past characterizes a postmodern society. I shall take aim at the condition and concept of modernity, which has lurked at the periphery of this introduction, shortly. For me, Jameson's statement resonates because I contend that a belief in the relevance of the past to comprehending the present, along with the application of the analytic skills that facilitate historical enquiry, appears to be waning within the 'west'. The concern that historical study, specifically, the pursuit of understanding human cultures, generally, is in the process of decline, even distortion, has appeared to increase in direct correlation with the advancement and adoption of digital communication technologies – social media especially – that facilitate the generation and dissemination of almost incalculable amounts of information that are challenging to process and store.[25] One corollary of this struggle to sort is that sources and types of information that are very different in conception and composition can be considered equivalent. 'Alternative facts', which have come to complicate people's understanding of contemporary news and other cultural narratives that frame the interpretation of their lived experiences, are one of the more disquieting examples of this occurrence.[26]

This premise requires a personal caveat to explain how I position myself within this book. I am a white, cis-gendered, non-disabled male. I was educated in single-sex schools from the age of thirteen, which included two years in a grammar school. My adult life has been spent in educational institutions. First, as a student within higher education, latterly as a teacher. For nine years I worked in a boys' secondary boarding school in the south of England; for the past four I have worked in a university in the north of England. As a gay person I have never felt wholly comfortable within the spaces that I lived and worked. I may feel that my experiences were typically lived in the third person, rather than the first, but I know that I have been shaped by the institutions I grew up in. Some were quite conservative, most had specific rules and daily rhythms, all were places of privilege and, however genially, 'western'-centric and overwhelmingly white. During my education, the study of history, which I loved, was considered highly academic, traditional, gendered towards male (pupils, students and teachers) and privileged. In some respects, it still is. Over 'the past decade, history has been declining more rapidly than any other major [in the United States], even as more and more students attend college'.[27] One exception may substantiate a troubling rule. Historian Eric Alterman observes that '[i]t's boom time for history at Yale, where it is the third most popular major, and at other élite schools, including Brown, Princeton, and Columbia, where it continues to be among the top declared majors'. There is perhaps something inherently privileged, and by implication white and 'western'-centric, to take a historical approach. Alterman suggests it is a 'luxury' to enquire into the past. It is for those who can 'afford' to see 'college as a chance to learn about the world beyond the confines of their home towns, and to try to understand where they might fit in'.[28] To use history as a means to interrogate the 'western'-centrism of the fashion industry could appear to be a zero sum exercise. Nonetheless, I contend that the role of histories in establishing 'western'-centrism within society and the fashion industry needs to be apprehended if the assumptions they underpin are to be defined and interrogated. The endeavour is especially important because the hurt caused by dominant 'western' histories is often overlooked by 'western' people who may consider these narratives familiar and consequently neutral.[29] Regardless of how we judge their motives, the dramatic changes that Wintour and Michele seek to make are unlikely to be tractable unless the problems they are conceived to remedy are more deeply understood. Consequently, whilst my enquiry is framed by and pursued through my lived experiences, the analytic skills of the discipline of history can help to make my approach dispassionate and critical.

Locating culture

Dwelling on history, this book is also deeply concerned with culture. Defining culture, which takes many forms, and understanding its effects, which are typically indirect and intangible, is a challenge. As with history, culture has become increasingly freighted because of its association with 'western' priorities, which it can appear to legitimate and reinforce. Contemporary culture wars have emphasized the extent to which the concept of culture catalyzes structural whiteness and perpetuates systemic inequalities.[30] Fashion scholars Adam Geczy and Vicki Karaminas recognize the complexity of cultural criticism. They cite philosopher Theodor Adorno, who claimed the pursuit 'shares the blindness of its object'.[31] Nonetheless, as fashion remains one of the more conspicuous and ubiquitous of human cultural practices, there is an imperative to include culture within an analysis of its impact.

My understanding of culture and its usage is informed by the work of two scholars, sociologist Ann Swidler and theorist Homi Bhabha. Swidler, an American, responds to culture from a 'western' and metropolitan perspective. She conceives of it as a series of 'symbolic vehicles of meaning, including beliefs, ritual practices, art forms, and ceremonies, as well as informal cultural practices such as language, gossip, stories, and rituals of daily life'.[32] Her approach leaves scope to apply the concept of culture broadly, both chronologically and geographically. For her, 'culture is not a unified system that pushes action in a consistent direction. Rather, it is more like a "toolkit" or repertoire from which actors select differing pieces for constructing lines [or "strategies"] of action'.[33] Emphasizing the role of culture in influencing human behaviour, Swidler repudiates a peculiarly 'western' perception, 'a more enduring feature of Protestant culture', that sees it as goal driven and a means to explain individualistic action.[34] She considers how culture frames people's thoughts and actions by contrasting its role in 'settled lives' and 'unsettled lives'.[35]

In settled lives, social structures are relatively stable. In these circumstances the role of culture is ambiguous because it is largely taken for granted. Stability and the perception of routine become stupefying. It reduces people's awareness of the socialized assumptions that frame their lives and increases the likelihood of complacency.[36] In settled lives Swidler suggests culture and social structures are 'simultaneously too fused and too disconnected for easy analysis'.[37] Established values and traditions are likely to be invoked as predictors of and justifications for people's behaviour even when there is an incompatibility between thought and deed: 'People profess ideals they do not follow, utter platitudes without examining their validity, or fall into cynicism or indifference with the assurance that the world will go on just the same.'[38] In unsettled lives, periods of 'social transformation', the role of culture in informing people's conduct becomes clearer. As 'competing ways of organizing action' are proposed to deal with the social upheavals at hand, there is a challenge between ideology, which purports to 'offer a unified answer to [the attendant] problems of social action', and traditions, which are 'articulated cultural beliefs and practices'.[39] Swidler's observation that an understanding of culture is contingent upon periods of social calm and commotion is instructive when applying the concept to an analysis of contemporary society and the fashion industry. The acknowledgement that culture is not a unified system helps to eschew the centralization of 'western' attitudes and actions. It permits an awareness that the 'west' might be the 'weird one' rather than the paragon, as Miller has suggested.[40]

The importance of emphasizing contingency and divergence when thinking about culture is highlighted by Bhabha. Negotiating the concept from his perspective as an Indian-English person, he argues that a focus on difference highlights boundaries, 'in-between' spaces 'that initiate new signs of identity, and innovative sites of collaboration, and contestation, in the act of defining the idea of society itself'.[41] It is within these interstices that cultural values are defined through an ongoing process of negotiation because there is an 'overlap and displacement of domains of difference'.[42] Fundamental to this process is Bhabha's concept of hybridity, which asserts that all identities – individual and corporate – are formed from a mixture of different cultures.[43] An emphasis on difference, or 'being in the "beyond"' as Bhabha terms it, complements Swidler's conception of culture because it challenges the notion of social and political 'fixity'. The 'enunciation of cultural difference problematizes the binary division of past and present, tradition and modernity, at the level of cultural representation and its authoritative address'.[44] Hybridity makes it possible to diminish Eurocentrism and the dominance of 'western' attitudes.[45] Consequently, Bhabha suggests it becomes possible to 'redescribe our cultural contemporaneity; to reinscribe our human, historic commonality'.[46]

In using history and culture to frame a study that seeks to elucidate the causes and consequences of the fashion industry's 'western'-centrism I am cognizant of polymath Audre Lorde's forceful analogy and admonishment that 'the master's tools will never dismantle the master's house'.[47] Both concepts have become increasingly associated with the furtherance of 'western' and largely white perspectives that perpetuate the structural marginality that has been starkly highlighted by the Covid-19 pandemic. I acknowledge Lorde's misgivings, and the invidious circumstances in which she made them. She was the only black person to receive an invitation to participate in a humanities conference that discussed systemic inequalities within American society.[48] Nonetheless, the extent to which history and culture are imbricated, even implicated, in the structures of 'western' society makes consideration of them necessary if a critical understanding of what they have built is to occur. Implicit within Lorde's metaphor is the suggestion that social structures and the ideas that galvanize them can be *either/or*; separable, dissolvable, replaceable. A solution as unorthodox and radical as that used to sever the mythical Gordian Knot is consequently possible for some of the more pernicious problems that confound human societies. A premise of this book, informed by Swidler's and Bhabha's writing, is that people's interpretation and use of history and culture are contingent. They depend on myriad factors from which they cannot be easily extracted, if at all. The attempt to solve problems with swords, physical or figurative, is consequently as fabulous as the ancient Greek legend. I take a *both/and* approach when discussing human social relations. This purposefully emphasizes 'connections and entanglements', 'oppositions' and 'contradictions'.[49] By dwelling on these complications, which are made explicit within feminist cultural studies, fashion scholar Susan Kaiser argues that dominant ideas within a society, not least its conceptions of power, are revealed to be multidimensional rather than unidimensional and oppositional.[50] This understanding is important because it facilitates a nuanced critique of the many 'western'-conceived binaries that frame human relations and which are starkly manifest in the conception and consumption of contemporary fashions.[51] The point is not to pursue the eradication of these oppositions, although they frequently become sites of contestation, because this is idealistic.[52] Here I part with scholars who pursue 'defashion' and seek 'to dismantle the current Fashion system'.[53] Rather, my aim is to understand the causes and consequences of these binaries with a view to developing more effective strategies to live with them, and limit them when we can.

The spectre of modernity

The knottiness associated with history and culture is compounded by the concept of modernity. Modernity and its cognates – modernism, post modernism and now post-post modernism – are so prevalent within 'western' discourses about contemporary society that they are often mentioned blithely and without comment. But modernity is not neutral. Nor should it be blithely accepted. Its origins and concerns conjoin peculiarly 'western' cultural and historical assumptions: to invoke modernity is to commence a dialogue – perhaps more, a monologue – skewed towards a 'western' perspective. There are many and varied definitions of modernity, but I favour and follow cultural scholar Elizabeth Wilson, who explains that it is 'oppositionalism and iconoclasm, [it is a] questioning of reality and perception, [it is an] attempt to come to grips with the nature of human experience in a mechanized "unnatural" world'.[54] The emphasis on mechanization is important because modernity is associated with the development of capitalism, consumption and industrialization in Europe. How European people adapted their values, private and public behaviours in response to these seismic social facts adumbrates the condition of modernity.

As Wilson's definition suggests, modernity is often perceived as troubling, dystopian. In her study of 'western' fashion in the 1990s and early Millennium, fashion scholar Caroline Evans refers to spectres, phantoms that haunt and scare people because modernity is uncertain, precarious, contradictory. She highlights the importance of opposites within it – 'despair and optimism, beauty and horror, fashion and mortality' – which come to frame people's lives.[55] Evans's study demonstrates how the condition and concept of modernity has informed an academic understanding of the global conception, creation and consumption of fashionable dress and appearance from at least the twentieth century.[56] This is problematic. Modernity is not so much the proverbial elephant in the room, but the elephant in a room built atop another elephant, akin to author Terry Pratchett's Discworld: a flat and circular world that is supported by four gigantic elephants who stand upon the shell of an even larger turtle. For the purposes of this book, the influence of modernity as both condition and concept is important to acknowledge because it has produced a particular way of thinking that I would most straightforwardly describe as insular and thoroughly 'western'-centric.[57] A preoccupation with the condition of modernity occludes a historical perspective because of its hybrid construction of time.[58] If modernism emphasized chronological linearity, within post-(post)modernism chronology is altogether more fragmented.[59] For this reason, modernity and its cognates can incline people to adopt a unidimensional view of culture because thinking beyond what is immediate and immanent becomes harder. The myriad choices and contradictions that characterize a modern society curtail the scope of people's (critical) thinking, arguably making it more selfish. At least two authors suggested the Covid-19 pandemic exacerbated people's selfishness.[60] Consequently, prevalent social values, many of which are framed by 'western' concerns, become entrenched.

My contention is that if 'western' scholars (of dress) were liberated from their 'mind-forg'd manacles' – an appropriate metaphor about the stultifying effects of increased commercialization and urban living from William Blake's eighteenth-century poem 'London' – and think around modernity rather than through it, nuanced discussions about the global relationships between history, culture and fashion might occur more frequently.[61] At the very least, it should be possible to right what designer Ken Kweku Nimo refers to as the 'predominant misconception of fashion as solely an agent of western modernity'.[62] First, it is necessary to elucidate the 'west's' fixation on modernity.

The origins of modernity are unequivocally European, although a *terminus post quem* fluctuates. A longer view of the multi-linear progression of human thought might seek its emergence in the seventeenth century, which saw the development of mercantile capitalism and the beginnings of the Enlightenment.[63] Conventionally, modernity is associated with nineteenth-century industrialization and the expansion of capitalism through increased global commerce and European colonialism. It was during the nineteenth century that new patterns of living, chiefly evidenced within the 'west's' expanded urban spaces, heightened the prominence of the individual and catalyzed the dissolution of traditional institutions, not least the church.[64] Eschewing authorities that prescribed appropriate forms of conduct, Habermas argues that people were tasked with finding their own sense of validation, a process made all the harder for them being cognizant of undertaking it.[65] According to sociologist Norbert Elias, the weakening of interpersonal bonds between people, which may have been underway since the sixteenth century, led them to think they had 'an inner-self inaccessible to others'.[66]

Resultant feelings of loneliness and despondency were experienced by many people. For younger people they were acute. Elias refers to the creation of a 'youth culture' because the time required to prepare adolescents for adulthood and gainful employment increased in correlation to society's complexity.[67] A prolonged novitiate had the potential to cause imbalances in people's personality, with biologically mature individuals remaining socially immature.[68] In the twenty-first century, the prevalence of social media, and what economist Noreena Hertz terms the 'pervasiveness of social comparison', may have compounded this dilemma.[69] The corollary of social estrangement was not wholly negative. Many people accepted the adverse consequences associated with the development of the modern state because they relished the potential for 'mass individualization' that was created through the ability to readily satisfy personal wishes.[70] Nevertheless, the potential for isolation increased as intrapersonal relationships became less permanent.[71] A sense of frustration was also heightened if personal goals remained unfulfilled.[72]

Changes in the role and perception of money compounded feelings of personal dislocation. In a compelling analysis Jameson considers the relationship between a society's conception of money and its cultural production. He questions whether people's engagement with culture is more patently realistic, more attached to thingness, when money is experienced materially, but he does assert that cultural production was affected by the advent of finance capital during the twentieth century.[73] Money became intangible and abstract, catalyzing 'dematerialization' and 'deterritorialization'. Jameson argues that a 'new stage of equivalence' occurred as money levelled the 'intrinsic differences' of things. The fragmentation of cultural production followed because objects became 'semiautonomous' and possessed 'independent existences'.[74] In the ensuing play of 'autonomized fragments' cultural products emitted 'a complete narrative message in [their] own right'.[75] For Jameson, this abstraction amplifies semiologist Roland Barthes's observation that meaning and existence, or the existential, are incompatible in the contemporary world.[76] The proliferation of digital technologies in the twenty-first century has exacerbated this conflict.

Jameson, along with many of the theorists quoted above, wrote after the Second World War when the experience of totalitarian regimes and the competing ideologies of capitalism and communism created a pronounced despondency with what might be termed human progress, but his sentiments were anticipated nearly a century earlier in an essay of 1903 by sociologist Georg Simmel. In 'The Metropolis and Mental Life' Simmel contends that a 'blasé outlook', characterized by an 'indifference toward the distinction between things', emerged within Europe's twentieth-century metropolises.[77] This insight was important in framing Simmel's influential essay of 1904, 'Fashion', in which he suggests that the development of fashionable dress and appearance is driven by people's equivocal desire to look similar to their peers and to stand out.[78] In the twenty-first century, Simmel's appraisal has become near orthodoxy. In Rebecca Arnold's phrase it is 'the dichotomy that has haunted fashion'.[79]

The implications of equivalency for people's dress and appearance are considered explicitly in a provocative study by sociologist Gilles Lipovetsky, *The Empire of Fashion*. Arguing that fashion became the preeminent social mechanism in the 'west' during the twentieth century, Lipovetsky suggests its 'reign' fostered 'flexible attitudes' in people:

> Its irrationality and its apparent wastefulness aside, fashion contributes to a more rational edification of society because it socializes human beings to change and prepares them for perpetual recycling. Capable of softening rigidities and resistances, the fashion form is an instrument of social rationality, an *invisible* rationality; while it cannot be measured, it is irreplaceable for a rapid adaptation to modernity, for the acceleration of transformations in progress, for the constitution of a society equipped to face the endlessly variable requirements of the future. The system of consummate fashion puts civil society in a state of openness with respect to historical movement; it creates receptive mentalities characterized by fluidity that are inherently prepared for the voluntary adventure of the new.[80]

The situation described is not utopian. It is uncertain and deeply paradoxical. Akin to Jameson and his focus on capitalistic processes, Lipovetsky argues that contemporary democratic processes, which include media consumption, have rendered knowledge 'increasingly elastic'.[81] Consequently, people are 'receptive' to information that 'dissolves the strengths of their convictions and makes [them] permeable, ready to give up their own opinions and systems of reference without much struggle'.[82] Indifference to knowledge and a tendency to acquiesce means that 'people's culture resembles a mobile patchwork, a splintered construction over which mastery is weak'.[83] The extent to which fashion 'generates a positive attitude toward innovation' is therefore illusory because it simultaneously 'freezes the ductility of the social body. Fashion society at once accelerates and rigidifies the tendency toward social mobility; paradoxically, it gives impetus to modernism, and conservatism alike'.[84] Social expectations or 'constraints' are caught between these extremes.[85]

The ambivalence within 'western' society is at once cause and symptom of its conception of time.[86] Lipovetsky argues that '[t]he time frame that has always governed fashion – the present – is being increasingly generalized . . . We are living in a time of short-term programs, perpetually changing standards, and exhortations to live in the moment. The present has taken over as the principal axis of social duration'.[87] He asserts that fashion 'goes hand in hand with a relative devaluing of the past'.[88] Lipovetsky would probably approve of theorist Jack Self's discussion of flatness, which describes how digital technologies have created a 'real-time, or total Earth time'.[89] The condition is not limited to the present, however. Self suggests that '[t]he ability to view vast volumes of data and records from the past, as well as grasp a variety of positions on the future, means that there is no longer any meaningful separation between other eras and our own. Indeed, history is today understood as a kind of alternative present, still happening somewhere else'.[90]

The contemporary fashion industry's preoccupation with the present is apparent in two respects. First, and most readily, pre-pandemic fashions were defined by the rapidity of their obsolescence and reinvention. Second, and more broadly, since the late nineteenth century when 'western' industrialized time became globally standardized, distinct forms of fashionable dress and bodily appearance have been liberally interpreted as evidence of epochal shifts and used to divide chronologies into periods of linear progression.[91] Regardless of intent, this process has tended to reinforce narratives of 'western' hegemony. Contributing to a socialized belief that fashion reflects contemporary concerns, as Lipovetsky asserts, the appealing idea that appearances articulate social progress may also provide a psychological salve for 'western' people seeking security and stability.

From at least 1863, when poet Charles Baudelaire suggested that the emergence of dandyism marked a decisive moment in the development of democracy, there has been an inclination to connect periods of social upheaval and the emergence of new forms of fashionable dress and appearance.[92] Seemingly neutral, even objective, this way of thinking constitutes a 'western' cultural chauvinism that binds culture, fashion and history only more tightly. As curator Patricia Mears and menswear author G. Bruce Boyer observe in their study of innovative interwar fashions, '[i]n times of crisis, various aspects of culture often come to assume a hyper-importance. Certainly in the 1930s, the cinema, jazz and the automobile played such a role. Clothing did too'.[93] Sociologist Fred Davis has cautioned against the deceptive simplicity of connecting fashion innovation and social change, but the apparent logic of this linkage means it continues to find expression in 'western' academic thought across many disciplines. For example, it is unlikely coincidental that the democratic and economic upheavals

INTRODUCTION 15

that occurred within the 'west' between the 1970s and mid-1990s sparked a period of soul-searching as the first generation of cultural critics and scholars after the Second World War queried the capitalist and democratic processes that military victory had appeared to legitimize. They produced an outpouring of anglophone literature that analyzed the connections between society, culture and fashion.[94] Aiming at criticism, the resulting literature also served as psychological salve and did much to affirm the essential rightness of 'western' values.

Asserting links between a society's internal feelings and external presentation continues today. Even this book, which seeks to interrogate dominant cultural ideas, at least partially reinforces this narrative because its genesis was sparked by the Covid-19 pandemic. Indeed, as debates about culture wars, the death of history and the appropriate name for the post-pandemic epoque intensify, there will doubtless emerge a literature as diverse and voluminous as that produced twenty to thirty years ago when economic and political crises precipitated a similar spurt of intellectual wrangling.[95] Hopefully, this time will be different and the peculiarity of the 'west' can be more seriously acknowledged. The peculiarity of the 'west's' conflation of fashion and time is a significant reason why the fashion industry struggles to decentralize and to convey the diversity of global cultures. Andrew Bolton, Curator in Charge at the Costume Institute of the Metropolitan Museum of Art, may be right to assert that fashion is a 'modish time machine', 'an acutely accurate and especially sensitive timepiece', in the catalogue to the institute's exhibition 'About Time: Fashion & Duration', which opened in 2020, but it is most accurate and sensitive to the constructs of time that have developed in response to the 'west's' preoccupation with modernity.[96]

Brief though the telling has been, it is apparent that the concept of modernity not only informs how ('western') people have lived since at least the seventeenth century, but it also frames how critics and scholars think about how they lived. Consequently, I see modernity as one of the major causes of the myriad social problems that Anna Wintour, Alessandro Michele and other fashion leaders have identified since the start of the Covid-19 pandemic. Unless the spectre of modernity is exorcized from the 'west', changes within the fashion industry will likely be illusory, certainly only temporary.

Hang-ups

This book analyzes the causes and consequences of the fashion industry's 'western'-centrism by focusing on nine concepts and binaries that frame contemporary ideas about the fashionable presentation of the human body: undress, gender, race, sexuality, age, religion, wealth, violence, shape. These concepts exist to varying degrees in many of the world's cultures, but their contemporary manifestation largely reflects how they originated in European discourses during the eighteenth and nineteenth centuries in response to the economic, political and social hegemony that European people established through the continuation of 'western' empire-building. These binaries enabled Europeans to comprehend, categorize and more easily control people subjugated to their rule through a process of othering. They also made it possible for Europeans to discipline themselves, a prerequisite to assure their assumed superiority. The chronological and cultural extent of Europe's overseas dominion meant these binaries became globally established. They remain prevalent today. Years of sustained social turmoil, chiefly between the economic downturn of 2008 and the beginning of the Covid-19 pandemic in 2019, emphasize how these binaries continue to be sites of negotiation as the 'west's' traditions and ideals are contested by divergent cultural perspectives and changing global realities.

The first three binaries were critical sites of negotiation within the 'west' during the eighteenth and nineteenth centuries and informed thinking about the binaries considered in chapters four through seven. Prior to the conclusion, the final two chapters, which dwell on the physical and psychological violence that fashions impose on the human body and, more fundamentally, contemplate the idealized shape this body should have, demonstrate how binaries frequently intersect. Paradoxically, this compounds their impact and the 'western'-centrism of the fashion industry because they appear camouflaged, neutral, and become more intractable. Each chapter considers three episodes, or case studies, linked to one of the binaries that demonstrate the pervasiveness of 'western'-centrism within the fashion industry. Examples, which include catwalk presentations and advertising campaigns from the 1980s to the present, are not necessarily, certainly not wholly, negative. They are chosen for being subject to widespread scrutiny because of the strong emotive responses they provoked when made public within the fashion industry and by the global media, which includes magazines, newspapers, news programmes, online forums and social media. International perspectives frame the analysis of all episodes, but examples purposefully centre the 'western' fashion industry. By emphasizing the binaries that so readily manifest themselves within the 'west', my contention is that they can be more deeply understood and more effectively challenged.

To interrogate how 'western'-centrism manifests itself within the contemporary fashion industry, I focus on how understandings of fashion are negotiated by conversations, which are sometimes discontinuous and discordant, between designers, brands and consumers. At this point it should be emphasized that the very word 'fashion', which derives from the Latin verb *facere* ('to make'), privileges 'western' perspectives.[97] More specifically, an anglophone perspective. Fashion scholar Heike Jenss observes that 'Romance languages as well as many Germanic languages [refer to fashion as] *mode* or *moda* derived from the Latin word *modus* for shape or manner, which is also the root of the word "modernity", associated with the fast-paced life in European capitals for which fashion (or *la mode*) became a symbol or metaphor'.[98] Again, the peculiarity of the 'west's' preoccupation with modernity is apparent. To mitigate against some of the implications of this point, I follow sociologist Yuniya Kawamura, who conceives of fashion as a belief that 'exists in people's minds'.[99] Conventionally, this is understood as a 'western' belief, heavily influenced by 'high' or 'elite' European designs, as fashion scholar Jennifer Craik has argued.[100] My arguments are framed by fashion scholars Linda Welters's and Abby Lillethun's contention that fashion is a global phenomenon, and a belief that can exist in the minds of people around the world.[101]

Throughout this study I seek to row against the tide of my socialized assumptions. There is an inevitably that I shall falter. Arguing against whiteness studies, which aim to confront white people with their complicity in a system that is largely of their making and exists principally to their benefit, sociologist Kehinde Andrews would probably urge me to hang up my oars.[102] He sees whiteness as a psychosis that is 'beyond rational argument'.[103] Whiteness is certainly ingrained within fashion's 'western'-centrism, but likening it to a form of psychosis places it beyond critical investigation, perhaps even understanding. By conceiving of this book as a series of interlinked investigative discussions that consider race in conjunction with other binaries, my contention is that themes and techniques can be identified to facilitate interrogation and make the task of reasoning with whiteness and 'western'-centrism meaningful, if still long-term. This book proposes no quick solutions, no manifesto, but I hope it will provide a spur for people to join me in the figurative boat so that we might row together.

In attempting to understand people's mindsets I make use of three sources that remain little used in academic discussions of the fashion industry: fashion journalism, designer and brand statements about dress collections, and social media and online forums. Fashion journalism, a form of 'soft news', is an ambiguous, amorphous source that includes print and digital commentaries and podcasts. It also has links to fashion illustration and photography.[104] Fashion scholars Rosie Findlay and Johannes Reponen argue that fashion journalism 'reflects all of fashion's polarities and contradictions, which is what tends to make it so suspicious to its critics'.[105] At the core of these suspicions is a concern about the intentions of the genre: how far can it be objective and critical when it is so imbricated within the industry it chronicles? Fashion journalism that aims at a greater criticality is a relatively new form of reportage that developed during the 1980s.[106] Consequently, it has changed greatly in response to technological advancements and remains under-theorized.[107] It is nonetheless apparent that 'journalist-activists', who speak truth to power, have become more vocal since the 1970s, at least in what might be termed 'high-quality newspaper[s]' and magazines.[108] Whilst it is increasingly acknowledged that fashion journalism exists along a spectrum, as Findlay and Reponen explain, the extent to which it perpetuates 'western' perspectives is not fully understood, although sociologist Monique Mulholland has considered the construction of beauty and Aboriginality within Australian media.[109] This is an important consideration because as fashion scholar Agnès Rocamora asserts, following Kawamura, fashion is not solely about the material object, but 'the fabrication of ideas about fashion, the creation of beliefs that give it meaning'.[110] Through my use of fashion journalism, I explore this issue.

Another key source to give fashion meaning is a brand or designer's statement about their collection. It is curiously rare for commentators, academic and generalist, to refer to contextual statements, oral and authored, when analyzing fashion collections.[111] These statements are invariably promotional, but they provide insights into how creators of collections and campaigns situate their work and how they want it to be understood. Attention to consumers' views is also sporadic beyond generalist fashion accounts that might include quotes from consumers' social media posts or short comments from interviews. I try to address this omission by utilizing social media – chiefly Facebook, Instagram and Twitter – and online forms, all of which are seldom used by scholars.[112]

There are challenges in using social media. Studies have highlighted how social media engagement tends to be greatest in richer countries, which may exacerbate a 'western'-centredness.[113] The nature of people's engagement with social media is also gendered, and therefore framed by a prevalent 'western' binary.[114] It is also dependent on personality type.[115] Specific challenges should also be highlighted. The provenance of comments and uploads to social media platforms are rarely fully verifiable because people tend to use pseudonyms. This underscores the performative nature of these digital spaces where 'seeming' can often appear to have greater validity than 'being'.[116] The veracity of opinions provided through digital spaces, on social media, blogs and forums, can also be impaired by the mutability of time. First, internet search engines prioritize new information. Content creators are increasingly adept at using keywords to steer people to their platforms and to ensure their material remains accessible for longer. Second, there can be an inverse correlation between the speed with which people's reactions are conveyed in a digital space and the length of time they remain accessible. Spontaneous and emotional outbursts that may not fully represent a person's point of view can be invested with greater meaning because of the length of time they are available for scrutiny. Third, broken and corrupted links mean information becomes irretrievable without warning. Conversely, old links might be rediscovered and the information they provide invested with new meanings when interpreted in response to different circumstances.

These points are not negligible, but they do not nullify the insights that can be gained from examining contemporary responses to fashion collections and campaigns. Immediate, oftentimes passionate, responses demonstrate how people's reception of fashions is contingent upon their immediate circumstances.

INTRODUCTION

Considering the profoundly visual and instant impact of fashion, an ability to gauge consumers' 'gut' responses can help to articulate how its communication relies upon socialized assumptions. Moreover, the timestamping of people's social media interactions, which sometimes includes rough geographical data, can show how attitudes vary chronologically and geographically.

A more conventional source also requires explanation. This book is interdisciplinary, and I draw heavily on the writing of scholars with diverse specialisms, including anthropology, art, economics, psychology and sociology. Many of these authors are 'western' and white. In large part this is a straightforward, sobering, reflection of the lack of diversity within the 'western' academy. It is also because many scholars who investigate European stories of colonization are themselves European. These perspectives are hugely useful because I seek to interrogate the origins of 'western'-centrism within the fashion industry, but I am aware of the limitations and partiality this creates. I hope the critical approach I adopt, the global voices of consumers that I bring into this study through social media and, fundamentally, the questions this study raises will encourage people, especially from beyond the 'west', to complicate the narratives I begin to sketch. Together, we can ensure a more complete series of histories emerges.

Three formatting choices require explanation. I place 'west' within inverted commas to emphasize the noun as a concept, rather than a specific and unified geographical region. I also eschew capitalization to avoid the suggestion that the concept should be invested with a singular status. I do likewise when using the adjective anglophone. In discussing race, I do not capitalize black and brown. I follow author Emma Dabiri, who suggests the capitalization of these social concepts tends to 'reinforce their fixedness' and highlight the people and practices they label as marginal.[117] Nor do I use the racial designation 'yellow' to refer to (East) Asians. Unlike black and brown, the usage of this term and concept, which was coined in the 'west' during the nineteenth century, has not been adopted by the communities it purports to describe. I refer to (East) Asian people as white. This is how they were initially described in travellers' accounts before the establishment of 'western' racial paradigms.[118] Throughout, translations are my own unless stated.

1
UNDRESS

The observation that 'naked people have little or no influence in society' is conventionally attributed to the nineteenth-century American author Mark Twain.[1] The reality is less simple, both for the quotation's origin and its sentiment. First, there is no direct source for the remark. The surest statement about undressed people that can be credited to Twain comes from a posthumous publication that includes excerpts from his notebooks. In one passage Twain contrasts the blissful state of being naked to the troubles that ensue when any form of adornment appears on the human body:

> Strip the human race, absolutely naked, and it would be a real democracy. But the introduction of even a rag of tiger skin, or a cowtail, could make a badge of distinction and be the beginning of a monarchy.[2]

From the perspective of an American born within sixty years of his country's independence from British rule, the prospect that clothes-wearing could prefigure the establishment of monarchy is a damning indictment about the perils of dress. This personal caveat raises a second, more pressing, concern with Twain's apparent and actual remarks about human undress. They convey a singularly 'western' perspective. In the passage, reference to evocative clothing materials that are trivialized for being like 'a rag' or 'a badge' is redolent of the curiosity and concern that permeates European travel accounts and costume books from the sixteenth century. These texts generally accept as axiomatic 'the more dress the more civility, the more nudity the more savagery'.[3] Twain's use of the word 'naked' most readily aligns his sentiments with 'western' patterns of thought. To reference nakedness sparks deliberation about its antithetical concept, nudity.[4] In absolute terms, nakedness and nudity appear to describe a similar, even identical, state, but in anglophone discourse the concepts are typically invoked as opposites, referring to divergent social circumstances and degrees of personal choice.

Nakedness is caused by an unselfconscious, unwanted or unintentional lack of clothing. It can be synonymous with naturality. Art historian John Berger asserts that '[t]o be naked is to be oneself'.[5] However, nakedness is conventionally associated with ignorance, impoverishment and encumberment.[6] By contrast, nudity is created through a deliberate absence of dress. To be nude is therefore to be confident, possibly desirable, certainly possessing of agency.[7] It is not clear when these concepts began to develop their divergent meanings, and in some cases naked and nude are still used as synonyms.[8] The assessments of nineteenth-century 'western' art historians, whose studies of ancient art, statuary in particular, galvanized long-standing assumptions about idealized human bodies, and the emergence of anthropology as a specific science during the first half of the century, are important factors. Both disciplines used comparative methodologies as a primary form of research, often – if inadvertently – to elucidate and affirm prevalent 'western' values. Both disciplines also contributed to the period's classificatory fixation, coining new terms and reappraising definitions of existing terms.[9]

The moralizing judgements that nakedness and nudity connote informs my decision to use the more neutral term of undress when referring to partially or wholly uncovered human bodies. In jettisoning at least some of the terminological baggage associated with nakedness and nudity, I follow scholars who emphasize that undress is a 'relative concept', 'socially produced' and dependent on 'who is looking'.[10] Acknowledging undress to be a culturally constructed and expansive idea is helpful in two respects. First, it clarifies the many and similar ways that unadorned bodies have been symbolically significant within the histories of many of the world's cultures. Among societies as diverse as ancient Greece, Rome and Egypt, the classical Maya, twentieth- and twenty-first-century Japan and Nigeria, undressed bodies have been conduits for expressing gender norms and socio-economic distinctions. They are frequently associated with physically adept men and valorized, or pre-pubescent girls, pregnant women, labourers and social outcasts, and problematized for existing betwixt and between defined social roles and for being, literally or figuratively, unclean.[11] A state of undress is typically avoided by a community's social and political elite, especially its female members.[12] Second, eschewing the concepts of nakedness and nudity highlights the 'west's' attitude to undress as peculiar. These antithetical concepts are informed by Hebraic and Hellenic beliefs that were largely crystallized by colonial experiences of the eighteenth and nineteenth centuries. Hebraic thought, conveyed through Jewish and Christian texts, typically considers the undressed body to be shameful because it is symbolic of Adam and Eve's Original Sin. According to the Book of Genesis, the couple's immediate decision on gaining the gift of knowledge was to dress their bodies (Gen. 3:7). They felt shame upon learning of their nakedness. Whilst there is potential for Adam and Eve's prelapsarian undress to be praised, because it stemmed from innocence, hindsight typically encourages a negative reading.[13] Hellenic thought, by contrast, transmitted through ancient Greek authors and artists, considered undress to be empowering.[14] Purposefully unadorned, the human nude becomes capable of revealing personal and social truths that clothing obscures.[15]

The product of different belief systems, these opposing views have been amalgamated within 'western' thought about human undress but not reconciled. They provide a perspective that is wholly unique, and disconcerting. The unease is apparent from Twain's passage. Within forty words, human undress is lauded for spawning a respected form of political organisation, and questioned, because of the implicit acknowledgement that different social roles, which are required for any political system to operate effectively, only become explicit through dress. The grammatical construction of the passage, written in the subjunctive mood, confirms Twain's remark as a thought experiment and gives lie to his argument: from a 'western' perspective the undressed body could never be considered a symbol of democracy because it is too discordant.

Such discordance has been emphasized by the Covid-19 pandemic. The irregularity of an increase in the amount of skin shown within the spring/summer 2022 collections of several 'western' fashion brands – notably Fendi and Prada – required 'western' fashion journalists to find an explanation.[16] Drawing upon the heavily gendered, and largely discredited, theory of shifting erogenous zones conceived by dress curator James Laver, fashion psychologist Dawnn Karen postulated that 'western' people's desire to show more flesh expressed a need to assert their personal autonomy after months of lockdowns, social restrictions, and adherence to mandates to wear face masks in public.[17] The 'exposure of skin', which fashion journalist Alexander Fury termed a 'trend', was also championed in Portuguese *Vogue*'s 'Forbidden' issue of April 2021. The magazine's cover featured a portrait of model Katrina Janickova, whose only item of dress was an open red shirt. Crosses concealing her nipples appeared on four variant covers in black, blue, pink and yellow. The quirky design ridiculed the continued censorship of women's mammaries on social media. The theme was pursued within the magazine in an article entitled '*São mamas, estúpido!*' ('They are tits, stupid!').[18]

The three studies in this chapter – the ready-to-wear collections of Rick Owens and MT Costello for autumn/winter 2015 and Brazilian ballerina Ingrid Silva's cover shoot for Brazilian *Vogue*'s digital issue for December 2020 – explore the negotiations that followed the presentation of two of the more problematic parts of the undressed human body in catwalk presentations and a fashion magazine: the flaccid penis, 'perhaps the most taboo image of all', and the pregnant female body, 'a source of abjection and disgust in popular culture'.[19]

Rick Owens, *Sphinx*, autumn/winter 2015

On 22 January 2015, Rick Owens's debuted his autumn/winter menswear collection *Sphinx* during Paris Fashion Week. Inspired by 'some random black and white submarine movie', designs reflected an 'eternal struggle' and recurrent theme in Owens's work, 'control and collapse'.[20] He explained that the claustrophobic conditions of a submarine create an intensified energy where 'things start [to get] a little deranged'.[21] Over time, feelings of 'bonding' fragment until there is a sense that things are 'falling apart'. The result is 'masculinity x3' and a 'primal element'.[22] The nine-minute catwalk show comprised forty looks each worn by a different black (3) and white (37) male model. In dark shades of monochrome, the clothes appeared to be divided into three sections. The show commenced with garments whose historical and maritime influences seemed certain, chiefly peacoats and cable knit sweaters. These evolved into outfits with more angular silhouettes that were futuristic and less obviously nautical. Six looks from the show's second and third sections, all worn by white men, sparked controversy among the 'west's' press because they featured garments with circular cut-outs and heightened hemlines that revealed the models' genitalia.[23]

The undress was partial. The looks that exposed the models' penises accounted for fifteen per cent of the collection. No model was wholly undressed, although some did wear garments that uncovered much of their torsos. Nevertheless, for journalists reporting on the show undress defined *Sphinx*. The titles of news articles and their accompanying texts were replete with provocative phrases about the penis. Within the UK, the heading of *The Independent*'s report was: 'Rick Owens Puts Penises on Show'.[24] *The Guardian* was more jocular and questioned, 'Penises on the Fashion Catwalk – a Flesh Flash Too Far?'[25] Commentaries that appeared in fashion publications were marginally less jittery, although they emphasized the theme of male undress. Journalist Susie Lau's article for *Dazed Digital* included a quotation from the designer in its heading, '"Nudity Is the Most Simple and Primal Gesture": The Designer Reflects on His Full-frontal Fashion Statement'.[26] In France, the title of *Grazia*'s article implied that Owens's show constituted a scandal by alluding to the Watergate affair of the 1970s that precipitated the downfall of US president Richard Nixon: '"Rick Owens Gate": *les mannequins dévoilent tout, vraiment tout* . . .' (the models reveal everything, truly everything).[27] In Australia, a short article that appeared in *GQ*, along with blurred out images of the models' genitalia, had a blunter title: 'Rick Owens Sends Models Down the Runway with Their Junk Out'.[28] Two hashtags, #dickowens and #freethepeen, trended on Twitter after the show. The first tag was coined in response to the collection. The second was pre-existing. Both were used by media organizations to promote articles about the collection on their digital platforms. During the days following Owens's show, they were co-opted by Twitter users who made sexually themed puns.[29]

There is some truth to journalist Zing Tsjeng's tongue-in-cheek observation that 'it's only in the retelling that the offending members took on larger-than-life proportions'.[30] Lau argued that 'there wasn't anything overt about Owens's choice to use full frontal nudity on the catwalk. You caught little glimpses from under the curved hemlines and strategically placed [holes] in the toga-esque gowns, but nothing was in yer face'.[31] According to journalist Hannah Marriott, models knew in advance what they would be wearing. One, whom she quotes, explained, 'It was not a thing at all.. . . Everyone knew what they would be wearing at early fittings . . . I just noticed it when I looked at the photo board and saw that there were cocks hanging about. Ha!'[32] Fashion commentators and their readers had also been primed for *Sphinx*.

Prior to the collection, Owens had spoken publicly about his love of bodies and, somewhat ambiguously, about his 'sex club past'.[33] In an interview with *i-D* magazine in 2013 he remarked that 'it's disingenuous to show your genitals so obviously and so provocatively. I love nudity, but playing with "don't look, don't look" is teenage'.[34] Eleven years earlier, in 2002, Owens had been the centre of controversy involving undress when a double portrait of him was published in *i-D* magazine.[35] The offending image, which was apparently banned in parts of the United States, showed a largely undressed Owens poised to urinate into his own mouth.[36] In reality, the image was composed from two separate portraits and Owens was holding a watering hose rather than his penis, but this was not made clear in the accompanying text. In short, for a designer termed the 'dark fashion Pope' (*pape de la mode dark*) who had spoken of his inclination to 'tease' because of his impatience with 'western' social conventions, Owens's incorporation of male undress into a catwalk collection seems more surprising for being a novelty in 2015.[37]

Cultural critic Alison Bancroft argues that *Sphinx* caused consternation because it disrupted the 'social conservatism' that assumes the catwalk is a feminized space associated with the display of attractive feminine bodies.[38] Framing her analysis with the psychoanalytic theories of Jacques Lacan, she suggests the furore caused by the models' undress was more apparent than actual. It was borne of journalists' belief that gender is anatomically determined, with masculinity 'located within a particular corporeal frame'.[39] In the case of Owens's models, this was their penis. Masculinity and femininity have a loose association with human anatomy in psychoanalysis. Lacan coined the term 'sexed subjectivity' to connote that people's identification with either concept can be independent of biological sex and societal expectations.[40] Following Lacan, Bancroft suggests the presence of the penis within the feminized space of the catwalk challenges 'its presumed inalienable relation to masculinity'.[41] If Owens's collection did convey this message, it refrained from pursuing Lacan's thought far. She suggests the garments did not sufficiently disrupt, or 'queer', dominant views about gender or sexual behaviour because they 'show[ed] and retain[ed] the limits of normative, gendered subjectivity'.[42] Adapting psychoanalyst Joan Rivière's suggestion that women's negotiation of their gendered roles is akin to wearing a veil, which masks non-normative behaviours, Bancroft argues that

Sphinx maintained 'fashion as a paradigm of the veil of femininity' because it did not propose new ideas about the role of dress in relation to concepts of gender.[43] The fashion on display remained feminine because it perpetuates the idea of 'masquerade and display', which Bancroft, following Rivière, sees as 'determinedly feminine'.[44] Consequently, *Sphinx* is little different to other fashion presentations.[45]

Bancroft appears disappointed by Owens's reticence, but her conclusion underpins remarks that he has made about his practice. In the case of *Sphinx* it is apparent that, contrary to Lacan (and Bancroft), Owens does equate masculinity with the penis. His comment that the collection was 'masculinity x3' in one interview reinforces his suggestion in another that 'every man wants to be walking on the street with his dick out, it is a great idea'.[46] In having some models show their penises, Owens seems to be pursuing a more elemental point – 'primal' in his words – than the one Bancroft seeks to ascribe to him. As fashion scholars Adam Geczy and Vicki Karaminas assert in their analysis of Owens's collections, 'the connecting thread in all of [his] runway performances is physicalization. It is here that gender finds space for expression'.[47] They invoke philosopher Judith Butler's concept of gender as performance to argue that the collection's premise 'was quite simple'.[48] The models' undress highlights the tension between men appearing in public as they should, framed by social mores, and how Owens assumes they want to. He emphasizes the personal complications that arise from the 'west's' ambiguous relationship with undressed bodies. In another interview about *Sphinx*, he explained:

> With the menswear I'm always thinking about decorum. It's about dignity. They don't want to look like they're trying too hard. I'm always thinking of that balance between control and self-discipline. And then on the [other] hand, it could all fall apart. What I do is about control and collapse. And sometimes getting tempted to do one or the other.[49]

Owens's discontinuous explanation of *Sphinx* accords with comments he had made in previous interviews. For him the fashion show is a 'sophisticated aesthetic arena where people expect a certain element of surprise or challenge'.[50] Consequently, he does not seek to be 'provocative'.[51] He suggests '[t]he most successful men's fashion is conservative with just a hint of rebellion'.[52] Whilst he likes artifice to be 'exaggerated and borderline ridiculous' that challenges 'the codes of good taste and notions of conversative beauty', it should do so 'in a good-humoured way'.[53] These comments indicate that Owens determines the effectiveness of his designs by the extent to which they are interpreted within social conventions. He does not seek to overturn them, as Bancroft might prefer. Moreover, the universal 'codes', 'notions' and 'humour' that Owens casually references are likely to denote the socialized practices of white 'westerners'.

Bancroft is not alone in being intrigued by the prospect of Owens's designs and reading more into them than may be warranted. Fashion scholar Hazel Clark and gender studies scholar Leena-Maija Rossi suggest that his work makes fashion 'more flexible and plural' because it 'typically def[ies] distinct gender identification'. Owens's creations are apparently similar to the work of designers identified by Fury as 'The Alternatives' because of their inclination to subvert luxury fashion conventions and erode any 'demarcation between genders'.[54] Visual analysis of Owens's designs can support this assertion. Owens coined the term 'glunge', a portmanteau of glamour and grunge, to describe his designs. Through this minimalist aesthetic, which is characterized by 'cloak shapes' and 'multiple layerings of long T-shirts, drop-crotch shorts and skinny pants', it could be thought that he champions gender fluidity.[55] Nevertheless, consideration of his work in conjunction with his documented discussions makes this evaluation less credible. Owens's designs, as evidenced by *Sphinx*, assert gendered roles more than they abrade them. This, I contend, is why they became subject to such public scrutiny.

The undressed models that appear in *Sphinx* caused consternation because they upset two tenets upon which the 'west's' conceptions of undress rest: first, that unadorned bodies reveal deeper truths; second, that the social body should remain covered, especially in the case of men. Within *Sphinx* the bodies of six male models were not fully covered, but neither were they wholly undressed. The wilful obfuscation regarding a sensitive issue that is almost always demarcated in 'western' art creates unease. Moreover, the genitalia that could be glimpsed through apertures and below heightened hemlines was, as Bancroft writes, 'flaccid, shrivelled and floppy'.[56] This presentation of the penis, which academic Peter Lehman suggests is 'perhaps the most taboo image of all' within the 'west', is a far cry from the decorous designs that adorn Greek and Roman statues.[57] To see a 'small, retracted' penis is to shatter the symbolic, valorized concept of the phallus and thus lay bare the fact that masculinity is a social construct that can be questioned.[58] Here, as Tsjeng observes, there 'is something to be ashamed of, laughed at and humiliated'.[59]

At least one scientific study has concluded that a 'western' man's physical attractiveness is determined by the relationship between his height, shoulder-to-hip ratio and flaccid penis size.[60] The research was conducted using virtual representations of white men and involved a majority of Australian women, presumably white, with a median age of twenty-six. The evidence is therefore suggestive rather than indicative. Nor does the study consider the genesis of socialized expectations of a man's physical appearance and the extent to which they have been shaped by artistic depictions, including 'western' classical statuary. Nevertheless, based on this research, the models in *Sphinx* may have seemed particularly unappealing because their oversized garments prevented onlookers from judging the size of their penis in relation to their shoulder-to-hip ratio. The image presented was consequently unsettling for being unreconcilable to people's socialized expectations. Feelings of unease, even ignominy, may have been amplified by the casting of thin, diminutive models and their dishevelled styling. This included several men with hair fashioned to look unwashed and unbrushed. This aesthetic recalls a comment Owens made in an interview that accompanied his controversial double portrait of 2002; namely, that his clothing is all about 'dirty habits'.[61] The undress within *Sphinx* is therefore at odds with the 'west's' Hellenic traditions and is far from valorous.

In sum, the parading of mundane male bodies, skinny, shabby, undressed, poses an antithesis to both Hebraic and Hellenic traditions, which are exposed as being wholly unreconcilable. An emphasis on the 'primal' also does much to question the applicability of some theories of undress. Rather than seeking to theorize, Owens seems more interested in the physical and quotidian, as Geczy and Karaminas note. He is concerned to comment on how 'western' people's bodies reflect negotiations between their self and social identities within a skewed cultural frame.

MT Costello, autumn/winter 2015

MT Costello's catwalk presentation for autumn/winter 2015 was shown as part of Mercedes Benz Fashion Week, New York, on 19 February 2015. The collection, comprising thirty-three looks, was conceived to assert the brand's commitment to 'unapologetically [break] the rules, rais[e] the bar and influenc[e] the power of sex, love and rebellion'.[62] Modelled by thirty-three black (5), brown (5) and white (23) women and two white men, a press release from the brand explained that garments were 'inspired by exotic reptiles and swampy grasslands, featuring earth tones, faux skins and unique hemlines. The theatrical performance signified the shedding of skin to convey self-confidence, revealing one's inner animal'.[63] The twelve-minute show became a focus for the world's 'western' media because of the undress it included. Commentary centred on twenty-three-year-old Charles Laurent Marchand. Marchand wore a knee-length hooded brown cloak that resembled a crocodile hide over his shoulders and back, a gold-coloured bracelet on his left wrist, and a similarly coloured item of jewellery set with stones in the form of a snake around his penis, which he covered with his right hand. The Frenchman was otherwise undressed. On completing his circuit of the runway, and before exiting, Marchand dropped the cloak to his ankles, exposing his posterior. Live streaming of the show was halted during his walk, although Marchand does feature in footage of its finale, when models returned to the runway in order of their initial appearance.[64]

Journalists' explanation of Costello's collection was defined by Marchand's appearance. It was also framed by the undress that had featured within Rick

Owens's *Sphinx* collection twenty-eight days previously during Paris Fashion Week. A second instance of catwalk undress within a month inclined several journalists to think they were observing an episodic fashion trend. Nevertheless, commentaries on the Costello show are curious for their lack of contextualization and explanation. The result is a series of reports, partial and sensationalist, that are at once more flippant and fretful than those that responded to *Sphinx*.

Many articles included puns about Marchand's appearance. He was a male model who 'let it all hang out'.[65] He was 'ballsy'.[66] In response to his undress, the audience were said to be 'gawping' and in 'shock'.[67] Most striking is the highly selective documentation of the catwalk presentation, which results in a distorted and prurient rendering of Marchand's undressed appearance. Three points can be made. First, Marchand was not the only model in the show to be undressed. The show began with an undressed female model, who is not acknowledged in any media report. Her appearance is mentioned in a press release from the brand, where she is unnamed.[68] Appearing at the top of the runway, the model wore a gold floor-length translucent hooded gown, what appeared to be black lace lingerie, a single finger-less black leather glove on her right hand, and gold open-toed high heels. After she had walked, falteringly, down the runway, the model stood before the audience and removed the gown. In so doing, she revealed that the lingerie and glove were *trompe l'oeils*.[69] Their appearance had been achieved through black and gold body paint applied by Mehron Cosmestics.[70] Walking the return length of the runway with the gown gathered in her right hand, the model was more obviously undressed than Marchand.[71] Second, Marchand was not the first model to appear on the catwalk as some edited clips of the show imply. He was the tenth model to walk. One clip of the catwalk presentation alters the sequence in which the models appear. According to this version of events, the female model who opens the show made her debut after Marchand.[72] Third, no commentator appears to have engaged with MT Costello's statement about the collection that asserted the brand's intention 'to break rules', which presumably referenced 'western' social conventions about undress. One explanation for this lack of engagement is the curiously late date at which the statement appeared on the Cision PR newswire website. Costello submitted their press release eight days after the catwalk show, on 27 February. This raises the possibility that the brand's explanation was conceived in response to the incomplete reporting of their presentation. Nevertheless, even before the publication of this text, no commentator considered the possible connection between the show appearing as part of an event hosted by the Los Angeles–based AIDS Healthcare Foundation, the world's largest AIDS organization, and the known homosexuality of Marchand and the brand's eponymous designer Michael Costello.

The disinclination to reflect on the implication of the undress in Costello's show is curious because, unlike the models in Owens's *Sphinx*, Marchand's look was more directly oppositional to 'western' concepts of undress because it appears to promote a Hellenic concept of valorous nudity over a Hebraic concept of vulgar nakedness. First, Marchand's appearance looks to have been informed by classical statuary.[73] The hooded garment that framed his shoulders resembles the *chlamys*, a cloak that recurs in sculpture from ancient Greece and Rome. His muscled physique and short tussled hair are another characteristic feature of gods and heroes immortalized in classical, and subsequently Renaissance, art. There is a particularly close resemblance between Marchand's appearance and the Vatican's white marble Apollo Belvedere from *c*. 120 to 140.[74] The model's covered penis even finds a parallel in the fig leaf that was added to conceal the statue's genitals from the eyes of shame-seeing pontiff Paul IV in the sixteenth century. Second, the serpent-shaped jewellery Marchand wore around his penis alludes to the story of humankind's Fall in the Old Testament and the commencement of a Christian narrative that considers undress objectionable. To adorn a snake motif with stones is to decorate, rather than disguise, the penis, and bring more attention to it. This decision surely pokes fun at the Hebraic conceit that undress is problematic. In referencing the Hellenic idea that undressed bodies convey truths, especially using a model with an athletic physique, in contrast to the skinny men in Owens's show, Marchand's performance supports the show's message of 'shedding . . . skin to convey self-confidence, revealing one's inner animal' by challenging the 'western' idea that undress is shameful.

One explanation for the lack of journalistic enquiry is that the theatricality of designs and their staging may have actively precluded it. In line with the brand's focus on sex and rebellion, many of the garments extenuated their wearer's silhouettes and revealed their skin. There was a profusion of gold and lustrous fabrics that flashed and shimmered as the models walked with exaggerated gestures. Their movements reflected the energy and self-assertion of the accompanying soundtrack, which included songs from American rappers I Love Makonnen, O.T. Genasis and Migos. Several of the models moved with long, deliberate strides. Some gripped the hems of jackets and dresses and made sweeping gestures with their hands to make garments billow behind them. Two models who wore similar black dresses mirrored one another's movements.[75] A consequence of this approach, which seemed to demand an immediate, visceral response from onlookers, is that garments appeared bold, perhaps beautiful, but bereft of deep meaning; 'gimmicky (and oh so Instagrammable)' in the words of *Los Angeles Times* correspondent Adam Tschorn in reference to Costello's spring/summer 2016 collection.[76] This judgement is not necessarily a criticism, but an acknowledgement that Costello's practice, the fame and commercial viability it has achieved, is rooted in his creation of red-carpet garments for A-list celebrities, including Celine Dion and Beyoncé, and his participation in the American reality shows *Project Runway* and *Project Runway All Stars*. Costello's career is predicated on an ability to design garments that stand out in large public arenas – on stage or through the small screen – where an immediate response is more important than incremental revelation. An unintended consequence of this practice may be that the clamour of the designs prohibits a deep consideration of their meaning. The potential for Costello's autumn/winter 2015 collection to interrogate the 'west's' socialized attitudes towards undress through its critical usage of Hebraic and Hellenic motifs was therefore unrealized and the fullest contemplation of the garments and show is contained within a press statement the brand issued a week after their debut.

The inclination to consider Costello's designs 'gimmicky' was heightened by an episode during the show, which was surely unscripted, and underscores the ambivalent response that catwalk undress provokes. During the finale, when models processed around the runway's perimeter, video footage shows the second male model, whose body was wholly and conventionally dressed in shirt, trousers, jacket and shoes, throwing his head back in laughter and reaching out towards Marchand, who passes him on the opposite side.[77] The trigger for the model's actions, along with the gesture he makes, is unclear, as is any reaction from Marchand whose back is towards the camera. This rupture, observable on film for just two seconds, disrupts the expectation of catwalk stoicism and Bancroft's assertion that the catwalk should only be thought of as a feminine space. It recalls Tsjeng's comment about the models who walked Rick Owens's catwalk with their flaccid genitals discretely exposed:

> [M]ale nudity – when it doesn't involve wink-nudge clothed bulges or hard-ons – is always a punchline. It's a joke. We don't have the vocabulary to even talk about cocks without turning into giggly schoolkids (hence the Dick Owens puns). A flaccid penis is something to be ashamed of, laughed at and humiliated.[78]

The conversational tone that Tsjeng adopts reflects that he is writing for a generalist audience, but his observation that people lack the vocabulary to talk about male undress is ostensibly reinforced by the presence of slang words in his prose – 'hard-ons', 'cocks' – and that of the other journalists cited above. Fundamentally, the point is not that 'western' people lack appropriate terms to contemplate and discuss undress. Tsjeng's paragraph alone establishes that the vocabulary is expansive and rich. The point is that colloquial and euphemistic terms have become preponderant because public and sustained contemplation of undress is typically disavowed in the 'west'. Discussing undress is permissible as a joke, which renders it unserious and harmless. It might be conceded that the use of theory within academic commentaries also acts as a pacifying mechanism, and psychological salve. To classify and explain troubling social behaviours through the comforting immutability of paradigms makes them appear safe and reconcilable to 'western' values.

Cover shoot, Brazilian *Vogue* digital issue, December 2020

The cover for Brazilian *Vogue*'s December 2020 digital issue features a portrait of thirty-one-year-old black Brazilian ballerina Ingrid Silva by Brazilian photographer Henrique Gendre. Silva's pose is taut, compact and complex. She sits upright, her body and gaze is positioned to face the viewer. Her right leg, bent at the knee with the flat of the foot resting on the ground, is held by her right hand at the shin. Silva's left leg, which supports the majority of her weight, is bent at the knee so that her shin, tucked behind her right foot, rests on the ground beneath her. Silva's left arm is draped across the front of her body, its hand rests on her right shoulder. The gesture conceals much of her torso and breasts. With the exception of her painted nails, underwear and pointe shoes, all of which correspond to her skin colour, and a Bulgari pendant necklace, Silva is undressed. She is also pregnant. Her distended navel is highlighted by soft white lighting. The portrait appears particularly striking because Silva is foregrounded by a gradient backdrop of light grey.

Silva posted the cover image to her Instagram account in November 2020 and wrote of making history for 'being the first Brazilian black ballerina on the cover of *Vogue*'.[79] Positive responses to Gendre's cover portrait and accompanying images were received when they were posted across multiple Instagram accounts in the same month, including those of Silva's husband, Zé Macedo, Henrique Gendre and Brazilian *Vogue*. By April 2021, five months after its upload to Silva's Instagram, the image had received 144,137 likes and 5,269 comments. Within the same period, Brazilian *Vogue*'s post had received 68,087 likes and 1310 comments. The majority of remarks were positive.[80] Chiefly made by women and often accompanied by emoticons – including red hearts, roses and crowns – they described the cover portrait in emotive terms: '*maravilhosa*' (wonderful), '*poderosa*' (powerful), '*linda demais*' (so beautiful).[81] Silva appeared like a goddess ('*que deusa!!!!!*'). Gendre's portrait was welcomed for depicting 'real women'.[82] It was praised for advancing the cause of racial equality:

> *Linda demais! Poderosa! e um exemplo para as futuras gerações negros, acreditando estudando e se superando, a nossa raça é linda e forte para sobreviver e brilhar sempre.*[83]👏👏👏😊😊

> [So beautiful! Powerful! and an example for future black generations believing in studying and excelling; our race is beautiful and strong to survive and shine forever.👏👏👏😊😊]

Nevertheless, Gendre's images sparked debate because they conjoined three topics that have been the subject of faltering negotiation within the 'west' and cultures where 'western' values have become socialized since at least the eighteenth century: a black, undressed and pregnant woman.

Two concerns predominated among people who commented on the magazine's cover image after it appeared within the Instagram grids of Brazilian *Vogue* and Silva. First, it was criticized for being tokenistic. One person queried if the team working on the shoot had been racially diverse.[84] Another observed that the positive message of Silva's portrait clashed with the scandalous images that had been taken of the magazine's former fashion director, Donata Meirelles, at a private costume party in February 2019. These photographs had evoked ideas of colonialism and slavery as Meirelles, a white woman, is shown seated on a chair flanked by black women. The hurt caused by the photographs forced her resignation.[85] Making a similar point, a third comment suggests that the 'misogynist magazine' had successfully met its 'quota' for featuring diverse people, observing that it would be utopic to think the decision to feature Silva on the cover was the choice of the editor alone.[86] A belief that Silva's body was being appropriated for mercenary reasons is conveyed most succinctly in the following remark:

> Not sure I like it for Brazil. I question the motive of Vogue in this cover. Artistically it [i]s good but knowing the heritage of slavery in Brazil, I feel like this is just a continuous portrayal of a black woman being a reproductive 'belly'.
>
> There is [*sic*.] so many more beautiful and powerful ways to show black women pregnant. I don't like it, sorry @voguebrasil @vogue
>
> A sister from BR 🇧🇷[87]

This comment, which suggests the motivation to feature Silva on the magazine's digital cover was ill advised for being oblivious to Brazil's racial histories, elucidates the second cause of disquiet about Gendre's shoot: its depiction of an undressed pregnant black woman. On the one hand, the shoot revived concerns about the morality of fashionable portrayals of undressed pregnant women that have become generalized following the publication of Annie Leibovitz's photograph of an undressed and pregnant Demi Moore on the cover of *Vanity Fair* in August 1991.[88] On the other hand, the shoot sparked a localized discussion about the race and skin colour of the child's father, framed by Brazil's freighted history of *branqueamento* (whitening) or *embranquecimento* (racial whitening). These concerns form the focus of the ensuing discussion.

Leibovitz's portrait of actor Demi Moore frames most academic discussions about the public portrayal of pregnant women. Sociologist Imogen Tyler has suggested the portrait 'could be argued to be one of the most significant photographs of its era'.[89] According to media scholar Carol Stabile, the cover image 'provoked the most intense controversy in *Vanity Fair*'s history: ninety-five television spots, sixty-four radio shows, 1,500 newspaper articles and a dozen cartoons'.[90] Within the United States, newsagents put the magazine 'on the top shelf alongside pornographic publications'.[91] Condé Nast also issued copies of the magazine in a plastic sleeve, 'leaving only Moore's face and the *Vanity Fair* title visible'.[92] Tyler argues that the difficulty of 'interpreting and classifying' Moore's image was due to the 'general invisibility of pregnant bodies in popular media' at the time.[93] Now widely imitated and spoofed – including a photograph of cis-gendered male actor Colton Haynes, who appeared to be pregnant in a monotone portrait by Tyler Shields to celebrate gaining four million Instagram followers on 31 March 2016 – it might be possible to agree with *i-D* magazine author Matt Glazebrook that the form of Leibovitz's image has become 'a pretty fail safe formula'.[94] This remark has greater validity considering the publication of pregnant singer Rihanna on the cover of American *Vogue* in April 2022.[95]

One of the people who commented on Brazilian *Vogue*'s Instagram feed certainly considered Leibovitz's image of Moore to be the antecedent of Gendre's image of Silva, remarking: 'And this is how we do it @annieliebovitz @voguemagazine'.[96] Acknowledging the photographic lineage of Silva's cover image does not necessarily aid its interpretation because the body being viewed is black. Silva is not the first black pregnant celebrity to appear undressed on the cover of a fashion-based magazine, although I contend that the treatment of her body is unique. In August 2017, *Vanity Fair* featured a Leibovitz portrait of pregnant tennis champion Serena Williams. The connection to the photographer's cover shoot of Moore that had appeared twenty-six years before was intentional. However, in placing Williams's body in a near identical pose to that of Moore, and with there being no explicit discussion of race in the accompanying interview with Buzz Bissinger or in reportage of the shoot, there is a sense that Williams's racial identity is occluded.[97] The shoot was conceived to portray a 'refreshing portrayal of modern, multifaceted womanhood'.[98] Style director Jessica Diehl wanted the images to demonstrate that 'power, motherhood, and athleticism are not mutually exclusive'.[99] Consequently, Williams's body becomes a carapace for her to represent something akin to an Everywoman. It is denied its own identity. Aligning the shoot with a photographic genre established by Leibovitz for white actress Demi Moore is fundamental here.

In her close reading of the Moore cover portrait, Tyler argues that it should be situated within the 'familiar lineage' of 'western' fine art.[100] The actress's diamond earrings and necklace make 'reference to the iconography of classical portraiture, in the fine art traditions of painting and photography'.[101] Her 'indeterminable gaze', 'neither looking at the camera nor away from it', is similar to that of 'the Virgin in Giovanni Bellini's paintings'.[102] In adhering to these same styling cues in the later portrait, Williams's body is therefore subsumed within 'western' traditions of depicting white undressed women. The use of drapery in one of the images of Williams marks a deliberate departure from the Moore shoot, but it confirms the subordination of her body to 'western' aesthetic values. The strategic use of cloth has been a characteristic feature of 'western' nude portraiture since antiquity. Diehl emphasizes how the treatment of Williams's body was representational rather than realistic when she explains the decision to use drapery, suggesting 'it felt more appropriate to bring in a bit of softness. Hence the caftan'.[103] Her remarks are framed by art historian Anne Hollander's observation, of 'western' art, that '[d]rapery near or on the nude figure in a work of art . . . makes it easier to take. It ensures both a high level of sensuous pleasure and a lowered quotient of disturbing, crude eroticism . . . its idealizing function has kept its authority: drapery automatically creates art out of life, and so it is self-justifying'.[104]

Gendre's portrait of Silva is informed by Leibovitz's image of Moore, but its portrayal of a pregnant black woman is fundamentally different, and also quite unlike that of Williams. To reconcile the image with 'western' art and canons of thought is consequently problematic and potentially undesirable. Two points can be made. First, Silva's gaze is not indeterminate. She looks directly into the camera, at the viewer. This form of presentation highlights the 'western'-centrism of Tyler's close reading of Leibovitz's portrait of Moore, and the insufficiency of applying it to Gendre's image of Silva. Tyler suggests that '[i]f Moore had been shot directly returning the gaze of the spectator, if her gaze had broken through the shiny surface of the photograph, this image would have been more difficult to accept, as it would have been more readily interpreted as inappropriately sexually inviting.'[105] In contemplating a difficulty of acceptance and an interpretation of inappropriateness, Tyler seems to privilege a 'western' audience because it is their socialized understanding of art that would be most readily challenged by these details. The point is amplified through her focus on Moore's whiteness; that is, of her skin and how it is lit, which she considers to be 'a crucial part of her ideality'.[106] Quoting film scholar Richard Dyer, Tyler argues that Moore is a 'glowing pure white woman'.[107] The difficulty here is that Silva's body is also 'lit in such a way as to glow' and it too possesses 'an intensely luminous quality'. The light similarly 'lingers' on 'the taut skin of her pregnant belly', but the effect is to emphasize Silva's blackness rather than conceal it.[108] This brings into focus the second feature that distinguishes Gendre's cover portrait from that of Moore and Williams: Silva's pose and the placement of her hands support herself; they do not '[cradle] her heavily pregnant belly'.[109] The resulting pose simultaneously facilitates the expression of Silva's personal identity and her role as a mother. Unlike the images of Moore and Williams, Gendre's portrait challenges 'western' visual conventions where, according to Rosemary Betterton, 'the maternal body has been conceptualized primarily as a container for the unborn child and its central modes of representation are the Christian maternal ideal, enshrined as the sacred vessel of divinity and the scientific concept of the pregnant body as a receptacle for new biological life.'[110] The detachment of femininity and maternity, which philosopher Julia Kristeva suggests has been most developed within

Christianity, makes Gendre's portrait less representational than the preceding images of Moore and Williams.[111]

Gendre's portrait espouses Silva's racial identity by eschewing 'western' visual and religious traditions. Nonetheless, because undress is a relational concept, dependent upon who is looking, 'western' attitudes did inform some of the responses to Silva's image within Brazil. One anglophone Brazilian blogger, Marques Travae, who created and edits *Black Brazil Today*, discussed Silva's portrait in relation to the 'rarity' of black women on the cover of Brazilian women's magazines and what he terms the 'Brazilian dream': 'the engineering [of] its non-white population into whitening itself'.[112] Travae was responding to comments from readers and friends who believed the Silva cover was a disingenuous celebration of race because Silva's husband, Zé Macedo, is white and their child would be mixed race. He quotes a 'friend' whose response to the cover was 'Too bad she doesn't want any black babies'.[113] This remark echoed comments made to Silva directly, which are addressed in her *Vogue* interview:

> *Ela tem sido constantemente questionada se existe pai, se ele é presente e até mesmo se é branco ou negro. "E se for uma produção independente? E se eu estiver em um relacionamento com outra mulher? Que diferença faz a etnia do pai? E se não tiver pai?", questiona.*[114]
>
> [[Silva] has been constantly asked whether there is a father, whether he is present and even whether he is white or black. 'What if it is an independent production? What if I am in a relationship with another woman? What difference does the father's ethnicity make? What if I don't have a father?', [Silva] asks.]

Discussion about the colour of Silva's unborn child highlights still further how race is recognized in Gendre's portrait and ignored in Leibovitz's portrait of Williams; the father of Williams's unborn child was her white husband, Alexis Ohanian.

The presumed importance of the ethnicity of Silva's foetus emphasizes how 'western'-centric assumptions that the pregnant body is a container have become globally prevalent. The development of visual technologies that permit examination of the developing foetus may have crystallized this outlook as Stabile suggests they have led to the 'erasure of woman's bodies'.[115] A belief that the black woman is 'a reproductive "belly"', to return to an Instagram comment, aligns with a Brazil's freighted history of race, chiefly stemming from its colonial occupation between the sixteenth and nineteenth centuries. In discussing the concerns about the ethnicity of Silva's child, and contemporary tensions around the concept of Palmitagem, which describes black people who prefer to date people 'outside of their racial group', Travae's blog documents racial disquiet that stems from the country's experience of European rule.[116]

Historian Petrônio Domingues argues that the abolition of slavery in Brazil in 1888 and the universalization of citizenship, which inaugurated the proclamation of the Republic in 1899, created long-standing tensions between the aspiration for and actuality of racial equality.[117] Brazil witnessed less overt racial segregation than the United States, where the 'colour-line' (*linha de cor*) was patent.[118] The country's experience of slavery was also considered to have been more humane than that of America.[119] Nevertheless, the compelling idea that Brazil was a 'racial paradise' (*paraíso racial*), which found expression in commentaries by civil rights leaders Booker T. Washington and W. E. B. DuBois, was illusory.[120] Racism within twentieth-century Brazil existed, but it was 'informal, plastic, disguised, in short, undeclared' (*informal, plástico, dissimulado, enfim, não declarado*).[121] It purportedly fostered a desire among the country's white elite, who 'had been educated since the colonial period to view blacks as inferior . . . to eliminate the "problem" of black people in the future, through miscegenation. By fostering miscegenation, the population would become increasingly white'.[122] The implication of Domingues's analysis is that whilst Gendre's portrait of Silva was viewed positively by very many people, and did indeed make history, it is nonetheless framed by a history that makes its meaning caustic as much celebratory.

Reflections

The infrequency with which undressed bodies are publicly encountered and considered may make them seem less contentious than dressed bodies. The uncommon sight of the undressed body – even of our own – more readily makes it an afterthought, something strange, even comedic. But undressed bodies are not *tabulae rasae* or culturally inert. They are sites of ongoing negotiation. The episodes considered in this chapter raise three observations. First, the communication of culturally sensitive topics within anglophone fashion discourse is uneven. The use of colloquialism and humour, predominantly by journalists, and the use of theory, predominantly by scholars, tends to confound more than clarify understanding of a designer's intent. A problematized issue – here, human undress – is obfuscated, either because it is trivialized or because it is rendered inert by association with malleable concepts and paradigms. This observation compounds sociologist Fred Davis's point about the inherent ambiguity – a word and its cognates that appears eighty-one times in his book – of contemporary dress, which makes the process of interpreting the causes and consequences of 'western'-centrism within the industry more challenging.[123] A linked point and question, to be pursued in later chapters, is what this reveals about 'western' people's perception of fashion's role: how far does fashion exist to critique or to convey culturally prevalent themes? Second, and pre-empting the discussion of the next chapter, journalistic and academic discussion of these episodes emphasizes a pervasive 'western' gender binary, where men appear active and women appear passive. Third, the physical catwalk is a fundamental means of communicating contemporary fashions within the 'west', but it can be a volatile platform. As the MT Costello show demonstrated, models can 'go rogue', live feeds can be cut and subsequently edited if aspects of a designer's work challenge socialized values.

2
GENDER

In the nineteenth century author Mark Twain suggested there was a positive correlation between human undress and people's propensity to cooperate. No amount of wishful thinking could make this fanciful claim tenable, and in explaining his position Twain unwittingly established the importance of dress in the construction of people's public lives.[1] The dressed human body is more obviously, if still ambiguously, laden with meanings than the undressed body. Consequently, it has been a more active site of negotiation within the world's cultures. Dressed bodies are the focus of the book's ongoing chapters. Three centuries before Twain, the English scholar-statesman Thomas More recognized that even the most perfect of societies would require a dress code, although tailors and dress-makers were forbidden from the community he imagined.[2] In his *Utopia*, published in 1516, More clothed people's public bodies in rough garments of linen and wool.[3] Adjustments were made for summer and winter, but everybody dressed alike.[4] Insisting on homogeneity of material and form, More nonetheless stipulated that Utopian clothing should vary according 'to sex and marital status'.[5] In his vision of a utopia, More could conceive of a scenario where people dispensed with gold and jewels, considering them playthings for children, and took no delight in rich silks, but he could not imagine a society where people's dress and appearance did not demarcate their biological sex and gendered roles.[6] For him, a gender binary – man and woman – was irrefutable. His resolution – or intransigence – stemmed from his Catholic devotion, which led to his execution in 1535 and canonization in 1935.

One of the most explicit ways that human bodies are socially recognizable and meaningful in the 'west' is through gendered dress. This is a deceptively simple remark. Following philosopher Judith Butler, who conceives of gender as a performance, it is now more readily accepted within academia that we are grappling with a concept that is socially constructed, culturally contingent, mutable.[7] Gender is understood, enacted and valued differently across communities, cultures and chronologies. Nonetheless, it remains challenging to separate gender from biological sex, especially beyond the academy.

This is because of the persistence of a 'western' binary that recognizes and differentiates between male and female only. The binary is most clearly manifest and maintained within the contemporary fashion industry. From a twenty-first century perspective, More's outlook, shared by many early modern European thinkers, appears conspicuous for its white, cis-gendered and heteronormative predilections. Nonetheless, it establishes that entrenched ideas about gender expectations existed within the 'west' before they were more rigidly defined during the Enlightenment and imposed and policed within and beyond Europe through subsequent colonial encounters and the establishment of empires.

The accounts of Europeans – largely authored by white, cis-gendered and heteronormative men conceiving of an identical readership – who participated in some of the earliest overseas voyages to territories that would become subject to colonial rule are characterized by a mixture of concern, contempt, always curiosity, about the gender and sexual practices of the people they met. Their unease reflected a socialized belief, articulated and authorized by anthropology – 'the science of man' – that bodily differences, most notably sex and race, necessitated specific rights and forms of citizenship. Consequently, there was an initial inability to recognize, and a longer-term struggle to reconcile, the fact that many societies beyond Europe did not conflate a person's sex, gender and sexual practices. For example, 'western' ideas of marriage, based on choice, 'personal desires and criteria', ran counter to societies within Africa where marriage was 'required as a fundamental obligation of kinship and citizenship, whether or not the partners [were] attracted to each other—or to each other's sex'.[8] The prominence of young boys who dressed in female clothing in Japan, Tahiti and Turkestan; the political importance of eunuchs in India, among other examples, suggested a 'topsy-turvy gender order' beyond Europe's borders. Europeans feared that sustained engagement with people whose beliefs and customs seemed very different to their own would be deleterious. Assuming the rightness of their position, desirous to establish their authority, and seeking to pre-empt contagion overseas and at home, European scientists and writers argued that contamination could be curtailed through a process of civilization. This early-eighteenth-century term, used in contradistinction to barbarism and savagery, justified the global imposition of European values and practices.[9]

The crystallization of the 'west's' gender binary during the eighteenth and nineteenth centuries drew upon long-standing ideas of difference and otherness. In More's *Utopia*, for example, women – 'the weaker sex' – undertook lighter physical tasks.[10] Science historian Londa Schiebinger argues that European men were as dominant in refining the concept of gender during the eighteenth century, and '[held] a tight rein on what was recognized as legitimate knowledge and who could produce that knowledge'.[11] Such homo-centrism led to curious classificatory foci that included the ability of white men to grow beards, which black and indigenous American men were apparently unable to do, and the extent to which a man's sphincter was smooth or his penis 'looked like that of a dog'.[12] Reasonably, Schiebinger questions, 'Had women and native Americans held chairs of anatomy in European universities, would the same question[s] have arisen?'[13]

Strange, arbitrary, uncomfortable as this reasoning may appear in the twenty-first century, it gained credence three centuries before as colonial encounters, interpreted through Enlightenment empiricism, seemed to demand the reconceptualization, or reassertion, of the 'west's' social norms and values.[14] The result was the demarcation of human roles and relationships into numerous, hierarchically ordered and seemingly rigid categories. Simultaneously, there was a renegotiation of human bodies, which became, in historian Kathleen Wilson's words, 'sites for constructing identities of insiders and outsiders'.[15] In particular, a 'two-sex' theory that established an essential biological difference between females and males became orthodoxy. This replaced a previous 'one-sex' theory that had considered female genitalia to be an inversion of male genitalia.[16] Concurrently, historian Ariel Beaujot argues that it was during the nineteenth century that 'western' 'clothing became exaggeratedly distinct for each gender – through careful tailoring, corseting, bustling, crinolining . . . women's bodies became hourglasses, and men's became long, straight, and cylindrical'.[17]

Classifications that spurred and legitimated changes in 'western' people's thought and actions were far from dispassionate and drew upon prevalent, if ill-defined, cultural allusions and metaphors that were 'elevated' to become 'self-conscious theory', and once '"naturalized" in the language of science . . . disguised'.[18] For example, gender-based references featured more prominently in colonial discourses as the notion of a masculine political sphere emerged in contradistinction to a feminized private and domesticated domain within Britain during the eighteenth century. Gender historian Jessica Hinchy links this development to a contemporaneous narrowing of the definitions of family and sexual respectability.[19] Historian Ben Barker-Benfield suggests 'the metaphor of the body-politic linked man's view of the state to his most personal and indestructible source of identity, his body'.[20] The metaphor was familiar. The linkage between conceptions of the body and state was current in Europe from at least the eleventh century.[21] The Enlightenment and onset of European colonialism during the seventeenth century meant it assumed a graver urgency, for two reasons. First, the ideal of a 'universal individual' that emerged during the Enlightenment, was, as historian Nancy Stepan adroitly observes, 'male and European'.[22] Second, the congruence, or more typically incongruence, between European gender and sexual practices and those of indigenous peoples became a litmus test upon which assumptions about social structures and cultural norms were based. Analyzing the initial encounters with indigenous peoples, European men of science tended to see what they desired and their writings frequently, and blithely, reinforced assumptions about their gender superiority. For example, long-standing views about women's frailty suggested they would be 'less able to withstand the lure of the exotic, bestial or sensual'.[23]

The importance of allusion and metaphor in clarifying scientific thought meant that men of the academy conceived parallels between black men, 'the dominant sex of an inferior race', and white women, 'the inferior sex of the dominant race'.[24] As Stepan explains:

> By analogy with the so-called lower races, women, the sexually deviate, the criminal, the urban poor, and the insane were in one way or another constructed as biological 'races apart' whose differences from the white male, and likenesses to each other, 'explained' their different and lower position in the social hierarchy.[25]

The resulting ideas about gender were complicated and contextual. They 'could be put to a variety of purposes'.[26] Moreover, the perceived need to establish and enforce European gender practices produced shifting typologies.[27] Both factors go some way to explain how these ideas remain tenacious in the twenty-first century. For, if they appeared fixed in their imposition upon Europe's colonial subjects between the eighteenth and twentieth centuries, they were in actuality fluidic, especially for their European (male) progenitors whose gaze – at once defensive, longing and domineering – informed the writing that would, and still does, frame so much of our thinking about gender. The dominance of these views is apparent from contemporary debates about the social recognition and legal rights of queer communities, specifically transgender people, that have become increasingly polarized and pernicious. The concept of gender is condemned as 'foreign' (i.e. 'western') within parts of eastern Europe, where, Butler explains, it is 'likened to "communism" or to "totalitarianism"'.[28] The challenge that gender poses in our present is also apparent in virtual spaces where organizations like the Institute of Digital Fashion suggest the blithe acceptance of a binary limits the utility of digital technologies and the experiences they can provide.[29]

The three studies in this chapter – the debut collection of Hedi Slimane for Celine, spring/summer 2019, Jimmy Choo's 'Shimmer in the Dark' television film for winter 2017 and American *Vogue*'s interview with Victoria's Secret representatives in November 2018 – seek to demonstrate how the negotiation of gender through contemporary fashions remains challenging and deeply emotive because of the persistence of patterns of thought that were defined in the crucible of the Enlightenment and through colonial encounters. If these thoughts are largely unquestioned, on account of the apparent neutrality that has been conferred upon them for being long-standing, the ensuing discussions seek to show how they are far being immutable when people's lives become unsettled. As Ann Swidler observes, it is at times of 'social transformation' when different ways of organizing social life are proposed that the socialized framing of people's beliefs and behaviours becomes most apparent.[30] Ideas pursued here will be developed in the following chapters, which consider race and sexuality, respectively.

Celine, *Paris la Nuit*, spring/summer 2019

Hedi Slimane's first collection for Celine, *Paris la nuit: journal nocturne de la jeunesse Parisienne* (Paris at night: the nocturnal journal of a Parisian girl), was presented on 28 September 2018 at *Les Invalides* within Paris Fashion Week. The collection consisted of ninety-six looks; forty-nine for men, forty-seven for women.[31] Six models were black (three men, three women); the remainder were white. The majority of garments, of wool and leather, were monotone with accents of metallic silver and gold. The collection was defined by three motifs. First, the pairing of jackets and ties, which comprised twenty-five of the menswear designs and three of the womenswear designs, including model Licett Morillo, who wore a bow tie. Second, quarter-thigh-length skirts and dresses, which featured in thirty-eight of the womenswear looks. Third, headwear with attached gauze veils that partially or wholly covered the model's face were paired with twenty-six of the womenswear looks. None of the menswear designs included headwear. The chief accessory worn by men, present in forty-eight of the looks, was a pair of dark sunglasses that wholly concealed the models' eyes. Sunglasses were included in five of the women's looks, two of which featured jackets and ties. Slimane's collection was markedly different to the pre-fall 2018 collection of his predecessor Phoebe Philo, which included forty-seven looks worn by four female models; two black, two white.[32] Philo's final collection for Céline – the accent on the brand's name was removed by Slimane – included a greater variety of colours, cloths and fabrics than that of her successor. Garments were cut to de-emphasize the wearer's silhouette and sex. The perception that Slimane's garments emphasized their wearer's sex and enforced a 'western' gender binary made it a deeply problematic, and much criticized, debut for Celine's new creative director.

The anglophone fashion press was excoriating about *Paris la Nuit* and its presentation. It was 'tacky' and 'ridiculous'.[33] Featuring 'skinny boys and cranky, baby-faced girls', it was said to channel apparel and attitudes from the 1980s, offering little that was new.[34] It was 'infantilizing' and offered no diversity 'of any kind'.[35] If the collection heralded anything, it was a 'dark dawn' for the brand. Suggesting that Slimane's talent was 'dulled', his collection was likened to a 'horror show'.[36] He was a 'house-wrecker' and a proponent of 'toxic masculinity'.[37] *The Hollywood Reporter* ran a story with the headline, 'Is Hedi Slimane the Donald Trump of Fashion?'[38] Negative responses to *Paris la Nuit* were so numerous within the anglophone fashion press that *Fashionista*, an online fashion news site, collated many of the more critical commentaries into a single post.[39] Concern around Slimane's collection centred on his 'blissful ignorance' about Philo's design philosophy, which was widely perceived to empower women.[40] Devotees of her 'transparency and believability' had become known as 'Philophiles'.[41] By contrast, Slimane 'wiped out' this 'streamlined vision'. Ruefully, Canadian fashion journalist Leanne Delap remarked, 'my first thought is that only a man would do that.'[42] Making a similar, but more considered point, editor Vanessa Friedman, writing for *The New York Times*, observed that Slimane presented an 'image *for* women, not *of* them'.[43]

For critics who thought Slimane had deprived women of their agency, making them avatars for men to steer and stare at, there appeared to be plenty of evidence. The location for Celine show, which Slimane had used to present his fall menswear collection when creative director of Saint Laurent in 2014, was considered a portent of his intent.[44] The *Les Invalides* complex memorializes France's military history and houses the tomb of the country's first emperor, Napoleon Bonaparte, whose armies subjugated much of continental Europe in the early nineteenth century. It is a space associated with the conventionally male, and increasingly freighted, topics of conflict and conquest. The emphasis on menswear within *Paris la Nuit* also seemed to herald a re-alignment of the brand's priorities away from women. The 'mainly black trapezoidal glasses' that were prominent in all but one of the menswear looks fuelled invective that Slimane had conceived his collection through a singularly male perspective. Darkened lenses liberated the male gaze by conspicuously occluding it.[45] The sombre colour palette and prominence of the men's suit, a garment lauded and lambasted for its representation of perfection, provided further grist for critics' mills.[46]

The concern that Slimane was unaware or indifferent to the aspirations of the women he dresses was presaged by remarks in an interview he conducted with French newspaper *Le Figaro* before the Celine show.[47] Asked how far his vision differed to that of Philo, Slimane's response was curious for referring to her obliquely as his 'predecessor'. He did not want to 'imitate' her work, but nor had he sought to 'go the opposite way'.[48] He was determined to start a 'new chapter'.[49] Throughout the interview, Slimane insists on following a personal code and style 'against all odds', questioning rhetorically 'why should I give up on what defines me?'[50] He asserts that 'a designer is someone who expresses himself authentically through what he feels'. They should be unafraid of 'making waves'.[51] A resolve for 'consistency, rigour, accuracy' makes Slimane resolute in his practice and uncompromising. He argues that '[t]wenty years ago, I put the shoulders back to where they should be and then redefined the waist line', seemingly oblivious to the possibility of different perspectives.[52] He similarly refers to a 'perfect black jacket' and 'perfect little black dress', content that their excellence is determined by him alone.[53] Reacting against 'nostalgia', desensitized to beauty, and pursuing a singular style for 'more than 20 years', Slimane's outlook is reminiscent of the European men of science who singularly, if inadvertently, (re-)defined notions of gender during the eighteenth and nineteenth centuries.

There is an analogy between Slimane's oblique assertion of power over women in the twenty-first century, and the power, similarly ill-defined but no less apparent, that European men claimed over women during the eighteenth and nineteenth centuries. Historian Joanna de Groot identifies three elements by which white European men of science established a male hegemony and the primacy of the white male body. Linkages can be made between these elements and Slimane's perspective and practice as a fashion designer. First, the scientists defined and prescribed human categories and social roles based on biological differences that were 'essential' and unreconcilable. There is an equivalence between this process of classification and segregation and the 'consistency, rigour, accuracy' that Slimane valorizes.[54] Three hundred years ago, the scientific method was underpinned by a second and supporting belief in the inherent inequalities between different peoples, specifically in relation to gender and race. Third, there was a perceived need for a superior sex and race to control, protect and nurture those deemed to be lesser, and to refute contrary views for the greater good.[55] These points are echoed in Slimane's pursuit of perfection and his championing of the skill and sentiment of 'handmade', which 'can only be found in Paris'.[56] These assumptions are predicated on inequalities within the fashion industry. Moreover, the assumption that he knows best how to clothe women and rejects models, whom he infantilizes as 'girls and boys', '[i]f a dress that I particularly love doesn't have a body that wears it', is redolent of a mindset that dismissed what it could not readily contemplate and control.[57] Nineteenth-century modes of thinking are obviously different to those of Slimane, but the divergence is one of degree more than kind. Slimane's vision for Celine, to prioritize an 'orthodoxy' and 'alignment' that he has conceived and seeks to establish broadly, appears to be similarly imperious:

> It's about putting the church back at the centre of the village. It's orthodoxy, quite simply. Installing language elements that are rooted in the original history of the house [of Celine], its foundations, returning to an architectural and graphic alignment is essential to the project.[58]

Scientific analysis during the eighteenth and nineteenth centuries shaped, and happily confirmed, European men's thoughts and the practices they facilitated, but de Groot argues that imagination was no less important; that is, men's desire for what they wanted the territories and peoples of their burgeoning empires to be like and to provide.[59] These fantasies, bolstered by obliging facts, enabled European men to survey and to judge all people that were considered inferior and beholden to their physical and psychological prowess: 'it invite[d] a *male* gaze.'[60] Slimane's assertion that he knows the correct placement of the female shoulder and waistline and the terms of perfection for items of women's dress, along with the assumption that he has the right to enact change and insist on it being followed, is similar to the self-justification of European scientists who clarified the 'west's' gender binary three centuries earlier. Delap's remark that Slimane's debut collection could only have been the work of man may read as glib, but it has foundation. Friedman's observation that his debut collection rejects the 'female gaze', and thereby privileges the male gaze, is similarly compelling.[61]

The concept of the male gaze was enunciated by art critic John Berger in a BBC television series and subsequent book, *Ways of Seeing*, in 1972. Berger argued that 'western' art, rather than dress specifically, was conceived from the perspective of what would now be termed a cis-gendered, heteronormative, white male gaze. Men viewed women as objects of desire. He argued:

> [M]en act and *women appear*. Men look at women. Women watch themselves being looked at. This determines not only most relations between men and women but also the relation of women to themselves. The surveyor of the woman is herself male: the surveyed female. Thus she turns herself into an object – and most particularly an object of vision: a sight.[62]

Similar ideas were pursued by film theorist Laura Mulvey. Three years after *Ways of Seeing* aired, she argued that women's appearances in Hollywood films connoted a 'to-be-looked-at-ness' as male 'phantasies' are projected on to them.[63]

These bold assertions, voiced four decades ago, are not without problems. First, they accept the 'west's gender binary as axiomatic. Second, they assume this binary frames people's gendered self-perceptions. The experiences of non-binary and transgender people belie this, although their voices were even more marginal in the 1970s when Berger and Mulvey wrote.[64] The substance of Berger's and Mulvey's points is nonetheless relevant when thinking about fashion broadly. Mulvey asserts that cinema is 'an advanced representation system' that elucidates, and enforces, 'dominant order structures', and this is no less true for the fashion industry.[65] Their points are particularly helpful when thinking about Slimane's collection specifically, which was inspired by his love of Paris by night.

In his *Le Figaro* interview, Slimane dwells on the enjoyment he felt walking voyeuristically through the French capital:

> I like walking in Paris for hours and hours, crossing the Seine, walking through the left bank . . . I love Paris by night. I grew up between the smoke of Le Palace and the white tiles of Les Bains-Douches. It's a pity that the city is eager to close down interesting places like those and turn its back on Parisian

nights. The lights still remain, though. The magic of the street lamps, the neons in the cafés, the sparkling Parisian youth and the energy of the streets.[66]

Evocative and captivating as these recollections might initially seem, they are indicative of a male privilege to be able to walk securely at night and to gaze. It is a privilege that evidences the persistence of 'western' gender inequalities that crystallized during the nineteenth century.

A legitimate question might be posed: why did Slimane's collection cause such consternation when it was framed by patterns of thought that have been ascendant in the 'west' for three hundred years? A response can be linked to Ann Swidler's discussion of unsettled lives, periods of time when the subconscious influences of culture become explicit. The complex, bitter negotiations that played out in the press in the days that followed the *Paris la Nuit* presentation were due to a period of transition that emphasized the disparity between Slimane's fondly remembered past and the fantasized Parisian female (*la jeunesse Parisienne*) who became the muse for his collection. At the time of the show, 'a new wave of feminism [was] coursing through Western society'.[67] The garments of *Paris la Nuit* were interpreted in conjunction with Senate hearings that had been convened in the United States to determine the veracity of sexual assault claims made by Professor Christine Blasey Ford against Supreme Court nominee Brett Kavanaugh.[68] More broadly, journalist Booth Moore mused that 'Donald Trump's politics of division, cable news and social media ha[d] made everything intensely personal, and turned public discourse into a daily shouting match'.[69] Not everyone derided Slimane. Anabel Maldonado, writing for *Business of Fashion*, was one of the few female fashion journalists to defend him. She argued that *ad hominem* attacks risked 'not only castrating creativity, but actually alienating a significant portion of the female fashion market. Not all women are Philophiles. Some of us, at all ages, actually enjoy wearing miniskirts'.[70] Positive though it was, Maldonado's argument is rooted in the same logic of 'to-be-looked-at-ness' that can be traced to the nineteenth century. The difference, which may not have been grasped by the disputants, is that Maldonado's stance seeks to upend its consequences. By conspicuously embracing, even exaggerating, the performance of femininity, linguist and philosopher Luce Irigaray has argued that 'a form of subordination [can become] assertion' by undermining men's fantasies.[71] Nonetheless, as fashion scholars Paul Jobling, Philippa Nesbitt and Angelene Wong argue in an analysis of Maria Grazia Chiuri's designs for Dior, such a performance can 'serve all the while as a strategic masquerade to bolster a traditional ["western"] kind of femininity'.[72] In sum, a disquieting conclusion might be that the cultural ideas within Slimane's debut collection for Celine were scrutinized and contested less because they were held to be inherently odious, but because a concatenation of factors made them appear so. The implication is that if *Paris la Nuit* had been shown at a different time when the 'western' gender binary was not subject to such critical negotiation, its reception could have been favourable. I seek to refine this point in the study of Jimmy Choo's television film, which was similarly criticized for valorizing the male gaze.

Jimmy Choo, *Shimmer in the Dark* television film, 2017

On 9 November 2017 Jimmy Choo released a television film as part of its winter cruise marketing campaign with British model Cara Delevingne. Directed by Lorin Askill the feature, just over a minute and a half in duration, follows Delevingne, who wears a scarlet red sequinned mini dress, blonde shoulder-length hair and dark eyeliner, as she walks alone through New York's bustling streets to a nondescript industrial building for an evening party.[73] The setting could be said to anticipate Slimane's *Paris la Nuit* collection, which was inspired by his memories of night-time Paris. The film opens with Delevingne admiring a pair of Jimmy Choo crystal embellished Maine boots in the window of a closed shop. As if by magic, the boots materialize on the model's feet as she stands outside. In the next frame she is shown wearing the boots, walking jauntily, presumably confidently, along a street. What follows in the film created a backlash, particularly on Twitter, that led its withdrawal by the brand on 22 December. During her walk, Delevingne's appearance elicits responses from five different men. The first man looks towards her as she passes him on the sidewalk. As he recedes into the crowd, Delevingne turns completely around to retain him in her view.[74] The second man, standing adjacent to the street and leaning on railings, wolf whistles at her approach and comments, 'Nice shoes, lady'. Delevingne smiles and instantly casts her eyes downward.[75] The third man, driving a yellow taxi, sounds his car horn multiple times as she crosses the road in front of him. Her casual demeanour and slow pace indicate the horn is being used to admire Delevingne rather than to admonish her for jaywalking. In response, she smiles and looks back at the taxi as it moves off behind her.[76] The fourth man Delevingne approaches is a hot dog vendor. Asking for her 'usual' and identifying the man as 'Sal', it is established that there is a pre-existing relationship. Nonetheless, Sal greets Delevingne with the remark, 'There she is', without using her name. When she departs, he scans her appearance from behind and calls after her, 'Hey, great shoes'. Throughout the transaction, Delevingne smiles. She describes Sal as a 'beautiful man' when he presents her order.[77] Finally, upon arrival at her destination, Delevingne catches the attention of a fifth man whose eyes can be seen to follow her as she enters the building, moving towards him.[78] During her walk, Delevingne engages with another woman, but beyond her feet, in Jimmy Choo strap stilettos, and lower legs she is otherwise unidentifiable. Her body is blurred after Delevingne has walked past her.[79] The facial expression Delevingne makes as she looks down at the woman's shoes – pursing her lips and blowing air – appears sexually provocative, as does the side-ways turn the woman makes when passing Delevingne.

The film was criticized in the anglophone fashion press for using 'unsophisticated sexist imagery' that would make 'any self-respecting woman curl up in embarrassment'.[80] It appeared to condone 'cat-calling'.[81] Twitter users, whose comments circulated within online commentaries about the film, described the feature as 'tone deaf'.[82] One woman, identifying herself as a former New York resident, wrote, 'when I watch it my stomach hurts'.[83] People's condemnation of Askill's film was unequivocal. It was gauged in terms that would be used to lambast Slimane's Celine debut ten months later. Nonetheless, criticism of the film was not immediate. Many of the most critical comments on Twitter, certainly those that were widely reproduced in online articles, were posted in mid-December 2017 and coincide with the appearance of reproving news reports.[84] At this point, the film had been showing globally for at least six weeks. Upon its release in November, the film had been received positively. In what follows, I want to suggest the Jimmy Choo television film became problematic, and sparked vitriolic public discussion, because of a shift in perceptions that heightened awareness of the 'west's' prevailing gender binary.

On the day of the film's release, William Hunt, writing for *Wonderland* magazine, described it glowingly. Situating the feature in New York was a 'perfect reference' for the city's 'pockets of glamour'. Delevingne was 'dazzling' and 'glamourous' as she walks 'to the kind of nightclub you definitely want to be on the guest list for'. Hunt includes a quote from the model to support his positive verdict. She explains how much 'the notion of celebrating togetherness and coming together with your family and friends' appeals to her at Christmas. The response of 'bystanders' who '[turn] their heads' to look at Delevingne's footwear amplifies this 'Christmas vibe' and demonstrates that this was the 'perfect time for Jimmy Choo to release such a collection'.[85] Hunt's assessment can be questioned. In much the same way that commentators claimed Slimane's inaugural Celine collection could only have been conceived by a man, it could be argued that Hunt's optimism is a consequence of his male privilege, which makes him oblivious to the film's sexist undertones. But Hunt's voice was not alone. A day after his article appeared, journalist Cassia Carter, writing for *Grazia* in France, praised Jimmy Choo's collection. She singled out the campaign for its flexible portrayal of gender.[86]

Focusing on Tom Craig's photographic shoot that accompanied Askill's film, and which features Delevingne wearing similar clothing and a range of Jimmy Choo footwear, Carter asserts that the model looks '*sexy, impérieuse, en minirobe à sequins et aux yeux revolver*' (sexy, imperious, in a sequined minidress with smoky eyes). Referring to an interview in which Delevingne speaks about her bisexuality, Carter contends that the collection and campaign 'respects the brand's codes, based on femininity (lots of sequins, and even more sequins)', but:

> [*la collection*] *présente aussi une sélection qui mêle les genres, et brouille les limites entre femme et homme. C'est donc par une gamme de chaussures unisexes, au nom espiègle "Emprunté aux garçons", que Cara revendique son côté boyish au sein de cette campagne.*[87]
> [[The collection] also presents a selection that mixes genres, and blurs the boundaries between women and men. It is therefore through a range of unisex shoes, with the mischievous name "Borrowed from the boys", that Cara asserts her boyish side within this campaign.]

To support her argument Carter quotes Delevingne from an interview she conducted as part of the brand's campaign:

> *L'opposition entre femme et homme n'est plus aussi grande de nos jours. Je ne pense pas nécessairement qu'il faille choisir quelque chose qu'un homme porterait afin d'être androgyne. Je pense qu'il s'agit de se sentir à l'aise, que ce soit une tenue féminine ou masculine.*[88]
> [The division between woman and man isn't as large these days. I don't necessarily think you have to choose something that a man would wear in order to be androgynous. I think it's about feeling comfortable, whether it's a feminine or masculine outfit.]

The confidence Delevingne appears to convey in the film, not least her suggestive interaction with another woman wearing Jimmy Choo shoes, could support the claim that the brand was seeking to move beyond the gender binary in its collection and campaign. Nevertheless, Carter's argument is hardly robust. Her association of femininity with sequins, reference to bi-sexuality and decision to cite Delevingne's remarks about androgyny, suggest a degree of uncertainty in using gender terms. More fundamentally, Carter's *jejune* commentary reflects the campaign's insecure and unconvincing treatment of a more expansive understanding of gender. This tends to underscore a point made by Jobling, Nesbitt and Wong that a heightened performance of femininity is more likely to 'bolster' socialized assumptions than abrade them.[89]

The turn against the film, which produced a diametrically opposed interpretation to that of Hunt and Carter, and led to its withdrawal, was a consequence of a sudden shift in 'western' responses to gender following the publication of reports that American film producer Harvey Weinstein had been sexually harassing women for thirty years. The first allegations against Weinstein were made on 5 October 2017, a month before the release of the Jimmy Choo film.[90] Weinstein issued an apology the same day, but over the next three months more women, many of them Hollywood actors, came forward to accuse him of sexual advances and rape. On 11 October, Cara Delevingne documented her experiences of Weinstein's sexual advances in a post on her Instagram account.[91] Legal claims against Weinstein were registered in courts on either side of the Atlantic throughout November and organizations and individuals affiliated with him began to publicly withdraw their support.[92] News coverage of the allegations intensified during December, at which point the first critical reports of Askill's Jimmy Choo film appeared. Criticisms were also made against Delevingne for participating in the campaign following her publicized remarks about sexual harassment.[93]

Reactions to the Jimmy Choo film demonstrate the contingency of gendered categories. Fundamentally, they show how gender remains a freighted concept in the 'west' because of the persistence of a binary that recognizes male and female and perceives the former to be superior. The final study in this chapter explores this point further by considering the treatment of transgender models, whose presence more patently challenges the entrenched gendered assumptions of the fashion industry.

Victoria's Secret, American *Vogue* interview, November 2018

On 8 November 2018, American *Vogue* published the transcript of an abridged interview between Nicole Phelps, director of Vogue Runway, Ed Razek, chief marketing officer of Victoria's Secret parent company L Brands, and Monica Mitro, executive vice president of public relations at Victoria's Secret.[94] Released prior to the annual fashion show of the American-based lingerie brand, the interview sparked criticism of Victoria's Secret's understanding and support for women's body positivity, age and racial diversity. It became widely controversial because of Razek's assertion that the brand would not include transgender models in its catwalk shows.[95] Reflecting on the diversity of Victoria's Secret, and public criticisms that the brand should do more to engage with different gender, racial and body-shape realities, Razek explained:

> So it's like, why don't you do 50? Why don't you do 60? Why don't you do 24? It's like, why doesn't your show do this? Shouldn't you have transsexuals in the show? No. No, I don't think we should. Well, why not? Because the show is a fantasy. It's a 42-minute entertainment special. That's what it is. It is the only one of its kind in the world, and any other fashion brand in the world would take it in a minute, including the competitors that are carping at us. And they carp at us because we're the leader. They don't talk about each other.

I accept that. I actually respect it. Cool. But [. . .] [w]e're their first love. And Victoria's Secret has been women's first love from the beginning.⁹⁶

Three days after the interview was published, on 11 November, Razek issued an apology via the Victoria's Secret Twitter account. He acknowledged that his remark about transgender models was 'insensitive' and explained, '[t]o be clear, we absolutely would cast a transgender model for the show. We've had transgender models come to castings. . . . And like many others, they didn't make it. . . . But it was never about gender. I admire and respect their journey to embrace who they really are'.⁹⁷ Criticism of the brand's position on transgender models, which included denouncements from its own models, was linked to a decline in views of their televised catwalk, which aired on 2 December, four weeks after the publication of the *Vogue* interview. Across the United States, 4.98 million people had watched the screening of the annual catwalk in 2017. Globally, Phelps states, 'some 1 billion people in 190 countries' engaged with the show, representing a 45 per cent increase on the previous year. By contrast, in 2018, audience figures for the United States dropped by just over one third to 3.3 million.⁹⁸ In 2019, Victoria's Secret did not release a televised catwalk. In another departure from its typical format, the brand appeared to distance itself from Razek's remarks by casting its first transgender model, Valentina Sampaio, for its VS Pink sports line.⁹⁹ Sampaio revealed the news through a post on her Instagram account on 2 August. On 5 August, Leslie X. Wexner, chief executive of L Brands, announced the retirement of Ed Razek; various newspapers suggested he had resigned.¹⁰⁰

The hurt caused by Razek's comments in the *Vogue* interview was conveyed by transgender model Andrea Pejic in a post from her Twitter account:

It's really sad when you see powerful people in our industry holding such backward views and being so comfortable in expressing them on a public platform [. . .] If we cannot set an example in what's supposed to be a progressive town and a progressive industry how can we expect change in the rest of the country? How can we expect this quasi-fascist administration to stop its cold blooded and unnecessary attacks on our community?¹⁰¹

The 'backward views' refer to Razek's and Mitro's remarks about gender and the persistence of a 'western' binary that recognizes only superordinate men and subordinate women. Pejic's disappointment was doubtless framed by moves within the fashion industry to proactively support and spotlight transgender models in previous years: she had appeared on the covers of *Elle* and French *Vogue*, Lea T had featured in a Givenchy campaign, Hari Nef had walked the runway for Hood by Air.¹⁰² By contrast, the stance of Victoria's Secret in 2018 seemed to hark back to the 1970s when transgender models like Tracey Norman concealed their gender identity to guarantee bookings.¹⁰³

Within the interview, Razek claims not to be 'defensive' about Victoria's Secret, but the tone he adopts, along with that of Mitro, suggests a discomfiture and unease talking about inclusivity, generally, and gender, specifically. For example, when Mitro mentions the cultural diversity of Victoria's Secret, she cites the brand's celebration of the models' backgrounds, which focuses on 'their routines, their families, their husbands, their children', seemingly unaware that these roles enforce a gender binary.[104] In a similar vein, Mitro refers to the age of Brazilian model Adriana Lima, asserting, 'She is 37 years old. She is so driven. And talk about age diversity. There aren't a lot of brands that continue to use models past a certain age. But she's an athlete; she boxes.' The framing of Mitro's response indicates she is unaware of her implied suggestion, and acceptance, that thirty-seven is atypical for a working model, or, that Lima's pursuit of fitness could be compelled by gendered and body expectations that Victoria's Secret perpetuates.[105]

This blithe outlook is shared by Razek. He recounts two stories about models' claims of sexual harassment in response to a question from Phelps about the brand's response to the #MeToo movement, which was initially founded in 2006 by Tarana Burke to raise awareness of and support for the survivors of sexual violence:[106]

> The two stories that broke, let me be specific about them, one of them was about a photographer who had dated a woman, had nothing to do with us, who was offended by him. We stopped working with him and did a full investigation. The other one—I had a model complain to me that she felt uncomfortable with him and I fired him an hour later. I didn't investigate it; I didn't do due diligence. I fired him an hour later, because the models' comfort is important to me. Nothing matters more. Over 25 years, 7,500 photo shoots, we had one incident and handled it immediately. I'd take that record. I had a hairstylist on a shoot who was rude to one of the models and I fired him on the spot. He asked, 'How do I go home?' I said, 'Swim.'[107]

Seeking to protect 'the models' comfort', Razek seems oblivious that his maverick actions, which were likely in defiance of employment law, perpetuate the gendered logic that has prevailed since the nineteenth century, in which men assumed a woman's fragility and their right to protect her. Without reflection, Razek and Mitro argue that because Victoria's Secret have a large market share in the lingerie industry – Phelp's suggests as much as one third – its brand values must be widely supported:

> Now tell me how it's possible that that bra would be the number one most popular bra in the marketplace if people didn't like the brand? Particularly if young people didn't like the brand?

To an extent, they might be correct, for as journalist Kyle Muzenrieder observes in an article for *W Magazine*, the fact that Victoria's Secret were the only brand to 'regularly broadcast [a fashion show] around the world . . . may [make it] the most important to the popular culture at large'.[108] To assert that Victoria's Secret and its fashion shows reflect prevalent gender attitudes will be uncomfortable for some people, but the suggestion is credible. After all, it was only after allegations of sexual harassment against Harvey Weinstein became widespread in December 2017 that people vocalized concerns about Jimmy Choo's 'Shimmer in the Dark' television film.

Razek provided two reasons for the absence of transgender models from the Victoria's Secret fashion show. First, he asserted that they threatened the 'fantasy' of these events.[109] Second, and in response to public criticism, he claimed that transgender models who had auditioned for the brand 'did not make it'; their gender being irrelevant.[110] Fantasy has echoed throughout this chapter. The fantasy of scientists who worked 300 years ago, idealizing and categorizing gender roles. The fantasy of the Hedi Slimane, whose debut collection for Celine included silhouettes that aligned with his conception of tailoring perfection, and the fantasies of both Slimane and Lori Askill, who imagined nocturnal metropolises inhabited by women whose appearance conforms to 'western' expectations of beauty. Different as they are, the fantasies are similar for being cis-gendered and heteronormative, for asserting a gender binary where males are subject and females are object, and where the male gaze has primacy. These are fantasies that enforce 'western'-centrism.

My interpretation of the role of fantasy in these examples differs to that Jobling, Nesbitt and Wong. In their reflections upon the changing place of transgender models within the fashion industry they invoke philosopher Michel Foucault's concept of the heterotopia. They suggest 'the heterotopia of fashion is akin to a space of dreams'.[111] It acts 'as a zone where differences that are otherwise unacceptable become accepted'.[112] Foucault differentiated between a utopia – a perfect and wholly 'unreal space' – and a heterotopia – an actual space possessing utopic attributes but 'absolutely different' and existing 'outside of all places' because it distorts reality through its representation, contestation and inversion of elements within a society's culture.[113] Nonetheless, focusing their interpretation on one of the six principles that Foucault conceived to explain the purpose of a heterotopia, Jobling, Nesbitt and Wong assert that its function in fashion is largely positive. With reference to the increased presence of transgender models in catwalk shows and campaigns since the 2010s, they suggest the heterotopia of fashion has become penetrable, 'allowing space for openly transgender models to enter'.[114] This is also true of fashion magazines, for model Ariel Nicholson became the first transgender model to appear on the cover of American *Vogue* in September 2021.[115] The authors make their judgement cautiously. They acknowledge the continued violence, physical and figurative, that transgender people continue to face as their bodies remain a political 'battleground'.[116]

Consequently, the heterotopia of fashion has an 'opening and closing dynamic', appearing variously more and less accepting of challenges to the gender binary.[117] This instability is important because in distinguishing between a heterotopia and a utopia, Foucault stressed that the former is a 'disturbing' space.[118] A heterotopia is not a paradise. It is a zone in which socially conceived structures can be challenged and reconceived. Whilst this gives the heterotopia of fashion scope to critique prevalent social attitudes, a point I explore in relation to Alexander McQueen's collection for spring/summer 2000 *Eye*, it can also galvanize them.[119] It can also do both concurrently. This is the case with the three episodes considered here. The complicated, plastic functions of the heterotopia are evidenced from public responses. For the most part, journalists and consumers repudiated the fantasies of Celine, Jimmy Choo and Victoria's Secret, but in the case of Celine and Jimmy Choo this was only after a cultural shift that reframed the implications of their respective campaigns and catwalk. The fact that heterotopias are rooted in actual spaces means the fantasies they present will always comprise elements of the socialized assumptions that frame people's lives. If they are a 'space of dreams', they are no less capable of being a space for nightmares.

Reflections

Gender is one of the most trenchant of the 'west's social binaries, and the fashion industry has long been associated with its preservation. The episodes considered suggest this pernicious practice continues, but not without complication. Three observations connect the above discussions. First, people's engagement with fashion, from conceptualization to consumption, is culturally contingent. Garments and campaigns that are accepted, even lauded, can become subject to criticism and cause intense hurt when they are interpreted in changed social circumstances. This point reinforces Yuniya Kawamura's stance that fashion is a belief existing in people's minds. It also leads to a second, paradoxical, point. Fashion's chameleon-like symbolism means that it can appear at once deeply revealing of people's contemporary concerns and ambivalent because it is sufficiently flexible to carry alternative, even wholly contrary, meanings in different circumstances. A cautious conclusion would be that fashion's ability to convey people's values is at best synchronic or partial. However, the characteristic of mutability, which makes fashion an unstable communicator of people's views, seems frequently to be interpreted by ('western') consumers as a sign of its deep meaningfulness, for it can always represent what they want to see. A third, and connected, observation is that fashion as it is conceived, created and consumed within the 'west' is rooted in the projection of fantasies. People use dress to help them negotiate the distance between their aspirations and the actuality of social norms and expectations.

3
RACE

Previous chapters started with a reflection on the role of human dress and appearance in the conceptualization of idealized human communities. Utopic imaginings, places where people visualize how they want their lives to be, are pleasing, sometimes pernicious, certainly pervasive. They are difficult to analyze, but the task is not impossible. Greek philosopher Plato, who considered another form of idealized community in the fourth century BCE, recognized that utopias, which often exist in words alone, find expression through people's conduct.[1] In a similar vein, philosopher Antonio Gramsci asserted that 'popular culture . . . takes the place of (and at the same time favors) the fantasizing of the common people'.[2] The terms 'popular' and 'common' confound more than they clarify, but Gramsci's point that culture, an aggregate expression of human conduct, enables people to reconcile their lived experiences and expectations through a form of wishful thinking is germane to a study interrogates the causes and consequences of the ideas conveyed through fashionable dress.

A premise of this book is that ideas associated with 'western' values and behaviours are frequently articulated through the fashion industry. Dress is very often the nexus where people's expectations and experiences converge and become manifest because 'corporeal display' is a fundamental part of human cooperation.[3] Consequently, dress possesses an immediacy of impact that warrants – even demands – interpretation. This is especially the case in the 'west' where people's clothing choices are considered to accurately connote their character. The potency the 'west' has attributed to race, which it has long fantasized, creates a particularly febrile situation when mediated through dress. The potential to spark bitter disputes is great as the gap between 'western', and predominantly white, expectations collide with the histories and lived experiences of people who are other than white. A challenging exception that underscores this general rule is the 'White Lives Matter' T-shirt that black American rapper-cum-fashion designer Kanye West – currently known as Ye – included within his Yeezy Paris Fashion catwalk show in October 2022. The garment, which appeared to marginalize the centuries-long degradation of black people within the 'west', was described by the Anti-Defamation League, a Jewish civil rights organization based in the United States, as a 'hate statement'.[4] Some of the most hurtful and intensely scrutinized episodes in the contemporary fashion industry stem from the 'west's' perpetuation of racialized fantasies that crystallized during the eighteenth and nineteenth centuries. The focus on race in this chapter is intended to be something of a foil to emphasize the place of fantasy, an emergent theme in the previous chapter that recurs in those that follow.

The role of fantasy in establishing racial otherness has been elucidated by literature scholar Edward Said. He argued that the Orient – a geographical region that initially included the Indian subcontinent and Eastern Mediterranean, but which can encompass Africa and Asia – was a 'European invention' in antiquity, 'a place of romance, exotic beings, haunting memories and landscapes, remarkable experiences'.[5] This utopic mythologizing – termed Orientalism – was as illusory as its consequences were harmful. A 'cultural enterprise' of the British and French, Orientalism became a 'style for dominating, restructuring, and having authority over the Orient' through how it was viewed, described, taught, settled and ruled.[6] Whilst this may seem abstract – like 'airy fantasy' – Orientalism 'created a body of theory and practice which, for many generations . . . [had] considerable material investment . . . [I]nvestment [that] made [it] . . . a system of knowledge about the Orient [and] an accepted grid for filtering through the Orient into Western consciousness'.[7]

The investment that socialized the 'west' to understand the Orient as separate, eccentric, backward, silently indifferent, feminine and penetrable, and possessing of 'supine malleability', in Said's terms, intensified during the eighteenth and nineteenth centuries because of a growing scientific belief in the biological inequality of races.[8] Ironically, it was the pursuit of egalitarianism, enshrined in the first article of France's *Declaration of the Rights of Man and Citizen* of 1789, that sparked questions about human inequality. As science historian Londa Schiebinger observes, 'an appeal to natural rights could be countered only by proof of natural inequalities'.[9] Influenced by the socialized belief in a great chain of being that had fixed sentient beings within a hierarchy since the Middle Ages, with an omniscient Christian God at its summit, eighteenth- and nineteenth-century authors, anatomists, politicians and legislators – white men for the most part – undertook, in Schiebinger's terms, an 'intense scrutiny of human bodies, generating countless examples of radical misreadings of the human body that scholars have described as scientific racism and scientific sexism'.[10] The urgency to establish the parameters of human parity during the eighteenth and nineteenth centuries was framed by the ongoing expansion of Europe's empires and their representatives' encounters with other peoples and new animal species. Discovery of the Orangutan, which tended to be used as a catch-all phrase for primates, and included apes and chimpanzees, was particularly important in shaping European ideas about human equality. This supposed 'missing link' entrenched scientific beliefs that humans had descended from apes and appeared to confirm emerging notions about biological and racial inequalities as African people, males especially, were thought to resemble these creatures, physiologically and psychologically.[11]

The hierarchical ordering of races was elaborated in various European publications that drew upon the idea of biological competition enunciated by Charles Darwin in his *Origin of the Species*, published in 1859. Arthur de Gobineau's *Essai sur l'inégalité des races humaines* (*Essay on the Inequality of Human Races*) of 1863 was particularly influential. In an early example from his four-volume work, Gobineau defaults to 'the highest natural law' and proceeds with a wilful interpretation of the history of Haiti, which he claimed amounted to 'a long account of massacres', to assert that 'the black variety belongs to the kind of branch of humanity that is unable to civilize itself'.[12] Odious as these ideas seem in our present, they persist. Anthropologist David Graeber and comparative archaeologist David Wengrove observe that historian Yuval Noah Harari depicts social relationships between early humans as being as 'tense and violent as the nastiest chimpanzee group'. They note, he 'could just as easily have written . . . nastiest biker group.. . . One might have imagined the obvious thing to compare one group of human beings with would be . . . another group of human beings'.[13]

To believe that race was biologically determined and that humans, existing in different racial groups, were inherently inequal facilitated racism. Racism was 'particularly powerful and its imprint on popular consciousness especially deep, because', as sociologist Stuart Hall observes, 'in such racial characteristics as color, ethnic origin, geographical position, etc., racism discovers what other ideologies have to construct: an apparently "natural" and universal basis in nature itself.'[14] These distinctions, which became the basis of scientific observation in the 'west', produced judgements that appeared to white Europeans 'value-neutral' and 'beyond reproach'.[15] The blithe acceptance of racial inequalities, more fundamentally the acceptance of whiteness as natural and impervious to critique, facilitated the creation of new 'historical subjects', who could ostensibly demonstrate the existence of a subordinate and superordinate relationship between races over centuries.[16] Consequently, race as biological fact seemed only more certain. The resultant racism, if it were even acknowledged as such, was an inevitable, if regrettable, corollary.

Distinctions between races were reinforced through fashionable dress. To broaden a point made by cultural scholar Sarah Cheang, the 'use of ["western"] fashion for self-distinction while remaining within a system that defined black [and brown] identities as subordinate and errant, resulted in [fashion from beyond the "west"] being criticized as a racial characteristic of pathological excess'.[17] Racialized forms of dress that were concocted in the 'west', like blackface minstrelsy, also operated to '[reaffirm] white social dominance' by mimicking and trivializing people because they were other than white.[18] Cheang explains that 'western' forms of dress could be accepted, adopted, undermined by the people they were imposed upon. They could also impose restrictions on their 'western' wearers.[19] Nonetheless, the establishment of European empires meant that for many people forms of dress accepted within the 'west' became globally preponderant during the eighteenth and nineteenth centuries.

The implication of these arguments is that the articulation of race and racism as we experience them today are relatively recent constructs. Author Emma Dabiri argues that race was invented in 1661 in Barbados, when a legal system distinguishing between black and white people became law.[20] *An Act for Better Ordering and Governing of Negroes* invoked the idea of racial difference to 'shut down . . . affinities and [a] sense of mutuality' between indentured Irish and enslaved Africans, who recognized that their labour was being exploited by English and Scottish overlords. The rhetoric of whiteness and blackness was a manipulation, predicated on the dubious assertion that skin colour was a truer determinant of allegiance and belonging than lived experience. It was conceived—a fantasy—to prevent the Irish from making common cause with the Africans. A similar occurrence followed in colonial Virginia after Bacon's Rebellion of 1675.[21] Prior to the seventeenth century Dabiri asserts, '[t]he idea that different features, hair textures or complexions [had] any intrinsic value or meaning, and that they constitute[d] *racial difference*, did not exist'.[22] Her argument is similar to that of Hall, who avers that racist practices are conceived and maintained to 'secure the hegemony of a dominant group over a series of subordinate ones, in such a way as to dominate the whole social formation in a form favorable to the long-term development of the economic productive base'.[23] Hall stresses that economic factors are not the sole constituent of racism; 'legal, political and ideological systems' are necessary to, but observes that the status of slaves as commodities is a racist characteristic of the nineteenth century.[24] Unlike Dabiri, Hall does acknowledge the existence of 'flourishing racisms in precapitalist social formations', even if they manifested themselves differently to later periods.[25]

Art historian Roland Bethancourt's study of intersectionality within late antique and medieval Byzantium establishes, contrary to Dabiri's arguments, that racial difference was understood and acted upon before the seventeenth century. He quotes from the Italian bishop Liutprand of Cremona, who described the Byzantine emperor Nikephoros II Phokas (r. 963–69) as 'in color an Ethiopian (*colore Aethiopem*)'.[26] Bethancourt also highlights semantic variations that reveal divergent attitudes to race within what is now eastern and western Europe. The Greek Testament version of the Song of Songs, used within Byzantium, included the line, spoken by King Soloman's wife, 'I am dark and beautiful' (*melaena eimi kai kalē*). In its Latin translation, used within western Europe, the same line became 'I am black, but beautiful' (*nigra sum sed Formosa*). The racializing of this passage 'underscores the presumption that beauty and blackness [were] mutually exclusive' within the western Christian Church.[27] These examples are synchronic and geographically specific, but they demonstrate well enough that ideas of racial difference, and with this, inequality, preceded the Barbados slavery code by at least seven centuries.

Language that demarcated people on the basis of race may have only became explicit and legally incontrovertible in the seventeenth century, but as Rictor Norton observes with regard to terms that define same-sex behaviours, the relationship between language and experience is complex and '[t]he absence of language does not necessarily indicate the absence of conceptual thought'.[28] Ideas of race had to exist, and arguably for a long time, before they could be written coherently and codified in enforceable laws. The ideological and logistical consequences of European colonization, which began in the seventeenth century, provided the catalyst for socialized thoughts and expressions about race to become action.

The studies in this chapter – Prada's Pradamalia collection of winter 2018, a focus on one garment – a balaclava sweater – from Gucci's autumn/winter 2019 collection *Cyborg*, and a Madewell photoshoot with black model Marihenny Pasible from 2017 – consider how racialized thinking, predicated on the belief that race is a biological distinction as opposed to a social construct, continues to operate within the contemporary fashion industry because of the correlative fantasies of exoticism and primitivism that are invoked in the conceptualization and consumption of products. The previous chapter emphasized how the interpretation of fashion catwalks and campaigns is culturally contingent. The point is pursued in the ensuing discussion because public scrutiny of the three episodes was either not immediate or wholly accepted by the supposed sufferers of the presumed infraction.

Prada, Pradamalia collection, winter 2018

On 14 December 2018, New York civil rights attorney Chinyere Ezie posted a 152-word description to her Facebook account in which she recalled an experience that had left her 'shaking with anger'.[29] Returning home from a 'very emotional' visit to the exhibition 'Blackface: The Birth of an American Stereotype' at the Smithsonian National Museum of African American History and Culture, Ezie explained how she felt 'confronted with the same very racist and denigrating blackface imagery' as she walked past the window of Prada's Soho shop.[30] The imagery that offended Ezie was a series of accessories from Prada's Pradamalia collection, two of which she described as being 'Sambo like', in reference to a nineteenth-century American caricature of a young black boy with large, protruding lips.[31] Pradamalia, a portmanteau of 'Prada' and 'animalia', included a range of earrings, wallets and keychains in the guise of seven creatures the brand described as 'one part biological, one part technological, all parts Prada'.[32]

Made from brightly coloured Saffiano leather, dark wood and polished metal, the $550 creatures included a slug and jellyfish and two monkeys, Otto and Toto, which featured large, bulbous lips that resembled blackface.[33] Larger versions of the Pradamalia creatures, including the monkeys, were created for the shop's window display. Entering the store, and seeking clarification about the products from an employee, Ezie was told 'in a moment of surprising candor' that a black employee had made a complaint about the imagery, but was no longer employed.[34] Asserting that '[h]istory cannot continue to repeat itself', Ezie concluded her post by asking readers to 'repost and retweet @Prada using the hashtags #StopBlackface #BoycottPrada #EndRacismNow'.[35]

The Facebook post was widely shared. It sparked outrage on social media as people accused Prada of racism. Anglophone commentators described the collectibles as 'extremely racist and dehumanizing'.[36] The brand was accused of 'racist crap' and urged to create a more racially diverse workforce.[37] In a news segment that aired on Canadian television channel *CTV News* on 16 December, one black man interviewed outside the brand's Soho store opined, 'They might as well have been selling nooses and, maybe, selling Swastikas,' a reference to the insignia of Adolf Hitler's National Socialist party that held power in Germany between 1933 and 1945 and whose policies led to the persecution of minoritized groups that were perceived to contravene many of the binaries that form of the focus of this book.[38] Prada responded promptly to the criticism and withdrew the offending items from display and sale. Nonetheless, their initial response did not include an apology. A statement released through the brand's Twitter account asserted that 'Prada Group abhors racist imagery'.[39] The imputed discriminatory associations were disavowed, and it was explained that '[t]he Pradamalia are fantasy charms composed of elements of the Prada oeuvre. They are imaginary creatures not intended to have any reference to the real world and certainly not blackface'.[40] Dissatisfied with what she termed Prada's 'non-apology apology', and clarifying that the employee from the Soho store knew the keychains could be associated with blackface – 'Why yes, our black employee told us this was black face' – Ezie surmised, 'The fact that this was green-lit at headquarters tells me, indisputably, there are no black faces, no one who looks like me, in the company's decision making tree'.[41]

In January 2019, Ezie filed a complaint about the Pradamalia collection and shop display with the New York City Commission on Human Rights. In February 2020, a settlement, described as 'landmark', was reached. The commission upheld Ezie's initial grievance. In a public statement they explained:

> The monkey figurine from the collection evoked images of Sambo, a caricature that, over generations, has been used to mock and dehumanize Black people. The display of such racist iconography manifests as discrimination on the basis of race, suggesting that Black people are unwelcome.[42]

As part of the settlement Prada accepted five rulings that included the guarantee that 'NYC employees and Milan executives receive racial equity training' and the establishment of a 'scholarship program for people historically underrepresented in fashion'.[43]

Whilst the comprehensive nature of the agreement between Prada and the Commission was lauded, the Pradamalia collectibles were not initially considered problematic. An advance feature about the collection that appeared in Singapore *Esquire* magazine in October 2018 described the creatures as 'sweet'.[44] The objects – the monkeys in particular – acquired a wholly different, and negative, meaning in response to Ezie's trip to the Smithsonian's Blackface exhibition and, doubtless, her lived experiences as a black person and civil rights attorney advocating for gender and racial justice. The circumstances in which the Pradamalia items were deemed hurtful and offensive demonstrates that the interpretation of dress is culturally contingent, and subjective. This is not to suggest that Ezie would not have voiced her concerns had she not visited the Smithsonian exhibition, or that other people did not feel as she did; the outpouring of support for her Facebook post, not least the ruling of the New York City Commission on Human Rights, indicates many clearly did. The point is that specific and highly personal triggers are often responsible for activating deeply held beliefs and thoughts that imperceptibly shape people's behaviour. As sociologist Ann Swidler contends, during settled lives the influence of culture on people is often impossible to discern. It is only when their lives become unsettled, when a trigger disrupts the status quo, that socialized thoughts and behaviours are more readily questioned. Moreover, the absence of comment does not signal acquiescence. The importance of bodily presentation to human interactions means that dress and adornment are prone to deliver an unanticipated visceral kick as widely felt and unexpressed values become manifest in a single garment or outfit. Ezie's Facebook post articulated an omnipresent hurt that many people feel about the persistence of racial disparity. It also revealed an obliviousness that many other people feel – perhaps especially white people – about the persistence of this inequality; Ezie's complaint established that Prada's Italian headquarters was indeed wholly white at the time.[45]

In defending the Pradamalia collection in response to Ezie's criticism, Prada's argument was twofold. First, the company abhorred racism. By implication, the racialized interpretation of their products was misplaced. Second, the Pradamalia collectibles were 'fantasy' and incapable of causing hurt. Both statements are examples of what English scholar Ayanna Thompson considers the 'inherent white supremacist logic of white innocence'.[46] In her study of blackface, which she defines as 'the application of any prosthetic – makeup, soot, burnt cork, minerals, masks, etc. – to imitate the complexion of another race', Thompson argues that white people's assumption of a black or brown person's appearance is typically self-legitimated by a belief that they are celebrating a racial minority through verisimilitude.[47] The appropriateness of this behaviour is predicated on two socialized, and thus largely subconscious, cultural blind spots. First, an obliviousness to how this form of aesthetic impersonation causes hurt. Second, a rationalization that the prevalence of blackface, from private parties to Hollywood movies, sanctions acts of assumption.[48] Drawing upon a history of white people performing blackface and blackface minstrelsy, which she traces to the plays of William Shakespeare in sixteenth-century England, Thompson argues that this form of exhibition emphasizes how white bodies, even before the Barbados slave act of 1661, were frequently considered the norm from which bodies of different appearance were judged. The psychological security this afforded white people meant that their bodies became 'Protean' and capable of 'tak[ing] on different identities and races'.[49] In commodifying and performing black bodies in this way, Thompson observes that '[e]xhibition, in fact, disempowers the person on display because all of the power resides with the viewer'.[50] Her point elides with that of cultural scholar Minh-Ha T. Pham, whose concept of 'racial plagiarism' is apt to describe the Pradamalia monkeys, which 'seize authorial identity, control, and capital away from the source community . . . [and diminish] the value of the source material itself'.[51]

Fundamentally, socialized assumptions about racial inequality emphasize that white people's motivation to wear and perform blackface is never solely to commend. This point was established by Ezie and New York's Commission on Human Rights when they explicitly connected the Pradamalia collectibles to the character Sambo and, in so doing, indirectly linked these figures to the nineteenth-century comedic tradition of blackface minstrelsy, which Thompson describes as 'imitat[ing], celebrat[ing], and mock[ing] the actions of black Americans'.[52] This performative genre was sustained by the 'radical misreadings' of eighteenth- and nineteenth-century scientists that had connected black people and apes through analogy. Sambo was a pickaninny, 'an imagined dehumanized black juvenile', popular in advertising and story book illustrations in the United States during the nineteenth century.[53] His appearance was characterized by a protruding jaw, enlarged lips and crooked posture. The nineteenth-century illustrator John R. Neill probably drew Sambo for Helen Bannerman's story *Little Black Sambo*.[54] He also created illustrations for Frank Baum's *Wizard of Oz* stories.[55] The connection is important because cultural historian Robin Berstein argues that the creation of fictional characters by nineteenth-century artists, which includes Sambo, Patchwork Girl, the Golliwog, Raggedy Ann and the Scarecrow from Baum's *Wizard of Oz*, drew, to varying degrees, on racialized depictions of black people through the performance of blackface minstrelsy.[56]

However playful, other-worldly, and harmless these fictitious characters seemed to their white creators and audiences, their genesis lay in the what Schiebinger has called 'the wildest fantasies of violent interspecies rape' where male apes, and African males, were considered physically and sexually powerful and brutish.⁵⁷ Since the Middle Ages primates had been labelled 'degenerate men' (*naturae degnerantis homo*).⁵⁸ This attitude was legitimated by the work of eighteenth- and nineteenth-century scientists. The features and traits of artists' creations – 'flat, geometric face', 'woolly hair', 'physical softness and floppiness', 'imperviousness to pain', 'tendency toward benign mischief', 'natural ability to entertain' – show how these ideas came to be more broadly acknowledged, such that an analogy between black people and primates became commonplace.⁵⁹

This history of racial dehumanizing continues in contemporary fancy dress costume. In a study of the Halloween costumes worn by university students in the southeast United States, Jennifer C. Mueller, Danielle Dirks and Leslie Houts Picca argue that the seasonal festivities have 'become a culturally tolerated, contemporary space for the racist "ghost" to be let out of the box [. . .] Halloween's combination of social license, ritual costuming and social setting make the holiday a uniquely constructive context for negative engagement of racial concepts and identities'.⁶⁰ The United States has a particularly freighted history of racial inequalities, but I have argued elsewhere that the festive licence that appears to exist for these white students, and other white people besides, is evident in other countries and exists beyond Halloween.⁶¹ Part of the reason for this is the heightened role of laughter and fantasy within the ludic performances of blackface. In the following passage I emphasize the role of laughter in facilitating people's (unintentional) communication of socially prohibited attitudes, but fantasy, which is germane to Thompson's argument and Ezie's complaint, is equally relevant:

> In a discussion on culture jamming – 'activist multimedia productions and performances' (Parameswaran 2019: 59–60) – Radhika Parameswaran quotes directly from [Mikhail] Bakhtin, who observes, '[l]aughter demolishes fear and piety before an object, before a world, making of it an object of familiar contact and thus clearing the ground for an absolutely free investigation of it' (Parameswaran 2019: 71). If laughter, perhaps specifically parody and irony, permits investigation, it also gives licence for people to communicate messages that might ordinarily be disavowed . . . Parting from Bakhtin, who considered this laughter ambivalent and subversive, subsequent academics and commentators tend to look upon it as benign (Bakhtin 1965: 11–18). It is the frequent references to laughter, of being carried away and seemingly forgetting oneself in accounts of costume participants, that encourage analysts to think that performances of dressing up lead to depersonalization, an increase in social awareness and reduction in self-identity. The sartorial form thereby reflects prevalent, if typically subconscious, cultural attitudes.⁶²

To assume laughter and fantasy are always benign is misguided. It is the very act of disavowing 'any reference to the real world', which Prada claimed of its

Pradamalia collection, that provides people and products with a figurative and physical space, akin to Foucault's heterotopia, that is distanced from social norms and behaviours and facilitates the communication of ideas that can reveal personal, possibly pernicious, certainly prevalent beliefs that their community would publicly disavow. Superficially, the Pradamalia monkeys might be viewed as 'sweet', 'fantasy' and 'imagined', but their saccharine appearance belies a sourer history predicated on racial inequalities that have become socialized among white people to such an extent that they pass unobserved until a change in circumstances forces reassessment and reflection. The point can be explored further with reference to a single garment within Gucci's ready-to-wear collection for autumn/winter 2018/2019, *Cyborg*.

Gucci, *Cyborg*, autumn/winter, menswear and womenswear, 2018/2019

On 6 February 2019, social media users reacted angrily to a roll-neck sweater from Gucci's *Cyborg* ready-to-wear collection, which they thought resembled blackface. Departing from a conventional design, the neck of Gucci's black wool balaclava jumper extended upwards to cover the lower third of the wearer's face. An opening in the neck for the mouth was framed by red wool. Resembling lips, the design recalled discriminatory caricatures of black people from the nineteenth century.[63] Gucci issued an apology on the same day, which was posted on their Twitter account on 7 February. The brand removed the jumper from sale and declared their commitment to diversity. They claimed the 'incident' would be 'a powerful learning moment for the Gucci team and beyond'.[64] Anglophone media on both sides of the Atlantic carried the story from 7 February. Documenting the episode, their coverage likely aggravated it.

Harlem designer Dapper Dan, who had a long history of coping styles by Gucci before more recently collaborating with them, criticized the brand in a post through his Instagram account on 10 February, stating they had 'gotten it outrageously wrong'.[65] He remarked, 'I am a Black man before I am a brand'.[66] Implying that his commercial relationship with the brand had been jeopardized, Dapper Dan's post explained that Gucci President and CEO Marco Bizzarri would travel from Italy to Harlem to meet with him, 'members of the community and other industry leaders'.[67] On 15 February, Dan posted a follow-up message on Instagram. Stating that 'great demands' had been made of Gucci, he wrote that it was 'time for [them] to answer'.[68] Answer Gucci did, with an initial four-point action plan that included 'hiring global and regional directors for diversity and inclusion, setting up a multicultural design scholarship program, launching a diversity and inclusivity awareness program [and] launching a global exchange program'.[69] Prior to the announcement of these measures, *Women's Wear Daily* published an exclusive interview with Bizzarri on 12 February. Echoing comments from an internal Gucci memo that he had authored on 9 February, Bizzarri claimed the offence was caused by 'ignorance of this matter'.[70] On the same day, Gucci's Creative Director Alessandro Michele circulated an exculpatory letter to employees. Writing that he felt 'the greatest grief' about the jumper's perceived racism, he explained:

> [It] actually had very specific references, completely different from what was ascribed instead. It was a tribute to Leigh Bowery, to his camouflage art, to his ability to challenge the bourgeois conventions and conformism, to his eccentricity as a performer, to his extraordinary vocation to masquerade meant as a hymn to freedom.[71]

Whilst defensive, Michele's explanation is important to acknowledge because no accusations of racism were made when the collection was debuted in Milan Fashion Week, almost a year earlier in February 2018. At this time, many anglophone fashion commentators remarked on the collection's cultural hybridity, which was variously described as 'weird',[72] 'unnerving'[73] and 'sensational—in a disturbing and creepy way', but none were overtly critical and they did not mention race.[74] The ninety looks that comprised the Milan show included one model holding a baby dragon, a white male wearing a turban, a white female wearing a Pagoda-style hat and textile designs from various global cultures.[75] Journalist Sarah Mower acknowledged that '[s]everal [models] had their faces covered in knitted half-balaclavas, surreally suggesting a postoperative state', but she made no reference to blackface. Her verdict of the collection was positive, and she seemed to welcome the 'zillion billion clothes and accessories guaranteed to stoke Instagram commentaries for weeks to come'.[76] Concluding her account, journalist Lauren Alexis Fisher appeared to approve of 'yet another boundary-pushing, conversation-starting show' from Michele.[77] Only journalist Tahmina Begum, writing for *The Huffington Post*, engaged with people's concerns that the designs constituted cultural misappropriation, but her report did not mention blackface.[78]

Akin to Chinyere Ezie's experience of the Pradamalia collection and the controversy that centred around the Otto and Toto monkeys, the diametrically opposed responses to the Gucci show in 2018 and 2019 were chiefly a consequence of circumstance. Whilst some of the masks and headwear in the collection could be thought to resemble blackface, the offending black balaclava jumper did not feature prominently on the catwalk in 2018, and it was not singled out for comment in coverage of the Milan show.[79] The garment became politically charged, and delivered its visceral kick, when it was photographed separately for the collection's retail launch in 2019, which coincided with Black History Month in the United States.[80]

Placing the public scrutiny of Gucci's jumper in a wider cultural frame, journalist Amy Held, writing for the American media organisation *NPR*, drew attention to contemporaneous race-related scandals in the United States involving politicians – Virginia's governor Ralph Northam and attorney general Mark Herring – who had worn blackface during the 1980s.[81] What connects the exculpatory remarks of Bizzarri and Michele, and those of Northam and Herring, is the assumption of a white innocence and insistence that they were 'ignorant' and unaware of the harm they were causing.[82] These men were harnessing the same 'white supremacist logic of white innocence' used by Prada. Michele's argument that the roll-neck sweater was inspired by ideas of non-conformity, 'eccentricity' and 'masquerade' elides with Prada's point that items conceived with reference to the imagination were benign and could never cause hurt. In another parallel, his remarks underestimate the potency of fantasy and its continuing influence within the conception, creation and consumption of fashionable dress.

Another point can be made about the brands' defensive, even dismissive, attitude when questioned about their commitment to racial equality. Implicit in the responses of Prada and Gucci is an assumption of cultural superiority, which places these brands beyond reproach. In suggesting that the racialized readings of their products were mistaken and unwarranted, Prada and Gucci, their creative directors in particular, presented themselves – however inadvertently – as cultural arbiters, who had licence to take ideas from different cultures and shape them as they choose. Akin to Said's framing of Orientalism, these 'western' brands were constructing a fantasy that reflected their socialized values, and this included the freighted histories of racial inequality.

In an article within the September 2017 issue of Italian *Vogue* Angelo Flaccavento dwelt on this point and suggested that Michele's 'hard and risky' approach to design was 'appropriationalist'. Markedly different to the designs of his predecessor, Frida Giannini, Michele's aesthetic, characterized by its patchwork incorporation of motifs from different chronologies, cultures and geographies, is at once a-cultural, a-historical and antilinear.[83] In 2017, he spoke bombastically with Flaccavento about his process:

> I am brazen. For me, creating means regurgitating, distorting and assembling everything that has passed through me and continues to do so.. . . For me, reworking the past over and over again is a way not to trivialise the garments and not to obsess over hem lengths. What I am interested in, as a matter of fact, is telling a story and, if someone sees fragments of other stories in it, be my guest. I don't have to justify myself. What is urgent for me is what I want to say.[84]

Michele's construction of self-referential narratives from different global cultures is encapsulated in the concept of Guccification. The term describes how Gucci seeks to become a 'cultural industry firm' and 'icon' through the expression of an immediately recognizable artistic style.[85] The brand's aesthetic is part of a broader shift within the luxury industry, described by marketing scholar Jean-Noël Kapferer, in which brands seek to manage growth and maintain their distinction through artification, a process by which non-art is re-constituted as art.[86] At least one implication of this development, which Kapferer does not consider, and which Flaccavento does cursorily, is an insistence on the omniscience of designers, who are sanctioned to assert their creative vision and fantasy. There is, perhaps, a parallel between the 'western' authors, anatomists, politicians and legislators of the eighteenth and nineteenth centuries whose personal views became public orthodoxy, and the contemporary creative designers and the boards they serve, who are instrumental in shaping global fashions. In both cases the people involved are, for the most part, white men.

The hubris apparent in Michele's assertion that he is not accountable culminated in nemesis when the jumper from his autumn/winter 2018 collection was widely criticized. Returning to his Italian *Vogue* interview after the Covid-19 pandemic, and reflecting how the global health emergency has heightened racial inequalities, his outlook seems especially callous. This interpretation is strengthened by a change in Michele's own thinking. One of the first and most strident of the fashion industry's high-profile designers to respond publicly to the pandemic, Michele posted a condemnatory message to his Instagram account in May 2020, in which he criticized his former mindset and the fashion industry:

> After all, the tragedy we are living is providing new reflections. We could never have imagined to feel so connected to life through a bond of trembling and heartbreaking tenderness. We could never have thought to reconnect, so deeply, with the fragility of our creatural destiny.. . . . Above all, we understood we went way too far. Our reckless actions have burned the house we live in.. . . . So much haughtiness made us lose our sisterhood with the butterflies, the flowers, the trees and the roots. So much outrageous greed made us lose the harmony and the care, the connection and belonging. We ravaged the sanctity of life, neglectful of our being a species. At the end of the day, we were out of breath . . . this crisis represents a fundamental test for soul. It's a test because there is sorrow, exertion, danger. Though also because there is an evaluation and judgement. Through sorrow we can look at our recent past with a critical eye.. . . . This present, then, entrusts us with important responsibilities.[87]

Michele's recognition of the responsibilities that he and his company possess is not without precedent. His remarks in May are similar to those expressed by Gucci in their statement as chief sponsor for the exhibition 'Camp: Notes of Fashion' that was held at the Metropolitan Museum of Art's Costume Institute in

2019. Here, Gucci acknowledged its role in eschewing 'cultural conservatism', and perhaps by implication forms of intolerance and discrimination, by providing an interrogative commentary on 'mainstream culture':

> Under the creative directorship of Alessandro Michele, [Gucci] has become a laboratory of audacious ideas, a celebration of extreme individuality, and an antidote to cultural conservatism. Each of these notions was also central to the evolution of camp as a transgressive commentary on mainstream culture.. . . Camp is animated by a faith in the power of the human imagination to transform, even liberate. Beauty can set you free. Gucci shares this faith, which underpins its ongoing support of the arts, the more maverick the better. Its sponsorship . . . is a reaffirmation of its commitment to creativity on the margins, now more crucial than ever.[88]

The statements from Michele and Gucci about the linkages between culture and fashion certainly present ambiguities. On the one hand, they suggest culture is being commoditized and used arbitrarily to drive marketing and merchandizing campaigns. On the other, they demonstrate that culture has an important place in challenging socialized values and behaviours. The mixed messages reflect the fact that these are public communications, aimed at divergent audiences to promote the brand, but they also underscore how changing circumstances effect people's interpretation of culture. Like the studies discussed so far, shifts in a person's or society's outlook, especially when unexpected, can manifest feelings that are otherwise subconscious, and this can considerably change their interpretation of a situation.

The ambiguity within Michelle's and Gucci's public statements raises a fundamental point about the place of fashion in contemporary society; namely, to what extent is its role to be 'socially responsive' and 'to contribute in a more substantial way' to people's lives, as Tim Blanks opined in his discussion with Virgil Abloh, which was discussed in the introduction.[89] This question was being asked with greater insistence in the years prior to the Covid-19 pandemic. In 2017, fashion scholars Adam Geczy and Vicki Karaminas conceived of the term 'critical fashion' to explain the interrogative and evaluative role they believe fashion now possesses. They argue that the populism of art and art criticism, which increased during the nineteenth century and became more apparent in the 1990s when art's 'collusion with the media, and its gravitational pull to mass appeal, became cornerstones of the art world', resulted in a 'devolution' of art's 'criticality'.[90] The commentative role that art relinquished was taken up by fashion and dress.[91] Gucci's assertion that they are an 'antidote to cultural conservatism' might be an example, albeit self-referential, of how contemporary fashions have come to query social norms.

If the work of brands stimulates consumers' heads, it also soothes their hearts. In July 2019, in a podcast interview with *The Economist*, Anna Wintour asserted the increased emotional value that people seek through fashion:

One big change I see right now, and particularly coming back from the collections as I just have done in Europe, is a sense that customers, CEOs, owners of big businesses, are really searching for what fashion means today and how that there needs to be an emotional connection, and that fashion cannot be seen as something that is in anyway disposable, that women need to look at fashion as not only an investment from a personal point of view, but an investment in terms of clothes that they can wear again and again. This idea that you wear something once and then won't be seen in it again seems completely out of step with the times.. . . It's much more about fashion, clothing, being emotional; something that you could give to your daughter or something that you could give to your son, as time goes by, and it having really meaning and connection, and reminding the wearer of moments in their life and I think it's important that all of us who live in a world where everything is seen so visibly, so instantly, by so many, that maybe a sense of value and connection is very meaningful right now.[92]

Fashion scholars Paul Jobling, Philippa Nesbitt and Angelene Wong consider the social role of fashion in an analysis of *Cyborg* that is framed by the pandemic.[93] The authors suggest the curious staging of the show and the polyvalent looks it featured probably had 'little or no impact on the lives of most people in society'.[94] However, in seeking to create a 'pluriverse'[95] in which 'mongrel' identities appeared, Michele is interpreted as a 'cultural intermediary',[96] who points the way for fashion 'to express how humans, posthumans and non-humans could live in harmony in the twenty-first century'.[97] His directions are nonetheless faltering for the authors acknowledge *Cyborg*'s racial plagiarism, even if they seem more inclined to interpret the problematized jumper as a form of 'terrorist chic'.[98] Their analysis underscores the challenges of the fashion industry becoming a critical conduit for social reflection and psychological salve, for as the remarks of Wintour and the underpinnings of Geczy's and Karaminas's concept make plain, they are wholly 'western'-centric.[99] The challenge of interpreting fashions, and of potentially investing them with too much meaning and significance, is picked up in the concluding episode of this chapter. I examine a situation where feelings of guilt about the prevalence of white innocence stoked concerns and controversy within the anglophone press that were not shared or endorsed by the purported black female victim.

Madewell advertisement, 2017

From 9 November 2017 Instagram and Twitter users began to comment critically on a campaign released by J.Crew-owned clothing brand Madewell. The advertisement included three colour portraits of black model Marihenny Pasible wearing one of Madewell's short-sleeved crew-neck tops in a ribbed marl fabric. Pictured against a white background, she smiles and appears relaxed. Her hair is styled into a top-knot. There appears to be an absence of styling product in Pasible's hair because strands remain loose, suggesting either a natural appearance, or as some commentators thought, a messy appearance.[100] As online reposts of Pasible's images increased, with many people assuming the model had been poorly treated by a white hairdresser who did not know how to style her hair, the anglophone media took up the story. In so doing, they appear to have sparked a debate between people who thought Pasible had been let down and those who thought natural hair styling should be embraced irrespective of race. On 10 November, J.Crew issued an apology through its Twitter feed. The brand stated that it 'strives to represent every race, gender, and background' and sought to reassure people that they would 'tak[e] steps to address [the complaint], and to prevent this from happening again'.[101] On 11 November, Pasible took to social media to respond to a post made by *The Shade Room*, an online news forum that encourages users to respond openly to contemporary news topics to promote 'positivity and substance' over negativity, colloquially termed 'shade'.[102] Pasible thanked people for their 'positive comments', and for attention that was 'flattering', but defended Madewell, explaining:

> [T]he concept of the brand specifically is to show that clothes can be comfortable wearable and naturally beautiful. So the natural hair and makeup fits right in. Also these days it is all about women embracing their natural looks so here it is! We as human beings are never satisfied with what we get we always want more and still complain![103]

Pasible's intervention did not immediately assuage people's concerns and stories about the Madewell advertisement continued to be published online by fashion magazines, including one story by *Cosmopolitan* with the headline, 'The Internet Is Mad at J. Crew over This Black Model's Hairstyle'.[104] Whilst Pasible claimed that her experience had been misconstrued, the debate sparked by her images drew attention to other black women whose hair had been poorly treated. Prior to this episode, in September 2017, model Londone Myers recounted a difficult experience she had faced during Paris Fashion Week. White hairstylists had appeared to 'avoid' styling her hair because they didn't know 'how to do [her] black hair'.[105] In November 2017, actress Lupita Nyongo'o expressed 'disappointment' at the 'unconscious prejudice against black women's complexion, hair style and texture' when she saw that her cover image for *Grazia* UK had been edited. Much of her hair, gathered into a pony tail, had been cut from the final image.[106] The resulting portrait appears to show her with a shaved head. Nyongo'o criticized the magazine for disregarding her heritage and for making her hair 'fit their notion of what beautiful hair looks like'.[107] Nyongo'o's experience recalls that of singer Solange Knowles, who had part of her braided hairstyle cut from the cover of London's *The Evening Standard* magazine in October 2017.[108]

These examples underscore Dabiri's point that the "managing' of black women's hair operates as a powerful metaphor for societal control over [their] bodies at both micro and macro levels'.[109] On the one hand, this is a metaphor that elucidates the subordination of black bodies to white, 'western' ideals, as Nyongo'o argued. Equally, it is a metaphor for the 'fantasies' that black people 'continue to uphold about what constitutes black beauty'.[110] Dabiri's personal narrative explains various hair-related tests that were performed within black communities to determine the extent of people's belonging. Membership of certain black churches depended on whether a comb could pass freely through a woman's hair. In South Africa, by contrast, a child's race was fixed according to whether their hair 'could hold a pencil'.[111] These two examples demonstrate how dominant black beauty ideals are subconsciously framed by 'western' values, chiefly because 'long, flowing hair' has been 'one of the most powerful markers of being a woman . . . [and] that is not how Afro hair grows'.[112] In the case of relaxed hair, a chemical process that straightens black people's hair, Dabiri considers the physical violence that black women endure to change their hair to align with 'western' norms. This 'brutal process' can burn the scalp, cause cancer and infertility.[113] The Natural Hair Movement, which began in the United States in the first quarter of the new Millennium, sought to celebrate black hair and develop awareness of how to care for it, but the prevalence of 'western' hairstyles, along with 'western' connotations of black hair, means black people's choices about growing and styling their hair remain politically charged.[114]

The freighted history and associations of black people's hair explain the controversy that Pasible's photographs sparked and why the ensuing negotiation about their meaning was protracted. Some commentators on social media claimed Pasible was being held to unfair beauty standards because she was black. Still others claimed this would not even be a point of discussion if Madewell had featured a white model.[115] Blogger Ayana Lage, writing for online media site *Bustle*, encapsulated the dilemma felt by some black women when she questioned, 'Do I have the right as a black women to be mad on Pasible's behalf, if she's not upset herself?'[116] Her comment hints at the persistence of 'internalised racism', which author and journalist Chaédria LaBouvier made explicit in her commentary for beauty website *Allure*. She argued that people's 'visceral reaction' when a 'black woman has "messy" hair', and their specific focus on whether Pasible's hair was 'presentable', was rooted in a racist discourse about the appearance and control of black women's bodies.[117] Responses to the Madewell advertisement, like those of Prada and Gucci, demonstrate the confusion and intensity of hurt that results when 'western' concerns, perceived to be at the heart of the fashion industry, engage – or more aptly collide – with the lived experiences of those of its consumers who reside, physically and figuratively, at its periphery.

Reflections

To connect race and fantasy might seem alarming, offensive, reductionist, but both concepts, as social constructs, are alike for drawing on people's visions of how they want their lives to be ordered. Conjoined, and made manifest through fashionable dress, they give rise to potent, frequently problematic negotiations about people's cultural values. Two observations follow from the preceding discussion. First, fantasies are never wholly utopic, nor are they harmless. The result of people's aspirations and assumptions, and predicated on a deeply felt sense of how things ought to be within a specific society, they are frequently impervious to rational analysis. Consequently, fantasies can be crucibles in which some of people's most intractable views and behaviours are formed. Fantasies become manifest through fashion because it is a prevalent, shared belief that most people around the world accept. This means that fashion is as adept at conveying the darkness inherent in people's longings, as much the delight. Second, and linked, the episodes question how much interrogation fashion can bear. As a belief, something that is aspirational, there is a sense to which it might be too ephemeral to be scrutinized. In their analysis of *Cyborg* Jobling, Nesbitt and Wong observe that most fashion journalists 'overlooked' the collection's theoretical framework. One person who did engage with it had a doctoral degree, but still claimed 'it was nearly incomprehensible'.[118] Consequently, instead of elucidating contentious issues that fashion may present, fashion journalists, academics too, potentially ignite, certainly entrench them, chiefly by establishing a false equivalence between perceived cultural infractions, as Minh-Ha T. Pham has argued.[119] Another perspective, which might explain why fashion analysis can be challenging to undertake and cursory in its presentation, is voiced by author Dal Chodha. He argues that fashion should not be used 'to correct our morbid reality'.[120] 'Fashion is or should be the distraction from daily life that focuses our minds on humanity and imagination. A place for beauty, not beast.' The extent to which this scenario is plausible or merely polemical underpins discussion in the chapters that follow.[121]

4
SEXUALITY

First impressions count, so they are almost always deceptive. 'Western' people's fixation on the association between a person's clothing and character often blinds them to a simple, complicated fact highlighted by sociologist Joanne Finkelstein: 'our tacit understanding of human character seems to be derived from a motley assemblage of contradictory ideas.'[1] This motley assemblage was explored, enjoyed and exaggerated by author Virginia Wolff in her novel *Orlando*, published in 1928. The eponymous protagonist of this fictitious biography cum autobiography lives for approximately four centuries and changes sex midway through the narrative. Naturally, this occasioned a change of wardrobe and permitted Wolff to reflect on the function of clothing.[2] Remarking that 'sexes intermix', she speculates:[3]

> In every human being a vacillation from one sex to the other takes place, and often it is only the clothes that keep the male or female likeness, while underneath the sex is the very opposite of what it is above.[4]

Wolff's musings about gendered clothing demonstrate how human bodies, undressed or dressed, become representative of cultural values, generally, and social structures, specifically. In the nineteenth century, when the white – typically male – body was invoked as a representation of the figurative body politic, it was readily understood that contamination of the former could lead to vulnerabilities in the latter.[5] Such logic demonstrates how far boundaries between fact and fantasy were elastic and porous during this period. It also establishes that 'alternative facts' is a twenty-first coinage for a long-standing phenomenon. English scholar Jayne Elizabeth Lewis argues that seventeenth-century historians and biographers were 'prone to see themselves less as faithful transcribers of a firmly distanced past than as mediators between competing desires and instincts of belief'.[6] Her verdict is apt to describe commentators two centuries later. She cites nineteenth-century English historian James Anthony Froude, who mused, 'It seems to me as if history was like a child's box of letters with which we can spell any word we please. We have only to pick out such letters as we want, arrange them as we like, and say nothing about those which do not suit our purpose.'[7] Writing technologies have changed, but Froude's sentiment is little different to that of President Donald Trump's political advisor Kellyanne Conway.[8]

The mutability of facts in the nineteenth century meant that many perils were perceived to weaken the sexual morality and normality of 'western' men, and thus the 'west'. Whether it was the 'male-power fantasy' noted by Edward Said of 'western' men possessing and penetrating the Orient, which was typically feminized;[9] the coordination of concubinage, which described the 'cohabitation outside of marriage between European men and Asian women';[10] the primal urges of black men that imperilled white women with sexual assault;[11] the myriad instances of young boys who dressed as women and consented, however unequally, in male-to-male sexual behaviour;[12] or the concerns that 'moral degeneration' would compromise European men who remained in colonial posts for 'too long',[13] encounters with people from beyond Europe's frontiers challenged the 'west's' cultural assumptions, particularly about gender, race and sexuality, risking their destabilization and the ruin of the society they upheld.[14]

The topics of gender and race were of grave concern, as previous chapters have suggested, but nineteenth-century discourses about sexual behaviours indicate that sexuality was a cause of acute anguish. Towards the end of the eighteenth century, historian and politician Edward Gibbon had argued that vice, which included what he considered to be sexual laxity, precipitated the demise of the Roman Empire.[15] Concerns that a similar fate could befall contemporary Europe created an imperative for power brokers, from scientists to statesmen, to solidify boundaries, figurative and physical, that would distinguish between what they considered to be normative and non-normative social practices. Showing an 'unlimited interest in the sexual interface of the colonial encounter', the purpose of these men – and white, heteronormative cis-gendered men they typically were – was to enshrine the former and eradicate the latter.[16] These actions, at once fearful and forensic, elide with cultural anthropologist Gayle Rubin's contention that '[d]isputes over sexual behaviour often become the vehicles for displacing social anxieties, and discharging their attendant emotional intensity'. Consequently, 'sexuality should be treated with special respect in times of great social stress'.[17] Then, as now, the clarification and condemnation of sexual behaviours becomes a particular preoccupation for power brokers during periods of acute social disquiet.

The concern to protect 'western' values against a perceived degeneracy meant that sexuality became, in author Rudi Bleys's phrase, 'a cornerstone of European constructions of a social utopia' between the eighteenth and twentieth centuries.[18] The difference Bleys observes across these centuries is one of degree rather than kind because sexuality, although unlabelled, had featured prominently in Thomas More's sixteenth-century *Utopia*.[19] Informed by his Christian convictions, More had been unable, or unwilling, to think beyond relationships that involved males and females who would marry and procreate. Prior to the nineteenth century, myriad terms in almost all of the world's languages had existed to define, sometimes to discriminate against, sexualities that were acknowledged as different. Their detail was often exacting.

In ancient Greece terms distinguished male-to-male sexual relationships with reference to partners' age and role. A 'passive partner' was a *pais* (boy).[20] *Pornē* or *pornus* described people who 'submitted to homosexual acts in return for money'.[21] Classicist Kenneth Dover also identified slang terms to refer to sexual organs. 'Barley' referred to the penis, as did 'rotten rope', if the man were older.[22] 'Cable' and 'lance' were also used.[23] Apparently, the Greek poet Aristophanes used seventy-five words to describe the male genitalia and over one hundred for sexual acts, including 'to spit', 'to jab', 'bump' and 'grate'.[24] Roman poet Catallus, who is not known to have practised male-to-male sex, used aggressive sexual language against male foes, including, 'I shall fuck you in the arse and in the mouth' (*Pedicabo ego vos et irramabo*).[25] Within West Africa, the Hausa term *K'awaye* is used by *yan daudu* ('feminine-identified men') to describe 'special, supposedly nonsexual friendship'.[26] In Central Africa Pangwe people tolerate male-to-male sexual behaviour involving adult men by describing them as a *bele nku'ma* ('he has the heart (that is the aspirations) of boys').[27] Within Angola, the Wawihé people have terms for various sexual practices and positions between people of the same and different sexes, but solitary masturbation is apparently so uncommon that it warrants no word.[28] Within India, the Sanskrit term *napumsada* ('lacking maleness') could describe a 'third sex' and terms like hijra referred to 'eunuchs, but also to transvestites and effeminate homosexual men'.[29] The richness of this language attests to the fact that people's sexuality and the performance of sexual acts have been cornerstones for the construction of social utopias across diverse chronologies and cultures. The establishment of European empires challenged these conceptions and constrained these words, the beliefs and actions they described.

Europe's 'great age of classification' during the eighteenth and nineteenth centuries included sustained attempts to isolate non-normative sexualities, particularly same-sex practices between men.[30] Academics, journalists, jurists and scientists worked to refine the lexicon that described same-sex relationships. During the 1860s, German sexologist Karl Heinrich Ulrichs coined the terms *Urning* and *Urningen* for men and women respectively, informed by Plato's *Symposium*.[31] He asserted that a same-sex desire was natural and developed within thirteen weeks of human conception.[32] In 1886, German psychiatrist Richard Freiherr von Krafft-Ebing published *Psychopathia Sexualis*. Using Ulrichs's terms, and acknowledging that same-sex desires could be inherent, his work was influential for distinguishing those that were 'acquired' and for insisting that any deviation from sex for procreation was degenerative.[33] *Homosexualität* (homosexuality) was conceived by German-Hungarian journalist Károly Mária Kertbeny. The term appears in one of his private letters from 1868 and in two publications from 1869.[34] In 1880, Kertbeny coined what remains its opposing term, *heterosexualität* (heterosexuality), in a publication that proved influential for the widespread adoption of both.[35] Reflecting on this semantic stratification, cultural historian Rictor Norton remarks that heterosexuals were '[t]hus . . . invented' later than homosexuals.[36] His comment is sardonic, but it emphasizes the pliability of language, which is reconfigured as people's ideas shift, and its power, which simultaneously defines concepts and confers validity upon them.

Kertbeny's terms and the emergence of sexology as a distinct discipline during the 1860s, which was overseen by scientists and buttressed by Christian doctrine, demonstrate how the classificatory imperative sparked by encounters with colonial subordinates at the frontiers of Europe had a significant impact within them. The process of defining sexual and wider social mores was fuelled as much by the cultures and histories of Europe.[37] As anthropologist Ann Stoler observes, '[u]ltimately inclusion or exclusion required regulating the sexual, conjugal and domestic life of both Europeans in the colonies and their colonized subjects.'[38] I would add, for Europeans at home, too.

The result was a regime of 'cultural hygiene' that was established throughout Europe and its colonies.[39] European concepts that purported to clarify sexual behaviours were enforced within and beyond its borders by policies and penal codes. This meant sexual behaviours that had previously been accepted, certainly tolerated, became restricted, stigmatized and punished. Bleys suggests a primary function of these legal measures was 'to safeguard male, white – I add, heterosexual – hegemony'.[40] His point is provocative, but Rubin's assertion that the consequences of 'nineteenth-century moral paroxysms are still with us' is compelling considering the number of former European colonies whose penal legislation in the twenty-first century remains unchanged since it was imposed during the eighteenth and nineteenth centuries, establishing 'western' heteronormative ideas.[41] At the time of reviewing this chapter – August 2022 – Singapore's prime minister Lee Hsien Loong has announced plans to repeal the country's colonial-era legislation that criminalizes same-sex relations between men.[42]

All of this means that two of the most enduring nineteenth-century terms to describe people's sexualities – homosexual and heterosexual – are freighted, for at least three reasons. First, neither term corresponds 'to the cross-cultural realities of "bisexual" practices and role-defined sexual identities' that existed within and beyond Europe during the eighteenth and twentieth centuries.[43] They occlude consideration of people who expressed their sexuality in diverse ways, 'sometimes exclusively heterosexually, sometimes with boys or with men and women alike'.[44] Their reflection of twenty-first-century sexual identities is even more askew. Second, usage of the term 'homosexuality' tends to prioritize male-to-male sexual behaviour, although authors like Norton do use it to describe female-to-female behaviours.[45] Accordingly, Bley avoids the term and favours 'same-sex behaviour' and 'male-to-male sexual behaviour', which I adopt.[46] Queer is increasingly used within discussions of sexuality, particularly within the academy. Author Mark Gevisser notes it is 'convenient', a 'catchall' that encompasses the people to whom the acronym LGBTQIA applies.[47] It is positive, 'having been reappropriated by people across the world to describe themselves'.[48] However, it is still used as a slur and 'remains awkward'; it does for me as a gay man, although I use the term when 'same-sex' seems too limiting.[49] Third, and perhaps most pressingly for discussions of sexuality today, the genesis of homosexuality and heterosexuality is conflated with 'western' ideas of modernity and capitalism to a greater degree than other concepts considered in this book. This point is important because contemporary support for LGBTQIA communities and the emergence of new terms to describe people's sexuality – including 'demisexual', coined in 2006, and 'abrosexual', possibly coined in 2013 – that have been popularized during the period I have worked on this book – have been linked to the continued social and economic dominance of the 'west'.[50] Perpetuating a nineteenth-century classificatory tradition, these concepts are also portmanteaus of English and Greek.

Focusing on male-to-male sexual behaviour, for which there is more readily available evidence in the contemporary fashion industry, I consider three studies. First, Dolce & Gabbana's *Love Is Love* advertisements that were published on social media and across the internet in February 2021; Burberry's *Time* collection for autumn/winter 2018, shown in February 2018; and Thom Browne's *Portraits* menswear collection for spring/summer 2019, shown in June 2018. These episodes consider the role – and right – of the fashion industry to undertake critical social commentary and reflect on responses to this that are predicated on notions of empire and 'western' cultural hegemony.

Dolce & Gabbana, 'Love Is Love' advertisements, 12–14 February 2021

Between 12 and 14 February 2021, in the run-up to Valentine's Day, Dolce & Gabbana released a series of seven short videos of couples kissing through its Instagram account. Conceived as part of the brand's 'Love Is Love' campaign, each film showed two people standing before a scarlet background wearing D&G-branded clothing and dress accessories. Seemingly oblivious to anything and anyone but themselves, the pairs were filmed embracing, caressing, even undressing each other. The couples were of different ages, races and sexes; four were male-female and three were same-sex (one female and two male pairings). On 12 February Dolce & Gabbana released a composite film on YouTube that included all the Instagram clips with two additional same-sex couples (one male, one female).[51] The campaign received little attention in the anglophone press following its release. This changed on 25 May, just over fourteen weeks later, when Reuters reported that Russian politician Mikhail Romanov, a member of the country's ruling United Russia party and State Duma, the lower house of Russia's Federal Assembly, had made a formal request on 14 May that the videos be removed. Romanov argued that the films contravened a Russian law of 2013 'for the Purpose of Protecting Children from Information Advocating for a Denial of Traditional Family Values', which forbids the dissemination of 'propaganda on non-traditional sexual relations' among young people.[52] His complaint apparently lacked supporting evidence, but it is possible the Dolce & Gabbana videos unsettled Romanov, and other people within Russia, because their explicit focus on kissing recalled the public kiss-ins that had been staged outside the State Duma in 2012 to protest the so-called 'gay propaganda law'.[53] The anglophone press immediately picked up the story and articles appeared on fashion and LGBTQIA news sites.[54] Somewhat ironically, the attempt to remove the Dolce & Gabbana films piqued people's curiosity about them, particularly within Russia.

Dated comments on Dolce & Gabbana's Instagram feed and YouTube site indicate that global discussion about Romanov's attempt to ban the films catalyzed debates, diatribes and dogma about them. From May 2021 onwards, remarks written by Russian-speaking viewers in response to the videos increased on both platforms. Along with comments from Arabic writers, they are among the most critical of the brand's campaign.[55] One comment, added by the same Russian speaker to two Instagram clips that feature men kissing is '🔧🚩'.[56] The comment received three likes across the two posts. Several of the comments express condemnation through satire. For example, one Russian writer claims they are 'tired' of the promotion of *heterosexual* relationships. They express a desire for people to 'love each other but not in public'.[57] Many comments are short – 'What nonsense, unsubscribe' (Чё за бред, отписка); 'Disgusting' (Отвратительно).[58] Russian-speaking viewers were not alone in voicing their disapproval. One Muslim commentator, writing in Arabic, quotes a hadith, or saying, of the Prophet Muhammad: 'Whoever among you sees an evil, let him change it with his hand. If he is not able to do so, then with his tongue. If he is not able to do so, then with his heart, and that is the weakest of faith.'[59] Another comment written by an Arabic speaker states, 'In Islam and in all religions homosexuality is forbidden because it is against instinct, I am against homosexuality, I am Muslim and I am proud.'[60] A Spanish-speaker considered the Instagram clips to be 'wholly unpleasant' (*Totalmente desagradables*) and suggested that a heavy financial penalty should be imposed for publication of same-sex content.[61]

Negative comments about the campaign were preponderant, but across Dolce & Gabbana's Instagram and YouTube platforms viewers did express support. A Portuguese writer considered the campaign to be 'video perfection' (*perfeição de vídeo*😎).⁶² An English writer opined, '[It i]s beautiful!!!♡😘😘😘😘😘'.⁶³ A German writer reflected stoically, 'yes it doesn't matter who you are' (*ja, es ist egal wer du bist*).⁶⁴ Several Russian speakers also expressed support for the campaign. One questioned why a 'normal video' should cause a problem (орм ролик, что не так?); another wrote simply, 'Beauty!' (красота!).⁶⁵ The majority of positive statements from Russian-speaking viewers mention that awareness of the campaign had been a consequence of Romanov's attempts to ban it:

> Если бы не Питерская прокуратура не знала бы про ролик этот.⁶⁶
> [If not for the St. Petersburg prosecutor's office, [I] would not know about this video.]

> Специально зашел глянуть и насладиться роликом. :-)⁶⁷
> [Especially came to look and enjoy the video. :-)]

> ♡ любовь есть любовь. Спасибо прокуратуре Петербурга за просвещение.⁶⁸
> [♡Love is love. Thanks to the St. Petersburg Prosecutor's Office for enlightenment.]

> Отличный бренд, отличный ролик 🍷 Пользуясь случаем, передаю привет российской прокуратуре 🙄👮 P.S. При просмотре рекламы ни одна семейная ценность не пострадала.⁶⁹
> [Great brand, great video 🍷 Taking this opportunity, I say hello to the Russian prosecutor's office 🙄👮 P.S. No family value was harmed when viewing ads.]

These satirical remarks, along with the negative comments of Russian and Arabic writers, show how Dolce & Gabbana's campaign became a site of global negotiation because it exposed a fault line, or a Pink Line to use Gevisser's term, between different understandings of sexuality that prefigure the acceptance or rejection of same-sex behaviours. Where tolerance can lead to the integration of queer people 'as full citizens' into a society, disavowal leads to an attempt to find 'new ways to shut them out'.⁷⁰ In particular, Romanov and the predominantly Russian commentators who responded critically to the videos baulked at what they perceived to be a 'western' form of sexual behaviour undermining their traditional values. This discourse had become increasingly public and trenchant within Russia, and its neighbouring countries, following Vladimir Putin's return to the presidency in 2012.⁷¹

Prima facie the belief that same-sex behaviours are a singularly 'western' phenomenon and pose an existential threat to Russian society is an inversion of the argument of eighteenth- and nineteenth-century Europeans, who feared for the consequences of their sexual morality following encounters with colonial subjects. Demonstrating the pliability of language, the changed geopolitical landscape following decolonization, and the freighted relations between the European Union and Russia specifically, this criticism of contemporary Europe has been made by others. Historian Joseph Massad has forcefully argued that 'western' sexual behaviours and the discourses that promote them distort the sexual morality and practices of other countries, particularly in the Middle East. Coining the term 'Gay International' to describe the 'western' organizations that defend and advance the rights of sexual minorities, the dialogues they produce and the actions they undertake, Massad maintains it 'both produces homosexuals, as well as gays and lesbians, where they do not exist, and represses same-sex desires and practices that refuse to be assimilated into its sexual epistemology'.[72] He has also highlighted the hypocrisy of 'western' countries who criticize contemporary Islam for its perceived sexual stringency, when they had, as colonial powers, berated Muslims for their apparent sexual licentiousness.[73] Massad's research shows that then, as now, no group of people have a monopoly on sexual behaviours that another might deem abhorrent. Gevisser has also drawn attention to the 'anti-colonial self-determination' of countries formerly governed by Europe whose officials defy 'western' politicians and organizations in sanctioning anti-same-sex legislation to demonstrate they are not 'neocolonial stooge[s]'.[74] At the time of writing this chapter, legislation that would constitute 'the first major step in criminalising the sexual minorities and their supporters since independence from colonial rule' is tabled for review by Ghana's parliament.[75] The bill apparently proposes a ten-year jail sentence for LGBTQIA people and their advocates, which includes expressions of support made through social media.

The tempestuous relationship between Europe's colonial past and its present was referenced by President Vladimir Putin when he forcefully asserted the connection between 'western' decline and the normalization of same-sex behaviours in speeches that coincided with the passage of the so-called 'gay propaganda law'. In September 2013, during a meeting of the Valdai International Discussion Club, he argued that 'western' Europe's endorsement of 'so-called multiculturalism' was a means of 'paying for the[ir] colonial past'. The inclusive measures that European countries sanctioned resulted in the denial of 'moral principles and all traditional identities.' To elucidate, Putin suggested '[t]hey are implementing policies that equate large families with same-sex partnerships, belief in God with the belief in Satan'. The 'moral crisis' he perceived was apparent in the inability of 'almost all developed nations . . . to reproduce themselves, even with the help of migration'.[76] Taking questions after his speech, Putin directly linked Europe's low birth rate to its acceptance of same-sex marriage.

> The birth rates are low, the Europeans are dying out; do you understand that or not? Same-sex marriages do not produce children. Do you want to survive on account of immigrants? . . . Your choice is the same as in many other nations: recognising same-sex marriages, the right to adopt, and so on. But allow us to make our own choice, as we see fit for our own nation.[77]

Putin emphasized the necessity for Russia to pursue its own course to mitigate the 'objective pressures stemming from globalization' in an address to the Federal Assembly in December 2013.[78] Highlighting the compromises made by 'many nations [who] are revising their moral values and ethical norms, [which] erod[e] ethnic traditions and differences between peoples and cultures', he explained that 2014 will 'be a year of enlightenment, emphasis on our cultural roots, patriotism, values and ethics'.[79] Simultaneously, he stressed, 'we are not limiting our sexual minorities' rights in any way. There are no limitations, we do not have laws limiting them in anything at all: at work, or in other areas of activity', and questioned, 'Why does everyone like to put so much stress on Russia?' Nonetheless, there seemed to be a clear message that same-sex behaviours were an unwelcome 'western' encroachment within his country. The apparent need for Russia and her closest neighbours to defend against Europe's 'eastward spread' has been discussed by Gevisser. He describes Ukrainian election posters from 2013 that were printed with the slogan, 'Association with the EU means same-sex marriage', and the promotion of the rhyming slogan, through Russian television: *V Evropu cherez zhopu* (The way to Europe is through the ass).[80] A more recent example includes Russian criticism of British diver Tom Daley during the 2021 Tokyo Olympics. *Attitude* magazine reported that Rossiya 1 Network's *60 Minutes* had described Russian diver Aleksandr Bondar as a 'normal guy' and Daley as a 'British homosexual'. Over images of Daley with husband Dustin Lance Black and son Robbie, 3, presenter Olga Skabeyeva said: 'In Britain, of course, they have their own values. If these guys weren't raising a child together, then it'd be their business.'[81]

The concern about same-sex behaviours and globalization within Russia and parts of Eastern Europe is likely rooted in the idea that homosexuality – both the term and the people it purports to describe – is a nineteenth-century creation, linked to the development of capitalism. Historian John d'Emilio makes the point unequivocally: 'gay men and lesbians have not always existed.. . . Their emergence is associated with the relations of capitalism.'[82] In outline, d'Emilio follows philosopher Michel Foucault and argues that industrialization prefigured new patterns of living and socialization, particularly in burgeoning urban spaces where people, possessing of loose connections and with disposal income, could uniquely explore their self and social identities. This included their sexualities. These freedoms were not universally welcomed. The recognition that industrialization and increased global connectivity required more labour, and so an increasing population, meant that same-sex relationships were stigmatized as 'fruitless pleasures', in Foucault's phrase.[83] The definition of normative and non-normative sexual behaviours during the nineteenth century was an attempt, led by scientists and the medical profession and sanctioned by politicians, 'to control sexuality in order to promote the reproductive capacity of the labour force'.[84] Framed by the metaphor of the male body representing the body politic, and the belief that the public sphere was male, these efforts elide with Ben Barker-Benfield's contention that:

> the underlying model for the operation of the whole man, psychological and physiological, was economic.. . . All of one's experiences were reified and quantified into a drum-tight economic system in which every gain was someone's loss, every loss someone else's gain. This seems to have been a projection of the intra-personal 'law of animal economy' on to inter-personal relations.[85]

These arguments about the genesis of Kertbeny's coinage are compelling because they link historical factors that seem plausibly contingent. Nonetheless, they are inaccurate. The judgements of d'Emilio, Foucault and other social constructionalists are ahistorical. They largely disregard the existence of same-sex behaviours prior to the nineteenth century by emphasizing discourse over 'experiential reality'.[86] Whilst it is credible to argue that industrialization and capitalism changed the nature of same-sex behaviours, this constitutes a difference of degree rather than kind to what had existed before. During the eighteenth and nineteenth centuries, and still today, the understanding and practice of same-sex behaviours could not but be influenced, however imperceptibly, by prior examples and incidents that have been recorded since antiquity.[87]

Of course, accuracy is determined by measurement, the criteria of which are subjective. As the chapters in this book demonstrate, an absence of intellectual validity is rarely sufficient to dislodge an idea that satisfies emotional longing. The elision between 'western' capitalism, globalization, homosexuality and moral decline may lack incontrovertible evidence but, following cultural anthropologist Gayle Rubin, I contend that its continued traction, particularly within parts of contemporary Russian society, is due to its ability to displace 'social anxieties'.[88] Anthropologist Tom Boellstorff's concept of 'political homophobia' can elucidate this point. Boellstorff defines political homophobia as 'an emergent cultural logic linking emotion, sexuality, and political violence'.[89] Charting the rise of violent homophobia at the start of the new Millennium within Indonesia, whose defence minister opined that the LGBTQIA movement was more threatening than a nuclear war, he argues that physical attacks against queer men by non-queer men have become a vehicle for the latter to expiate the 'shame' of living in a country with 'a nationalized masculinity' (i.e. male-to-male sexual behaviours), which they deem to be 'a psychic threat to proper masculinity'.[90] Advancing the pessimistic and chilling argument that these attacks constitute the 'working out of cultural logics of inequality and exclusion to their horrific but comprehensible conclusion', Boellstorff acknowledges how the advancement of globalization and the attendant spread of 'western' mores can appear to undermine traditional beliefs and power structures. This is analogous to the situation in Russia, which the Dolce & Gabbana 'Love Is Love' campaign called attention to. Framed by an increasing concern about the pace of globalization and the concomitant spread of 'western' social and political ideas that can appear to undermine a society's traditional values, I contend that Dolce & Gabbana's support for same-sex behaviour was interpreted as an episode of neocolonialism.

The concern and suspicion generated by the brand's campaign within Russia, and presumably across other parts of the world judging from the different languages used on social media to comment on the videos, demonstrate how the 'in-between spaces between cultures' that elaborate 'strategies of selfhood – singular or communal' can result in disagreement.[91] For Homi Bhabha as a post-colonial theorist, one of the chief sources of disagreement, if I understand him correctly, stems from the challenge of reconciling the 'jarring of meanings and values' that persist from the colonial past with the circumstances of the present.[92] Here: the paradox of a contemporary 'western' fashion brand utilizing its commercial and social authority to publicly embrace same-sex relationships, and implicitly criticizing those who do not, when 'western' imperial powers had used their economic and political authority to eradicate, at least suppress, the very same relationships.

Burberry, *Time*, autumn/winter 2018, 17 February 2018

On 17 February 2018 Burberry presented its autumn/winter 2018 collection *Time* within London Fashion Week. It was the final collection to be overseen by Christopher Bailey who had served as the brand's creative officer and president since 2014. The twenty-one-minute show comprised eighty-four looks – fifty-one for women and thirty-three for men. It was more racially diverse than many contemporary catwalks with just over one-third (seventeen) of the women's looks and just under one-third (nine) of the men's looks worn by other than white models. Reflecting upon Burberry's 'past, present and future', the collection included the brand's recognizable check across a range of garments, including baseball caps, coats and trousers. In homage to the 1980s and 1990s – 'the licensing part of Burberry's history' – there were sweatshirts, puffer jackets, bucket hats and bold, primary colours.[93] The show's soundtrack comprised five songs by the gay pop groups Bronski Beat and The Communards, including 'Infatuation/Memories', 'I Feel Love' and 'Don't Leave Me This Way', which had been released between 1984 and 1987. The vibrancy of the collection reflected its emphasis on youth and support for the LGBTQIA community. Several garments featured rainbow stripes in reference to the colours of the Pride flag, as it then was. The show's final look, a floor-length faux fur coat in the Pride colours, lined with the Burberry check, was worn by model Cara Delevingne.

The anglophone press considered the show's explicit support of the LGBTQIA community, which was presaged by catwalk invitations that included an amalgamation of the Pride colours and Burberry check, appropriate. During his seventeen-year tenure at the brand, Bailey had been the first openly gay chief executive among the UK's FTSE 100 companies. Consequently, journalist Amanda Arnold, writing for women's online journal *The Cut*, suggested this was the 'perfect last show for Bailey'.[94] It was fitting that his 'highly emotional' final collection was dedicated to LGBT Youth. Burberry also made donations to three international organizations that support members of the queer community: the Albert Kennedy Trust, Trevor Project and International Lesbian, Gay, Bisexual, Trans and Intersex Association (ILGA).[95] Consequently, whilst the theme of *Time* had been conceived to reference Burberry's history, commentators applied it to Bailey's biography as well. Journalist Sarah Mower described the show as 'autobiographical'. It was:

> an honest, symbolic revisiting of the place of his first fashion awakening, a dive club in a basement in Halifax, Yorkshire, and all the DIY teen-tribe styles that rolled through British street culture in the '80s and '90s. Of course, Bailey said it with music, too. What more perfect an opening anthem could there be than 'Smalltown Boy,' the Bronski Beat hit from 1984, sung by the gay working-class pop hero Jimmy Somerville?[96]

Not all commentators were positive. In contrast to the critical reception of Dolce & Gabbana's 'Love Is Love' campaign, the issue was not the deleterious effects of globalization that facilitated the spread of same-sex behaviours and the work of the 'Gay International', although Massad would certainly consider the organizations that benefitted from Burberry's largesse among its members. He has argued that the ILGA - the 'most well-known' body of the 'Gay International'- launched an 'aggressive universalization campaign' for the acknowledgement of same-sex rights in 1994.[97] By contrast, *Time* was criticized in some quarters for not doing more to reflect the sexual diversity that globalization was making possible.

The anglophone press reported that the collection 'featured zero transgender women' or men, and no gay models.[98] This claim was not wholly accurate because Delevingne had spoken publicly about her bisexuality in 2015.[99] In 2020, she described herself as pansexual.[100] Repeated use of the rainbow colours throughout the collection was deemed a 'little gimmicky' by SHOWstudio's Georgina Evans, who queried, 'The rainbow is supposed to be an international symbol of pride and diversity, so where was the diversity?'[101] In a live SHOWstudio discussion about the collection chaired by Evans on 18 February, I made a similar, if less eloquent, point:

Do you need this amount of channelling [ie. repeat use of the Rainbow colours] because you don't actually have a clear identifiable message coming from the collection itself? . . . If you hadn't told me about the LGBT+ connection before, in terms of the colours, I was sort of thinking of the old Apple Mac. logo, which [had] horizontal bars in bright colours, or the old Channel 4 [television] logo. There was a lot; that sort of colour was almost indicative of the eighties and nineties generally, so I think . . . for this influence of LGBT+ . . . they could have done more; the clothes I do not think necessarily conveyed that for me.[102]

For Evans – and for me – the 'collection fell a little flat'.[103] A perception that *Time* had not done enough to champion LGBTQIA communities warrants critique. Akin to Dolce & Gabbana's 'Love Is Love' campaign, rueful analysis of the show is predicated on the assumption that Burberry had an obligation to articulate values associated specifically with its 'western' consumers. The arguments of Bandana Tewari, editor-at-large for Indian *Vogue*, who wrote about *Time* in an article for *Business of Fashion*, can help to refine this point. Tewari praised Bailey's final collection and his character. She argued that he was the antithesis to the 'archetype alpha-male that symbolize[s] brutal masculine force'.[104] She claimed he was 'a shining example of how far men have evolved to be sagacious, mindful and willing to embrace a different type of masculinity that is quietly empowering for the entire LGBTQ+ community'.[105] Without citing Boellstorff's concept of political homophobia, or referring to globalization, Tewari's panegyric of Bailey essentially envisages two forms of masculinity to represent binary stances towards globalization. If Bailey's characterization represents people on one side of Gevisser's Pink Line, who seek the integration of queer people 'as full citizens' into a society'; her 'archetype alpha-male', whom she likens to Emily Brontë's Heathcliff, represents those, like Romanov and the perpetrators of violence in Indonesia, who seek 'new ways to shut them out'.[106]

Tewari acknowledges the fraught situation for queer people around the world. Remarking on the situation in India before the repeal of Section 377 of the country's penal code in July 2018:[107]

Section 377 of the Indian Penal code still bans 'carnal intercourse against the order of nature' . . what's little known is that it is a 16th century English law, imposed during the British colonisation of India, which makes this an unforgivable play of irony.[108]

Nevertheless, in arguing that *Time* 'was about mobilising ourselves to serve those who have suffered deeply and quietly', and invoking Mahatma Gandhi's belief in Ahimsa ('non-violence') to demonstrate the 'power of an individual to catalyze change', Tewari appears unaware of the deep emotional resistance towards globalization and 'western' behaviours, which Boellstorff's study of Indonesia elucidates, and which the Russian response to Dolce & Gabbana's campaign demonstrates. Whilst she mentions the violent attacks committed against queer communities in Russia, Uganda and Nigeria, her suggestion that fashion, 'the most ready means through which individuals can represent themselves in their everyday lives and make visual statements about their identities', can lead to an 'exploration of truth' analogous to Gandhi's campaign of non-violence is, at best, optimistic. Moreover, her argument, which emphasizes the importance of individual agency to overcome adversity, is framed by a peculiarly 'western' belief that time, people's lives specifically, follow a linear chronology. The same thinking underpins Bailey's show, as its name and the horologically themed songs make clear. Fashion scholars Caroline Evans and Alessandra Vaccari refer to this chronological concept as 'industrial time'.[109] They describe it as 'rationalized', 'disciplined', 'modernist' and datable to 1884, when Greenwich Meantime was globally established.[110] The accuracy of industrial time has been contested, but rooted in 'the period of post-Enlightenment modernity and the nineteenth-century colonial expansion of global capitalism', it is entrenched.

On 4 July 2018, Burberry posted three identical images of Cara Delevingne wearing the faux fur rainbow cape from *Time* to its Instagram account.[111] In the photograph, Delevingne stands in three-quarter profile with her back to the viewer so the rainbow stripes can be clearly seen. The portrait is captioned,

> Happy #Pride 2018
> Celebrating the rainbow, a global symbol of inclusiveness and joy. Showcased in our February 2018 collection, dedicated to some of the best and brightest organisations supporting LGBTQ+ communities around the world
>
> You always have our support!
> @AlbertKennedyTrust, @ILGAWorld and @TrevorProject

The posts generated a lot of interaction – respectively, 62,676 likes, 540 comments; 30,626 likes, 229 comments; 24,457 likes, 208 comments – but there are a large proportion of negative comments alongside the more positive responses, including:

> From today no for Burberry 👋[112]
> This is so political now ! Keep it to making Clothes rather than post on sexual preference[113]

> Жаль, что такой замечательный бренд поддерживает это безобразие. Я разочарована.[114]
> [it's a pity that such a wonderful brand supports this disgrace. I am disappointed.]

This small selection of comments emphasize how Tewari's arguments, and those of the other commentators cited above – including my own – focus on whether the fashion industry could be a vehicle for changing global perceptions about same-sex behaviours. They do not consider whether it should be. Burberry's *Time* collection and the critical commentary about it is predicated on the assumption that the 'west' should mobilize itself to champion same-sex behaviours around the world. Without wishing to make a moral argument, I would nonetheless reflect that 'western' assumptions about presumed obligations might explain why it is difficult to reconcile viewpoints on either side of the Pink Line and why, following Bhabha, accusations of 'western' neocolonization by former colonies continue to gain traction. The point is pursued in the final episode.

Thom Browne, *Portraits*, spring/summer Menswear 2019, 23 June 2018

On 23 June 2018 Thom Browne unveiled his spring/summer 2019 menswear collection, *Portraits*, within the École des Beaux-Arts during Paris Fashion Week. Like many of his catwalk shows that which introduced *Portraits* was theatrical and playful. The runway was a technicolour garden, lined with turf. White picket fencing created an outer perimeter.[115] An inner garden, around which the models walked, was demarcated by a rainbow-coloured picket fence. This space was decorated with flowers and ferns in pots, bunches of white helium-filled balloons and enlarged wind spinners of various shades. A wooden shed, its panels painted in clashing colours – yellow, red, pink, light blue – was positioned in the middle of the garden. A male model, wearing a light grey knee-length jumpsuit, matching tie and pointed gnome hat by milliner Stephen Jones, dark shades and a fake beard, was seated on its floor, looking out.[116] The fourteen-minute catwalk presentation commenced with two men appearing to trim the grass with white, hand-operated lawn mowers.[117] They were dressed identically to the model in the shed. As they worked, the model from the shed ventured from his colourful compound with a wheelbarrow containing brightly coloured picked flowers.[118] Pausing at the edge of the turf, he handed small bouquets to members of the audience seated in the front row.[119] The three grey gnomes continued to wander around and wave from the garden as models, wearing sixty looks, started to walk the green catwalk. Most of the models were white (57 per cent), leading one fashion journalist to suggest the show presented a version of 'White Anglo-Saxon Protestant America'.[120] Just under one third of the looks were worn by black men (27 per cent); seven looks (12 per cent) were worn by Asian men.

Luke Leitch, writing for British *Vogue*, divided Browne's collection into two halves. Inspired by the American Ivy League of the 1950s, looks 1–30 consisted of tailored shorts, jackets and coats, in pastel colours embroidered with marine-themed motifs – anchor, crab, lobster, sailing boat, whale. The clothes were characterized by their oversize proportions. Looks 31–59 were a 'shrunken version of the first half' using the same palette and patterns for decoration.[121] All models wore bowler-style hats designed by Stephen Jones decorated with a different coloured gerbera; their chins had a smudge of brightly coloured make-up, matching the flower's colour, as though depicting a 'buttercup reflection'.[122] As the models walked, slowly because they wore platformed high-rise derbies, David Bowie's 'There Is a Happy Land' played.[123] To conclude, models wearing corresponding colours from each half of the show came together to complete a final circuit of the garden. They held hands, linked arms or draped their arms over one another's shoulders.[124]

Many anglophone commentators found the show confusing. It was 'kooky', 'surreal', a demonstration of Browne's 'wacky savoir-faire'.[125] Leitch was franker than most about his bewilderment:

> Because it's poor form to open whatever bag or box a house might leave on your chair at a show – you check the loot in the car afterwards – the vast majority of the audience at this preppily pogonophile, gnomo-exotic, Technicolor kaleidoscope of a Thom Browne show watched it with bare eyes. Most of us did not connect the note Browne left that read, 'Please see the world through my eyes . . . please . . .' next to a sunglasses box and a lollipop.[126]

During the show, no one from the audience appears to have worn the glasses that Browne provided. Consequently, few seem to have grasped what the presentation was about. Tim Blanks, writing for *Business of Fashion*, went so far as to suggest, '[a] talk with Thom can occasionally leave you with the frustrating sense that he genuinely has no idea of the subtexts that give his work its resonance'.[127] But Browne did have a message, and he did want his work to resonant with those who saw it. Speaking about the catwalk presentation, he explained:

> [W]e started with gnomes because they are funny, just nonsense.. . . It was really taking where it all began and playing with the proportions.. . . It was just nonsense and ridiculous and I wanted it be all that. And pride . . . a world where everybody gets along.[128]

Despite the repeat use of rainbow colours, which featured in the collection and decorated the catwalk; the Bowie sound track; the pairing, and embracing, of male models at the conclusion of the show; Browne's reference to pride and his request that the audience see the world through his eyes, just two journalists, to my knowledge, grasped the intended message. Samantha Conti, writing for *WWD*, acknowledged the collection's 'big theme of diversity and tolerance', albeit without elucidation.[129] Only Charlie Porter, writing for *The Financial Times*, acknowledged that '[t]he day of the show was Pride in many cities around the world'.[130] Whilst he pursues a similar point to other journalists and asserts that Browne was 'reaching for extreme idealism', Porter nonetheless recognized the purpose of Browne's theatrical presentation, observing that 'in queer communities, nonsense is often used as a tool to make a serious point'.[131]

It intrigues me that few commentaries on *Portraits* considered the possibility of a link to Pride when the evidence is suggestive, if admittedly ambiguous, from a known gay designer. The inclusion of *Portraits* in this chapter is consequently something of a foil. If Dolce & Gabbana's 'Love Is Love' campaign and Burberry's *Time* catwalk make it possible to span the Pink Line and see how contemporary fashions are understood and negotiated differently because of contrasting cultural experiences, the messages of Browne's designs and their display were not only unproblematic, they were almost entirely overlooked.

The chief reason Browne's collection did not communicate a clear message of support for queer relationships is because it was enigmatic. Summarized in an academic text after the fact, the prompts that Browne conceived to convey his ideas become apparent, but in the atmosphere of a fashion week this did not happen. Nor did it happen online. Between 23 and 27 June, twenty images and short clips of the *Portraits* collection and catwalk show were posted on the brand's Instagram account. None of this content referred to Pride. Many of the images were accompanied by ambiguous captions. One post of a model wearing a pink coat decorated with embroidered crabs has the sexually provocative caption, '. . . i got crabs . . . yeah'.[132] One viewer responded with a row of five different-coloured hearts (♡♡♡♡♥), but it is speculative to connect this to Pride. A short film of the catwalk finale that included the male models linking arms and hands was captioned, '. . . come one, come all . . .'.[133] The lack of explanation created confusion among the 138 viewers who made comments. Whilst many remarks were positive, it is unclear from verdicts like, 'I'm so in love with this idea!' what was understood from the catwalk or enjoyed.[134] More common are responses that indicate bewilderment. One viewer wrote, 'so many clowns, scary a[s] f[uck]', although no clowns appeared on the catwalk.[135] Another wrote, 'Shiaparelli's and Dali's 🤡😍♡' [*sic*.], although neither designer is known to have inspired Browne.[136]

Only on 27 June 2020, two years after the catwalk show, was a direct connection between *Portraits* and Pride made. A post on the brand's Instagram feed features three of the *Portraits* models standing side-by-side and facing the camera, their heads cropped out.[137] The model on the left of the image holds a Pride flag in his right hand. The accompanying caption, which wishes followers a 'Happy Pride', asks them to 'please support' three US-based organizations whose work supports members of the LGBTQIA community: Audre Lorde Project, Marsha P. Johnson Institute and Ali Forney Center. The post received 12,879 likes and eighty-two comments. Many of the remarks were positive, but explicit reference to Pride did elicit negative remarks. In three separate posts, one viewer responded with a series of vomiting emojis (🤮); three in the first post and five in the second and third posts. One person wrote, 'Block & bye bye'; another wrote, '👆 f**k'.[138] The fact that Browne's *Portraits* collection faced homophobic comments only when its connection to Pride was made explicit suggest that its inherent ambiguity rendered its message obtuse. Discussing the collection in relation to its performativity and links to fancy dress costume, I have previously argued that Browne's use of humour and recourse to 'nonsense' and the 'ridiculous' 'surprised audiences' and 'confound[ed their] attempts at decipherment'.[139]

Nonetheless, the disconnect between intention and reception could still be considered odd, especially as there had been a number of global incidents, widely reported in the anglophone press, that reflected the fragile position of queer people prior to the catwalk show in June 2018. Following Donald Trump's inauguration as president of the United States in 2016, his administration had worked to remove the legal rights of transgender people, twice seeking to ban them from military service, in August 2017 and March 2018.[140] In April 2018, China experienced its 'largest protest' pertaining to LGBTQIA issues after its Twitter equivalent, Sina Weibo, began 'to censor gay-themed images, videos and cartoons'. The hashtag '#Iamgaynotapervert', which was used to protest Sina Weibo's actions, was apparently viewed more than 1.35 million times within China.[141] In May of the same year, the prime minister of the UK, Theresa May, vowed to streamline the process by which transgender people could legally change their gender identities.[142] On 1 June, a law banning same-sex marriage came into effect in Bermuda, only to be struck down five days later by the country's Supreme Court and nullified on 23 November through the Court of Appeal.[143] These few examples establish that there was a global frame in which Browne's appeal for 'a world where everybody gets along' could resonate in response to contemporary LGBTQIA experiences. As it was, audiences and subsequent viewers only seem to have made a connection to Pride if they were paying close attention, or purposefully willing there to be one.

This point is not as flippant as it may appear, and it gives rise to two reflections about the conveyance of sensitive topics within fashion, which are germane to all themes considered in this book. First, fashion has long made use of humour and laughter, the incongruous and uncanny, to convey messages and interrogate issues that people might find challenging and unpalatable. The studies of fashion scholars Caroline Evans and Rebecca Arnold, and more recently those by Francesca Granata, Adam Geczy and Vicki Karaminas, show how people's anxieties about modernity have been mediated through arresting designs.[144] As I have argued elsewhere:

> The role of laughter . . . is particularly important. In a discussion on culture jamming – 'activist multimedia productions and performances' (Parameswaran 2019: 59–60) – Radhika Parameswaran quotes directly from [Mikhail] Bakhtin, who observes, '[l]aughter demolishes fear and piety before an object, before a world, making of it an object of familiar contact and thus clearing the ground for an absolutely free investigation of it' (Parameswaran 2019: 71). If laughter, perhaps specifically parody and irony, permits investigation, it also gives licence for people to communicate messages that might ordinarily be disavowed. (2019: 71)[145]

Nonetheless, whilst the disarming power of laughter can spur people to reflect and respond, the subjectivity of humour can also create confusion and ambivalence, which is evident in the case of *Portraits*.

Second, and more hesitatingly, I wonder to what extent the ambiguity of *Portraits* is predicated on an assumption of Browne's, and that of his brand, that same-sex behaviours were sufficiently tolerated around the world, or at least within the 'west', to make elucidation unnecessary. To use nonsense 'as a tool to make a serious point' akin to queer communities of the past is to assume the collection's immediate and subsequent audiences would be conversant with this strategy, like Charlie Porter. It is also to assume, and to take for granted like Bandana Tewari, that 'western' fashion brands have a right, even duty, to advocate for the acceptance and support of same-sex relationships worldwide. For, akin to Burberry's *Time*, which supported three LGBTQIA organizations, Browne used *Portraits* to do the likewise. Browne and his brand may not have been alone in making these suppositions. The unknowing responses of many 'western' fashion commentators may reflect their assumption that same-sex behaviours were sufficiently accepted so as to make a Pride-themed collection unnecessary. The point I am raising is similar, if less polemical, to that of historian Martin Duberman, who queries, 'has the gay movement failed?' in a book of the same title published in 2018. Dwelling on the observation that the most prosperous and public members of LGBTQIA communities within the United States are 'white' metropolitans, Duberman laments that the radical nature of the gay movement generally, the Gay Liberation Front specifically, was 'never entirely [able] to free [itself] of the wraparound tentacles of socialization'.[146] A gap opened between 'rhetoric and practice' as the very concepts and social structures that had been opposed during the 1970s became objectives, notably the legalization of same-sex marriage.[147] The corollary of this 'establishment status' is that British prime minister David Cameron could proclaim in a speech of 2011, 'I support same-sex marriage because I am a conservative'.[148] Fragile as they can still seem, the acceptance of gay rights within the 'west', which Cameron's statement assumes to be axiomatic, may have obfuscated the message Browne was making through *Portraits*.

Reflections

People's sexuality was a source of anguish during the eighteenth and nineteenth centuries. It remains so today because how people love and live, and the extent to which they have a choice in doing either, is deeply associated with a society's core values. Three observations can be made. First, the episodes in this chapter consider the extent to which a primary purpose of fashion is to legitimate and spread 'western' values. Non-'western' people can disapprove of this apparent cultural hegemony, interpreting it as a form of neocolonialism. Conversely, 'western' people often consider it necessary and liberating. Their assumption that fashion can, and should, be used to proselytize 'western' values can make them ambivalent or wholly unaware of the negative consequences that can result. Second, and irrespective of motive, effective fashion communication depends on people being able to distinguish between medium and message. In the case of Thom Browne's collection, a poorly understood method inhibited understanding of the designer's message. Third, the three episodes re-emphasize that the experience and interpretation of fashion is culturally contingent and markedly different depending on who is looking. The motivations and expectations of consumers, journalists and politicians, among others, do not necessarily coincide, which can result in contrary responses to the same clothing and campaigns.

5
AGE

A concern, curiosity, often outright fear of human mortality has existed across diverse global cultures for centuries. Some of the earliest surviving human stories, which typically feature gods characterized by their immortality, dwell on the inevitability of people's death.[1] Prosaic or philosophical, reflections on human ageing frequently emphasize dress and appearance. In William Shakespeare's late-sixteenth-century comedy *As You Like It* the melancholic Jacques adumbrated seven ages of man: first, the 'mewling and puking' infant; second, the 'whining school-boy'; third, the lover; fourth, the soldier, 'bearded like a pard'; fifth, the justice with 'fair round belly', 'good capon lined' and 'beard of formal cut'; sixth, an older man, defined by the spectacles on his nose, 'youthful hose, well saved', but loose-fitting because of his 'shrunk shank', and finally a decrepit in the midst of a 'second childishness', who is 'sans everything': teeth, eyes and taste.[2] For the Bard, a person's age was signalled by keenly observed changes in the shape and dress of their bodies. Implicit within this sober summary of human mortality is a correlation between people's increasing infirmity and sensitivity to their dressed appearance. The connection between age, apparel and body is a recurrent, often explicit, theme in factual and fictional accounts of human societies by 'western' authors. In the second century Roman poet Ovid poked fun at women's attempts to remain youthful in his satirical, rhyming work *Ars Amatoria* (*The Art of Love*):

> Beauty is fragile. As the years go by
> your looks diminish; finally they die.
> Lilies and violets don't always blow,
> the rose's thorns remain when petals go,
> and you, sunshine, will notice whiter hair,
> as wrinkles plough your body with a share.
> Enhance your beauty: feed your soul. It stays—
> only the soul survives the funeral blaze.[3]

A recurring reason why moralizers and pundits wouldn't condone the pursuit of beauty is because it emphasized traits that most obviously stymy human cooperation – jealously, narcissism, vanity. Fundamentally, people's efforts to stay youthful were also foolhardy because human mortality is immutable. Philosopher Giacomo Leopardi contributed to this literature in the nineteenth century with a satire that imagined a conversation between the daughters of Caducity, Fashion and Death. Fashion, the younger sibling, seeks desperately the approval of her big sister:

> I have already told you about some of my doings that are of great assistance to you. But they are trifles in comparison with what I am going to tell you now.. . . . I have caused the neglect and the elimination of the exertion and those exercises which favour physical well-being, and I have introduced innumerable others that weaken the body in a thousand ways and shorten life and have caused them to be valued highly. In addition to this, I have put in the world such orders and such customs that life itself, both of the body and of the soul, is more dead than alive, so much so that this century can truly be called the century of death.[4]

Leopardi's contribution emphasizes how perceptions of anti-ageing within the 'west' are heavily gendered and assumed, much like fashion broadly, to be pursued most ardently by women. These attitudes, which remain persistent and pernicious in the twenty-first century, crystallized during the eighteenth and nineteenth centuries because of a concatenation of factors, some possessing a direct link to a person's age, others with more diffuse connections. All contribute to an explanation of why 'western' attitudes towards human ageing have become globally preponderant.

First, the feminization of the domestic sphere. This had three main catalysts. First, industrialization created many new jobs that were more readily undertaken by men than women. Whilst women did avail themselves of the opportunities for employment that industrialization provided, there was a distinction, typically framed by wealth and perceived social standing, between the home-based tasks they undertook and the labour men did beyond the homestead.[5] Second, influenced by the writings of philosophers John Locke and Jean Jacques Rousseau, there was a reappraisal of the meaning and role of childhood during the nineteenth century. Believing that children were born innocent, there was a requirement for society, mothers particularly, to guide the development of the young.[6] Consequently, the home became an important space for childrearing in conjunction with the classroom, attendance at which became mandatory from the late nineteenth century on both sides of the Atlantic.[7] Third, and connecting both points, the development of department stores with specialized sections for children meant women and mothers became important agents in the 'west's' expanding consumer society.[8] The consequence of these changes in relation to the feminization of the domestic sphere is that they heightened awareness of the purity of the very young and the moral responsibilities of mothers, who were expected to prioritize the needs of dependents over their own. Any woman who put personal consumption before caring for children was unlikely to garner the respect of their peers.

A second change that effected attitudes to ageing was the 'west's' reconceptualization of time in both a practical and philosophical sense. Practically, the onset of industrialization from the 1860s, and the acceptance of Greenwich Meridian Time in 1884, which established a universal ordering and measurement of time around the world, emphasized the profitability of efficiency.[9] At least one corollary of these developments is that senescence became problematized and strategies to marginalize the elderly from public life were pursued. The translation into English of Jean Martin Charcot's *Clinical Lectures on the Diseases of Old Age* in 1881 (United States) and 1882 (England) was influential in associating advancing age with physical frailty and incapacity.[10] Charcot's book contains descriptive accounts of patients who suffered from ailments associated with older age, from arthritis to rheumatism. Medical insights like this, galvanized by the creation of geriatrics as a specific speciality in the nineteenth century, provided answers to incipient queries about the role of older people within the workplace. In the United States, the American Express company introduced the first private pensions in 1875.[11] Whilst they did reflect a 'genuine humanitarian concern for unwillingly retired employees', pensions 'gave managers the moral cover they needed to fire workers merely for the crime of superannuation'.[12] Running parallel to these pragmatic concerns was the philosophical reconceptualization of time.

The surety with which Europeans asserted their values and behaviours over other parts of the world was predicated on the assumption that their social structures, their civilization – another term coined in the crucible of empire – were older and consequently possessing of greater legitimacy.[13] These alternative facts were often unverified, although throughout the nineteenth century newly formed or revived antiquarian associations attempted to demonstrate the long-standing existence of 'western' cultural rites and pastimes in what historian David Cannadine has termed the invention of tradition.[14] During the nineteenth century an emphasis on national histories and the biographies of national heroes, whose greatness was often demonstrated in the maintenance of empire, evidences still further the utility of history to clarify and champion the importance of the past to the present. According to historian Kathleen Wilson, history was a 'primary vehicle of national self-understanding and identity as well as philosophical reflection, promoting a cosmopolitan perspective and a deeply grounded sense of national specificity'.[15] People and cultures beyond Europe were often considered to be deficient and lagging on some fictional chronology that charted human progress because their social structures were younger and lacking a credible history. In a similar vein, black people were likened to apes, an early proto-human, in an attempt to explain their perceived lack of rectitude. The instability of such a comparison, in addition to its invidiousness, is apparent from the fact that elderly people within the 'west' could also be likened to monkeys by scientists, who appeared to subscribe to Shakespeare's view that old age was a second childhood.[16]

What results from these shifts is, to say the least, confusing. During the nineteenth century, age could confer authority on cultures, institutions, and the nations to which they pertained, but it was decried when associated with humans because contemporary industrial and technological developments favoured attributes more readily linked to youth. Associated with children, innocent representatives of a society's future, women were expected to hone their maternal skills rather than invest time in the selfish preservation of their appearance. Men, linked to industry and empire, could negotiate the passage of time more freely, although the pursuit of productivity and profit meant such privilege was not infinite. During the mid-twentieth century, when the concept of the "golden years" was invented by real estate developer Del Webb, the founder of Sun City retirement community in Arizona, it became easier to associate all elderly people with the 'old and needy' or 'old and greedy' stereotype that Joseph Coughlin, director of the Massachusetts Institute of Technology AgeLab, claims has become a global commonplace through the establishment of 'western' capitalism and the concept of retirement.[17] The corollary is that many people around the world, including Costa Rica, Israel, Japan and South Korea, see the elderly as warm but incompetent.[18] The fuzziness of thought about age, which can inhibit effective critique, likely accounts for the persistence of contrary and ambivalent attitudes about human mortality. Whilst a nuanced – perhaps more sympathetic – picture about the relative power and powerlessness of ageing people is gradually emerging, the Covid-19 pandemic emphasized the persistence of stereotypes and the divides they entrench.[19] Public debates about the efficacy of prioritizing the elderly for vaccinations and prolonging their time in social isolation frequently pitted the young against the old.[20]

If Europe's empires acted as catalyst more than cause in the global proliferation of 'western' attitudes towards ageing, post-colonial discourses have a more explicit role in reappraising their place within contemporary academic discussions. Ethnologist Harm-Peer Zimmermann suggests the essentialism that frames the 'western' gaze and excludes subaltern voices through othering and alienation is akin to that which marginalizes older people. Informed by 'the main progenitors of Postcolonial Studies' – Jean Améry, Simone de Beauvoir, Frantz Fanon and Jean-Paul Sartre – Zimmermann posits that 'one of the lessons to be drawn . . . is that research on aging needs to be subject to its own gaze (basic distinctions, axiological premises, normative impacts and normalizing consequences) to critique.'[21] In particular, 'it is important to develop responsible structures in Ageing Studies which acknowledge the Other in his/her alterity and not, for example, to bind them to certain norms and demands using labels such as responsibility and shared responsibility.'[22] The need for nuance is important as increased life expectancies, particularly within the northern hemisphere, make people's designation as 'old' less straightforward.[23]

The three episodes in this chapter – the '*Cadeaux*' editorial in Parisian *Vogue*'s December 2010/January 2011 issue, Carmen Dell'Orefice's modelling for Guo Pei's spring/summer couture show *Legend*, 2017, and Lauren Hutton's appearance in the 'Calvin Klein, or Nothing at All' campaign of 2017 – consider the role of fashion in manifesting the 'west's' 'deterministic binarism that leads to individuals and groups – and indeed entire cultures and cultural regions (as in "the West and the rest") – being despised, excluded, regarded as an unsettling and threatening Other, and condemned to subalternity (othering, alienation).'[24]

'*Cadeaux*' editorial in Parisian *Vogue*, December 2010/January 2011

The December 2010/January 2011 issue of Parisian *Vogue* was guest-edited by American fashion designer Tom Ford and Dutch model Daphne Groeneveld. The pair appear on the magazine's cover photographed by Mert Alas and Marcus Piggott. The issue includes a *Vogue Enfant* supplement featuring the ten-year-old model Thylane Loubry Blondeau along with two unnamed pre-teen female models in an editorial titled '*Cadeaux*' ('Presents'), styled by Mélanie Huynh and photographed by Sharif Hamza. Across fifteen full bleed pages the child models appear in joint and single portraits.[25] Their clothing, dress accessories, hairstyling and cosmetics imitate that of an affluent 'western' woman preparing for an evening out. In the photographs the models wear dresses of varying degrees of formality, lipstick and eyeliner. Their necks, wrists, fingers, foreheads and ankles are variously adorned with jewellery that is set with large stones and diamonds. They wear garments from Balmain, Jimmy Choo, Valentino, Versace and jewellery from Boucheron, Cartier, David Webb and Harry Winston. Reclining against leopard-skin print cushions within wood-panelled and elaborately wallpapered interiors, we might imagine the trio to be staying in an expensive hotel. One image, in which Blondeau sits in a shiny red, vintage-style peddle car from *Au Nain Bleu*, alludes to childhood, but the trench coat, feather boa, darkened sunglasses and drop earrings that adorn her body, still more the leopard-skin throw that is wrapped behind her, emphasize the premature ageing and sexualization that characterizes Hamza's shoot.[26] The fifteen portraits are interspersed with advertisements that appear on alternating pages. These are aimed at *Vogue*'s adult female readership but feature several of the brands included within the '*Cadeaux*' editorial, including Jimmy Choo and Harry Winston.

An accompanying two-page article, authored by Frédérique Verley and Théodora Aspart, is headed with the statement and questions:

Quel maquillage à quel âge

Comment se maquiller à 13 ans? Et à 70? Sûrement pas comme à 20 ans. Les make up artists sont catégoriques et portent un regard acéré, divergem parfois, sur la question.[27]

[What makeup at what age

How to wear makeup at 13? And at 70? Certainly not like at 20. Make up artists are categorical and take a sharp, sometimes divergent, look at the issue.]

The text includes responses from five make-up artists – Tom Pecheux (Estée Lauder), Peter Philips (Chanel), Aaron de Mey (Lancôme), Karim Rahman (L'Oréal), Charlotte Tilbury (Charlotte Tilbury) – who offer reflections and recommendations about the make-up that females could, and should, wear at the ages of thirteen and seventy, respectively. Photographs of eight women, famous white celebrities, including Sophia Lauren, Jane Fonda and Lauren Hutton, accompany the article. The guidance offered by the make-up artists also assumes the teenager and octogenarian are white. Another assumption is that cosmetics are acceptable for the young and old alike. At thirteen, Tilbury asserts that a girl's make-up should not make her look like a lady. Philips insists that make-up is 'obviously not a seduction tool'. Rahman goes further, proclaiming the 'golden rule' is to avoid a total look, which he deems 'frankly vulgar' (*Règle d'or: éviter le total look yeux + bouche + joues, franchement vulgaire à cet âge*).[28] The make-up artists' views of what constitutes an attractive, even acceptable, look for pubescent children demonstrates the prevalence of Enlightenment thought, which established a child's innocence and purity. Their views nonetheless run counter to the application of cosmetics within the '*Cadeaux*' editorial, which realizes '*le total look*' and includes smoky eyes in seven of the portraits and red lipstick in two, which Pecheux suggests is 'disturbing' (*dérangeant*) for a 'little girl': '*Donc, à cet âge, on oublie l'œil charbonneux et le rouge à lèvres qu'on laisse aux grandes*'.[29]

Make-up worn by girls is apparently acceptable as a preparation for adulthood. It enables teenagers 'to learn the right gestures and to look a little prettier' (*A cet âge, on se maquillage juste pour apprendre les bons gestes et être un peu plus jolie*).[30] The recommended use of pink blush (*de blush rose*) by Pecheux, and 'a bit of brown mascara' (*un peu de mascara brun*) by Tilbury, suggests a white girl is envisioned in this scenario.[31] At seventy, the colours suggested for a woman's eyes – black, brown, soft grey, taupe – and lips – red and 'very red' – suggest the imagined client remains white. Assumptions are also made about the physicality of this older woman. Pecheux proposes that eyelash tinting is more practical because eye make-up is difficult to apply without spectacles (*On oublie le maquillage des yeux difficile sans lunettes et on opte pour la teinture de cils, plus pratique*).[32] A degree of incompetence may be assumed by de Mey's caution to prevent make-up from appearing 'over-powering': '*Il faut tojours sur-hydrater sa peau pour que le make-up rayonne sans cartonner*'.[33] The stereotypical view of older people being inept and harmless may also inform Philips' somewhat patronizing suggestion that 'extravagance' (*l'extravagance*) is permitted.[34]

'*Cadeaux*'s' portrayal of the three girls was problematized in the 'west' because it appeared to contravene socialized expectations of children's innocence. The images were variously described as 'discomforting',[35] 'oddly adult',[36] 'troubling', 'destructive psychologically'[37] and 'a little creepy'.[38] The article by Verley and Aspart condoned of children wearing make-up, but the views expressed in it by 'western' make-up artists do not fully endorse the portrayal of the girls in Hamza's shoot. Within the UK, *The Daily Mail* published a story under the heading, 'Far too much, far too young: Outrage over shocking images of the 10-YEAR-OLD model who has graced the pages of Vogue.' The article included a statement from psychologist Dr Emma Gray, who asserted that the images were 'the antithesis of what childhood in our society should be; a child being exposed to a world she is not yet equipped to deal with solely to serve the needs of the adults around her'.[39] A similar point was made in November 2022 in response to Balenciaga's 'Toy Stories' campaign for spring/summer 2023. The inclusion of child models who held handbags by the brand in the shape of teddy bears that wore bondage and BDSM gear was deemed 'disgusting'.[40] Anglophone media commentary emphasized the campaign's purported links, and apparent condonement, of child pornography.

Emotional and unequivocal, denouncements against the '*Cadeaux*' editorial were nonetheless not instantaneous. Some bloggers linked the announcement of Carine Roitfeld's resignation as editor-in-chief of Parisian *Vogue* on 17 December 2010 to negative responses from the shoot, but this is unlikely.[41] Many of the more critical comments about the images and their implications appeared in articles published between May and December 2011, at least six months after the magazine first went on sale.[42] It was only in August 2011 that Blondeau's mother closed her daughter's Facebook fan page because of increasing public scrutiny sparked by the editorial.[43] Véronika Blondeau attributed her decision to a 'bad personn in usa', writing in faltering English on the page that 'Thylane doesn't know about the buzz and i want to protect her from the deapest of my heart . . . she's so young . . . so we are going to close this accompte for a while'.[44]

The time lag between the magazine's publication and protestations about its content can be attributed to a confluence of three factors. First, the images appeared in Parisian *Vogue*, which may have slowed their transmission among an anglophone audience. The models were French – Blondeau has an English father but resides in France – image captions and the article authored by Verley and Aspart were written in French. Second, within the United States, the online magazine *BlackBook* published a story in July 2011 under the heading, 'This 10-Year-Old French Model Has a Tumblr Dedicated to Her'. The article, which appears to have been sparked by the author's curiosity to learn more about the pre-teen model, provides one of the earliest, and critical, anglophone discussions of the *Vogue* shoot.[45] In early August, *BlackBook* published a follow-up story, asserting that they had precipitated the ensuing 'media frenzy'.[46] Third, at the close of 2011 UK prime minister David Cameron announced his intention to convene a summit that would address concerns about the sexualization of children in advertising. Seeking to contextualize this initiative, anglophone commentators and journalists on both sides of the Atlantic invoked the '*Cadeaux*' shoot as one of the more egregious examples of child models' increasing vulnerability and exploitation.[47] The *Vogue* editorial had included three young models, but Blondeau became the *cause célèbre* for people arguing that political reform of the advertising industry was necessary. News stories about 'Cameron's crackdown' included biographies of Blondeau that explained how she had modelled for Jean Paul Gaultier at the age of five, as if to evidence the long-standing nature of her exploitation, which was now being more widely discussed, and the ills of the industry.[48]

Hamza's images, which came to be listed among the top five 'most controversial' published by *Vogue* in 2014, only became a site of debate when a specific interpretation of them could be supported by concurrent political events.[49] The implications of this are twofold. First, and following Ann Swidler's observations about culture, socialized views, in this case the 'west's' essentialist ideas about age, become clearer at times when they are tested. Second, the internet acts as a repository, preserving experiences that can become examples to support myriad viewpoints. The importance of the clothed body in making and maintaining human relationships means experiences related to dress are more likely to serve the needs of disputants seeking to make their arguments compelling. It should also be noted that the opinions and judgements recorded in the article by Verley and Aspart were no less objectionable towards older people than Hamza's images were towards the young. However, because of the marginalized status of older people within 'western' society, and other countries that have adopted 'western' forms of living, there was no public attempt to challenge their portrayal as warm and incompetent. The depiction of older people through fashionable dress forms the focus of the next two episodes.

Carmen Dell'Orefice modelling for Guo Pei spring/summer couture, *Legend*, 2017

On 22 January 2017 Guo Pei presented her spring/summer 2017 couture collection *Legend* at the *Conciergerie*, a former courthouse and prison where

Marie-Antoinette was incarcerated before her execution on 16 October 1793.[50] The show's nineteen looks were inspired by ecclesiastical and royal dress from the Middle Ages and Renaissance along with murals within the Stiftskirche St. Gallus und Otmar in the Swiss town of St. Gallen, which were printed on specially created fabrics.[51] The final model to walk Guo Pei's glittering horse shoe-shaped runway was 85-year-old model Carmen Dell'Orefice. Replacing the 'bride' who traditionally ends a 'western' couture show, Dell'Orefice wore a sleeved floor-length gown of red silk and lace, matching gloves and shoes. The front of her dress was embroidered with asymmetric and angular swathes of black and red metallic thread and adorned with crystals of the same colours. A red lace train with an intricate floriate design cascaded from her shoulders. Lengths of matching lace were suspended from each of her wrists. A large semi-circle of ruched red lace embroidered with metallic thread, crystals and sequins of black and red, framed Dell'Orefice's shoulders and head. This foregrounded a headpiece made from an assortment of red-stemmed pins of varying heights affixed with red crystals in gold-coloured settings. For the duration of Dell'Orefice's runway appearance, the *Conciergerie* was lit with a soft red light. The octogenarian walked to an adaptation of the first verse of Edvard Grieg's 'Solveig's Song' by Celicia. The score had originally been composed as incidental music for Henrik Ibsen's nineteenth-century play *Peer Gynt*. The effect was especially dramatic because the music commenced with the sound of a wolf pack howling. The audience responded to Dell'Orefice's appearance with a round of applause.[52] Walking to her left and right, two wavy-haired blonde male models acted as escorts. Dell'Orefice clasped their lower arms, possibly for support, as she processed along the runway. The models wore grey ballet-style tights and double-breasted, shawl-collared jackets of pale yellow. Dell'Orefice did not participate in a final runway walk with other models from the show, but she did return to the catwalk after Guo Pei had received the audience's applause and embraced the designer with affection.[53]

The execution of Guo Pei's designs were lauded in anglophone fashion reports, but the appearance of Dell'Orefice, which one blogger claimed was a 'surprise', dominated written commentaries of the couture show and the headlines they appeared beneath.[54] Journalist Erica Gonzales, writing for *Harper's Bazaar*, used quotation marks to describe Dell'Orefice as the 'World's Oldest Working Model', a curious usage of punctuation that was likely conceived to emphasize the model's maturity. The title of the article, at once deferential and bemused, included the model's age: 'Carmen Dell'Orefice, 85 Years Young, Closed a Couture Show'.[55] An edited version of Gonzales's article was published in *Harper's Bazaar* Arabia, which included a similar focus on the model's age and an identical subheading: 'Fashion Has No Age Limit'.[56] A report in *The Cut* claimed Dell'Orefice existed among 'an older cadre of models'. Author Véronique Hyland appeared to suggest the 'fashion veteran' had been especially chosen to conclude *Legend* because she was one herself.[57] French online magazine *Benude* made this connection explicit, albeit for the purpose of good copy rather than accuracy.[58] Journalist Daisy Murray, writing for *Elle* magazine, was marginally less deferential. Under the subheading, 'Here's to Closing Couture Shows When You Have a Free Bus Pass', she emphasized the model's seniority by invoking humour and 'western' stereotypes of the elderly:

> What do you see yourself doing when you're 85?
> Really getting into your rose garden upkeep, knitting lots of cute hats for your grandchildren, or closing a couture show?
> Well, that's what Carmen Dell'Orefice does on a Wednesday afternoon – she closes Chinese couture shows at Paris Fashion Week.
> We should all be so lucky.[59]

In October 2020, nearly four years after closing *Legend*, Guo Pei spoke of her admiration for Dell'Orefice, whom she claimed as her style icon; at the time of her couture show, she had described her as 'the queen of models'.[60] Dell'Orefice's age was cited as the chief reason for Guo Pei's respect: '[she] is now 89, but she has not been diminished by time, which I think makes her even more elegant'.[61] The designer's sentiment reflects Chinese traditions of reverence for people's age.[62] Prior to *Legend*, Dell'Orefice had appeared in Guo Pei's couture runway for *One Thousand and Two Nights* in November 2009. Wearing a long dress and cape that required two men and two boys to support, her outfit anticipated that which she would wear eight years later. On this earlier occasion, the model likened Guo Pei to the twentieth-century English-American couturier Charles James.[63] Dell'Orefice herself, then seventy-eight, was described as 'the legendary model'.[64]

The attitudes to ageing, specifically, and time, generally, that *Legend* conveyed and evoked emphasize the paradoxical nature of 'western' attitudes to age and its depiction within fashionable dress. First, the accolades Dell'Orefice received for her appearance in *Legend* contrast with the concerns and criticism that followed Blondeau's appearance in Parisian *Vogue*. Where Blondeau was generally considered too young to feature in a fashion shoot, Dell'Orefice was revered because of the length of her career, which began in 1947 when she was fifteen.[65] The Guo Pei couture report that appeared in *Harper's Bazaar* was keen to emphasize the magazine's support of Dell'Orefice during her career and explained how the model had been their May 1959 'cover star' when she was twenty-eight.[66] Respect for the model's longevity, her 'spirit of dedication and devotion' as Guo Pei described it, was emphasized by remarks that she was a legend and looked like a 'queen'.[67] Gonzales concluded her commentary with the hope and instruction that Dell'Orefice 'Slay queen'.[68] Murray ended her report with the prognostication that she would be 'slaying and sashaying her way into her 90s'.[69] Comparison of the public discussions about Blondeau and Dell'Orefice reveals double-standards. Whilst the latter was praised for transcending traditional gender and ageist stereotyping and presented as a 'successful ager', commentators overlooked the obvious fact that the length of her career is a consequence of it commencing when she was young, a scenario that was considered negatively in the case of Blondeau.[70] Even allowing for the fact that Blondeau began her modelling career before her teens whilst Dell'Orefice started hers in her twenties, arguments about child innocence, geriatric indolence and respect of elders were applied inconsistently.

Inconsistency with respect to time was also apparent in the staging of *Legend*. Multiple chronologies are referenced. The collection was inspired by images from the Middle Ages and Renaissance, presented in a location associated with Marie-Antoinette and accompanied by music from the nineteenth century. *Prima facie*, these rifts could be attributed to Guo Pei's ignorance of 'western' histories. The designer was born at the start of China's Cultural Revolution, which sought to remove capitalist and other 'western' influences from China. She has spoken in interviews about the absence of 'western' knowledge among her schoolteachers.[71] Convenient, this argument is not compelling, given the specific visual references *Legend*, and other of Guo Pei's collections, contain. Instead, it is possible to suggest the designer was seeking to convey a particular and empowering message about (older) women. A positive reading could go as follows: To stage *Legend* in the *Conciergerie* connected the collection to a 'western' historical narrative of tragic heroinism that regards Marie-Antoinette as 'the martyr queen'.[72] The medieval and Renaissance references catalyzed a broader theme of women heroically confronting adversity for these were periods when only strong women and some successful agers were able to wield effective political and social authority: Queen Eleanor, wife of England's Henry II; Mary Queen of Scots, and briefly queen of France; Elizabeth I; Catherine de'Medici. The theme of female endurance viewed over an expansive chronology is clarified with the choice of Grieg's 'Solveig's Song' from *Peer Gynt*. Solveig is the long-suffering supporter and would-be partner of the play's eponymous protagonist, a lazy peasant who embarks on a series of unfulfilling adventures that take him from Norway to North Africa. On returning home, Gynt is welcomed and supported by Solveig, despite her abandonment. In so doing, he finds solace and redemption. At the time of its publication in 1867, and subsequently, Ibsen's play was lauded and lambasted for blurring chronological and geographical boundaries and for combining fantasy and factual critique.[73] Consequently, it becomes an apt score for the expansive references that seem to frame *Legend*.

If this interpretation is correct, Dell'Orefice perhaps literally becomes the queen, a role fashion commentators only suggested in jest. Through her age, which Guo Pei acknowledges respect for, she becomes an embodiment of every women's adversity and the achievement they derive in confronting this. The wholly red ensemble worn by Dell'Orefice, which was itself bathed in red light, contrasts with the white *chemise* that Marie-Antoinette wore at her execution, and the white gown that brides typically wear in 'western' couture shows.[74] The colour is redolent of blood, which could reference the literal and figurative strength of women and the sacrifices they are expected to make, particularly as wives and mothers. This reading of *Legend* is weakened by the absence of any explanation from Guo Pei, the dearth of critical analysis in contemporary reports and the fact that it prioritizes a 'western' schema. Whilst my analysis is inevitably framed by my 'western' cultural outlook, and must remain tentative, the explicit use of 'western' historical motifs and location makes it plausible that Guo Pei sought to convey an empowering message about women's agency, with a specific remark about the value of and respect due to older women in accordance with Chinese traditions. If this were Guo Pei's intention, it went unrealized. The fact that no commentary of the show went so far as to interpret Dell'Orefice's involvement or the multiplicity of themes referenced within it reflects, first, a lack of deep analysis within fashion reporting and, second, the marginality of the elderly, such that people would not expect a fashion collection to impart a gerontologically informed message. Contemporary reports imply Dell'Orefice was lucky and exceptional to be modelling in her eighties. Fundamentally, because her presence was emphasized and considered separately to the collection and runway presentation, the effect of *Legend* was to reinforce 'western' essentialist binaries regarding the peripheral status of older people, women especially. The intersection between age and gender forms the focus of the chapter's final episode.

Lauren Hutton for 'Calvin Klein, or Nothing at All', 2017

In the third week of April 2017, Calvin Klein launched its spring/summer women's lingerie campaign. Cast, directed and photographed by American filmmaker Sofia Coppola 'Calvin Klein, or Nothing at All' included portraits and films starring American-based female actors whom Coppola had previously worked with or admired, including Kirsten Dunst, Maya Hawke, Lauren Hutton, Rashida Jones, Nathalie Love and Chase Sui Wonders.[75] The campaign was shot in black and white and recalled the aesthetic of Calvin Klein commercials from the early 1990s. A more immediate visual influence for Coppola was the brand's spring/summer 2017 menswear underwear campaign. Shot by Belgian photographer Willy Vanderperre, and featuring male actors from the film *Moonlight* that had opened across American cinemas in September 2016, there was an identical use of black-and-white portraiture.[76] The theme of 'coming of age' provided another link between the two campaigns. *Moonlight* is based on the semi-autobiographical play 'In Moonlight Black Boys Look Blue' by Tarell Alvin McCraney that follows the life of black orphan Chiron from childhood to early adulthood. 'Calvin Klein, or Nothing at All' features a series of short films in which Coppola's chosen actors talk blithely about 'pick-up lines, self-presentation, and first kisses'.[77]

The campaign was lauded by the anglophone fashion press because it 'celebrate[d] women of all ages'.[78] It was 'brilliantly age-diverse'.[79] *Vogue* praised '[Calvin Klein's] more pointed stance to include people of different cultures, age demographics, and ethnicities in its campaigns, providing a more inclusive look at American culture'.[80] Coppola explained that she 'wanted cool, smart women. And I was very proud that we had two Harvard graduates in our group. They have real bodies. And I think they relate to me, and to the camera, in a different way – they're not so much like goddesses; they're more approachable.'[81] This inclusive approach, along with the strong visual impact of the campaigns by Coppola and Vanderperre, was attributed to Raf Simons, who became the brand's creative director in 2016.[82] It was considered more evidence of Calvin Klein going from 'strength to strength' following his appointment.[83]

Reporting of 'Calvin Klein, or Nothing at All' in the anglophone press, which occurred four months before the release of the campaign, was not entirely balanced. Akin to coverage of Guo Pei's *Legend*, which focused on Carmen Dell'Orefice, much of the discussion centred on the age and presentation of model and actor Lauren Hutton, who, at seventy-three, was the oldest woman to feature. She was variously described as '[t]he most striking [star]',[84] the 'true star', 'inimitable'[85] and 'muse to the lingerie brand'.[86] Author commentaries make it clear that Hutton's age, which was included in the headings of several reports that covered Coppola's campaign, was the chief reason for these accolades.[87] Nor was the reporting of the campaign wholly favourable. The New Zealand–based online magazine *Stuff* criticized Calvin Klein and highlighted the inverse correlation between the media's coverage of Hutton's involvement in the campaign and the length of time she actually appears within the film: 'Much has been made of Hutton's presence as she's several decades older than your typical underwear model. However, her appearance in the ad is brief, a fleeting two-second shot.'[88]

Ostensibly, Hutton is another example of a successful ager. Twelve years previously, she had appeared undressed in a series of photographs published in *Big* magazine. Nonetheless, on being asked to model, she expressed shock.[89] She agreed to participate after speaking with her godchildren and determining – apparently after some persuasion from the magazine, who told her, '[t]his is going to be inspirational' – that 'I don't care. Th[is is] really important that women understand not to listen to a 2,000-year-old patriarchal society'.[90] Explaining that 'my generation of "60"s women are not going to stop wanting to be attractive', there is some sense that as a Third Ager – someone between their mid-fifties and early seventies – Hutton subscribes to the view adumbrated by writer Jenni Diski and summarized by fashion scholars Paul Jobling, Philippa Nesbitt and Angelene Wong, that 'membership of the post-war . . . youth culture . . . seemed to confer one with the status of eternal youth'.[91] However, despite her defiant stance, Hutton's initial concerns about appearing undressed reflect the persistence of the 'west's' essentialist views about age and the unclothed body. These concerns, and constraints, are evident in other aspects of Coppola's campaign, and become more apparent when compared with Vanderperre's work.

Journalist Kate Dingwall, writing for the online magazine *Fashion Network*, opined that Vanderperre's images were 'a stark contrast from the flashy, influencer-focused #MyCalvins campaign of the last few years', but in reviving 'all the elements of a classic Calvin Klein underwear ad, from the classic black and white photographic style down to the signature logoed brief', they nonetheless enforced a hegemonic masculinity.[92] Where the male actors photographed by Vanderperre strike poses emphasizing their physicality and musculature, the women in Coppola's film are watched while they pose. Seeing them perform seems more voyeuristic, even though models in both campaigns sit and lie against chairs and a bed. This aesthetic emphasizes art critic John Berger's contention that 'men act and women appear. Men look at women. Women watch themselves being looked at'.[93] The conformity to essentialist binaries is equally apparent in the presentation of age because the youngest and oldest stars are the most clothed, ostensibly to preserve their innocence and modesty, respectively. Alex Hibbert, who was thirteen at the time of the Vanderperre shoot, features in the campaign wearing a T-shirt. The portraits of him are cropped to only include his head and torso. The rest of the cast that feature in the campaign – Ashton Sanders, Mahershala Ali and Trevante Rhodes – are adult males and wear T-shirts and, in some images, just briefs in full-body portraits. In Coppola's campaign, Hutton, the oldest women, is the most covered as she is the only star to wear a dressing gown. It is also interesting to note how the styling of Hibbert exemplifies what philosopher Susan Sontag has called the 'double standard of ageing', whereby women are expected to maintain their looks as they get older.[94] Hibbert and Thylane Blondeau were the same age when they were photographed for their respective campaigns, but Blondeau's female body was presented in an overtly sexualized way, as though enunciating make-up artist Peter Philip's point that a young girl's youthful engagement with beauty is to prepare her for adulthood.[95] By contrast, in being wholly covered and cropped, Hibbert's body was almost sexless.

The conformity to 'western' age and gender binaries frames a complaint that was made against the 'Calvin Klein, or Nothing at All' campaign seven months after its launch. A blog post on the website of the UK's Data & Marketing Association accused Calvin Klein of condoning of 'inappropriate sexual behavior'.⁹⁶ The members-only association describes itself as 'the driving force of intelligent marketing'.⁹⁷ The anonymous, colloquial article focuses on Kirsten Dunst's interview that features her talking 'sheepishly about her first kiss when a guy landed a non-consensual kiss on her mouth'.⁹⁸ The author asserts that '[t]he context [of the kiss] might be understood better, if she wasn't telling the story half naked and although she says she was upset, her nonchalant attitude about it speaks volumes and not good volumes'.⁹⁹ Citing comments from concerned social media users, one of whom described Dunst's experience as 'sexual assault', and previous occasions where they believe Calvin Klein had 'pushed the boundaries of what is acceptable', the author queries why no complaints were made to an advertising body.¹⁰⁰ The concern reflects the campaign's manifestation of the 'west's' socialized norms about both age and gender.

Reflections

People's concerns about ageing, immortalized by Ovid 2,000 centuries ago, have died hard. In large part, this is because the 'west's' binary that pits young against old is not as straightforward to grasp as it might initially appear. Two observations can be made. First, 'western' approaches to age are contradictory. Where the participation of an older person within the fashion industry appears to be treated with respect and valorized, the involvement of a younger age, pubescent, person is derided. These positions appear contrary to consumer's experiences based on the opinions of commentators. Moreover, attitudes to age are heavily influenced by the 'west's gender binary. Where a female should prepare for adulthood as a child and learn how to pre-empt ageing, a male tends to be protected from adulthood by having his childhood innocence protected. Second, the perceived topicality and meaningfulness of fashion means it can be harnessed by social and political causes. The episodes discussed highlight the adaptability of fashion to elucidate contemporary concerns. In part, the flexibility with which fashions can be reinterpreted is connected to their limited analysis within media reports. A lack of contextualization makes it easier to deploy catwalks and campaigns as examples to support myriad social and political agendas.

6
RELIGION

Faith and fashion, human dress broadly, have a knotty relationship. Both involve complicated sets of ideas and values that find their clearest expression in a tangible form. Fashions are inherently material, constant and yet ever-changing as people's ideas shift. By contrast, faiths typically eschew the physical and temporal in their pursuit of the incorporeality of eternal salvation. A resulting paradox is that many of the world's religions utilize material cultures, dress particularly, to convey teachings that admonish possession and the privileges it can create. Some of the largest, costliest and most intricate of the material forms to be created by humans are an attempt to communicate physically the numinous and symbolic in a form and scale that makes the figurative graspable and relevant.[1]

Within the 'west', the early Christian Church denounced materialism.[2] The Bible – the Books of Luke and John especially – speaks ill of possessions and a life of greed. During the Middle Ages, moralizing texts exhorted aristocrats, who were most able to sin through excessive spending, to live frugally. In thirteenth-century England, the Bishop of Lincoln Robert Grosseteste wrote a series of rules for the household of the Countess of Lincoln that stipulated sobriety and thrift as part of Christian observance.[3] In fifteenth-century Florence, Dominican friar Girolamo Savonarola presided over a would-be Christian republic for three years. Seizing on public fears of imminent social collapse, he denounced the deposed Medici family, the material preoccupation and licentious ways of many Florentines. Annual bonfires of vanities were convened on Shrove Tuesday in which people were urged to burn their material possessions, including costumes, 'ostentatious' clothing and wigs.[4] Many centuries later, the pontificate of Benedict XVI between 2005 and 2013 confirmed the challenges of reconciling divinity and dress. The Vatican issued one of its most unusual public statements in 2013 when it asserted that the pope was 'not dressed by Prada but by Christ', in response to media speculation about the provenance of his red leather footwear.[5] One of the more enduring legacies of Benedict XVI's pontificate was his perceived penchant for 'flamboyant' and 'unusual' garments, which resulted in him being named 'Accessorizer of the Year' in 2007 by men's fashion magazine *Esquire*.[6]

Difficult as it was to achieve, the repudiation of materiality became acute after the ascendancy of Protestantism within Europe during the sixteenth century. Believing that a person's salvation was achieved through faith alone, Protestants admonished the Catholic Church for its physical wealth and expressed suspicion at what they perceived to be the more mystical elements of its doctrine, chiefly the veneration of saints through icons and transubstantiation, the belief that the wine and bread literally became the blood and body of Christ during the Eucharist.[7] In the early twentieth century, sociologist Max Weber argued that a focus on individual accountability and agency to secure eternal salvation imbued Protestants with a singular outlook and work ethic. Their 'spirit of progress' was characterized by inquisitiveness, acquisitiveness, and grit.[8] In developing his argument, Weber was really providing an answer to a question of his own devising; namely, why was there a 'greater proportion of Protestants (far exceeding the percentage of Protestants in the total population) represented among owners of capital, management and the higher grades of labor in the large modern [i.e. twentieth-century] business and trade enterprises'?[9] The singular focus of his enquiry means that its conclusions have been challenged and modified.[10] Nonetheless, in appearing to define and legitimate Protestant values, Weber's ideas have proved attractive and enduring, not least because they purport to explain how the sacral can be reconciled to, and even valorize, the secular in contemporary life.

The social and political consequences of the secularization of people's faith were profound within Europe. They were equally decisive, and destructive, beyond its borders when trading posts and colonies were established by Europeans around the world. English scholars Bill Ashcroft, Gareth Griffiths and Helen Tiffin assert that a 'Eurocentric stress on the secular has been part of the exported baggage of colonization'.[11] The reason for this is succinctly explained by English and feminist scholar Laura E. Donaldson, who observes that '[w]hile many countries occupied and dominated foreign territories, only the group of nations claiming Christian identity implemented a global colonial system upon which the sun never set'.[12] The country possessing the largest number of colonies was Protestant Britain. By 1820 26 per cent of the world's population were ruled from London.[13]

In the sixteenth century, historian Carolos Eire suggests that religion was 'a language of sorts . . . a way of conceiving and of expressing, and a way of interacting with one's neighbors, near and far'.[14] This was no less true three centuries later when European missionaries worked to spread Christianity throughout their colonies. Theologian William Baldridge asserts that the establishment of Christianity in these locations rested 'on its power to monopolize definitions: who is godless, godly, and most godly, all stemming from Christianity's definition of the essential nature of God'.[15] Acceptance of this language was most readily conveyed by converts through the adoption of 'western'-style dress.[16] Historian Robert Ross quotes from British missionary John Williams, who expressed delight at seeing people from Rarotonga, the largest of the Cook Islands, 'clothed and in their right mind'.[17] As previous chapters have noted, the acceptance, certainly dominance, of Christian values within Europe's colonies was fundamental in clearing the ideological ground for the establishment of the 'western' essentialist binaries upon which imperial rule was justified and maintained. Another corollary of the 'muscular imperial Christianity' that operated during the nineteenth century is that branches of the Christian faith that were dominant within Europe came to be established across much of the world. Faiths that were less prevalent and culturally accepted within Europe, chiefly Judaism and Islam, were marginalized; a situation that persists today.

The differential impact of the Covid-19 pandemic has highlighted the complicated relationship between faith and fashion in the 'west'. As some people joined or returned to their local congregations to seek solace during a period of uncertainty, still others turned to popular culture, and fashion, for meaning.[18] Whilst very different, these behaviours show that religion remains a compelling language in our present and, continues to be a 'social glue', even if its adhesiveness has diminished over time.[19] In August 2021, British *GQ* published an article under the sacrilegious heading, 'Prayers Up: How God Became the Hottest Thing in Fashion'.[20] Author Ari Lisner explains how 'God has been on the rise in popular culture' since 2016, citing the popularity of community group-cum-brand *I NEED GOD*, the Metropolitan Museum of New York's Costume Institute exhibition 'Heavenly Bodies: Fashion and the Catholic Imagination' that opened in 2018, and the launch of Kanye West's invitation-only 'Sunday Service' series in 2019, as evidence.[21] The article is tongue-in-cheek in tone, but a serious argument is made. Lisner shows how pseudo-faith-based groups, events and brands have emerged as a form of psychological salve in correlation with the economic and social instability, political polarization and legitimation of alternative facts that have come to define the twenty-first century for many 'westerners'. Through parody, satire and provocation, Lisner suggests that 'western' Christians have begun to deconstruct their faith's doctrines and to reinscribe them with new, pointedly secular meanings to find a sense of orientation within their lives. Two implications from Lisner's article are relevant for the discussions that follow. First, there is an assumption that Christianity is the *de facto* religion of the 'west', and thus much of the world. Second, Christianity has been secularized as people's quotidian concerns, framed by capitalism, inform their understanding and engagement with faith.

The three episodes within this chapter – the 'Heavenly Bodies: Fashion and the Catholic Imagination' Costume Institute Benefit held at the Metropolitan Museum of Art, New York, on 7 May 2018; Jean Paul Gaultier's *Les Rabbins*

Chics (*Chic Rabbis*) autumn/winter collection for 1993, which was informed by Judaism; and Alexander McQueen's womenswear collection for spring/summer 2000, *Eye*, which was influenced by Islam – purposefully look at three different faiths – Catholicism, Judaism, Islam – to consider how 'western' conceptions of religious belief inform the fashion industry's portrayal and usage of the numinous and symbolic.

'Heavenly Bodies: Fashion and the Catholic Imagination' Costume Institute Benefit, Metropolitan Museum of Art, New York, 7 May 2018

Continuing a tradition that began in 1948, on the first Monday in May 2018 New York's Metropolitan Museum of Art hosted celebrities from around the world for its annual Costume Institute Benefit.[22] The fundraiser coincided with the launch of the Institute's exhibition 'Heavenly Bodies: Fashioning the Catholic Imagination'. Garments worn by guests, crafted by some of the fashion industry's leading designers, drew inspiration from the ecclesiastical theme. Organizing an exhibition that aligned fashion and faith was contentious. As if to allay people's concerns Andrew Bolton, the Institute's lead curator, emphasized the long-standing connection between divinity and dress in press interviews. In an essay published in the show's accompanying catalogue he argued:

> Dress . . . is central to any discussion about religion: it affirms religious allegiances and, by extension, asserts religious differences. Throughout the history of the Roman Catholic Church, dress has functioned to distinguish hierarchies (and to express the related concepts of power and authority) as well as gender (and to express the related concepts of virtue and modesty). And whilst some might regard fashion as a frivolous pursuit far removed from the sanctity of religion, most of the vestments worn by the secular clergy and religious orders of the Catholic Church have their origins in secular dress.[23]

The adaptation of Catholic imagery to create couture costumes for an exclusive party with a $30,000 ticket price had the potential to be avowedly problematic. Curiously, this was not the case. Costumes worn at the Benefit became fodder for journalistic judgement, but remarks were characterized by their vacillation between concern and comedy. Reporting was generally ambivalent about the appropriateness of guests' garments. Within the UK, *The Daily Telegraph* reviewed the celebrity costumes under the derisory heading, 'Oh Good Lord, Did They Really Wear That?'[24] The cover of *Times 2*, a segment within *The*

Times newspaper, carried the headline, 'Hail Mary! Saints, Sinners and Heavenly Bodies at the Met Gala'. The paper's lead story by journalist Hilary Rose had a similarly tongue-in-cheek title: 'Lord! What Happened at the Met Ball, Fashion's High Altar'.[25] Only journalist Piers Morgan, writing for *The Daily Mail*, was explicit in his criticism of the Benefit, describing it as 'brazenly disrespectful' towards his Catholic faith.[26] The dresses of actor Sarah Jessica Parker and singer Rihanna feature prominently in commentary about the event, and descriptions of them convey the mixed feelings it stirred.

Sarah Jessica Parker wore a floor-length belted gown and train from Dolce and Gabbana's *Alta Moda* 2018 collection. The garment was embroidered with a repeat floriate design in gold brocade that resembled acanthus leaves. Three bands of red sequins decorated the skirt of the dress. The size of the hearts increased incrementally with those decorating the hem approximately double the size of those at the thigh. Red hearts were also added to the train and the sleeves of the dress above an appliqué depiction of a genuflecting female saint, executed in multi-coloured sequins, who may have been a representation of the Virgin Mary. A singular red heart appeared centrally on the bodice, another was positioned at the apex of the costume's headpiece, which featured a miniature three-dimensional Nativity scene. Resembling a bejewelled icon, Parker's headwear was decorated with costume stones in elaborately wrought gold-coloured casings, pearls and white faux-enamel flowers. She carried a Dolce and Gabbana *Alta Moda* handbag and wore jewellery by Fred Leighton and Jennifer Fisher.[27] Rose quipped that Parker 'got over-excited and put a pergola on her head'.[28] Morgan was excoriating. He described Parker as 'comfortably the worst offender' at the Benefit because of her decision to wear 'an entire Nativity Play scene on her head'.[29]

Rihanna wore a white and silver mini dress, ankle-length coat and headpiece by John Galliano for Maison Margiela. The entire ensemble was embroidered with intricate floriate patterns and embellished with faux pearls and costume stones of deep red. Strikingly contemporary and feminine, the outfit was clearly inspired by Catholic vestments. The headdress recalled an episcopal mitre. The coat, with its wide, drooping collar was a loose interpretation of ecclesiastical robes that appear in manuscript illustrations and paintings. Rihanna wore two necklaces; the pendant of one appeared to be in the shape of a dove and resembled artistic depictions of the Holy Spirit. Rose claimed the singer 'came as the Pope'.[30] A student writing for a University of Oxford blog described the outfit as 'immodest and clearly a political statement about women's ordination rather than a celebration of Catholic art'.[31]

As with Sarah Jessica Parker's costume, critical comments about Rihanna's dress were tempered by others of a more comedic and jovial nature. The inclination of onlookers and participants to speak with levity about guests' interpretation of the ecclesiastical theme is reflected most clearly in remarks by the cardinal archbishop of New York, Timothy Michael Dolan, who attended the Benefit in his cassock. Speaking on *SiriusXM*'s The Catholic Channel the day after the event, which he described as 'glitterartissima', he joked that he was the 'only one that didn't have to go out and buy something, because [he wore his] Sunday duds'.[32] He quipped that Rihanna had borrowed his mitre, returning it to him that morning.[33] Seemingly enjoying the raillery provoked by his attendance, Dolan explained that he had, in jest, rebuked his auxiliaries for their complaints about the singer's appearance because 'she's volunteered to do some confirmations'.[34] Ambivalence about the exhibition's theme and its playful interpretation by Benefit attendees is of more than passing interest. It emphasizes the 'western'-centric nature of the exhibition and Benefit, specifically, and highlights the pervasiveness of Catholicism within the fashion industry, broadly.

Dolan's interview clarified that the Costume Institute had conceived of an 'interfaith' exhibition before deciding to focus on Catholicism:

> That's right, it was, it was supposed to, initially, be ecumenical and inter religious, and then they found, oh, there's so much in Catholicism, maybe we'll postpone the others to another year, which they well could; our Jewish brothers and sisters are high in imagination too; we borrowed a lot of it from them. So it's not just ourselves.[35]

Through his cursory reference to Judaism, Dolan acknowledges that at least another of the world's religions has similarities to Catholicism, but his commentary on 'Heavenly Bodies' is framed by a narrative that situates the Catholic Church as the first among faiths that might, perhaps, be considered equal. Explaining why he supported the exhibition and its launch event, Dolan asserted:

> It's because the church and the Catholic imagination are all about three things: truth, goodness, and beauty. That's why we have great schools and universities, to each the truth. That's why we love to serve the poor and to do good. And that's why we're into things such as art, poetry, music, liturgy, and, yes, even fashion, to thank God for the gift of beauty.[36]

Nothing in this statement is unique to Catholicism, but the impression created suggests otherwise. Dolan assumes Catholicism has an omnipresence that other faiths lack. This is an outlook that Bolton and the Costume Institute appear to have shared and which influenced the decision to eschew an interfaith exhibition. In an interview with American *Vogue* journalist Osman Ahmed, Bolton observed that:

> [a] lot of Catholic imagery has been so absorbed in Western culture that it is as much a cultural symbol as it is a religious symbol.. . . The cross and rosary

beads are located within the Catholic faith, but they are also located within a Western cultural tradition at the same time.³⁷

Consequently, in Ahmed's phrase, 'when it comes to the Catholic church, it's seen as fair game'. The implication is that people's assumed familiarity with Catholicism, whether believers or not, persuaded organizers that a Catholic-focused exhibition would be culturally and political neutral, safe. By contrast, Ahmed suggests 'there would be uproar and one could be vilified for insincere cultural misappropriation' if the imagery and ideas of another religion were utilized in a similar way.³⁸

The normalization of Catholicism to which Bolton and Ahmed allude contextualizes the vacillating commentary about the guests' costumes, which invoked ideas and images that are culturally prevalent, to the extent that they might be considered a cultural white noise, on the one hand, and deeply admired and possessing of an emotional charge on the other hand. The *Vogue* interview also emphasizes how the diffusion of Catholic imagery has become a characteristic of 'western' culture. The point is amplified by Dolan's discussion of the Benefit. His jovial recollection conveys how Catholic sentiments and motifs have become deeply imbricated within contemporary 'western' society. He did not see anything 'sacrilegious' and 'didn't detect anybody out to offend the church',³⁹ but his jokes about Rihanna, the small food portions being served – 'I had to tip one of the waiters to go out and give me a couple hotdogs'⁴⁰ – the lip-stick stains on his cassock – 'All the women were sort of crowding around me, I really didn't get much of a chance to see men'⁴¹ – and his trivializing of the fashion industry through the implication that he was previously unaware of the annual Benefit and Anna Wintour's role as *Vogue* editor suggests he was not likely to have done:

> I didn't know about it, to be honest with you, apparently it is the social event of the year; the Metropolitan Museum of Art, which is a magnificent museum right here in New York, every, is it the first Monday of every May? And it's sponsored by Anna Wintour. Got me! She edits *Vogue* magazine, and it's to benefit her fashion design at the Museum.⁴²

Dolan's participation in the Benefit and his reflections upon it are framed by socialized values and patterns of behaviour that might be considered characteristic of 'western' cis-gendered heterosexual white men; namely, where simple fare is favoured over fancy, where men are attracted to women and trivialize fashion as feminized, peripheral and unworthy of prolonged consideration. It was presumably in response to this stance that one listener to Dolan's interview with The Catholic Channel wrote the following comment:

> Cardinal Dolan is the kind of Ledership [*sic*.] in the Catholic Church that is leading the faithful on the wrong path, away from the teachings of the church.⁴³

The extent to which Catholicism is imbricated in 'western' culture is readily apparent from the minimal criticism of the Benefit's costumes that appropriated it. For journalist Daniella Greenbaum the passive acceptance of guests' attire reflected an 'unfairness' in ('western') people's understanding and application of the concept of cultural appropriation. She argued that tolerance for Rihanna's costume, which 'could easily be seen as offensive by religious Catholics', meant believers were 'left . . . out to dry' because few people were prepared to argue that their faith had been misappropriated.[44] Her opinion was shared on Twitter. By contrast, Native American academic Adrienne Keeve, opined, 'I can't handle the Met Gala Catholicism appropriation hottakes this morning. It's so clear white folks weren't listening the 100 million times BIPOC [Black, Indigenous, People of Colour] explained that appropriation is about POWER.'[45] Another Twitter user commented, 'Laughing @ all the white ppl calling Met Gala theme "cultural appropriation." To appropriate, a dominant culture takes from a marginalized culture. Not happening here. In fact, Catholics FORCED their religion on Black/brown ppl all over the world – it's called colonialism.'[46]

Greenbaum's analysis is perceptive, but the point is less that people misunderstood cultural appropriation, or cultural misappropriation, for as she observes 'the concept of cultural appropriation as a whole is deeply misguided because it ignores the reality that ultimately, every culture, tradition, or religion borrows slightly from those that surround it'.[47] The point is surely more that the 'western' attendees and the designers who clothed them did not think it possible to misappropriate Catholicism because its symbols and imagery were so diffuse, and, as the above tweet asserts, dominant. Implicit within this outlook is the assumption that Catholicism has a clear, established and thus uncontested global position. Unlike other religions, Catholicism is not oppressed.[48] With its singular focus, 'Heavenly Bodies' augmented this status and, simultaneously, hinted at the precarity of other faiths, which are the focus of the remainder of the chapter.

Jean Paul Gaultier, *Les Rabbins Chics* (Chic Rabbis), autumn/winter 1993

Before Jean Paul Gaultier presented *Les Rabbins Chics* in March 1993, the forty-year-old designer had a reputation for his avant-garde designs and catwalk shows that challenged 'western' conventions by highlighting communities routinely marginalized within the fashion industry. Contemporary eulogies of Gaultier make much of his early status as a disrupter, an *enfant terrible*, and recount stories of his disregard for convention. In one story, he placed a modelling call in the French daily newspaper *Libération* that stipulated the 'conventionally pretty need not apply'.[49] Whilst it might have been expected that *Chic Rabbis*, as the collection became widely known, would provoke, the garments and catwalk were problematized because this was the first occasion that Judaic motifs were incorporated into the work of a known, if still relatively junior, 'western' fashion designer.[50] The collection was inspired by men's traditional Hasidic clothing and included tailored outerwear, trench coats and textured knitwear. Some of the garments and accessories were directly influenced by Hasidic dress. Large fur hats resembled *shtreimel*, which are worn on the Sabbath. Skull caps with bands of embroidered decoration recalled *yarmulkes*, which Jewish men wear in public. Leather and fur-covered pouches suspended from the neck by metallic chains were like *tefillin*, small boxes containing verses from the Torah that are worn on the head or around the arms, typically by men. Models' hair styling was patently influenced by the Hasidic tradition of *payots*, curled sidelocks that frame the face. The catwalk presentation was particularly overt in its appropriation of Jewish culture or, perhaps more accurately, its appropriation of 'western' depictions of Jewish culture. Referring to the show as a 'campy sendup', *The New York Times* journalist Amy Spinder described how 'menorahs lined the runway; Maneschewitz wine was served; the invitations were lettered in Hebraic script (Hebraic-looking clothing labels, it was decided, were uncommercial and, so, removed)'.[51] At the start of the show, a solo violinist led models onto the catwalk, playing the theme from Jerry Bock's musical 'Fiddler on the Roof'.[52] At its end, Spinder observed that 'Mr. Gaultier himself came out wearing a blue-and-white-striped [*yarmulke*], to match his signature Breton fisherman's shirt'.[53]

In drawing sartorial inspiration from the Jewish community, Gaultier explained that he 'wanted to celebrate religious diversity, to pay homage to religion without focusing on any one in particular'.[54] He attributed the genesis of his collection to an experience in New York: 'I saw a group of rabbis leaving the New York Public Library on Fifth Avenue. I found them very beautiful, very elegant, with their hats and their huge coats flapping in the wind. It was a fantastic scene.'[55] In a television interview after the *Chic Rabbis* show, Gaultier spoke of his intention to use the collection to challenge racism and antisemitism, although he did not elucidate how his designs and their catwalk presentation facilitated this:

> Why? Because I think it's coming a lot of, like, racism and antisemitism again; you know, coming in all Europe, and also in all the world, so, so, so I wanted. I think it was the right moment to show that and to take [a] position.[56]

Gaultier may have wanted to show respect to the Hasidic Jewish community, but responses to the collection were mixed. Model Christy Turlington, who participated in the catwalk show, claimed there was booing at the end.[57] *Artforum* editor Ingrid Sischy, who was in the audience, disagreed:

I didn't hear any booing at the end, but I certainly heard afterwards, 'Now he's done a thing about Hasidic Jews and people are gonna, you know; Jews are gonna be upset and people are gonna say, you know, this is a sacred thing'. I completely, completely disagree. I think what was so fantastic about it, and what is so fantastic about Gaultier, is that he incorporates politics and culture into his fashion. I think to take something that none of us understand necessarily and mix it up; and incorporate it into the culture and show all sorts of different people wearing it is a way of removing strife. And I think that was really great.[58]

Critical reactions to *Chic Rabbis* were reported, and amplified, within the anglophone press. The controversy sparked by the collection focused on two areas. First, and specifically, the adaptation of men's clothing into womenswear and second, and broadly, the apparent trivialization of Judaism and the Holocaust. Within the Jewish community, Rabbi Morris Shmidman, executive director of the Council of Jewish Organizations of Borough Park, New York, considered the collection to be 'very offensive'. He explained that it was 'extremely inappropriate in this community . . . [t]o take men's mode of clothing and make that into a modish thing for women'.[59] Editor Bernadine Morris was forthright in her denunciation of *Chic Rabbis*, stating, 'I was offended. I was strongly offended. I don't think it's time for jokes about the Holocaust'.[60] In August 1993, images of the collection, photographed by Ellen von Unwerth, were published in Paris *Vogue*. In response to the editorial, five members of the French branch of Ford Models spoke of being 'painfully embarrassed that two of our models were involved in such out-and-out mockery'. The quintet described von Unwerth's 'portrayal of models in Hasidic dress in their community [a]s blatantly racist and anti-Semitic'.[61] The co-president of Ford Models demurred, asserting that she felt the 'pictures were beautiful'.[62] Similarly, fashion journalist Richard Buckley offered support for Gaultier, suggesting, 'I don't think he meant to offend anyone'. He explained, 'You know, it was [Gaultier's] way of styling a show, which is making it a little bit; taking very tailored clothes and making them look; giving them an edge.'[63]

Whilst *Chic Rabbis* elicited diverse reactions, the underpinning assumption of critics and champions from beyond the Jewish community was that Judaism is a marginal faith within the 'west'. In defending his work, Gaultier acknowledged that he was 'afraid' it would be 'poorly received' and considered 'ridiculous', but despite recognizing that 'some' [people] might be offended', he did not explicitly mention the Hasidic community. He did, however, dwell on Anna Wintour's approval of his designs, the fact that 'top models' were photographed wearing them, and his belief that 'many considered [*Chic Rabbis*] one of my best collections, for the cuts, fabric, and the idea'.[64] In a similar vein, whilst Sischy applauded Gaultier's work for 'removing strife' through his sartorial bricolage, she averred that Judaism remained 'something that none of us understand necessarily'; the 'us' either being 'western' people generally or members of the fashion industry specifically. Even Morris, who repudiated *Chic Rabbis*, seems to misunderstand the offence she felt had been committed. In explaining her position, she argued:

> I have thought about it, and I know we use other ethnic groups, but other ethnic groups did not die – five million of them – in Europe. I spoke to one important fashion editor in New York, and asked her about it before I wrote this thing, and she said 'It's OK because it's in Europe'. Well, it's not OK because it's in Europe; possibly if it happened in the north of Canada, it might be appropriate. It is not appropriate in Europe. I feel this very strongly.[65]

Deconstructed, Morris's argument appears to suggest that the appropriation – 'use' – of minority cultures by the 'western' fashion industry is routine, even if it is not wholly acceptable. She considers the adaptation of motifs from Jewish culture to be less tolerable because of the Holocaust, but this is geographically contingent. Appropriation of Jewish culture that occurs beyond Europe constitutes a lesser offence, although the reason for this is unclear. Fundamentally, her explanation overlooks genocides perpetrated against other minority groups and the fact that Jews from beyond Europe were also casualties of the Holocaust, chiefly those who lived in France's African colonies.[66] Morris's preoccupation with place over people emphasizes a 'western', certainly Eurocentric, outlook and a limited awareness of the global extent of the Jewish faith.

Ayanna Thompson has written of white innocence to describe how white people justify wearing blackface.[67] Adapting her argument, it could be suggested that a 'secular innocence' is evident in responses to *Chic Rabbis* from beyond the Jewish community. Similar to the blithe acceptance of white dominance and sensibilities in respect to race, responses to Gaultier's collection presume the ascendancy of 'western' secularism, in which a person's faith is cultivated privately and curtailed publicly. Consequently, the experiences and feelings of Jewish people are overlooked or marginalized. This outlook is most evident in Buckley's redemptory remarks that Gaultier did not mean to offend. In the case of fashion critic Suzy Menkes's verdict of *Chic Rabbis*, a secular innocence frames a repudiation of Judaism, specifically, and a denigration of religion, generally. She asserts that the rabbis who inspired the collection are 'like other religious zealots . . . a counterpoint in the freedom of expression – particularly sexual – that Gaultier champions'.[68]

Menkes's sentiment, which prioritizes the intentions of an individual designer over divergent social groups and asserts fashion's role in promoting 'western' values, is not uncommon within the fashion industry. Nor is it uncommon in 'western' fashion journalism. As fashion scholar Katie Baker Jones asserts, the genre 'often singles out and celebrates the *sui generis* individuals commenting on the industry's outputs and practices'.[69] This attitude is apparent within Hedi Slimane's *Le Figaro* interview that was published prior to his debut collection for Celine in 2018.[70] It is apparent from John Galliano's dismissive response to criticisms of his *Les Clochards* collection in 2000.[71] To conceive of fashion, broadly, the fashion designer, specifically, as a cultural conduit, is to perpetuate a 'western' notion that accords respect and gives latitude to artists from various genres who pursue art for art's sake and in so doing exist singularly as a 'romantic genius' or clarifier of the zeitgeist.[72] When explaining the rationale for hosting an exhibition of Jean Paul Gaultier's clothing designs within the Montreal Museum of Fine Arts in 2011, Chief Curator Nathalie Bondil wrote of the 'world of Jean Paul Gaultier' that 'provides an open-minded view of society, a realm of extravagance, sensitivity, humor and impertinence, where all can affirm themselves as they are'.[73] In the specific case of *Chic Rabbis*, the process of affirmation was not unanimously positive and resulted in people defining themselves through opposition to Gaultier's works. In large part, criticism of his designs stemmed from a rejection of his personal practice, which Bondil lauds. She suggests that he 'systematically questions stereotypes, standards, codes, conventions and traditions, which he reroutes, shifts, inverts and destroys, the better to reinvent them'.[74] Referring obliquely to *Chic Rabbis*, she avers that 'his leitmotiv is the need for all families, tribes, coteries and minorities to open themselves to others in order to revitalise themselves'.[75] Convinced of the necessity of his own work, which is validated by members of the 'western' fashion industry, including curators, journalists photographers and models, Gaultier 'blithely forges' ahead; a description redolent of eighteenth- and nineteenth-century European colonialists. Blondil's argument is underpinned by an uncritical acceptance of the virtue of 'western' values that leaves no possibility for the harm that unwanted rerouting, shifting, inverting, destroying and reinventing can cause. Insistence on the rightness of Gaultier's approach also obscures reflection on whether fashion is an appropriate medium to convey such views.

The point is especially pressing considering the antisemitic slurs and threats made by American rapper Kanye West in October 2022. In a public tirade that followed the reporting of several racist remarks by West, the singer-cum-fashion designer asserted, 'I can say anti-Semitic things, and Adidas can't drop me.'[76] His belief, erroneous as it proved, is a disconcerting example of how the fashion industry's tendency to vaunt certain designers as *sui generis* diminishes accountability and, far worse, provides a platform for the conveyance of some of the 'west's' most intolerant perspectives. Adidas did sever its commercial ties with West, but anglophone media criticized the brand for its lack of transparency in responding to public concerns.[77]

Alexander McQueen, *Eye*, womenswear, spring/summer 2000

On 17 September 1999, Lee Alexander McQueen presented his fifteenth collection, *Eye*, at Pier 94 during New York Fashion Week. The twenty-nine-minute show, his first in the United States, was divided into two sections and included seventy-eight looks. The collection used a limited palette of black, blue, red, silver, white and included Islamic motifs and 'westernized' interpretations of the Middle East. During the first part of the show, which included sixty-eight garments, female models walked a black, dimly lit and water-covered runway. Moving swiftly, their feet, sometimes hemlines, agitated the water, creating ripples and shimmering reflections. McQueen's ninth catwalk show *Bellmer La Poupée*, shown on 27 September 1996, had also included a water-covered catwalk.[78] Commentators speculated that this well-received design was revived to impress an American audience. The blackened water used for *Eye*, which apparently symbolized 'Middle Eastern oil', suggests the designer had a more subversive motivation.[79] References to Islam were apparent throughout the collection in the repeat use of the crescent moon and star and draped body coverings that resembled the burka and niqab. Heeled shoes with pointed vamps, voluminous bell-shaped sleeves, gilt embroidery on thigh-length jackets, and dark, elongated eye make-up, adapted motifs the 'west' has long used to portray the exoticism of 'the east' in art, media and film. Two pailleted garments made by jewellery designer Shaun Leane, which fitted around the wearer's head and torso, resembled armour. They conjured associations of the Crusades, when Christians and Muslims fought for control of Jerusalem and its adjacent territories between the eleventh and thirteenth centuries.[80] Some of the more striking garments within the collection were those that concealed models' heads and faces and exposed their arms, legs and torsos. One model was bare-breasted. When standing at the end of the runway, she cupped her breasts within her hands in a sexualized gesture that emphasized her undress.[81] Several looks were made from translucent fabric that showed the models' breasts.[82] Still others included the crescent moon and five-pointed star, which symbolizes the five pillars of the Islamic faith, in logos that seemed to draw inspiration from American sportswear and the Ivy League look of the 1950s. This incongruous bricolage of Islamic and American motifs was apparent in garments that simultaneously resembled burkas, because of their silhouette and cut, and referenced the American flag, because they were made from fabrics woven with vertical stripes.

The second part of the show was more unconventional in its staging. After a pause of approximately sixteen seconds, when the entire catwalk was plunged into darkness, pairs of models wearing burka-inspired garments, 'some striped red, others colored black', appeared.[83] Suspended in the air by concealed harnesses, the models seemed to float, wraith-like, towards the front of the runway. Their bodies convulsed, sometimes violently, as they moved. These agitated acrobatics were performed above rows of spikes that had risen through the blackened water of the catwalk during the interval. To conclude the show, after the models had completed a final walk of the runway's perimeter, McQueen took his bow of thanks. As soon as he had done so, he lowered his trousers to reveal that he was wearing a pair of boxer shorts printed with the Star-Spangled Banner, the flag of United States.

Eye caused consternation for two reasons. First, the show probed the freighted relationship between the United States and the Middle East through its provocative appropriation and reinterpretation of Islamic motifs. Commentators were nonetheless uncertain about the extent to which McQueen had used these symbols to convey a specific message. Russian journalist Ekaterina Lysenko considered *Eye* to be 'like a commentary or reaction to what is happening in the world'. Its 'main theme [was] the growing tension between the Eastern and Western worlds'.[84] Asserting that McQueen 'was deliberate with [the] statements' he made with his collections, author Ana Finel Honigman has argued that *Eye* 'juxtaposed fraught references from Islamic and Christian traditions as a critical commentary on America's foreign policy following Al-Qaeda's bombing of US embassies in Nairobi and Dar es Salaam'.[85] By contrast Kate Bethune, a curator for the Victoria and Albert Museum, London, locates the inspiration for *Eye* in Turkish music that McQueen had heard whilst riding in a taxi.[86] The suggestion that the collection had a mundane origin is attributed to McQueen, although it is an outlier. Bethune's opinion is not necessarily the weaker for this. Her remark appears in a book edited by Claire Wilcox, who was chief curator for McQueen's posthumous exhibition 'Savage Beauty' which was staged at Victoria and Albert Museum after first showing at the Metropolitan Museum of Art's Costume Institute. It is repeated by Dana Thomas in her biography of McQueen.[87] The provenance of Bethune's statement is therefore compelling. The challenge of reconciling divergent views about the collection's genesis highlights a general difficulty of locating fashion commentaries before the creation of contemporary social media platforms and their routine publication online. It should also be acknowledged that political readings of *Eye* have increased over time: Honigman's account, which is the most explicit about McQueen's subversive intentions, was published in 2021. This is most likely a reflection of the worsening relationship between the 'west' and the Middle East following the attacks against New York's World Trade Centre in 2001, the subsequent 'War on Terror' and the banning of Muslim face and head coverings in multiple European countries. Fundamentally, shifting interpretations of *Eye* provide a reminder that the meanings of human dress are mutable. They are as contingent as the cultures they are conceived, created and consumed within.[88]

Another reason the catwalk show caused consternation in 1999 is because it occurred during Hurricane Floyd. An extratropical storm that killed eighty-six people within the United States, the hurricane was ranked as the third costliest at the time for the physical damage it caused.[89] Whilst some designers postponed their shows, for pragmatic as much as philosophical reasons – pavilions hosting Fashion Week events had been flooded and a festal occasion during a declared state of emergency is ethically dubious – one commentator surmised that McQueen enjoyed the 'added spectacle'.[90] In an interview the designer quipped, 'The wind and rain will not stop us.'[91] Reflecting on the show's reception, journalist Mimi Spencer, writing for London's *The Evening Standard*, observed that 'Alexander McQueen shook New York more than Hurricane Floyd'.[92] Spencer's flippancy is echoed in a cursory review of *Eye* that appeared online for *Vogue* magazine. The anonymous author suggests McQueen showed 'cheeky insouciance' for 'dropping trou'.[93] They refer to the aerial models as 'good and bad angels', with those wearing red stripes possessing positive attributes and those in black possessing negative attributes.[94] The inference is oblivious to the possibility that the contrasting dress intentionally represented the United States and Middle East, or to the fact that the concept of fallen or errant angels is less prevalent in Islam than Christianity.[95]

The absence of criticality is a recurrent theme within anglophone fashion commentary about culturally sensitive topics. In the case of McQueen's collection, the superficiality of analysis suggests most commentators did not consider the title relevant to its comprehension or an inducement to see the designs as presenting a different perspective about Islam and 'western' understandings towards the faith. This is despite acknowledgement among many of the commentators that McQueen's work was laden with meaning and meticulously researched. The limited evaluation of the designer's work, which can be considered a lack of accountability, elides with a 'western' view that sees artists as being beyond reproach because they are pursuing a singular creative vision. Nonetheless, whilst McQueen's practice could be likened to that of Gaultier, who largely imposed his aesthetic vision on Hasidic Jewish culture, it does seem that he was seeking to make a critical comment on the 'west's' relationship with Islam.

Art historian Alma Hernández Briseño has used Michel Foucault's concept of the heterotopia to elucidate McQueen's intentions within his ninth catwalk show *Bellmer La Poupée*. Considering that McQueen adapted a central element of this show – the use of a water-covered runway – for *Eye*, there is reason to extend the use of Foucault's work to analyze the designer's practice in this later show. Within *La Poupée* Briseño suggests that 'McQueen presented the tension that exists between reality and fiction from the idea that these two concepts are not opposed and that if there's a line that divides them it's blurry and can be erased through fashion'.[96] Consequently, she argues that the runway operates in a similar way to Foucault's mirror: 'it functions as an unreal space constructed by the designer in the reality in which fashion narratives are inserted.'[97] In *La Poupée* and *Eye* the runways literally became mirrors because of the water covering them. Foucault referred to the mirror as 'a sort of mixed, joint experience' that connects utopias and heterotopias.[98] The mirror is a utopia because it presents a 'placeless place' where people can see themselves existing in a wholly unreal space. It is simultaneously a heterotopia because it is real and because it enables people to interrogate themselves along with the actual and virtual spaces they inhabit. The creation of an unreal space existing within a real one was amplified by McQueen's anamorphic designs. Briseño defines anamorphosis as 'an illusion, a new way of seeing a deformation, a visual unreality. [It] transcends the bi-dimensional space; we can see it in textiles, patterns, textures, materials, and objects, all which McQueen used to dress and distort the body'.[99]

Briseño's application of Foucault's thought results in a largely positive analysis. Through the creation of a heterotopia, the intentions and impact of McQueen's designs are clarified and the tensions between reality and fiction are effaced. In the case of *Eye*, however, interpretations remain mixed two decades after its debut. This lingering uncertainty is less to do with differences between *La Poupée* and *Eye* as collections and catwalk shows, although these exist, but more to do with Briseño's partial application of Foucault's concept. Her evaluation dwells on the form of a heterotopia and does not fully consider Foucault's explanation of a heterotopia's function, which is to critique established knowledge. Primarily, they show how socially conceived structures can be challenged and reconceived.[100] Foucault argues that heterotopias:

> secretly undermine language, because they make it impossible to name this *and* that, because they shatter or tangle common names, because they destroy 'syntax' in advance, and not only the syntax with which we construct sentences but also that less apparent syntax which causes words and things (next to and also opposite one another) to 'hold together' . . . [T]hey dissolve our myths and sterilize the lyricism of our sentences.[101]

This qualification means the manifestation of a heterotopia within fashion is perhaps closer to that proposed by English scholar Julia Emberley. She uses the concept of the heterotopia to analyze a photograph of designs by John Galliano from the March 1985 issue of *Harper's and Queen* magazine. Studying the presentation of Galliano's work through a single image and its accompanying caption, Emberley argues that fashion functions like a heterotopia because it is 'a multiple and diverse field of discontinuous and incongruous spectacles lacking in syntactical continuity'.[102] In a similar way, McQueen created 'discontinuous and incongruous spectacles' through *Eye* by sexualizing the female body through undress in a religiously themed collection, adapting 'western' stereotypes of Islam and rendering Islamic motifs as American sports insignia. For the duration of the show 'a unitary effect of congenial pluralities that apparently "hold-together" without contradictions' was achieved, but, like Galliano's designs analyzed by Emberley, the images presented by McQueen 'cut across traditional barriers of limits of representation and efface[d], along the way, differences and historical specificities'.[103] This more critical account of heterotopias manifesting in fashion certainly captures the confusion evident in different commentaries of *Eye*, but, like Briseño, Emberley focuses on how a heterotopia appears rather than what it seeks to achieve.

A possible means of thinking about the impact and influence of a heterotopia within fashion is provided by sociologists Angharad Beckett, Paul Bagguley and Tom Campbell, who suggest that:

> Heterotopias can be understood as real experiments in thinking and being differently, lived in the present. They provide escape routes from the norm, enlarging the possibilities for self-determination. They are spaces that facilitate and organize resistance practices. In enabling practices that are rule-breaking, they have the potential to effect a rupture in the current order of things.[104]

Approached from this perspective, the purpose of the incongruities and appropriations within *Eye* was – perhaps – to highlight and challenge 'western' attitudes about Islam. If this were the intention, the divergent and flippant views of the collection and catwalk presentation suggest it was not successful, chiefly for two reasons. First, commentators' remarks reveal a limited knowledge of Islam, and by implication, they indicate that 'western' secularized attitudes prevail within the fashion industry. Second, the use of satire confounded understanding. Commentators recognized the juxtapositions McQueen had created within his designs, but the use of this ambivalent form of communication meant they did not sufficiently grasp his intentions. There are parallels with Thom Browne's use of humour in his *Portraits* catwalk presentation of 2018, which confounded journalists' interpretations because of its use of 'discontinuous and incongruous spectacles'.[105] More fundamentally, the decision to use an inherently subversive form of expression to analyze a topic as emotive as people's faith underscores the secularity of the 'western' fashion industry.

Reflections

The rich symbolism within Christianity, Islam and Judaism make these faiths fascinating sources for 'western' fashion designers. Nonetheless, the incorporation of religious motifs within fashionable designs is problematic because it highlights deeply felt and long-standing political and social tensions that underlie contemporary cultural inequalities. Two observations emerge. First, the theme of appropriation raises two points. On the one hand, anglophone news and media discussions about the three episodes assume that fashion reflects the views of the 'west' and that Catholicism is a 'western' religion. Consequently, argument that fashion appropriates from the Catholic Church are difficult to sustain. By contrast, as Islam and Judaism are considered to be non-'western' religions, certainly not fully understood 'western' religions, they can be subject to appropriation. The implications of this appropriation vary. Practitioners of the faith consider it sacrilege, an expression of the 'west's cultural hegemony. By contrast, 'westerners' tend to think their actions are meritorious because fashion is being used to channel democratic and tolerant values. The extent to which 'western' motives are altruistic is complicated by a second point. Commentaries on *Chic Rabbis* and *Eye* emphasize the singular role of the designer. A perception that these individuals are steadfastly pursuing their craft appears to insulate them from criticism. Their work might be presented as a paragon of 'western' values by contemporary fashion journalists, but it is evident from the designers' personal comments that ego and concerns of reputation play out in the fashions they produce. Consequently, appropriation may be less noble than some 'western' commentators are prepared to accept. A second observation, which emphasizes remarks made in previous chapters, is that interpretations of fashion within contemporary journalism are often cursory. They are certainly changeable. Contemporary commentary about each of the episodes includes elements of humour and trivialization. Moreover, analyzes of *Eye* have made the collection more political over time to reflect the deteriorating relationship between the 'west' and 'east'. Twenty one years after its debut and eleven years after McQueen's death, interpretations of the show continue to galvanize 'western' attitudes about other global cultures.

7
WEALTH

In the final year of the nineteenth century, economist Thorstein Veblen published *The Theory of The Leisure Class*. One hundred years later, his survey of 'western' consumption patterns is possibly the most influential, probably the most quoted, to examine the motivations and meanings of contemporary dress. The social mores and structures that supported Veblen's thinking have long since changed, and reappraisals of his work, even denunciations, have been made.[1] Nonetheless, the intellectual legitimacy attached to centuries-old concepts mean its foundational ideas continue to be cited. Few clothing textbooks and readers are without some comment on his writing.[2] Phrases from the essay – 'conspicuous consumption', 'vicarious waste' – and those inspired by it – 'Veblen good' – have entered a rich anglophone lexicon to describe the causes and consequences of 'western' spending habits. One of the more pernicious and persistent sentiments from Veblen's text is the 'requirement of expensiveness'. He asserts that 'without reflection or analysis, we feel that what is inexpensive is unworthy. "A cheap coat makes a cheap man." "Cheap and nasty" is recognized to hold true in dress with even less mitigation than in other lines of consumption.'[3] In the twenty-first century, costly status expenditure continues to be valorized because one of the 'west's' more enduring cultural narratives insists that a person's character and social worth is established through their dress and appearance. Such is the persistence of this belief that even as 'western' economic and political influence diminishes, the nations and regions emerging to challenge, even dominate, demonstrate their assent through prolific status expenditure.[4] One quixotic example is the 'flaunt your wealth' challenge that became viral in parts of China after appearing on Weibo during 2018. The trend 'encourage[d] people to pose amid luxury goods as if they've just fallen out of a car'.[5]

The idea that seeing is believing, more perniciously that 'apparel oft proclaims the man', as Polonius asserts in William Shakespeare's early-seventeenth-century tragedy *Hamlet*,[6] has a long history. Briefly sketched, it derives from two peculiarly 'western' attitudes. First, an insistence on human individuality, which is something of 'an eccentricity among cultures'.[7] Second, an essentialist belief in human inequality, which can be traced to ancient Greece.[8] This ordering of humans was endorsed by Christian doctrine. Medievalist Colin Morris describes Christianity as an 'interior' religion in so far as it encourages introspection and an awareness that the actions of one person will always affect another.[9] Such human-centeredness is reflected in the curious fact that the Christian Church framed its liturgical year with stories of saints, rather than the seasons, despite Europe's reliance on agriculture.[10] Consequently, 'the key to the understanding of the world lay, not in the natural order', according to Morris, 'but in the history of man'.[11] This history was explained with recourse to a hierarchy that came to be known as the great chain of being. Derived from the work of Greek philosopher Aristotle, the Christian chain descended from heaven to hell and proposed a vertical order into which all living organisms could be slotted. Humans resided in the middle. Christianity's co-option of this hierarchy socialized a belief in inequality and the immutability, certainly rigidity, of social position. Whilst the concept of a great chain has weakened over the centuries in direct correlation to the waning authority of religion, psychologists suggest an analogous 'vertical moral hierarchy' might continue to operate within the 'west', subconsciously informing a person's quotidian social interactions.[12]

If the notion of a vertically organized society and a belief in attitudes and actions that are inherently good or bad remains compelling, this is arguably because they have been appropriated by capitalism. Taken at face value, this premise seems counterintuitive, but capitalism sanctions personal assent through the private accumulation and exploitation of resources as a means of providing social order and prosperity. What this linkage lacks in intellectual vigour, it makes up for in being a pragmatic compromise between human idealism and intent. It was a compromise struck by Protestants during the sixteenth and seventeenth centuries as they tried to balance their craving for profit with their chances of eternal salvation. In his study of the Dutch Republic, historian Simon Schama explains:

> In this working compromise, the [Dutch] regents acknowledged the need for some sort of antipecuniary ethic to retrain capitalism from anarchy and abuse, and the church recognized that, however perilous for a godly Republic, Dutch wealth was a fact of life and could be made to work for righteous ends.[13]

Rough around the edges it may have been, but this compromise tacitly sanctioned the accumulation of wealth and the privileges it conferred, which Christianity had always denied. Whilst questioned by philosopher Fredric Jameson, there is some sense that a more explicit, condonable, interest in profit and exchange value spurred 'a new interest in the physical properties of objects'. Over time, these 'new interests develop[ed] new kinds of perceptions, both physical and social – new kinds of seeing, new types of behaviour'.[14] My contention is that one of the more important consequences of this pecuniary gaze is that 'western' people began to perceive greater differences between one another based on their wealth from the sixteenth century.

Dress provided one of the clearest manifestations of human inequality. From Antiquity to the eighteenth century, sumptuary legislation – the name derives from the Latin word for expense, *sumptus* – placed material and monetary limits on people's consumption. One of the expenses most heavily regulated by these laws was dress. Sumptuary legislation stipulated the type, grade, colour and quantity of materials that people's social status entitled them to wear. Laws were typically ineffective because they lacked specificity and because forms of dress changed constantly. Fundamentally, they demonstrated the futility of 'freezing material life', which was contingent upon a society's changing circumstances and values.[15] Nonetheless, the continued existence of sumptuary legislation, which purported to show that human conduct could be regulated by the state's hold over its citizens' purse strings, emphasized a compelling falsehood that a person's appearance was an accurate gauge of their compliance with socially accepted norms. This explains why dress and fashion became so important during the sixteenth century. Historian Rachel Worth notes how members of the Regent class within the Dutch Republic – 'stately and powerful merchants and magistrates' – commissioned portraits in which they appeared arrayed in formal, fashionable clothes with expensive embroidery and lace ruffs.[16] In many of their portraits, the wealthy wear black. This was ironic in two senses.[17] First, it showed the Republic's indebtedness to Spanish fashions during a time when they were seeking political independence from Spain. Second, the wearing of black, whilst a signifier of wealth because it was a hard colour to achieve prior to the creation of synthetic black dyes, has associations with Christian sobriety.[18] The profusion of this colour in many portraits painted by Rembrandt van Rijn is an apt manifestation of the reconciliation that had been achieved between soul and specie.

Embryonic during the sixteenth century, the connection between commerce and conscience was enshrined during the nineteenth century because of the physical and figurative consolidation of European empires. Two factors were important here. First, the establishment of empires was coterminous with the development of a new consumerist culture within Europe, facilitated by department stores and fuelled by advertising. This meant the act of consumption was often imbricated with imperialist ideologies. Focusing on soap, historian Anne McClintock asserts that '[t]he new economy created an uproar not only of things but of signs'.[19] A 'scarce and humdrum item' in the eighteenth century, 'little more than a mundane object to be bought and used', soap acquired during the nineteenth century a 'privileged place not only as a fundamental form of a new industrial economy but also as the fundamental form of a new cultural system for representing social value':[20]

> The emergent middle class values – monogamy ('clean' sex, which has value), industrial capital ('clean' money, which has value), Christianity ('being washed in the blood of the lamb'), class control ('cleansing the great unwashed') and the imperial civilizing mission ('washing and clothing the savage') – could all be marvellously embodied in a single household commodity.[21]

Second, industrialization, which spurred the new economy that McClintock references, contributed another dimension to the signification of things by crystallizing the concept of class. The term was not a new coinage in the nineteenth century. It had been used to describe 'a social division or grouping' from at least 1772, and, as I suggest, the inclination to identify markers of wealth that divided people had become more apparent since the sixteenth century.[22] Nonetheless, the development of the factory system, initially within England, produced clearer divisions between people on the basis of their occupation, place and conditions of habitation, along with their ability and inclination to participate in the emergent consumerist society. Consequently, class became at once more tangible and urgent, as contemporary narratives, both factual, like those from Karl Marx and Friedrich Engels, and fictional, like those from Elizabeth Gaskell and Charles Dickens, demonstrate.[23]

The coincidence of an increased awareness of social stratification and an increased realization that people could elevate themselves with conspicuous status expenditure resulted in a bind that has in many respects come to define modernity in the 'west': the conflict between identity and choice. On the hand there was an increased reliance on material possessions to demonstrate a person's social position and, on the other, an increased suspicion that looks could deceive because people could purchase beyond their means. This mental miasma contributes to explain why dress became such an important issue in the colonies, and why the imposition of sumptuary laws increased in territories controlled by Europe during the eighteenth century when they were being relegated or retracted within Europe.[24] For people to look like a European was to provide some comfort that they were beginning to think as Europeans wanted them to and had begun to adopt their cultural language. Colonial subjects would always be positioned lower on the great chain, but the gap would be bridgeable; such was the belief in the transforming nature of civilization. By contrast, to frustrate European sartorial norms by displaying bodies that challenged their social hierarchies was to painfully expose the limits of imperial rule and the ideas that underpinned it.[25]

The connection between wealth, class and fashion, perceived to be indissoluble in Veblen's day, has become increasingly unstable as social hierarchies have toppled. Worth suggests the linkage may have entirely dissolved, although the 'flaunt your wealth' challenge suggests otherwise. For Worth, the corollary of today's 'democratisation', which is fuelled by online shopping and social media, is the end of fashion.²⁶ Lacking clear hierarchies, fashion is denuded of its essential purpose: to define and divide. The three episodes in this chapter – Fendi's *Haute Fourrure* show for autumn/winter 2015, which valorizes the conspicuous display of affluence; Dior's *haute couture* show for spring 2000, '*Les Clochards*', which appears oblivious to the pernicious consequences of social inequality, and Vivienne Westwood's menswear spring/summer 2009 collection, which purports to challenge socialized notions of the Romani community – are all rooted in the 'west's' idiosyncratic conception of wealth and class, which I suggest fashion continues to play an important role in manifesting and negotiating.

Fendi *Haute Fourrure* autumn/winter 2015

The presentation of Fendi's autumn/winter *haute fourrure* collection on 8 July 2015 was unique and contentious. Unique, because the brand had never organized a presentation solely focused on fur. Its decision to include the show in the same season as an *haute couture* display was unprecedented in the history of the *Fédération Française de la Couture*.²⁷ Contentious, because the *haute fourrure* collection spurred acrimonious debates about the use of fur within the fashion industry. It also rekindled a long-running feud between PETA (People for the Ethical Treatment of Animals) and Karl Lagerfeld, who was celebrating his fiftieth year as artistic director for Fendi. If the *fourrure* collection was the apogee of the designer's vision for the brand and something of an indulgence to commemorate his corporate birthday, there had been clear antecedents. Under Lagerfeld's steer, fur had become synonymous with Fendi. To offer just one example: the show notes for the brand's autumn/winter 2014 womenswear collection had been printed with a sketch by Lagerfeld alongside the assertive caption, 'Fur is Fendi and Fendi is Fur'.²⁸ The vexatiousness of Lagerfeld's endorsement of fur and the deeply divisive relationship he had with PETA became patent following his death in 2019. The organization responded to news of the designer's demise with the following statement: 'Karl Lagerfeld has gone, and his passing marks the end of an era when fur and exotic skins were seen as covetable. PETA sends condolences to our old nemesis's loved ones.'²⁹ So ardent was Lagerfeld's patronage of fur that fashion scholar Jonathan Faiers believes his death marked a 'serious blow to the fashionable status of contemporary fur design'.³⁰

The 2015 *haute fourrure* collection was shown in Paris's *Théâtre des Champs Élysees*. The runway, a narrow horseshoe, projected in front of a mural-sized reproduction of Giorgio de Chirico's painting '*Piazza d'Italia*'. The original and diminutive work, completed around 1955, purposefully confuses chronological and physical spaces. A centrally placed statue of the Grecian princess Ariadne is set against loggias, suited men and a steam locomotive, which are positioned at oblique angles. This uncanny scene reflects Chirico's interest in the relationship between antiquity and modernity, nostalgia and identity.[31] These were appropriate themes for a fashion show that celebrated Lagerfeld's half-centenary with Fendi and gave prominence to a material possessing of so many problematized histories. The interplay between past and present was underscored by the thirty-six looks worn by one black female model and thirty-five white female models.[32] Heavy, textured furs of chinchilla, fox, mink and sable were fashioned into coats, dresses, skirts, 'moon-age daydream jumpsuits of gold and silver', and bags. Some garments had required up to 600 hours of labour to create.[33] One coat of 'silvered sable' was reported to have cost €1 million, making it the most expensive fur coat ever to be made at the time.[34] In all of the show's looks furs were contrasted with patent leather footwear, purses and tops. Natural materials and artisanal skills were juxtaposed with modern materials and processes of manufacture.

Faiers suggests the dichotomy between ancient and modern is fundamental in explaining the continued appeal of fur. Oscillations between these chronological extremes determine the extent to which the material is perceived as 'fundamental' and 'fashionable', signifying the 'primitive' or 'progress'.[35] He adapts philosopher Henri Lefebvre's concept of space as a social construct that is 'contradictory, conflictual . . . political', to argue that the wearing of fur is akin to a 'cinematic space' that conjures fantasies that are at once luxurious, violent and powerful.[36] Conceiving of an imagined 'Furland' that advocates and wearers of fur create for themselves, Faiers posits that this psychological space provides a unique environment for the 'constant re-imagining and re-creating of identities necessary in an increasingly artificial world. Fur in its realness provides authenticity in a climate of escalating simulation. Occasionally Furland takes on specific national identities, and not always the imagined identities of western fashion's continuing project of cultural appropriation.'[37] This imagined safe space is necessary because Faiers contends that fur advocates are 'haunted by the misunderstood remnants of ritual and seduction' before the material became an 'unspeakable object' during the twentieth century.[38] In defining this space, Faiers might have done better to borrow the term Lagerfeld used to describe Fendi's autumn/winter 2014 *Made in Italy* collection: 'fur escape'.[39] 'Escape' is perhaps a more accurate term because the fictive space envisioned by Faiers is the opposite of the heterotopia conceived by Foucault, which engenders critical reflection.[40] Adapting Lefebvre's concept, Faiers conceives of a space that offers patrons of fur a psychological salve, free from censure and guilt.

The extent to which Fendi's *haute fourrure* collection existed in its own space and time is apparent from other elements in the show. The discordance that could be seen on the catwalk through the contrasting use of materials was reflected in what could be heard as the models walked, almost robotically, along it. The artful distortion of time was reflected in the soundtrack, which included Igor Stravinsky's ballet score 'Rite of Spring' (*Le Sacre du Printemps*) interspersed with the more contemporary 'Hammers' by Nils Frahm and 'Acid Reflux' by Dimitri Motofunk and George Libe. The choice of accompanying music could be interpreted as a joke by Lagerfeld. In his review of the catwalk presentation, fashion editor Tim Blanks notes that when Stravinsky's premiered 'Rite of Spring' at the *Théâtre des Champs Élysees* in 1913 it had sparked a riot for being considered too avant-garde.[41] It is very likely the location for the Fendi show – in the same venue – its art and music, were conceived by Lagerfeld to make a darkly humorous statement in defiance of the consternation he knew his collection, which had been widely anticipated in the anglophone media, would spark. If correct, Faiers's concept of Furland is misplaced in this context. The staging of the show suggests Lagerfeld was seeking a sartorial showdown and was wholly disinclined to slink into a psychological safe space.

If the presentation of the *haute fourrure* collection had been conceived to adumbrate Fendi's modernity and heritage, it certainly heightened the brand's outlier status as an advocate of fur. Since the start of the new Millennium, many fashion companies had ceased to use real furs, particularly within the luxury sector. Fashion houses that had banned the use of fur widely publicized this fact.[42] Several British fashion editors refused to attend Fendi's *haute fourrure* show. PETA supporters protested outside the *Théâtre des Champs Élysees* as it took place.[43] The UK director of PETA Mimi Bekhechi had previously described the concept of a fur-focused show as '*haute horreur*'.[44] Blanks was stoic in his commentary, but seemed bemused by the amount of fur shown: 'Without a detailed guide, it was all but impossible to nail what it was we were looking at'.[45] PETA's disavowal apart, the silent protest made by absent editors was reflected in the passivity of journalists' commentaries, which tended to view the protesters' actions as an inevitable part of the fashion panoply.[46] Their response elides with an observation made by journalist Alex Williams, writing for *The New York Times*, about 'the curious state of fur in 2015: So many people seem happy to sell it and show it, but nobody wants to talk about it'.[47]

It was not just the fur that journalists were silent about. None of their commentaries connected the disparate elements of the show to wonder if Lagerfeld sought to convey a specific message through the collection and its presentation. Blanks and at least one other journalist suggested he was aware of the scandal caused by Stravinsky's score, but neither pursued this point to speculate on intentions. One commentator linked the collection's aesthetic to 'Games of Thrones', a mediævalesque popular drama then airing on television.[48] Another suggested, '[t]his was not a collection with a theme or a particular starting point'.[49] Seeing no message or malevolence within the garments and their staging, several reports endorsed the show. French online magazine *Crash* opined that the decision to stage a *haute fourrure* show 'completely falls into sense when we consider Fendi's history with the luxurious material'.[50] Whilst I maintain that a lack of criticality characterizes many contemporary fashion commentaries, the disinclination to fully interrogate Lagerfeld's *haute fourrure* show when elements within it provoked questions among journalists writing from different publications and in different 'western' countries implies the continued existence of what Faiers terms 'a western rationalising gaze'.[51] In the nineteenth century this gaze had facilitated the construction of a patriarchal and gendered hierarchy that sanctioned colonial dominance in such as a way as to appear incontrovertible. In the present, the gaze accepts as benign the wearing of fur to convey status and gender. Within Julia Emberley's feminist reading of fur, the material '[a]s commodity fetish . . . appears to fulfil the needs of a "modernizing" capitalist and patriarchal society' and remains bound up with signs of 'absolute power and mastery' that is only temporarily, and then unstably, exercised by women.[52] The lack of critical reflection about the Fendi show challenges Worth's view that contemporary fashions are no longer stable symbols of class, at least for items of high prestige like fur, which her study does not consider in detail.[53] The show's looks, which were voluminous on account of the cut and pile of the fur, were almost entirely worn by white women, who looked similar – their faces were angular and their hair was styled to be parted on the right. This made the clothes appear more prominent than the models wearing them and suggests a central premise of Veblen's thinking about class and its manifestation remains current: 'the office of the woman [is] to consume vicariously for the head of the household; and her apparel is contrived with this object in view'.[54]

Dior *haute couture* spring 2000, *Les Clochards*

On 17 January 2000, John Galliano presented his couture collection for Dior at the *Petit Palais* art museum during Paris Fashion Week, *Les Clochards* (*The Tramps*). The twenty-minute show included forty-five looks – forty-two worn by white women; two by black women; one by a white male – that ostensibly drew inspiration from three sources. First, the homeless people of Paris, whom Galliano passed on his morning runs along the Seine. Second, Diane Arbus's final photographic series, *Untitled*, which depicts the mentally infirm.[55] Third, early-twentieth-century rag balls, nocturnal entertainments in which the wealthy donned the dress of the destitute to experience a form vicarious escapism through fancy dress costume. These discordant themes were amplified through the show's staging. During the first eleven minutes, twenty-nine models walked the dimly lit runway accompanied by Madonna's cover of Don McLean's 'American Pie' and Tom Traubert's 'Four Sheets to the Wind in Copenhagen'. Both songs are framed by concerns associated with metropolitan living, but neither dwells on homelessness or mental well-being. After a short pause, the second half of the show commenced with the appearance of three models (two female one male), walking in single file and holding between them a distressed and holed sheet, which presumably represented a homeless person's blanket. Accompanied by Fun Boy Three's song 'The Lunatics Have Taken Over the Asylum', the models were followed by others whose clothing was influenced by dress conventionally associated with mental illness, notably the straight jacket.

Using a palette of putrefaction, with hues of black, brown, grey, red, yellow, and white, garments of silk taffeta, lace, tulle and wool, were cut at oblique angles, distorting the wearer's silhouette. Seams and hemlines looked variously frayed and torn. Enlarged safety pins, threaded eyelets and tied rope appeared to hold the ensembles together. An assortment of incongruous objects that included a comb, compass, cork, fork, cheese grater, small whisky bottles, a spool of thread – 'garbage' in the words of reporter Court Williams – were hung from some of the models' waists.[56] Silk printed with pages from *The International Herald Tribune* had been used to make a pair of baggy trousers. The inspiration for this design apparently derived from Elsa Schiaparelli, who had observed Danish women making hats from newspaper.[57] The Christian Dior couture label could be seen on several garments, which looked like they had been turned inside out. Throughout the show there was a sense that the models' dress would fall apart as they walked and posed. Make-up heightened the feeling of decay and disarray. Models' faces were whitened, their eyes blackened. One report suggested their skin was literally smeared with dirt.[58] The result was a series of ghoulish Pierrots, reminiscent of the doleful paintings of Antoine Watteau and Edward Hopper.

Reflecting on *Les Clochards* for *Women's Wear Daily* ten years after its presentation, journalist Bridget Foley described the show as 'one of the most controversial . . . ever staged'.[59] Her verdict is an example of how responses to fashions are contingent upon the people, spaces and times in which they are interpreted. Foley's opinion differed markedly to that of her predecessors at *Women's Wear Daily*, whose contemporaneous response to the collection was complimentary. The form and staging of Galliano's designs were considered inoffensive because he 'shows such great affection and respect for his subjects, and even falls in love with them a little.'[60] In a similar vein, Suzy Menkes described the show as 'brilliant, imaginative and extraordinary'. She raised two concerns about the collection – first, that '[t]here wasn't a thing 'for customers' to wear'; and second, that the 'deconstruction theme . . . has been around for years from *avant garde* designers Rei Kawakubo and Martin Margiela' – but had no qualms about the subject matter, which she interpreted as Galliano returning 'to his roots: to the maniacal mix of sex, romanticism and chaos of his own early collections'.[61] In *Libération*, Pierre Marcelle expressed fatigue at the continued use of deconstructive techniques, which were no longer scandalous (*même pas scandaleux!*), but, unlike Menkes, pondered if this meant people had become desensitized to the suffering of others.[62]

Several contemporary commentators were forthright in their condemnation. Journalist Maureen Dowd, writing for *The New York Times*, linked the show to other forms of 'tasteless chic': 'from heroin chic to Hasidic chic to Kosovo chic. So why not homeless chic?'[63] Referencing *Le Monde*'s criticism, which had likened the collection to the whimsy of Marie-Antoinette, who dressed as a shepherdess in her make-believe rustic retreat *Le Hameau de la Reine* during the eighteenth century, Dowd drew parallels between the insouciance of Galliano and the then mayor of New York, Rudy Giuliani, who had recently sanctioned the clearing of homeless shelters across the city.[64] Mary Broshahn, executive director of Coalition for the Homeless, remarked, '[t]he fact that this is a matter of life and death seems lost on Galliano and his Eurotrash following'.[65] In Paris, homeless activists entered Dior's flagship store, which caused it to be shut for two hours until riot police restored order.[66]

Other commentators were sanguine, or at least more inclined to balance their interpretation of the show with recognition of Galliano's technical skill and ability to increase Dior sales. In *Harper's Bazaar* Spain, Vicente Benavent wrote of Galliano's attempt to create pieces that were 'daring and crazy, but impeccably crafted' ('*Galliano proponía piezas diferentes, atrevidas y alocadas, pero de una factura impecable*').[67] To support his argument, Benavent quotes a letter of Bernard Arnault, CEO of Dior's parent company LMVH, who praised Galliano's ability to turn fashion parades into profits: *una fuerza del diseño irrefutable, que con sus creaciones aporta una visión nueva que se traduce en un incremento de los beneficios* ('an irrefutable design force, who with his creations brings a new vision that translates into increased profits').[68]

As Foley's judgement demonstrates, opinions of *Les Clochards* have not remained static. Five years after the show, fashion editor Laird Borrelli-Persson argued in a short commentary published in American *Vogue* that Galliano was purposefully thinking about 'transgression' at the start of the new Millennium. She seemed uncertain of his intent, however, observing, '[w]hether [he] was upending ideas of class and privilege, or making fun of the dispossessed was part of the debate'.[69] Journalist Virginie Mouzat, reflecting eleven years after the show, was similarly equivocal, but opined that there was 'too much irony, bordering on contempt'.[70] Only Galliano's views remained unchanged. Addressing criticisms made of *Les Clochards* shortly after its debut, and speaking to Dowd's remarks, he stated:

> The critics have a slightly bigoted view. One is allowed to have women mincing about in high heels and combat trousers and a scarf around their head, inspired by the war in Bosnia. One is allowed to be inspired by India, even though there is enormous poverty there. One is allowed to be inspired by Africa, even though the Masai tribe is a disappearing race. One is allowed to have bohemian chic inspired by Gypsies even though we all know now where Gypsies are coming from.

> I don't get why, just because this is on their own doorstep, it's any different. Because they don't want to know about these people?
>
> Children are brought up to watch Lady and the Tramp and Charlie Chaplain and The Little Rascals. I didn't set out to make a political statement. I am a dressmaker. But jogging around the Seine has thrown Paris into a whole different light for me. I call it the Wet World. There are shades of Tennessee Williams and Marlon Brando.
>
> Some of these people are like impresarios, their coats worn over their shoulders and their hats worn at a certain angle. It's fantastic.[71]

In response to the protest, Galliano explained that he did not intend for his collection to be 'offensive to anyone', but he did not issue an apology.[72] His stance was little different in 2007, when he was interviewed by *L'Express*:

> I find it beautiful, why not? When others imagine Gypsies, no one takes offense, because it is a usual reference, but this was the first time in fashion . . . When I look back, [my collections] all seem relevant to me in the evolution of the house. I want to be the best and move forward without regrets.[73]

Ruminating on the theme of being the best, Galliano emphasized the praise his collection had received for its technical accomplishment. At the time of its debut, he claimed it was 'the most spoken-about topic at dinner parties in Paris'.[74] The periodic applause from members of the catwalk audience, including one person who shouted 'Bravo!' would support Galliano's assertion that his work was lauded, at least by its immediate viewers, acolytes and employees of the fashion industry.[75]

Central to the shifting interpretation of *Les Clochards* is the role of signification: How far should the colours, motifs and silhouettes used by Galliano be understood as signifiers or enjoyed as spectacle? Asserting that he is a 'dressmaker', a curiously humble self-definition that jars with the bombastic assertion that his collection had become the talk of Paris, Galliano repudiated criticisms of *Les Clochards* by implying that negative remarks about his work derived from people's inclination to over-interpret and see significance where none was intended. It is possible that he genuinely believed his cultural bricolage to be no different, and similarly inert, to that of other – presumably 'western' – designers, who incorporated combat trousers, headscarves, African and Indian motifs into their work. An exculpatory analysis of *Les Clochards* would be predicated on Galliano's fashion education and understanding of Punk, and go as follows:

Galliano completed his fashion design studies at Central Saint Martins, London, during the 1980s. Referring to himself as a 'club demon', he experienced a city with a dynamic fashion and music scene that embraced a wide range of cultural references. Bricolage and deconstructive techniques were employed by contemporary musicians as much by contemporary fashion designers in response to England's social and political upheavals: mass unemployment, miner strikes and periodic power outages.[76] Fashion scholar Shaun Cole describes a 'Hard Times style' that was worn across the city's clubs, catwalks and sidewalks. It was especially evident in the influential designs of Malcolm McLaren and Vivienne Westwood which they sold through their King's Road shop SEX.[77] Cole signals out their 1982 'Buffalo' and 1983 'Punkature' collections that 'featured oversized, distressed, mismatched and layered garments that were presented in a seemingly thrown-together mix of historic and multicultural influences'.[78] This abundant visual stimulus became a characteristic of Punk as it developed in England during the 1970s and 1980s. Punks adorned their bodies with a surfeit of incongruous historical and cultural motifs, chiefly relating to class, gender and sex, because they 'did not want their bodies to be legible'.[79] Through multiplication and exaggeration, or 'hyper-spectacle', English scholar Stacy Thompson argues that Punks wanted 'to demonstrate that the surface markers of fashion, and by association all clothing, [were] purely spectacle and, as such [did] not correlate with their supposed social referents'.[80] Galliano was familiar with Westwood's designs, and saw her 1984 autumn/winter collection, which he apparently liked.[81] Assuming this appreciation for 'one of the key architects of punk in the 1970s' translated into a long-standing influence, a positive appraisal of Les Clochards could suggest that Galliano was similarly aiming for the 'destruction of the status quo' and using the 'hyper-spectacle' of his designs to interrogate the relationship between fashionable dress, class and social hierarchies.[82]

Feasible as this reading is, it is nonetheless scuppered by Galliano's recollection of his student days. Reflecting on his research in the Victoria and Albert Museum's archives, where he learned about the Incroyables and the Merveilleuses, French revolutionary subcultures that performed their gendered identities through elaborate dress and staged entertainments, Galliano romanticized his penury by suggesting, 'I was looking like this down-and-out French tramp . . . I could imagine these creatures marching, running across the wet shiny cobblestones of Paris.'[83] His sentiment here is little different to that which he expressed after the catwalk show, when he described the homeless of Paris as being 'like impresarios'. Consequently, it would appear that Galliano conceived of his collection through the same 'rationalising gaze' that Faiers speaks of in relation to fur. The extent to which Galliano's work is framed by a 'western' conception of social and political hierarchies is emphasized by his loose vocabulary, where he becomes a 'tramp' and the homeless are variously 'creatures' and 'impresarios'. People and concepts are displaced and invested with meaning according to Galliano's intentions. This artful role-playing, which can be considered analogous to the methods of nineteenth-century European anthropologists and biologists, is most apparent in his invocation of cartoons and comic characters – Lady and the Tramp and Charlie Chaplain and The Little Rascals – to justify his appropriation of people's destitution.

Galliano's apparent indifference to people's impoverishment, which Pierre Marcelle links to a wider desensitivity within the 'west', appears to elide with an observation made by philosopher Gilles Lipovetsky in *The Empire of Things*. This is a beguiling book. In his foreword to the English edition sociologist Richard Sennett suggests it is 'as maddening as it is stimulating'.[84] Nonetheless, it contains some clarion insights and superb soundbites that seem apposite to an analysis of *Les Clochards*, and also to Lagerfeld's *haute fourrure* show. One such is that '[n]othing is taboo any longer; all styles are accepted and exploited unsystematically. There is no longer a fashion, there are fashions'.[85] According to Lipovetsky the pluralization of fashions during the mid-twentieth century, which gave way to 'a patchwork of disparate styles', means that contemporary clothing designs are more akin to modern art, which is a 'free, untrammelled creation'.[86] He asserts:

> Just as, in the contemporary theater, directors feel free to appropriate the official repertory and transgress it, abolishing the authority of the text and of any principles extrinsic to creation for the stage, designers have done away with the implicit reference to universal taste and have reinvested ironically and anarchically in styles from the past. The theater of texts has given way to a theater of images, intensities, and poetic shocks; fashion, for its part, has turned its back on discreet parades in haute couture salons in favor of the 'podium effect', sound-and-light shows, the spectacle of astonishment. As Rei Kawakubo writes, 'fashion has no reality except in stimulation.'[87]

The result is that '[e]clectism is the supreme stage of creative freedom' and fashion 'entails the combining of absolutely incompatible criteria'.[88] This reflects the 'open society' in which new designs are conceived and consumed. Consequently, 'fashion no longer arouses the interest or passion it used to elicit. How could it, when such a broad tolerance rules in matter of dress, when the most heterogeneous styles coexist, when fashion is no longer uniform?'[89] There is much that appears compelling about this analysis when applied to the form and staging of *Les Clochards*, and also to Lagerfeld's *haute fourrure* show. Nonetheless, what Lipovetsky does not seem to grasp – and what provided the vituperative source of criticism within both designers' shows – is that the 'disparate', 'heterogeneous', 'eclecticism' was interpreted as a kind of cultural chauvinism, whereby 'western' designers indiscriminately appropriate motifs associated with marginalized and voiceless communities to clothe wealthy consumers. Interpreted in this way, the indifference and desensitivity are borne of an overriding desire for people to achieve greater material distinction for themselves by claiming, however unselfconsciously, hegemony over divergent groups of people and their cultures.

Vivienne Westwood menswear spring/summer 2009

Vivienne Westwood's menswear collection for spring/summer 2009, shown during Milan Fashion Week in June 2008, was inspired by the Roma community. Roma men, described by the brand as 'rough, stylish and hardened', were selected to model the collection's fifty-four looks.[90] Commentators were franker about the casting, labelling the 'not so regular models' 'brutish he-men', 'bruisers', 'muscled, tattoo-covered, greasy-haired m[e]n'.[91] The apparent incongruity of the models was emphasized by their gait, which involved quick, deliberate strides and, in many cases, exaggeratedly oscillating shoulders. Many models walked with at least one hand in their pockets. Pausing and posing at the end of the first stretch of a U-shaped runway, several of them appeared to scowl, presumably to heighten their rough and hardened demeanour.[92] Those wearing grills bared their teeth to flash the gilded jewellery adorning them.[93] One model walked the runway with a white bulldog on a leash. Any attempt at aggression was scuppered by him grinning; an apparently spontaneous response to the situation.[94] The men's choreographed nonchalance was underscored by their clothing, which was replete with juxtapositions: clashing patterns of vertical stripes and paisley prints; pastels mixed with vibrant hues; jackets, albeit casual, worn with boots. All garments were styled with a studied insouciance. One model walked with the buttoned fly of his trousers undone; another wore shorts with an exposed vertical button fastening. Chests, some tattooed, were visible beneath shirts and jackets that were not fully closed. The shirt of one model was deliberately designed to make it look like the collar and cuffs were torn and hanging by threads.[95] Dress accessories were as conspicuous as the golden grills and included oversize belt buckles, thick chains and medallions.

Invitations to the show included a short stanza that seemed conceived to provoke, although Westwood was clear that her collection, which was largely designed by her husband and creative partner Andreas Kronthaler, conveyed a message of 'tolerance':

> My mother said that I never should
> Play with the gypsies in the wood
> If I did she would say
> You naughty girl to disobey.[96]

The stanza is the chorus from an anglophone children's rope-skipping song that was prevalent within Britain and Northern Ireland during the first half of the twentieth century. American academic and children's author Francelia Butler argues that this genre, which exists in many global cultures and includes commentaries on social roles and interpersonal relationships, enables 'unconscious elements in the personality to surface'.[97] By selecting this stanza for her invitation, Westwood was almost certainly declaring her intention to subvert socialized attitudes about a marginalized group. Nevertheless, the suggestion that 'gypsies' lived apart in the 'wood' and constituted a nefarious and corrupting influence may explain the responses of fashion commentators, which seem at once wary and dismissive of the models. If journalists struggled to connect the invitation's text to the catwalk presentation, the reactions from audiences lacking any steer were understandably more diverse. Comments posted to the anglophone online forum *The Fashion Spot* indicate that people who viewed the collection after its debut did not fully understand its purpose. Commentators responded in various ways but their remarks focus on the style of the clothes that were shown and the attractiveness of one of the models:

It's kind of funny. I like it[98]

love the bottoms! and the chunky guy![99]

The baggy pants are *adorable*!! She can cut a mean cut, never underestimate her tailoring! I love that she's using real-looking men to model, and they look good too!! ♥ Westwood! ☺[100]

The collection seems to have no conceptual basis but for what? Vivienne westwood does not need it. From one look to the other there's always a reminder of her action and ideology: politics, human thinking, body power, etc. And I always see a piece that nobody else could nor design nor produce. I'll see you at the shop white sandals!!![101]

One forum user posted an article from *The Guardian* that explained the collection's theme of tolerance, but apart from a general remark (quoted above) about the political nature of Westwood's work, the specific intention of the collection was not considered by any of the forum users.[102]

In Milan, where the collection was shown, there was a backlash. The region's long-standing antipathy towards the Roma community meant the appearance of Romani men on the runway was criticized by local officials, who interpreted the gesture as an outside intervention in local politics. Tiziano Maiolo, a member of Milan's council, spoke out against the show. He argued that Westwood had 'a romantic notion about gypsies that [was] one hundred years out of date'. He explained that 'I worked in the Gypsy camps around Milan and believe there is no chance for integration while the men play cards instead of working and the women and children steal and beg'.[103] He extended an offer to 'take [Westwood] on a tour of the nomad camps. These people do not want to work, they live by thieving and they have no respect for the law'.[104]

In contrast to Galliano's *Les Clochards*, it is possible to interpret the motifs and incongruent imagery within Westwood's collection more securely as hyper-spectacle. The oversized chain necklaces, gilt grills, exposed and tattooed skin repudiate the 'west's' insistence that adorned surfaces of the human body are readily legible.[105] The choreographed and comically aggressive presentation of Westwood's and Kronthaler's collection suggest their designs were specifically conceived to challenge negative stereotypes about the Romani community, examples of which appear in Maiolo's invective when he refers to workshy men who play card games and women who steal. By featuring men who perform exaggerated versions of their contemporary stereotypes, the designers aimed to demonstrate the instability and intolerance of such reductionist outlooks. To use stereotypes in this way is as clever as it is difficult because audiences are required to understand their critical function. If audiences do not comprehend that stereotypes are being used subversively, there is a risk their subject matter will be reified rather than reappraised. Whilst limited, comments cited earlier from journalists and the public indicate the designers' interrogative use of stereotypes was not widely fathomed, especially beyond Milan where the place of the Romani remains contested. Consequently, the effectiveness of the collection in using Punk-era strategies to frustrate socialized ideas about class appears limited.

The challenge of divesting culturally potent symbols of their meanings is an inherent limitation of hyper-spectacle. Thompson's analysis identifies two obstacles that beset Punks who sought to use this form of visual communication during the 1970s. First, a surfeit of images creates polyvalency as multiple interpretations of symbols become possible and equally plausible. If this creates ambivalence, the strategy's impact will be nugatory. Second, Thompson suggests there is an inverse correlation between the adornment of the body with multiple or exaggerated motifs associated with economic, gendered and political power and the effective authority that wearers of these symbols possess. The more that authority symbols are disassociated from their source of power and desecrated, the greater the outlier status of their despoilers becomes and the sharper their powerlessness is perceived. Thompson suggests Punks may have experienced a 'masochistic delight' in making their marginalized status public to highlight the brutality of the class system.[106] Whilst this may be true in some cases, it nonetheless confirmed Punks' peripheral position within English society. In a similar way, it could be argued that the exaggerated clothing and dress accessories in Westwood and Kronthaler's collection confirmed the pariah status of the Romani men who wore them.

Applying Thompson's concept of hyper-spectacle to a fashion catwalk presents an additional issue. Where Punks had used material objects to highlight the problems of class and capitalism, Westwood and Kronthaler were using Punk strategies to sell material objects. Thompson elucidates the conundrum continually confronted by Punks as they sought to eradicate capitalism by harnessing capitalist tropes. Through their collection, Westwood and Kronthaler probed two counterintuitive issues. First, they used strategies from an anti-capitalist movement to sell fashionable designs. Second, they used a commercially driven brand to advocate a message of tolerance towards a socially marginalized and financially deprived community. The complexity, if not simple incompatibility, of the collection's aims may explain why audiences were unable to discern a clear – or perhaps genuine – message about the Romani community. Even if it is the case that Westwood and Kronthaler genuinely wanted this collection to effect positive change for the Roma community, its framing by 'western', more specifically English, ideas of class limited its impact.

Reflections

The episodes considered challenge two arguments that Rachel Worth makes in her study of fashion and class. First, that social hierarchies are no more, and, second, that fashion has come to an end. Fashion continues to exist, and thrive, because social hierarchies do, even if they are less explicit than in the nineteenth century. Two observations can be made. First, the episodes emphasize at least three contrasting roles that fashion can serve in clarifying people's socio-economic status. Lagerfeld appears to have mocked, studiously, concerns about excessive consumption by asserting that a primary function of fashion is to demarcate people's social and gendered positions. Galliano's outlook was romanticized, but his collection was equally clear that clothes define people's social position. Sentimentally he demonstrated an unsentimental fact that the wealthy are at liberty to take, often with impunity, from others. Westwood and Kronthaler attempted to use their collection to challenge socialized views predicated on wealth but in seeking to do this through an industry so deeply associated with consumption their impact appears nugatory. A second observation, linked to these remarks and the reflections of previous chapters, is that fashion, so imbricated with 'western' values and structures, struggles – when it tries – to convince consumers of its social consciousness. Underpinning discussions of each episode is an assumption that disparities of income and wealth exist and that these are most readily and conventionally conveyed through people's public appearance. This has become an axiom of capitalism.

This ambivalent, despondent, attitude is also reflected in the consideration of spectacle. In 1967, philosopher Guy Debord published *La Societé du Spectacle* (*Society of Spectacle*), a critique of modern life conveyed through 221 reflective paragraphs. Debord believed that 'unrealism' had come to define contemporary 'western' society because a surfeit of visual communication, of images, had privileged representation over reality.[107] This resulted in people developing a blasé outlook akin to that observed by Georg Simmel in 1903.[108] Debord asserts: 'In a world which is really *topsy turvy*, the true is a moment of the false.'[109] The implication of these reflections for the episodes considered here, and in other chapters, is potentially unsettling. Fashion's reliance on visual motifs and spectacle demonstrates the extent of its immersion – perhaps subjugation – within modern modes of thought. Consequently, its images exacerbate the unrealness of society because they emphasize signs over signification, fantasy over fact. In this sense, the insouciance of Lagerfeld and Galliano becomes comprehensible and their play with images becomes just that: a playful performance. Consequently, their work can cause no offence because it involves the reorientation of pre-existing signs and symbols. Mercifully, the critical responses from fashion journalists and protesters indicate that people's stupefaction is not as prevalent as Debord feared. Nonetheless, his text is important for reminding us that images are rarely devoid of meaning; they have potential and power to inspire and to injure. In a society that is becoming saturated with images, his work clarifies the imperative to analyze them, rather than to blithely accept them as another facet of the modern condition.

8
VIOLENCE

The French expression *il faut souffrir pour être belle* (it is necessary to suffer to be beautiful) encapsulates a pernicious idea that has long been pervasive in the 'west'. Fashion historian Alison Matthews David suggests that clothing 'is our lifelong companion'.[1] She cites nineteenth-century French author Auguste Debay, who likened dress to a house that protects people from 'harmful influences on the outside world'.[2] These metaphors are reassuringly pleasant, but in the case of fashion, which sociologist Yuniya Kawamura considers a belief 'manifested through clothing', the relationship between wearer and wardrobe is often far less nurturing.[3] The French mantra alludes to this. The pursuit of beauty, fashionable appearances and living are unreasonable because their conception, which is fantastic, informs modes of creation and consumption that are frequently capricious, divisive and painful, physically and psychologically. The suffering induced by fashion is caused by two main factors. First, social processes – often framed by 'western' concepts – determine fashions. Consequently, people need to comply with what is recognized within their community as fashion if they wish to be judged fashionable.[4] Second, the manifestation of fashion through dress is exclusionary because of the requirement that people possess sufficient agency and resources to acquire products and services deemed fashionable. Paradoxically, these prescriptive and prohibitive circumstances mean the French expression has become axiomatic within the 'west' rather than arguable: a person's suffering becomes necessary and meritorious if their fashionable status is to be incontrovertible.

This sentiment, which follows a similar logic to Thorstein Veblen's adage that a cheap item of dress designates a person as cheap, crystallized during the nineteenth century as industrialization facilitated what historian Frank Trentmann terms the 'birth of total shopping' in the 'west' and wider world.[5] Consumers were not uncritical, and the proliferation of new vogues in dress, which became more cognizant of sex and gender, was challenged by reformers.[6] In a period that historian Aileen Ribeiro has called the 'great divide', on account of the social transformations that were occurring during the eighteenth and nineteenth centuries, philosophical and political texts questioned the morality of the society that was emerging.[7] The physical pain that people appeared willing to accept to participate in the latest fashion's in dress was a frequent subject for naysayers, moralists and satirists who tended to interpret this self-inflicted violence as a doom-laden harbinger of things to come. It was, perhaps, a portent of the 'unrealism' that would come to trouble Guy Debord. In his nineteenth-century satirical dialogue between sisters Fashion and Death, Giacomo Leopardi adumbrated the various ways that the younger sibling, Fashion, had imposed physical violence on people around the world:

> It is quite true, however, that I haven't refrained – nor am I refraining now – from playing many games comparable with yours, such as, for instance, piercing ears, lips, or noses with holes and causing them to be torn by the trinkets I hang in those holes; charring the flesh of men with red-hot brands, as I make them do for beauty's sake; misshaping the heads of babies with bandages and other trappings, making it a custom for all the men of a country to have their heads in the same shape, as I have done in America and in Asia; crippling people with tight shoes; cutting off their breath and making their eyes pop out because of their tight corsets; and a hundred other such things. As a matter of fact and generally speaking, I persuade and force all genteel men to endure daily a thousand hardships and a thousand discomforts and often pain and torment and I even get some of them to die gloriously for love of men. I won't tell you about the headaches, the colds, the inflammations of all kinds, the quotidian, tertian, to quartan fevers that men catch to obey me, agreeing to my wishes, by protecting their shoulders with wool and their chests with cloth, and by doing everything my way, no matter how much it hurts them.[8]

Today, fashion narratives that dwell on the physical discomfiture caused by fashions tend to focus on innovations that occurred within the 'west' during the nineteenth century, most notably the corset.[9] Chemicals long used in beauty regimes that were successfully, and fatally, popularized during this period, including arsenic, lead and mercury, are also highlighted.[10] People's proclivity to endure pain in the pursuit of fashion is most commonly evinced through their footwear. In the opening catalogue essay that accompanied the Victoria and Albert Museum's exhibition of 2015, 'Shoes: Pleasure & Pain', curator Helen Perrson opines that 'shoes have been the most consistent example, across socio-economic groups, of fashion that ignores actual human anatomy – distorting the feet'.[11] During the nineteenth century, several tales authored by the Grimm brothers and Hans Christian Andersen, much darker than their Disney adaptations, included grisly accounts of shoes torturing their wearers, with amputations and death providing their only release.[12]

The pain caused by fashionable dress is most obviously physical, but a central premise of this book is that some of the most grievous and long-lasting harm caused by people's acceptance, or alienation, from fashionable forms of appearance is psychological. The point can be refined by thinking about descriptions of pain caused by fashions beyond the 'west' that are used to demonstrate the cultural inferiority of their wearers. One of the most cited examples in 'western' fashion texts of a non-'western' fashion causing physical pain is the Chinese practice of binding aristocratic females' feet, which occurred between the seventh and twentieth centuries.[13] 'Western' authors variously describe foot binding as 'notorious', the cause of 'deformation' and a 'mincing gait'.[14] Accounts typically invoke the example to explain the lengths that even 'civilised people' will go in the pursuit of a fashion appearance, except within the 'west', because 'no such extreme practices are indulged in by Western nations'.[15] The accounts cited date from the twentieth century, but contemporary fashion studies perpetuate an idea that followers of fashion paid a higher physical price if they lived beyond Europe. Perrson assumes her twenty-first-century readers will react with incredulity upon hearing about foot binding. She writes, '[h]owever impossible it may seem to us today, women with bound feet did move about'.[16] Fashion commentator Colin McDowell goes further than most accounts, and without evidence, to assert that foot binding 'was a deliberate and permanent attempt to remove women's freedom of movement'.[17] He includes the prurient, also unreferenced, suggestion that the 'crevasse between the heel and the sole was so highly sexualized it was reputedly used to masturbate men'.[18] 'Western' authors do compare 'western' and non-'western' forms of fashion-induced pain. Perrson likens the 'mincing gait' of foot binding to wearing a high heel.[19] Nonetheless, the physical pain endured by 'western' people – women for the most part – is valorous, as per the French maxim quoted above, because it evidences their involvement, and agency, within a consumerist society. This is important because it elides with a central 'western' premise that clothes convey character. In contrast, beyond the 'west', fashion-induced pain shows how people – again, women for the most part – lack agency and are usually subordinate to the whims and wiles of men. Their physical pain is conceived to be directly proportionate to their psychological suffering. The logic invoked here does not stand scrutiny, but it emphasizes how 'western' fashion norms create psychological violence through people's conformity to them, or, through the shame and hurt caused by people's inability or unwillingness to follow them.

I deliberately choose the word violence for this chapter over hurt or suffering because unlike these terms, which can describe unintended human agony, violence more commonly refers to distress that is intentional, knowingly caused and endured. The episodes considered – Dolce & Gabbana's, spring/summer womenswear campaign for 2007 shot by Steven Klein, a bogus United Colors of Benetton domestic violence campaign from 2007 and Burberry's autumn/

winter 2020 ready to wear collection *Tempest* – aim to clarify how fashions can sanction violence through their manifestation of socialized 'western' attitudes. In so doing, this penultimate chapter, and that which follows, brings together some of the threads – here, gender, race, religion – that have been raised in previous chapters by showing how the binaries considered separately intersect in the conception, creation and consumption of contemporary fashions.

Dolce & Gabbana, spring/summer womenswear 2007 campaign

Dolce & Gabbana's campaign for their spring/summer 2007 womenswear collection, photographed by Steven Klein, was the subject of opprobrium within north-western Europe for its depiction of females in exploitative and physically vulnerable positions. One image, removed from French and Spanish fashion magazines prior to publication, appeared to show a woman about to be gang-raped. Before a cloud-filled blue sky, four white, athletic, dark-haired and tanned men, perhaps in their mid-twenties, stand upon white plinths of differing heights, their bodies facing the camera. Two of the men are shirtless, their bodies oiled. A third man wears a shirt that is unfastened to his navel. His oiled sternum is visible. Silver pendants hang from the necks of two men, directing attention to their pectorals. All four men wear dark blue denim and belted jeans. Silver key chains are attached to two of the belts. Associations of hegemonic masculinity underpinned by physical labour, sweat and toil abound. The men occupy positions to the left and right of a woman who is lying against another white plinth. In contrast to the men's utilitarian attire, the woman wears a black silk body suit and black ankle tie stilettos. Her hair is tied back. She wears mascara or false eyelashes and red lipstick. The scene is charged by the fact that woman has her left hand held down by one of the men, shirtless, who kneels over her. As if in response to this aggressive-looking gesture, the woman's back is arched upwards. Her head, shoulders and stiletto-clad feet are the only parts of her body, along with her pinned arm, to connect with the surface beneath her. The awkward, uncomfortable position suggests she is resisting. Her gaze is cast downwards. By contrast, the man looks directly towards the woman. His line of sight is unambiguous, although his eyes are concealed behind a pair of sunglasses. The three other men look towards the woman. Their gaze and posture – hands on hips or in pockets – suggest they have no intention of intervening. They intend to watch. The physical encirclement of the woman is completed by the viewer of this scene who occupies a position directly opposite the four men. Like them, we watch.

The campaign's emphasis on machismo, sexual provocation and the playing out of these themes along a gender binary where men are physically dominant, was echoed in the staging of the collection's Milan catwalk show.

The rectangular runway was constructed of transparent glass panels. Models' access to the runway involved two dramatic elements. First, a moving platform brought them up from concealed dressing rooms below. Second, alighting the platform, the models descended four glass steps. Tiered staircases of varying heights on either side of the catwalk and lift acted as backdrop. Across the top of the staircases, six female models, illuminated by individual spotlights, posed on revolving turntables. On a lower level, three male models stood in a niche immediately behind the lift. Looking along the length of the runway that projected before them, the men were identically dressed in black trousers, a collared shirt and black necktie.[20] The design of the catwalk, which appeared to impede the female models' movements – through the use of stairs – and emphasize the scrutiny that was already upon them – through the use of spotlights and the constant surveillance of the three male models – seemed to be framed by a socialized 'western' sexism that is expressed in art historian John Berger's remark that 'men act and women appear. Men look at women. Women watch themselves being looked at'.[21] It was unclear whether Dolce & Gabbana were blithely accepting of this outlook or seeking to interrogate it.

One 'western' blogger, 'Fashionattheedge', opined that the collection's message was 'clear'.[22] The combination of 'skin-tight' garments, which included corsets fashioned from synthetic materials, created a 'masculine femininity'.[23] References to Stanley Kubrick's film *2001: A Space Odyssey* are claimed, without foundation, to manifest themselves in allusions to robotics, humankind's pursuit of technological advancement, and convey our species' 'natural quest for perfection'.[24] The future visualized is not utopic, however, for the author claims the show suggests '[f]emales will loose [*sic*.] their status and gain controlled freedom'.[25] This interpretation of the collection and its staging runs counter to that of the brand. Responding to the concern sparked by Klein's campaign, Dolce & Gabbana released a waspish statement in which they appeared to reject, certainly to question, concerns raised about the campaign. They asserted that '[w]e have decided to cancel . . . the advertising image that has caused such repercussions within human interest groups and individuals'.[26] Designers Domenico Dolce and Stefano Gabbana claimed their intention had been 'to recreate a game of seduction in the campaign and highlight the beauty of our collections'.[27] Gabbana described Klein's shoot as an 'erotic dream, a sexual game'.[28] In response to the media scrutiny generated by Klein's image of the apparent rape scene, he equivocated, asserting that 'evil is in the eyes of the beholder'. He invoked the shifting association of women's corsets to imply that any outrage was untenable because it was culturally contingent:

> 'El mal está en los ojos de quien mira. En el 87 nuestra publicidad sobre sujetadores fue muy criticada [. . .] Nosotros habíamos diseñado esas prendas con inocencia, recordando la corsetería de nuestras madres', añade.[29]

['Evil is in the eyes of the beholder. In 1987 our advertising on bras was highly criticized [. . .] We had designed those garments with innocence, remembering the corsetry of our mothers,' he adds.]

The designers also spoke out against what they deemed to be 'a strong censorship feeling' within Spain under the premiership of the socialist politician José Luis Rodríguez Zapatero.[30]

The response of the design duo is similar to the sentiments expressed by other 'western' designers when confronting criticisms of their work; namely, because no harm was conceived, feelings of offence are unsustainable, certainly without moral foundation. The apparent frustration in the rebuke of Dolce and Gabbana also emphasizes the peculiarity of the situation in Spain during the time of the campaign's launch. *The New York Times* journalist Victoria Burnett argued that Klein's image, which purports to condone of a woman's violent rape, appeared at a moment when Prime Minister Zapatero was spearheading initiatives 'to change Spain's macho culture and do away with outdated female stereotypes'.[31] Interpretation of Klein's image was further problematized by the release of government data that indicated sixty-eight women had 'died [the previous year] at the hands of their partners or former partners, despite a 2004 law against gender-related violence'.[32] Burnett acknowledges that some Spaniards criticized Zapatero for creating 'an oversensitive climate', but she is likely correct to suggest that his measures to '[defend] people's rights', in the words of the Socialist Party's equality chief, account for the critical reaction to Klein's image in Spain.[33]

Within Italy, thirteen senators along with equal opportunity minister Barbara Pollastrini wrote a letter to the country's Advertising Self-Discipline Institute, which subsequently banned the image because of 'the passive and helpless position of the woman relative to the men around her, and the representation of abuse or the idea of violence towards her'.[34] Their ruling emphasized that the woman was 'immobilised and subjected to a man's will', had an 'alienated expression, with an absent look' and appeared in a 'degrading manner' that offended her dignity.[35] The senatorial action might usefully be seen in the context of the divisive ruling made in 1999 by Italy's highest court, the *Corte di Cassazione*, when it overturned the conviction of a regional court that had successfully prosecuted a male driving instructor for raping his female pupil. The so-called scandalous decision was predicated on the argument that '[i]t is a fact of common experience' that tight blue jeans cannot be removed 'even in part, without the active cooperation of the person who is wearing them'.[36] The ruling was widely condemned across Italy, within the media and by politicians from the right and left of the political spectrum. In her analysis of the court's judgement, criminologist Kitty Calavita has written of 'the pervasiveness of the intense negative reaction' that was 'at odds with the gender ideology . . . for

VIOLENCE

153

what, for lack of a better label, might be called the dominant culture'.[37] It is conceivable the appearance of the Klein image in 2001, reignited at least some of the negative feelings from this event eight years earlier.

The importance of circumstance and the contingency of cultural fault lines was emphasized by a revived interest in Klein's image eight years later, in 2015. By this point, much of the anglophone media coverage of the campaign from 2007 had become difficult to access online, if it remained. Consequently, a new audience was encountering the image of the apparent rape scene for the first time in relation to another controversy that was then engulfing the brand. In March 2015, Domenico Dolce and Stefano Gabbana were widely criticized for describing IVF babies as 'chemical children' and 'synthetic'.[38] Their opinion was presumably framed by their Catholic faith. Singer Elton John urged people to boycott the brand over the designers' remarks through an Instagram post that has now received over 26,000 likes.[39] He condemned the duo for suggesting that his 'beautiful children' were synthetic and declared that he would never wear the brand again.[40] Seeking to contextualize the furore, London's *Metro* newspaper reported that Kelly Cutrone, a publicist and judge on the television reality series *America's Next Top Model*, had 'brought to light' the 'controversial shoot from 2007'.[41] Cutrone posted Klein's photograph of the apparent rape scene on Twitter with the caption, written in capitals: 'I GUESS SIMULATING GANG BANGS ARE FINE – BUT IVF AND SAME SEX MARRIAGE ARE NOT – LIFE ACCORDING TO @dolcegabbana.'[42] The re-ignited debate about Klein's eight-year-old image was picked up by other global news sites from India to the UK.[43] A report published in *Metro* summarized the ruling of Italy's Advertising Self-Discipline Institute against Klein's 2007-image, which they republished. The article also included a second image from Klein's shoot, which appears to anticipate another rape scene. This image is not discussed in the article text and did not, to my knowledge, become the focus of criticism in 2007. It is referenced and published in online articles from business news platform *Quartz* in 2014 and *The Daily Mail* newspaper in 2015. The *Quartz* article implies this image was also banned, but *The Daily Mail* account merely states, by way of caption, 'The duo also depicted a group sex scene featuring all men in another ad that was slightly more graphic, though the man was not being restrained'.[44] An article published on the blog 'Sex in Fashion Advertising Campaigns' states that this second image was banned.[45]

The image in question appears to depict male-to-male rape. Set within a space that resembles a plush hotel interior, the image shows four men occupying positions to the left and right of a fifth, who lies with his back against the ground. Two men on the right appear to be getting dressed: one, perched upon a chair, is fastening his necktie, the other, whose body is cropped just above his navel, is zipping the fly of his trousers, his shirt undone and open. His shoes, unworn, are placed behind him. The men on the left appear to be in conversation. One sits with his legs widely parted. He wears a cream suit and white shirt like the men on the left. His eyes are downcast and follow the pointing finger of the fourth man who leans forwards and gesticulates towards the man on the floor. In contrast to these men, who express agency through their actions, the recumbent man is undressed. His right leg is raised and bent at the knee. His hands rest on his torso. His head is tilted back, his mouth closed. The man is not physically restrained but appears to be incapacitated. The implication of the scene is that he, like the woman of Klein's other image from the same campaign, is at the mercy of the men's sexual desires. He is certainly presented in a vulnerable position in contrast to his peers whose poses convey physical energy and authority.

The physical violence that is perceived in the second Klein photograph is less graphic than that featuring the woman because the reclining man is not restrained. Nonetheless, subjugation and humiliation are suggested through the implied use of coercion and intimidation. The furore over the Klein image in 2007 and 2015 focused on the violence perpetrated against a woman and the extent to which this image was demonstrative of what feminist writer Louise Pennington termed 'the dehumanisation of women's bodies in our pornographic mainstream media'. Pennington argued that:

> [r]epresentations of women in fashion are inherently misogynistic. Women are represented as objects – increasingly we're seeing campaigns which depict women as victims of violence and murder.. . . This particular image is representative of an increasingly misogynistic construction of women in the fashion industry demonstrating very clear links between the fashion-beauty industry and the mainstreaming of pornography.

Calling out Dolce & Gabbana, specifically, and the fashion industry, broadly, in response to Klein's image is explicable considering that women are more likely to be the victims of physical violence at the hands of men than *vice versa*.[46] Gender scholars Lori Heise, Mary Ellsberg and M. Gottmoeller are unequivocal: '[v]iolence against women is the most pervasive yet least recognized human rights violation in the world'.[47] Nonetheless, Pennington's critique implicitly, and surely inadvertently, entrenches what she perceives to be the heteronormative and patriarchal nature of the contemporary fashion industry by not remarking on a second image from the campaign that appears to depict the rape of a man by other men. Her argument is perhaps framed by philosopher Tommy Curry's observation that feminist theory has tended to emphasize men's 'proximity to patriarchal power'.[48] The absence of a specific and sustained commentary about the apparent gang rape of a man by his peers, even the uncertainty about whether this image was banned in 2007, hints at a belief that men are not, possibly cannot be, victims of rape, or domestic violence broadly. This sentiment is borne of a socialized view, long prevalent in the 'west', that assumes men are physically stronger, victors rather than victims. The point is recognized by Heise, Ellsberg and Gottmoeller who explain that '[j]ustifications for violence frequently evolve from gender norms – that is, social norms about the proper roles and responsibilities of men and women,' and in many global societies the rights of men are typically more patent and secure than those of women.[49]

United Colors of Benetton unofficial domestic violence campaign 2007

On 13 May 2015 *Dazed Digital* published an online article titled 'Fashion v Censorship: A History of Banned Ads' written by journalist Emma Hope Allwood.[50] The article features eighteen advertising campaigns by seven European-based fashion brands that were reported to the UK's advertising regulator, the Advertising Standards Authority, between 1992 and 2011 – Calvin Klein, Gucci, Miu Miu, Sisley, Tom Ford, United Colors of Benetton, Yves Saint Laurent. Allwood's text is playful, at times tongue-in-cheek. She suggests the composition of the Authority's jury is 'entirely middle-aged' and consequently not representative of popular opinion.[51] The decision to focus on a small number of European fashion brands and to include multiple campaigns from them makes Allwood's argument limiting.[52] In one respect at least, it is also inaccurate because one of the four featured campaigns by United Colors of Benetton is a spoof.

Under the direction of Oliviero Toscani United Colors of Benetton produced a series of culturally sensitive and visually arresting advertising campaigns between 1992 and 2000. Allwood focuses on four, although only three are genuine. The first, from spring/summer 1992, is a photograph by Thérèse Frare that depicts the approaching death of David Kirby from AIDS. Ravaged and weakened by his illness, Kirby reclines in bed surrounded by his immediate family.[53] The second image, from autumn/winter 1992, is a photograph of an empty electric chair by Lucinda Dean.[54] The third Benetton image, a composite from the brand's UNHATE campaign of November 2011, depicts Pope Benedict XVI and Imam Sheik Ahmed el-Tayeb in a kissing pose.[55] All of these images and the campaigns to which they relate are genuine. The fourth image that Allwood features, from May 2007, is a spoof. It depicts two brown women with long, wavy dark hair staring directly towards the viewer. Both have facial injuries. The woman on the left has a bruised left eye and cheek; the woman on the left has an inflamed scar above her right eye. The double portrait is presented in the style of Toscani campaigns with a solid white background. Nonetheless, three clues identify it is as anomalous. First, the models wear Benetton clothes. Toscani campaigns are characterized by their lack of explicit fashion imagery. Second, the brand name has been replaced with the text 'Colors of domestic violence'. The white text in a green box mimics the presentation of the United Colors of Benetton branding from other advertising posters, but in no previous campaign had the company's name been removed or altered. Third, the text 'Issued in public interest by United Colors of Benetton' is printed in the bottom left corner of the image. This notification does not appear in other campaigns issued by the brand. In a caption, Allwood's article suggests that 'United Colours of Benetton replaced their title with "colours of domestic violence" to highlight abuse'.[56] The image was released with two others that are presented in an identical style.

Upon their release, the images sparked debate. One online blogger claimed to be 'speechless' that a brand known to champion 'a good cause' was using the topic of domestic violence to sell clothes:

> But, yes, they really are using models made to look like the victims of domestic violence to hawk their clothes. Yes, domestic violence is bad, but why not buy this jumper I'm wearing?[57]

A similar stance was taken by another blogger, who erroneously claimed the campaign was the work of Italian-based communications agency McCann:

> The United colors of Benetton seems to be scoring at both ends while drawing Victimized picture of women it satiate its social responsibility and dressing them up in stylish apparel will satiate its commercial hunger. However, following this endeavor the campaign seems to be loosing direction as it's impossible to join both ends [sic.].[58]

A third blogger acknowledged that the campaign 'was [. . .] claimed to be a hoax', but describes one of the images they republished – a brown woman with a bruised lip wearing a purple sweater tied across her torso – as 'really well shot'.[59] They observe that 'the colour of bruises matches the sweater's. Definitely, an interesting image'.[60]

Confirmation that the campaign was bogus was shared by American Jill Miller Zimon through her blog 'Writes Like She Talks'. Zimon explains that she contacted Benetton about the campaign and received a reply from their Senior Fashion Public Relations Manager Anissa Nouhi, who asserted:

> I would like to inform you that the images you are refering [sic.] to with the logo 'Domestic Colors of Violence' are a FAKE and are NOT an adverting campaign of Benetton Group.[61]

A thread attached to Zimon's article that captures readers' comments includes the opinion that the campaign images emerged in Russia and India.[62] Zimon responded with shock to the news that the campaign was unsanctioned, and possibly a hoax. By contrast, the response of blogger Steve Hall was sarcastic.

He had initially praised the campaign for its frank engagement with the topic of domestic violence, writing in a tongue-in-cheek tone:

> Benetton is back and they have a message. And as a bonus, maybe the campaign itself will deliver its own version of violence in the form of a slap upside the head of fashionistas who are more concerned with how they look than the plight of women around the world. Damn, that was bitchy.[63]

Learning the campaign was unofficial, he updated his post with the addendum: 'UPDATE: Surprise, surprise. They're fake. Yawn.'[64]

The perpetrators of this hoax have not been identified. In large part this is because their images were still thought to be genuine eight years later when Allwood featured one of them in an online article that remains live. Consequently, their decision to imitate a Toscani campaign is unclear. It might be linked to Hall's remark that the brand had not produced any notable campaign for several years and, in his view, was thought to have gone 'out of business'.[65] Benetton's perceived inactivity could have made them an easier target for a spurious campaign because consumers and commentators possessed no recent advertisements for comparison. After a long hiatus it might have been thought that people would respond more readily, and less critically, to a new campaign. The anglophone bloggers cited above certainly reacted with an eagerness that confounded their ability to identify details that marked the images as suspect. Nonetheless, whilst the campaign was unofficial, it raises three issues about the conveyance of culturally prevalent messages through fashion, broadly, and fashion's relationship with physical violence, specifically.

First, the fashion industry is a recognized conduit for communicating culturally relevant topics, albeit with the caveat, based on the above commentaries, that sensitive themes are addressed infrequently. This is largely because consumers appear wary of a brand's motives and tend to perceive such messaging as tokenistic. Second, the profoundly visual nature of messaging through fashion means people tend to respond quickly, emotionally, and not always critically to what they see. Three implications follow from this point: spurious campaigns can be deemed legitimate; fashionable items of dress and their associated campaigns typically initiate widespread debate, more especially if they engage with culturally freighted topics, and responses to fashion communication are highly dependent on contemporary cultural themes. The third issue, specific to the fake Benetton campaign, is that the fashion industry is not doing enough to use its platforms to raise awareness of domestic violence. Perhaps of greater concern, even with the acknowledgement that the 2007 campaign was unofficial, is that fashion campaigns seeking to raise awareness of social ills tend to compound assumptions that engrain social inequalities. The sole depiction of brown women throughout the fraudulent campaign as sufferers of domestic violence implicitly galvanizes a message that lawlessness of this nature occurs beyond the 'west'. Whilst the campaign was illicit, the fact that it was initially received and critiqued as genuine suggests people are accustomed to see 'western' norms championed within the discourses of the contemporary fashion industry. In much the same way that Louise Pennington's critique of Steven Klein's shoot for Dolce and Gabbana galvanized 'western' assumptions about male strength and authority by implying they have immunity from the violent crime of rape, the images from this campaign posit that domestic violence is a graver issue beyond the 'west'.

Burberry, *Tempest*, autumn/winter 2020 ready to wear

On 17 February 2019, creative director Riccardo Tisci showed Burberry's autumn/winter 2019 collection *Tempest* during London Fashion Week. Framed by the 'contrasts in British culture and weather', the collection was dedicated to the 'youth of today' and sought to be 'including, not excluding'.[66] According to *Vogue*'s online coverage and images of the collection, there were 101 looks: 27 for men and 74 for women. This statement is inaccurate. Three looks – two worn by black men, one worn by a white woman – are omitted from *Vogue*'s online slideshow between 'Look 21' and 'Look 22' and the accompanying commentary by journalist Sarah Mower.[67] The expunged garments and the models wearing them are clearly visible in live footage of the catwalk presentation.[68] These looks, that worn by the female model in particular, were the subject of public concern within the UK because they invoked motifs associated with the noose and lynching. The brand appeared oblivious to the implication that their garments could be linked to the trauma of suicide or the ritualized murder of black people in the United States.

In a post made to her Instagram feed on 17 February, model Liz Kennedy, who participated in the Burberry runway but did not wear the offending items, showed two photographs that she had presumably taken backstage. The images featured the taupe-coloured hoodie with its dark brown draw string closure worn by the white female model. The knot and fastening method of the hoodie resemble a noose. Kennedy uploaded the images along with the following paragraph that included the Instagram handles of Burberry and Tisci. Burberry was also tagged at the end of the text:

> Suicide is not fashion. It is not glamorous nor edgy and since this show is dedicated to the youth expressing their voice, here I go. Riccardo Tisci and everyone at Burberry it is beyond me how you could let a look resembling a noose hanging from a neck out on the runway. How could anyone overlook this and think it would be okay to do this especially in a line dedicated to

young girls and youth. The impressionable youth. Not to mention the rising suicide rates world wide. Let's not forget about the horrifying history of lynching either. There are hundreds of ways to tie a rope and they chose to tie it like a noose completely ignoring the fact that it was hanging around a neck. A massive brand like Burberry who is typically considered commercial and classy should not have overlooked such an obvious resemblance. I left my fitting extremely triggered after seeing this look (even though I did not wear it myself). Feeling as though I was right back where I was when I was going through an experience with suicide in my family. Also to add in they briefly hung one from the ceiling (trying to figure out the knot) and were laughing about it in the dressing room. I had asked to speak to someone about it but the only thing I was told to do was to write a letter. I had a brief conversation with someone but all that it entailed was 'it's fashion. Nobody cares about what's going on in your personal life so just keep it to yourself' well I'm sorry but this is an issue bigger than myself. A look so ignorantly put together and a situation so poorly handled. I am ashamed to have been apart of the show. #burberry. [*sic*.].[69]

On 19 February, Burberry chief executive Marco Gobbetti said he was 'deeply sorry for the distress' caused by the garment and advised that it had been removed from sale, along with all associated imagery.[70] He acknowledged the design was 'insensitive' but claimed its inspiration had been marine-based, and was not intentionally malevolent.[71] Tisci followed suit with a similarly worded apology.[72] As I opined at the time in an interview for *The Daily Beast* when asked about fashion's relationship with human death, '[w]hile Burberry said they were working a nautical theme, the presentation of the cord around the model's neck was suggestive of violence'.[73] Anglophone commentators from around the world described the garment as 'horrific' and 'disappointing'.[74] *The Huffington Post* refused to publish an image of the item in case it proved triggering, as Kennedy said it was for her.[75]

Kennedy criticized the brand and garment specifically for its invocation of suicide and lynching, but few commentators explored these complaints further. It is noteworthy that anglophone commentary on the controversy was characterized by list-like accounts of recent transgressions by fashion brands. Most articles compared this transgression to Gucci's so-called blackface sweater that had been the focus of media reports in the week prior to the Burberry show.[76] On social media, commentators followed suit. On Twitter, American writer Saaed Jones posted a link to CCN Style's article about the offending garment with the caption, 'Y'all have lost your goddamned minds'.[77] In a linked tweet, he posted a composite image of model Claudia Schiffer wearing different hairstyles and cosmetics. Two images depict her wearing blackface and yellowface. Jones encouraged people to append similarly offending images to his thread, presumably to provide a form of visual accountability for the fashion industry with the hope of atonement: 'Shout out to Karl Lagerfeld putting Claudia Schiffer in blackface AND yellowface in 2010. Do continue with your memorial posts.'[78] Whilst Kennedy's reference to lynching explicitly invoked racially motivated violence, in connecting this incident to the wearing of blackface, anglophone commentators, perhaps inadvertently, minimized the trauma signified by the noose-like fastening. The wearing of blackface and lynching are examples of racial ignorance and hatred, but they are not otherwise comparable. In blackface a black body is temporarily sequestered and typically trivialized by a white body.[79] In lynching, white people act in concert to violently traumatize and take the life of black people.[80]

The naïve reductionism evinced by the conflation of these two forms of racism is compounded by the equally limited acknowledgement of suicide, despite Kennedy's stern rebuke. An interview with Dr Antonis Kousoulis, associate director of research for the UK's Mental Health Foundation, was included in *The Huffington Post*'s report. It was reprinted by *The Independent*. Kousoulis explained that '[t]here are thousands of people who have been impacted by suicide. At the very least, brands should be thoughtful that images can be triggering,' but there was no analysis of this point.[81] Nor was there consideration of Kennedy's claim that global suicide rates were rising. The lack of analysis likely reflects the fact that suicide remains a taboo subject within the 'west'. Perhaps more than this, studies of suicide often appear to critique ways of living that have become characterized as part of modern 'western' society. In a comparative study of suicide, psychologist David Lester explains that attitudes to and instances of suicide vary considerably among and between the world's global cultures.[82] Nonetheless, in the twentieth and twenty-first centuries, '[l]ower suicide rates were found for nations with less economic development and where Islam was the dominant religion'.[83] Furthermore, his research establishes that there is an 'issue' with 'the impact of the pervasive western culture on the suicidal behaviour of those living in less modern cultures'.[84] In short, suicide appears to be a specific, and negative, consequence of modern 'western' values and social structures. Lester's findings resonate with echoes of the sociologist Émile Durkheim, who published *Le Suicide* in 1897, the first study of this social fact. Durkheim's undertaking was framed by his belief that suicide rates had increased significantly across Europe within the first half of the nineteenth century. Observing that '[a]t each moment in its history . . . each society has a definitive aptitude for suicide', he was concerned to understand why this 'aptitude' appeared marked at this moment in Europe's history.[85] During a time when 'western' social commentators, scientists and politicians were seeking to differentiate and protect their values and social structures from the people they had colonized, evidence of suicide rates appeared to indicate a troubling fault in their assumptions of infallibility. It is interesting to speculate if a similar concern to eschew difficult, dangerous information that hints at problems within the 'west's values persists. How far does journalistic silence about suicide and the expunction of the offending garments from Sarah Mower's *Vogue* article demonstrate an unwillingness to question 'western' values in the face of evidence that they might be harmful?[86]

Reflections

For many people around the world getting dressed is a natural, seemingly neutral, act because it is largely unselfconscious. Previous discussions suggest this is never the case. This chapter makes the point forcefully by highlighting the physical and psychological trauma that the pursuit of fashionable appearances, as defined by 'western' values, can cause. Two observations focus on the interpretation of fashion and what it communicates. There is a clearer articulation of the point raised in previous chapters that fashion communication, though imbricated within 'western' patterns of thought, is frequently ambiguous. In the case of Dolce & Gabbana's campaign, one person's assertion that inspiration derived from a Kubrik film seems patently incorrect, despite their surety. Simply put, this is an example of misinterpretation. However, it is a mistake that results from what appears to be a common methodological flaw in the decipherment of fashion shows that relies on visual, sometimes thematic, equivalence. In the case of Burberry's *Tempest*, journalists' interpretation was predicated on a comparison made with Gucci's *Cyborg*, which had also included an offensive garment, albeit one linked to race and not suicide. The problem of seeking sameness between different collections and campaigns is that anomalies and anxieties become more difficult to understand. But this may be the point. Finding similar examples makes an anomaly usual, or at the very least less irregular. Consequently, the need to explain something that may initially be troubling is lessened, if not wholly nullified. In short, given the various instances throughout this study where fashion commentary has lacked critique, where colloquial or jocular language has been used, and where, in the case of the disturbing topics raised by the episodes considered here – domestic violence, suicide and rape – there has been cursory commentary, a question could be asked: to what extent does fashion journalism exist to critique fashion? The query appears combative, but it is pertinent given the decision by *Vogue* to remove three looks from its online discussion of Burberry's *Tempest* without explanation. At the very least, the episodes emphasize fashion scholar Katie Baker Jones's point that 'fashion media players are integral to the process of importing meaning to fashion goods as they move from production to consumption'.[87] Fundamentally, it is also apparent that the 'theme of intellectualisation' within fashion journalism, which fashion scholar Aurélie Van de Peer claims to be more apparent within the genre from the later twentieth century, is not prevalent.[88] A second point, derived from this, is that the presentation of the three episodes and the discussions they sparked consider it axiomatic that fashion conveys 'western' norms. Without intending to suggest there is (always) conscious collusion, it is interesting to ponder how far the work of designers, brands and journalists within the fashion industry has developed to foster the elucidation of 'western' values.

9
SHAPE

In its edited and published form *Das Klaidungsbüchlein* (*The Little Clothes Book*) has been called *The First Book of Fashion*.[1] It was conceived and commissioned by Augsburg accountant Matthäus Schwarz and contains a series of hand-painted portraits by Narziss Renner of the banker's fashionable, expensive appearance between 1520, when he was twenty-three, and 1560, when he was sixty-three and a half.[2] The book includes two facing portraits of Schwarz undressed at the age of twenty-nine in 1526. The paintings were clearly conceived as a pair. In one image Schwarz's body faces towards the viewer. Leaning slightly to the right, his right arm is held away from his body, its hand slightly clasped. His left arm is bent at the elbow so its hand can cover his genitalia. In the second image, which shows him from behind, the pose is repeated, although Schwarz's body inclines to the left. The scrawling annotation Schwarz has made above this painting, that he 'had become fat and round', conveys a sense of shock, perhaps disgust, towards his body, as if he had been unaware of its changing shape.[3] The remark hints at social stigma, a concern about the thoughts and words of people regarding his self-perceived corpulence. The concealed genitalia presumably reflect Catholic qualms about human undress.[4] Historian Ulinka Rublack asserts that this 'deeply human' portrayal was innovatory.[5] 'No one had ever done this before.'[6] This isn't quite right. Whilst original in form, Schwarz's critical portraits were not unique in conception. Twenty years earlier, *c*. 1500–5, and 146km north, artist Albrecht Dürer produced a self-portrait of his undressed body. Art historian Norbert Wolf suggests this pen and brush drawing evinces a 'profoundly penetrating and merciless self-interrogation'.[7] His judgement is similar to that of Rublack's. She considers the self-centred depiction of Schwarz to be 'a specifically Western invention [that] occasioned new ways of exploring personhood – in the West, and soon in other parts of the world'.[8]

The timing of the Dürer and Schwarz portraits may be attributable to 'western' concerns during the first half of the sixteenth century, not least the questioning of Catholic doctrine and the social structures and values it buttressed, but their premise that a human body should conform to an idealized shape drew upon long-standing artistic and political principles that had been conceived in ancient Greece and consolidated during the European Renaissance of the fifteenth and sixteenth centuries.[9] Fundamentally, discourses about ideal body shape are not exclusive to the 'west' and exist in most global cultures. Often connected to faith, a person's physical shape has long determined their suitability for socialization and salvation. In Confucianism, Judaism, Islam, traditional religions within Africa, as well as Christianity, there are established associations between a person's departure from an expected norm through a physical disability, their perceived sinfulness and infantility.[10]

A narrative that emphasizes the peculiarity of 'western' attitudes about body shape is a consequence of the pervasiveness of the 'west's' body ideals in contemporary culture, a corollary of eighteenth- and nineteenth-century colonialism. Edward Enninful alluded to this narrative in his editor's letter for the May 2023 issue of British *Vogue* that featured nineteen disabled people and the assertive text, 'Dynamic, Daring & Disabled' on its cover. Reflecting on these people's lives, he questioned, 'we all engage with fashion, but does fashion engage with us?'[11] Insular reflection about the shape of the human body can be attributed to the 'west's' emphasis on reason, which has framed discussions about ideal humans and human communities since antiquity.[12] The ancient Greek philosopher Plato argued that a society's leaders should possess the highest amount of reason. Their mental acuity was to ensure dispassionate governance, which could involve the removal of people from a community, even by murder, if they were judged to be physically or psychologically deficient. Plato recommended laws to prevent the upbringing of crippled children.[13] The Twelve Tables, the font of ancient Rome law, obligated citizens to 'kill the baby visibly deformed; the monstrosity is impossible because it is not tolerated'.[14] Self-centred reflection about physical appearance can also be attributed to Christianity, which has been described as a human-oriented, and 'interior', faith.[15] Disability scholar Tim Stainton highlights biblical passages that reproached people with physical ailments – dwarves, hunchbacks, the blind, lame and mutilated (Lev. 21: 17–23) – from approaching God, although he argues that the doctrine of Grace offered some protection to disabled people.[16] Whilst reason and religious sentiments were not unique to the 'west' they were important in framing a way of thinking that came to peculiarize 'western' attitudes about ideal human bodies during the nineteenth century.

During a period when Europeans sought to clarify, classify, contain and control parts of the world they had incorporated into their empires, there was a need to demarcate inside and outside, the same from the other, and to erect boundaries, figurative and physical, to prevent despoliation of the former by the latter. Language contributed to this effort, so did statistics, which developed as a discipline during the nineteenth century. Disability scholar Lennard J. Davis opines that '[w]ith . . . statistics comes the idea of a norm'.[17] Previous chapters have argued that many of the fantasies and fears that imperialism presented were mapped on to the human body, physically, in terms of how it should look and behave, and conceptually, as a metaphor for society.[18] Reason and religion were used, sometimes spuriously, oftentimes uncritically, to legitimize these projections. A popular, invidious way of conveying these ideas was the so-called freak show. Communication about the 'physical Other' in the form of artistic depictions and exhibitions can be traced to the Stone Age, but American literature and culture scholar Andrea Zittlau asserts that public interest in the staging of 'abnormal bodies' became widely popular within the 'west' during the second half of the nineteenth century.[19] She contends that the exhibition of bodies that 'violated the rules of civilization' and the purposeful manipulation of fact and fantasy, science and spectacle to highlight people as atypical were a form of psychological salve that permitted 'western' audiences 'to view science at its limits and reassure [them] not only of the[ir] collective physical identity but also of their intellectual capacity'.[20] The proliferation of monsters in nineteenth-century literature, which included Frankenstein's Modern Prometheus, Quasimodo and Mr Hyde, served a similar purpose, although these figures also enabled their creators to question the morality of the expectant, expansionist society that was emerging in the 'west'.[21] The monstrous, derived from the Latin words for monster (*monstrum*) and warning (*admonitio*), was being used to substantiate the mundane.[22]

The presence of physical ailments and differences within societies encountered by Europeans, whether natural or the result of political and social practices, justified colonization and the ensuing process of civilization.[23] Motivated by their faith as much their confidence in being able to improve the lives of other people, European missionaries provided rudimentary support for the disabled. This assistance was decidedly double-edged. Scholar Shaun Grech explains how it entrenched European dominance and isolated disabled people still further, as their 'bodies were examined in isolation, including of their own history'.[24] Provisions within the colonies reflected developments within Europe. Commercialization, colonization and the classificatory imperatives that followed from both as people were increasingly defined and segregated by age, gender, race, sexuality and wealth had many consequences. At least two factors are germane to explain the 'west's' shifting concerns about the shape of the human body. First, increased evidence of social stratification catalyzed the work of social reformers whose aim, sometimes expressed condescendingly, was to narrow the gap between people who resided at the centre and periphery of society. This included greater support for the physically disabled.[25] During the eighteenth and nineteenth centuries new branches of medical support were conceived to support disabled people.[26] In regions beyond Europe, similar methods were adopted, partially to pre-empt European intervention, as was the case for the Ottoman Empire.[27] Second, increased consumption of foods and fashion within the 'west', and increasingly public and anxious discussions about body shape, framed by the Christian condemnation of gluttony, produced what historian Peter Stearns has termed a 'major new modern code' that valorized thinness.[28] During the nineteenth century the term 'calorie' was first associated with the energy capacity of foods; it had previously referred to a measurement of heat.[29] Medical concerns about weight gain lagged behind public qualms, but myriad products were produced and peddled to people who wanted to avoid perceptions of public shame.[30] Today, the consequence of being overweight and obese, conditions that define bodies with a mass index exceeding 25 or 30 respectively, are discussed more frankly. The World Health Organization asserts that 'globesity' 'is taking over many parts of the world'.[31] A 'social and environmental disease', the United Nations' claim of an obesity epidemic is largely a consequence of how human lives have changed since the nineteenth century.[32]

Elucidation of the 'west's' growing concerns about body shape during the nineteenth century is provided by contemporary responses to a particular argument made by naturalist Charles Darwin. Darwin's books *The Origin of the Species by Means of Natural Selection, or the Preservation of Favoured Races in the Struggle for Life*, published in 1859, and *The Descent of Man and Selection in Relation to Sex*, published in 1871, constitute a turning point in the 'west's' understanding and approach to the conception and ordering of human life, especially as they were interpreted by polymath Herbert Spencer, who coined the phrase 'survival of the fittest'.[33] For Zittlau, Darwin's ideas about natural selection were played out in the freak show.[34] His writings are conventionally interpreted as the legitimation *sine qua non* of contemporary scientific and social ideas that justified the superiority of white people, their values and social structures. In his discussion of physical beauty, however, Darwin pursued a highly original, even idiosyncratic, argument. Citing comments he gleaned from travellers' reports, which explained how people around the world responded to one another's physical appearance, he asserted that physical beauty was particular rather than universal. As evolutionary developmental biology scholar Armand Marie Leroi summarizes, Darwin believed that '[d]ifferent people in different parts of the world each have their own standard of beauty'.[35] This element of Darwin's theory, which challenged essentialist theories that were being defined during the eighteenth and nineteenth centuries to the benefit of white bodies and people, has never been widely adopted and was omitted from some academic discussions of his work.[36] Then, as now, beauty is generally considered to be a universal concept that conforms to 'western' ideals that were galvanized and globalized through empire. What this missing or marginalized aspect of Darwin's work demonstrates is that attitudes to the shape of the human body, and to disabilities, are, like all the concepts considered within this book, social constructs.[37] It emphasizes that the qualms 'western' people have had about the physical appearance of their bodies, whether it be Matthäus Schwarz in the sixteenth century or Americans in the nineteenth century, are contingent upon circumstances and, furthermore, that their global prevalence was not inevitable.

Darwin would likely be bemused, perhaps disappointed, even troubled by a *New Yorker* article of 2019 that describes the emergence of Instagram Face. Journalist Jia Tolentino explains that this female visage, which is 'ambiguously ethnic', is a composite image of the face filters and most-liked portraits from the social media platform. She describes it as 'a young face, of course, with poreless skin and plump, high cheekbones. It has catlike eyes and long, cartoonish lashes; it has a small, neat nose and full, lush lips'.[38] It displays an 'algorithmic tendency to flatten everything into a composite of greatest hits [that] had resulted in a beauty ideal that favored white women capable of manufacturing a look of rootless exoticism'.[39] The fantastic allure of Instagram Face elides with anthropologist Joanne Finkelstein's point, informed by the work of sociologist Jean Baudrillard, that 'the social value of beauty in the contemporary era is unrelated to any ideals of physical attractiveness but is, instead, attached to the means by which the individual has been able to secure such an appearance of beauty or attractiveness'.[40] This commodification of the body leads Finkelstein to suggest, pessimistically, that people in the 'west', and those who adhere to 'western' mandates about body shape, have a 'contingent self' that 'demonstrates time and time again how little we value the contemplative and how much we value the performative. This view shows that the modern self is contingent, that in the authenticating narrative of the contemporary epoch, it has no enduring substance, it is simply treated as an icon'.[41] Finkelstein's argument has echoes of Guy Debord's concerns about the proliferation of signs over signification.

Pursuing a similar approach to the previous chapter, the three episodes considered here – Brazilian *Vogue*'s November 2020 body positivity cover shoot with singers Duda Beat and Preta Gil and model Rita Carreira; French *GQ*'s March 2021 cover shoot with model Grant Douglas and the launch of the world's first non-binary avatar, Catty 8.1, in June 2021 – draw upon earlier discussions to consider the consequences of 'western' attitudes to body shape. The inclusion of Catty 8.1 provides an opportunity to ponder how future fashions will be shaped by 'western' ideas as we move into digital spaces where the concept of bodies, human or otherwise – or even at all – is being negotiated.

Duda Beat, Preta Gil and Rita Carreira cover shoot, Brazilian *Vogue*, November 2020

The November 2020 print issue of Brazilian *Vogue*, guest edited by influencer and *Vogue* contributor Juliana Ferraz, was published with three variant covers that featured portraits of prominent Brazilian women: singers Duda Beat and Preta Gil and model Rita Carreira. The images, taken by photographer Fernando Tomaz and directed by Pedro Sales, were connected through the theme of body positivity. The bodies of Beat, Carreira and Gil are distinctive for being larger than conventional *Vogue* cover stars. Ferraz asserted that they were published 'without any touches or tricks', but they are stylistically similar.[42] The cover stars all wear monochrome garments by Dior, with Carreira and Gil wearing matching houndstooth. Each woman wears a hat, dark lipstick and eyeliner. There are some unique styling choices: Carreira wears temporary tattoos, Beat embodies the singer Madonna. Images of the women feature the same backdrop of crashing waves and a single prop, a miniature white Doric column. An identical waist-height column appears in the covers of Duda and Gil, which is respectively sat upon and leant over. By contrast, Carreira stands on a column base. The cover layouts are also comparable. The 'g' of *Vogue* has been removed from each to enable the central placement of a full-height portrait of the women. The caption '*A cantora/modelo fazode ao corpo livre*' (The singer/model frees the body) appears on each cover along with the woman's surname. All text is formatted in a red serif font.

Articles within the magazine include summarized interviews with the cover stars, who reflect upon their experiences, often dispiriting, of achieving professional success against a backdrop of fatphobia. Beat considers the pressures of conforming to 'western' fashion conventions, although she does not label them as such:

> 'I was always a chubby teenager. I fell in love with the boys, and they chose the slimmer ones', she recalls, who years later, still feeling pressured, ended up surrendering to cosmetic procedures and put silicone in her breasts. 'Today I wonder to what extent it is worth giving in to the pressures for a norm that, in the end, is not even a genuine desire of ours? Everyone has the freedom to do what they want, but I think it is important to question whether they are doing it for you or to please the other', she warns. And she reflects: 'Free body is this: if you love yourself the way you are and don't follow rules that don't make sense to you. Fashion is there to serve us. And not the other way around.'[43]

Gil also speaks of having 'mutilated' (*mutilato*) her body with surgeries because of a compulsion to conform to prevalent beauty canons.[44] In her interview, Carreira discusses the challenges of being black and fat:

> 'Being fat will never be more difficult than being black, but I make a point of carrying on discussions about fat phobia. Nobody thinks how this unfolds in health, for example, while obese people do not have access to hospital equipment to support their weights', she explains.[45]

Asserting that she does not 'put [herself] in any situation that can impose any change on my body', Carreira nonetheless discusses how she altered her body's physical appearance, and continues to do so, explaining that she wears wigs to enable her to have straight hair.[46] In an interview with online magazine *Universa*, she had previously spoken of purposefully gaining weight to become a plus size model.[47]

Ostensibly, text and images within the magazine present a powerful message of body positivity, but there is no explicit consideration of the pervasiveness of 'western' attitudes towards acceptable body shapes that frame the varied experiences of the cover stars. On Instagram, where Brazilian *Vogue* published images of the three magazine covers in consecutive posts on 3 November 2020, viewers' written responses highlighted the tension. One person, responding to Gil's cover image, suggested that her previous surgeries made her a less authentic advocate for body positivity:

Faz ode ao corpo livre, mas não aceita seu próprio corpo. Se submeteu a inúmeras plásticas e lipoaspiração, sempre tentando parecer mais magra. Vá entender esse empoderamento.[48]
[She is an ode to the free body, but does not accept her own body. She has undergone countless plastic surgeries and liposuction, always trying to look thinner. Go figure out this empowerment.]

A chief concern of many commentators was the disparity between the stated purpose of the issue, to promote body positivity, and the perceived values of *Vogue* as a fashion brand. Misgivings were manifest in people's suspicion that the cover images had, contrary to claims, been edited:

Ela se aceita, pois suas fotos publicadas nas redes sociais dela são naturais, sem Photoshop.
Mas parece q vcs revistas, n aceitam de verdade. . .olha o tanto de tratamento q fizeram nessa foto, ficou outra pessoa!
[She accepts herself, because her photos published in her social networks are natural, without Photoshop.
But it seems that you magazines, do not really accept . . . look at the amount of treatment they did in this photo, it turned out to be someone else!]

Kkkk.. cheio de photoshop😂[49]
[Lol . . . full of photoshop😂][50]

A cantora faz ode ao corpo livre. A REVISTA NÃO 👎👎👎👎
[The singer makes an ode to the free body. THE MAGAZINE DOES NOT 👎👎👎👎][51]

Questions were also raised about the use of fake tattoos on Carreira's body:

I understand posting a positive body image but why add the fake tattoos? Being tattooed is a lifestyle it's not clothing it's not something you take off at the end of the day.⁵²

A capa tá bem bonita, mas so uma pergunta, porque não uma tatuada real?! Há tanto model tatuado que tem duas [sic.] tattoos apagadas por clientes em Photoshop.

Parabéns mais uma vez pela capa.

[The cover is very nice, but just one question, why not a real tattooed woman?! There are so many tattooed models that have [their] tattoos erased by Photoshop clients.

Congratulations again for the cover.]⁵³

The occlusion of any explicit acknowledgement of the 'west's' influence on body shape and appearance is most apparent in the presentation of the cover portraits, which feature white Doric columns. Inadvertently, perhaps, but no less instantly, this prop situates the images in relation to Grecian statuary and its interpretation during the nineteenth century to valorize 'western' concepts about the appearance of an idealized human body. One commentator on Instagram also remarked on the women's poses, which mimic those of 'western' fashion images and are themselves redolent of Classical artforms:

Fotos cheias de pose que afinam a silhueta, roupas que dão a impressão de mais magra, posições que valorizam as curvas e escondem as gordurinhas! Isso é aceitar a gordura? Ou seja, HIPOCRISIA!!😒

[Pictures full of poses that slim the silhouette, clothes that give the impression of being thinner, positions that enhance the curves and hide the fat! Is this accepting fat? In other words, HYPOCRISY!😒]⁵⁴

There were three orders, or standard forms, of architectural column within ancient Greece. Doric was the earliest.⁵⁵ Sheena Wagstaff, chair of the department of modern and contemporary art at the Metropolitan Museum of Art, New York, explains that a 'western' assumption that these structures and the statuary that appeared alongside them had initially been white, as they were in their rediscovered form, was a 'misidentification'.⁵⁶ They would have originally been polychromatic. Nonetheless, colour-blindness became an orthodoxy within the 'west': 'This perception, which defined the Western artistic canon as it was created and sanctioned during the Renaissance, persisted well into the nineteenth century and notably inspired the eschewal of practices that could be seen as too real.'⁵⁷ The point is important in understanding the placement of the truncated white Doric columns in the *Vogue* portraits because it evidences that 'western' sentiments, even those linked to ancient architecture, continue to loom large in the twenty-first century. Paraphrasing Wagstaff, whose analysis is informed by the nineteenth-century art historian Jacob Burckhardt, the appearance of this prop in Tomaz's shoot could be said to demonstrate 'an "egotism" [that] pervade[s] European art and culture to the exclusion of other cultures worldwide'.[58] So pervasive and exclusionary is this egotism that it is reflected in the work of a non-European photographer who questions expectations of the human body's appearance that stem from 'western' values. The egotism evinced by the choice of prop appears even more pernicious considering art historian Aileen Ribeiro's observation that the body form most idealized by the Greeks was male, rather than female.[59]

The influence of 'western' aesthetics on Tomaz's cover shoot is also apparent in the decision for Duda Beat to 'embody' (*encarna*) Madonna. To effect this transformation Beat's hair has been dyed partially blonde and styled to imitate the singer's peroxide curls from the 1980s. A mole, which Madonna extenuated during the first decades of her career, has been drawn between the upper lip and right nostril on Beat's face. A short, silent and looping video of Beat, which focuses on her face, involves her mouthing words, presumably lyrics from one of Madonna's songs, and moving her hands in a sensual manner, as if she were dancing.[60] No editorial content explains the reference to Madonna or the curious phrase *encarna*, which seems misplaced in an issue seeking to encourage body positivity. The Portuguese language can express the concept of imitation and impersonation (*para imitar*), which implies a superficial, temporary homage, so the decision to refer to embodiment and suggest the effacement of Beat's identity seems an unsettling oversight. Beat's embodiment of Madonna also gives lie to Juliana Ferraz's remark that the images of the women were presented 'without any touches or tricks'. Madonna's mole is on the right side of her face, as it is on Beat's in the short film. However, on the cover of the magazine, the mole appears on the left side of the singer's face. This either means the cover portrait includes an image of Beat that has been flipped, or the mole was added to the other side of her face for this photograph. In any case, editorial changes have been made, presumably to make her appearance elide with the editorial team's expectations of how a cover model should appear.

Fundamentally, the decision of a Brazilian woman to 'embody' a white woman conflates ideas of body shape and appearance with Brazil's freighted history of race. Interestingly, these issues were explicitly referenced in the digital issue of Brazilian *Vogue* published in December 2020, one month after the body positivity issue featuring Beat. Questions about the race and skin colour of the unborn child of the digital cover star, ballerina Ingrid Silva, were framed by the country's history of *branqueamento* (whitening) or *embranquecimento* (racial whitening).[61]

Negative comments about the cover portraits indicate that some people within Brazil, and around the world, felt uneasy about the images, but even direct comments, about poses that slim the silhouette, the use of fake tattoos and Photoshop, remain generic. The triggering issue remains unspecified. In short, it is as though the pervasiveness of 'western'-centrism, which frames the cover shoot and perhaps more broadly notions of body size and appearance within Brazil, creates a situation where there is insufficient scope for a more comprehensive critical appraisal to be made. Whilst some people did question *Vogue*'s motives, many more appear to have regarded the brand and its publication as a neutral messenger, conveying self-evident, if troubling, realities. Consequently, the magazine's communication about body shape was received and accepted in good faith even when people could not reconcile all parts of it to their lived experiences. The fact that people within Brazil do believe *Vogue* possesses authority to express, and influence, social mores is evidenced by comments from two Instagram users, approving of the November issue, who suggested the publication was seeking to challenge a 'standard' (*padrão*) by acknowledging a 'new normal' (*novo normal*):

> *Ah!!! Ler e ver sobre atitudes assim, nos enche de coragem. Quantas pessoas se sentem mal com o seu corpo por não seguir um padrão que não condiz com a realidade das mulheres?! O padrão tem q ser desmascarado. . .*
> [Ah!!! Reading about and seeing attitudes like this fills us with courage. How many people feel bad about their bodies for not following a standard that does not match the reality of women? The standard has to be unmasked. . .]
>
> *Que bom que a Vogue está atualizando o 'novo normal'!*[62]
> [Glad Vogue is updating the 'new normal'!][63]

The 'standard' and 'normal' being referenced is not clarified, but as these remarks respond to the cover images of Beat and Carreira respectively, it is apparent the authors endorse the magazine's attempt to dismantle hegemonic views about body shape. A corollary of these comments is that as much as *Vogue*'s perceived authority can dismantle dominant social attitudes, so too can it reinforce them. Neither agenda is mutually exclusive, which the use of the white Doric column and the channelling of Madonna demonstrate. Cultural and fashion scholar Djurdja Bartlett explains that 'serving the existing social and economic order, fashion pretends to participate in the traumas of the Other, keeping instead a safe distance in order not to alienate its well-off customers'.[64] The simultaneity of empowerment and disempowerment is paradoxical and can appear unsettling, but it has become more apparent within the contemporary fashion industry as brands seek to demonstrate cognizance of identity politics and eschew many of the social binaries that dress and appearance traditionally manifest and galvanize.[65] This point is explored further in discussion of France *GQ*'s cover shoot for March 2021.

Grant Douglas cover shoot, French *GQ*, March 2021

The March 2021 print issue of French *GQ* features a cover shoot with 27-year-old American model Grant Douglas photographed by James Brodribb. The cover portrait is cropped mid-thigh. Douglas looks directly towards the camera and stands in a contrived position that confounds expectations of a 'western' cover model. His body inclines to the left, his torso stretches upwards, his head is raised, he leans slightly back. Douglas's right arm is elevated, bent at the elbow, with his hand placed behind his right ear and head. His left arm, also bent at the elbow, is positioned at his side, away from the body. Douglas wears a snap back, a white crew-neck T-shirt and a thin madras overshirt. The right elbow of the shirt is patched, its cuff torn and frayed. The look is completed with a pair of beige khakis. Douglas wears a brown leather key fob around his neck; the pouch, which contains several brass keys, hangs across his stomach. The pose Douglas adopts causes his T-shirt to lift, exposing a section of his abdomen, which protrudes over the waist band of the trousers. The cover text, written in white sans serif capitals, proclaims: '*BIEN DANS SON CORPS: LE NOUVEAU COOL*' (HAPPY IN HIS BODY: THE NEW COOL).

The magazine's editor in chief, Olivier LaLanne, explained that Douglas had been found through Instagram.[66] The decision to make him their first anonymous cover model (*le premier cover boy anonyme*) was driven by a desire to 'end of decades of normative tyranny and conditioning' (*pour siffler la fin de décennies de tyrannie normative et de conditionnement*) concerning the human body's acceptable appearance.[67] In his interview within the magazine, Douglas explains the anguish he felt gaining weight because of his height: 'when you're as tall as I am [1.96 metres] and gain weight, you become even more <<out of the norm>> in other people's eyes'.[68] LaLanne acknowledges that most men's magazines encourage 'a singular model' (*d'un modèle unique*) of male appearance and masculinity that is symbolized by 'a gleaming sixpack' (*un Sixpack rutilant*).[69] He concedes that men's fashion publications lag behind women's magazines that have been 'spearheading a crusade against overly normative representations of the body and beauty' for several years (*ardent fers de lannce d'une croisade contre les représentations trop normées du corps et de la beauté*).[70]

The language of the editorial and interview appear hyperbolic. Douglas is described as sage and heroic: '*Grant le sage fait figure de héros*'.[71] On the one hand, this reflects the emotive nature of discussions about body shape. An article in the magazine summarizes conversations with fat men who recount stories of bullying and stigma.[72] On the other hand, the dramatic language, which invokes the 'crusade', demonstrates the pervasiveness of 'western' ideas about body shape because they frame both the shaming of fat people and the support that is offered to them. A crusade might signify the resolve of the fashion industry to reappraise socialized attitudes to the body, but it remains a problematic term, linked to ignorance, intolerance and an inflexibility of thought that has long defined how human bodies should look and behave. The tension between what is meant, said and written about fat bodies in the magazine is apparent from some of the responses appended to Douglas's cover image on *GQ France*'s Instagram. People queried whether the cover shoot constituted a change or gesture:

> *Il va falloir pl's d'une couverture et d'articles pour se placer en initiateur d'un mouvement "Body Postitive" au masculin et se permettre de faire la leçon aux autres en édito... On tient le bon bout quand même!*[73]
> [It's going to take more than one cover and articles to position yourself as the initiator of a 'Body positive' movement for men and allow yourself to lecture others in an editorial..... We're on the right track though!]

> *Sage décision mais sa sincérité dépendra des numéros suivants. 'Si c'est comme dans ELLE qui met une femme ronde en couverture tous les trois ans en se focalisant le reste du temps sur la minceur,' ça n'aura pas servi à grand chose à part avoir fait le buzz. On compte sur vous GQ!*[74]
> [A wise decision but its sincerity will depend on the following issues. If it's like *ELLE* that puts a curvy woman on the cover every three years and focuses on thinness the rest of the time, it won't have served much purpose except to have created a buzz. We count on you *GQ*!]

These remarks echo misgivings about Brazilian *Vogue*'s body positivity issue. Reader's perceived there to be a tension between the magazines' association with valorizing 'western' beauty and body norms and their claim to support exceptions to this narrative. The sincerity of *GQ*'s editors was questioned in the anglophone online forum *The Fashion Spot*. Amidst positive comments, including some that suggested Douglas looked 'hot', there was concern that the shoot's styling was 'lazy'.[75] One commentator queried why he had not received the 'same type of H[igh] F[ashion] styling a top male model would've gotten?' He looks like your average American on his way to or coming from a 'game'.[76] Another wondered if the magazine was deliberately playing to a stereotype:

> The styling with the torn shirt, exposed gut, keychain-worn-as-necklace, and what appears to be some sort of khaki cargo pant definitely feels very much like an unflattering American 'bro' stereotype.[77]

There is a concern within these comments that Douglas's casual appearance could be perceived as lacklustre, which would catalyze a long-standing and negative stereotyping of fat people, defeating the purpose of the issue.[78] Another forum participant took a different stance. Ostensibly bypassing the topic of body positivity, they criticized the cover image and interior portraits of Douglas because the casual styling and portrait appeared 'average'. This was diametrically opposed to the aspiration they believed fashion magazines exist to instil:

> Average images should not be on the cover of FASHIONNNNNNNNN magazines sorry. It hurts my eyes seeing this gosh. Where's the luxury? Where's the passion for fashion? W'ere's the aspirational factors???[79]

Discussion of Douglas's apparently unfashionable appearance could reflect an attitude to fat that is either more prevalent in France or at least perceived as being so. In his loosely comparative study of American and French attitudes to fat, Stearns suggests that since the late nineteenth century, when affluent 'western' people became increasingly anxious about the appearance and effects of gaining weight, doctors and social commentators had been less inclined to link 'fighting overweight and combating the evils of a consumer society' in France than they were in the United States.[80] There was a social pressure to appear beautiful in France, particularly for women, but less shame and guilt was attached to fat than was the case across the Atlantic.[81] Assuming this way of thinking became socialized within, and about, France, it may account for the bewilderment expressed about Douglas's cover shoot. First, Douglas's clothes, styled to deliberately reveal his abdomen, highlight a topic that may not resonate so deeply and urgently as a contemporary issue within France as it does the United States. Second, in revealing his abdomen and appearing to prioritize comfort in his choice of clothes, *GQ*'s cover seems to adopt a position that not only runs counter to how fashion is conceived and created within France but also challenges how people assume fashion is conceived and created within France. Many of the comments on *The Fashion Spot* express confusion about why a French fashion magazine would be espousing a way of life more conventionally associated with the United States. One blogger even questions if the magazine was 'taking the mickey out of Americans':

> He's just built like an American footballer or a Rugby player, so at least in American GQ, men like him are a dime a dozen,
>
> . . . I hope they're seriously trying to have a conversation and not just taking the mickey out of Americans, lol.
>
> . . . I had hope after the debut issue but now it's look like they following their awful direction of their U[S] edition. Is there of plus size French actors available? Is there no budget around this time? [*sic.*]

That's why part of me thinks it's so shady. Let's do a splashy cover about men's body positivity, but let's get an American instead which ironically otherise the movement for GQ Fr readers. They're so true to form with the shade, lol. [*sic.*][82]

Cumulatively, these comments suggest *GQ*'s decision to spotlight Grant Douglas was not only perceived by some people to be un-French, it was unremarkable. It was interpreted as evidence of syndicated magazines – in this case, those owned by Condé Nast – producing regional derivations that published similar content. Potentially important contemporary issues consequently became anodyne because of their cursory treatment and presentation to ambivalent audiences. Whilst the remarks made in the forum may constitute a broad critique of the fashion industry's 'western'-centrism, they could indicate specific misgivings about Condé Nast's move to appoint global editorial directors from December 2020.[83] This change of leadership is not mentioned in the discussions about Douglas's shoot, but the appointment of Will Welch, editor in chief of American *GQ*, to Global Editor Director may go some way to explain the concerns about the Americanization of French *GQ* sparked by this issue.

The negative implications of such a narrow cultural perspective were emphasized by one forum commentator, who speculated that an Asian male on the cover would have had a more positive impact:

I wonder when people would come to realize that subcategorizing each and everything in [an] American way just create[s] controversy[,] which leads to chao[s] rather than provide solutions[.] And yeah[,] if these global editions would dare to put an Asian male subject to their perspective value of beauty[, i]t might be more interesting.[84]

Ostensibly, the solution proposed here would redress the grievances made by other forum users, but in all likelihood they would persist. This is because although the critical comments appear to rue *GQ*'s presentation of Douglas, their inclination to interpret his images with reference to conventional 'western' male stereotypes that include his physical build, athleticism and attire suggests their unselfconscious commitment to a hegemonic masculinity, which fashion scholar Ben Barry describes as 'the most exalted form of masculinity in a society that works to legitimize unequal power relations between men and women and also among men'.[85] In short, in appearing as a 'normal' American man – an 'American footballer', an 'American "bro"' – Douglas was judged as a 'normal' man. Had he adopted Barry's notion of fabulous masculinities, which is informed by the writing of cultural critic Madison Moore, it is interesting to speculate how the reaction would have differed.

Barry asserts that 'fabulousness diminishes the allure and power of hegemonic masculinity through original looks on bodies that cannot be classified into binary gender categories'.[86] He cites Moore, who explains how '[t]he brilliance of fabulousness as an embodied aesthetic . . . actually exposes the bland, boring nature of rote masculinity [that] lets us tap out of toxic masculinity'.[87] Consequently, it inhibits the connection of 'clothes and bodies with specific masculine archetypes, such as "the cowboy" (i.e., denim jacket, snap-front shirt, paisley bandana) and the "Ivy Leaguer" (i.e., varsity jacket, button-down shirt and khaki pants)', which is what commentators of Douglas's shoot were doing.[88] In conceiving of fabulousness, Madison is primarily thinking of 'eccentric style' that is 'dangerous' and a 'spectacle', but interpreted through Barry's research about fat and disabled bodies, it can be present wherever people seek to defy 'the fashion industry and society's regulation' through their dress and appearance.[89] Had Brodribb's images of Douglas done this, it may be that responses would have been more expansive and accepting.

The world's first non-binary avatar, Catty 8.1, June 2021

On 28 June 2021, the Institute of Digital Fashion (IoDF) and 3D content and software company Daz3D released 'the world's first [white] non-binary and photorealistic double, Catty 8.1, for Pride' to coincide with the anniversary of the Stonewall riots in New York City in 1969.[90] The avatar bundle was immediately available to purchase from Daz3D's online marketplace for $44.95.[91] The launch was announced in three consecutive posts on IoDF's Instagram account that described Catty 8.1 as a 'gender non-conforming digital double of IoDF's Creative Director & Co-Founder', Cattytay.[92] In each of the images, which are styled to resemble a fashion portrait, Catty has a different appearance.

The first portrait is cropped to focus on Catty's upper body and face. They are undressed. Their arms are raised; the right is positioned behind their head, the left in front of it. Catty's gaze is fixed on an indeterminate space, beyond the viewer. They wear blue eyeshadow, its edges blurred to create a smoky effect, deep red glossy lipstick and what appears to be a beauty mark high on their right cheek. Catty's face appears whiter than the rest of her skin, which may also be the result of cosmetics. The lobes and tragus of their ears are pierced with multiple, small silver-coloured loops. They wear an indistinct tattoo on their right arm. Catty has hair under their arms and a dense, neatly trimmed moustache that follows the line of their upper lip.[93] Their body hair, which is dark brown, matches the colour of their head hair, which is cut short and worn in a three-quarter parting. The text, 'IoDF Institute of Digital Fashion w/ Daz3D; Catty 8.1: A digital double in celebration of Pride month', is written across the portrait in a white sans serif font.

The second portrait also focuses on Catty's upper body and head. Their arms are again raised. They adopt the pose of a weightlifter performing a chest press. They wear a black crew-neck sleeveless top. On their lower left arm they have a monochrome tattoo of a tiger; on their upper right arm, they have a monochrome tattoo of a non-binary humanoid, which has two horns protruding from either side of its head. Their left hand is clothed in a black leather glove that is trimmed with white stitching and decorated with silver-coloured, cone-shaped rhinestones. They wear earrings, but no cosmetics; the colour of Catty's face more obviously corresponds to that of their body. They do not look directly at the viewer. Their glance is cast downwards, and they stick out their tongue in a playful gesture that may connect with the image's caption, written in capitals, 'CATTY 8.1: BIG DYKE ENERGY'.[94]

The third portrait released on 28 June is a three-quarter length portrait of Catty, cropped just below the groin. They wear a pair of loose-fitting black jeans but are otherwise undressed. More tattoos can be seen on Catty's body: they wear tattoos on the upper and lower parts of both of their arms and have two stylized line designs below each breast. Their nipples have been blurred by a skin-coloured rectangle. Their breasts are further obscured by the placement of text in front of them, which replicates that from the first portrait. Catty does not wear cosmetics or a moustache. Akin to the other images, their direction of sight looks beyond the viewer.[95] A different portrait of Catty 8.1, in monochrome, announced the avatar's launch on Daz3D's Instagram account. Focusing, again, on the avatar's upper body and head, the portrait shows Catty wearing a hooded sweatshirt. Studs are worn in their left ear and right nostril; hoop rings are worn in their lower lip and sternum. They hold their hands clenched and raised in front of their body. The webbing worn over them suggests they are boxing.[96]

The online fashion communication platform *SHOWStudio* placed the creation of the Catty 8.1 avatar on an evolving trajectory of digital fashion exploration that had commenced with catwalk shows by Alexander McQueen and Lady Gaga's 'slew of little monsters [that] broke the internet'.[97] The partnership between IoDF and Daz3d would 'further the promotion of digital diversity to ensure underrepresented communities in the physical world are not left behind in the digital world'.[98] According to its creators, the avatar was designed by a team of largely queer developers 'to represent queer voices and represent them in the digital sphere'.[99] The perceived need for equity within digital spaces was framed by an online diversity survey undertaken by IoDF in 2021 that involved 6000 global participants and five semi-structured interviews.[100] In a report that presented the survey's main findings, co-founder of IoDF Leanne Elliott opined, 'it is clear that current options are not doing enough to represent people who do not conform to biased, superficial and capitalist societal norms.'[101] Participants' responses, so far as they related to body shape, are more equivocal than this punchy summary suggests.

The survey established that participants' engagement with digital worlds had increased 68 per cent during the Covid-19 pandemic.[102] Their main reason for entering a digital space was 'escapism', although a connection with reality remained strong: 'There was a dual importance of both reality and imagination, accuracy and fantasy.'[103] If participants wanted to represent themselves in 'numerous, potentially conflicting ways – creatively, accurately, uniquely and imaginatively', they did not want their real world identities to be wholly effaced.[104] Retaining their appearance and shape as a human was important. Seventy per cent of participants claimed that gender representation was 'vital' to them in a digital space.[105] Here, there is an interesting echo from the sixteenth century and Matthäus Schwarz. Whilst he reacted to his painted body with shock, he nonetheless valued it as his 'proper figure'.[106] Participants were also wary about crossing the threshold into a digital arena and relinquishing disabilities that had come to frame their physical lives. Whilst not all survey participants identified as having a disability, and expressed misgivings about speaking for a community they did not represent, others identified the importance of 'avatar customisation options that take into account bodily differences, limb difference, mobility aids such as canes and wheelchairs, and clinical equipment such as oxygen tanks'.[107] The desire for real-world accuracy and the retention of physical supports for a disability that would be wholly symbolic in a digital space are complicated by the fact that 60 per cent of participants voiced concerns about 'the potential for bullying and discrimination against disabled people within virtual worlds'.[108] This paradoxical finding evidences a common-sense critique by design and material scholars Juyeon Park and Jennifer Paff Ogle; namely, that 'we know relatively well the factors that influence a person's body image in the real world, [but] are still discovering the mechanisms associated with the construct of body image in virtual space'.[109]

The tension between reality and recreation, and the extent to which the binaries considered in previous chapters shape the conception and creation of avatars, are apparent from the presentation of Catty 8.1 by IoDF and Daz3D, in three respects. First, within their online marketplace, Daz3D suggest that 'Compatible Figures' to Catty are 'Genesis 8.1 Female'.[110] The implication is that this non-binary avatar was constructed from a female template. Second, the physical appearance of Catty 8.1 is recognizably female. The censorship of their nipples in the third Instagram portrait responds to 'western' qualms about female undress.[111] Third, in the second Instagram portrait, the caption 'BIG DYKE ENERGY' associates Catty 8.1 with a specific gendered and sexual label. Linguistics scholar Richard Spears suggests the term 'dyke' is 'usually glossed as 'lesbian' or 'an aggressive, mannish lesbian', or a 'mannish woman'.[112] This bellicose and masculine characterization is emphasized in the portrait because Catty is shown wearing black, has studded gloves and adopts a pose – sticking out their tongue and performing what might be termed a victory pose: arms outstretched either side of their body, raised upwards at the elbow, and with fists clenched. In popular culture the wearing of a moustache above their upper lip by men and the absence of other facial hair have also had associations with homosexuality since the late twentieth century.[113]

To suggest that the creation of Catty 8.1 has been framed, however inadvertently, by 'western' cultural expectations of dress and appearance is a critical comment. It is not a criticism. The recognizability of the avatar's appearance may help to explain people's responses to the Instagram portraits of Catty, all of which were positive. Many people appeared to consider the creation of the avatar a turning point, although it is unclear to what extent they were referring to the technical accomplishment of Catty or its social importance in promoting digital diversity. Most comments consisted solely of emoticons. Some views were unequivocal ('😻🏳️‍🌈🙀'[114] and 'Damn 😍 so realistic it's mad!🔥'[115]), but the majority were unspecific:

👏👏👏👏[116]

ICONIC[117]

Amazing 🔥🔥[118]

😍😍😍[119]

This is wayyyy too cool[120]

In accordance with findings from IoDF's diversity survey, the positive reception of Catty 8.1 may be a gauge of how far their appearance conforms with social expectations of a non-binary person's self-presentation. Whilst the avatar can be considered innovatory for being the world's first non-binary avatar, it is nonetheless sufficiently realistic and similar to a human's appearance to be readily understood and accepted. At a time when the virtual presentation of human beings remains in its infancy, fidelity to real-world bodily appearances within a digital space is important. Research undertaken by Park and Ogle that considers people's responses to their virtual avatar 'based on actual body dimensional information' underscores the IoDF survey's discovery that there is a close correlation between a person's perception of their physical self and their virtual self.[121] Moreover, this relationship is not straightforward. Park and Ogle observe that '[p]articipants shared diverse responses to the experience of engaging with their clothed virtual avatars, characterizing the experience as "weird", "cool", and "pleasantly surprising" and suggesting that the experience prompted a range of emotions, including comfort, nervousness, and self-consciousness'.[122] They explain that 'not all participants regarded their avatars in a "singular" way (i.e., as patently "better" or "worse" than their "real" bodies').[123] The experiment was limited to 18- to 21-year-old females from the United States with 'body image concerns', so its results are interesting more than they are indicative.

The findings are, nonetheless, important for emphasizing the disparity between real and recreated versions of self. Participants' experience of seeing their virtual avatar ultimately resulted in 'some positively-charged self-body perceptions, increased body confidence/acceptance, and enhanced self-esteem /self-esteem-related traits', even if many people initially believed their digital double fell short of an idealized or obligated body shape and appearance.[124] The rehabilitation of people's views was due to the intervention of a 'body positivity program[me]' that formed part of the experiment.[125] The programme comprised four biweekly classes that enabled participants to '(a) appreciate an inclusive conceptualization of beauty, (b) develop media literacy skills, (c) develop self- esteem and skills to proactively cope with or filter negative body image information, and (d) create messages of body acceptance and self-compassion'.[126] The impact of these educational sessions was reportedly mixed, but they enabled some participants to reconcile, seemingly to overcome, initially negative responses to their digital double.[127] This conclusion is important because it emphasizes how socialized attitudes frame notions of how a human body should appear. It also demonstrates that these values are carried across the threshold into digital spaces.

Reflections

The physical and figurative shape of the human body bears the imprint of all the binaries considered in this book. Fittingly for a final chapter, two observations that distil remarks made at the close of previous chapters can be offered. First, 'western' values frame the conception and creation of a fashionable, more fundamentally acceptable, body shape and appearance. These values are so ingrained that they are not only unquestioned in some instances but also unobserved. The use of Doric columns in the Brazilian *Vogue* shoot, which associate the cover portraits with ideas totally opposed to their purpose, indicates how 'western' values can be considered neutral when the contrary is closer to actual their impact. Second, the three episodes highlight the dynamic tension between fantasy and reality. This tussle is acute as fashion enters the digital space because the (unwritten) social rules for negotiating what constitutes a person's fashionable shape and appearance can, if people desire it, be wholly recast. Interestingly, the creation of Catty 8.1 suggests there is an aversion to change these rules too much. The binaries that have come to frame 'western' people's understanding of their public selves cause physical and psychological pain, as the three episodes here and those discussed in previous chapters attest, but they also confer security by helping them to navigate who they are. This book has considered various paradoxes and uncomfortable realities, and this could be the root of them all: It has become convention – it is certainly convenient – to demonize the 'western' fashion industry for manifesting and maintaining social binaries and the inequalities they cultivate, but in contemplating the future we – especially those of us in the 'west' – should be cognizant of the past and reflect that the fashion industry exists as we have made it.

CONCLUSION

The essentialist paradigms, the binaries that form the focus of this book, are not unique to the 'west'. Their global omnipotence was not inevitable. Within Egypt, for example, sometime around 3500 BCE, the burial of male dwarves in royal tombs evidences a preoccupation with body shape.[1] Within Mayan civilization, dress distinguished people by gender and wealth from at least the seventh century.[2] Social critic Minna Salami follows philosopher Sophie Bosede Oluwole and wonders 'why Socrates, who did not produce any written work, can be considered the father of Western philosophy when Orunmila [author of the Yoruba compendium of knowledge known as Ifa], who also transmitted his ideas to his disciples without writing them down, could not'.[3] The reason for this outcome, and doubtless others from different disciplines, is linked to the cultural hegemony that was established by European nations through the political and social control they exerted with their empires. In a word: colonization. Between 1492 and 1914, 84 per cent of the world was governed from a handful of European cities.[4] A premise of this book is that the 'west's' cultural hegemony persists today.

Anthropologist David Graeber and comparative archaeologist David Wengrove assert that many arguments from the nineteenth century, staged for the most part between and before white 'western' men, 'never really ended; they keep resurfacing in different forms'.[5] One of the main forms that continues to manifest these debates is fashion. Historian Robert Ross is surely right to assert that '[i]t would be mistaken to believe that the [global] adoption of European attire was inevitably or even primarily a consequence of colonialism'.[6] Nonetheless, it is hard to conceive of the essentialist thought that manifests itself within the contemporary fashion industry being so extensive without the classificatory schema that colonialism spurred during the eighteenth and nineteenth centuries. It was during this period that many of the terms and concepts we grapple with now and seek to inscribe with new meaning and relevance – civilization, homosexuality, heterosexuality – along with certain disciplines – anthropology, geriatrics, sexology, statistics – were coined and defined.

Fact and fantasy

There are two main reasons why fashion is an ideal conduit for the continued negotiation of centuries-old debates. The first is pragmatic and relevant to all forms of human dress: adornment of the body has become a fundamental requirement for people to participate meaningfully in most societies, as author Mark Twain opined. The ubiquity of a material and predominantly visual medium readily facilitates the exchange and negotiation of complex ideas between different groups of people. The second reason, specific to fashion, links to one of the key themes, and complications, to emerge through this book: people's belief in fashion, as it has come to be understood within the 'west' during the twentieth and twenty-first centuries, appears to be predicated on two seemingly irreconcilable forms of information that are deeply intertwined: fact and fantasy.

In many of the episodes considered, there is an ongoing negotiation between an expectation that fashions reflect and reaffirm socialized values – life as we know it – and an equally strong feeling that fashions should be aspirational – life as we want it. This may not seem a particularly revelatory point, but it is important. It raises at least three implications that go some way to explain why 'western'-centrism within the contemporary fashion industry persists. First, the combination of fact and fantasy is compelling. The beliefs that fashion reveals are sufficiently understandable to make them relatable and reassuring, and sufficiently aspirational to make them desirable, at least for people who share the dominant culture. Second, fantasy is generally considered to be idealistic and harmless. Consequently, appeals to people through fantasy can obfuscate the conveyance of facts that might otherwise appear objectionable. Third, ideas conveyed by fashion, which blend fact and fantasy, are often diffuse. This means they can be plausibly re-interpreted in different circumstances. Such ambivalence poses challenges for effective criticism. Fundamentally, it means that consumers and commentators tend to understand fashions in conjunction with dominant cultural values. This is not to say that fashions are vacuous, but to highlight that the dominant groups who determine what constitutes fashion also influence the meanings they want it to convey.[7] This is a deceptively simple point. Sociologist Ann Swidler's remarks about how people understand and engage with culture can help to make it clearer. Swidler contends that people's use of culture – of which fashion is one expression – follows a tripartite continuum from ideology to tradition, to common sense. Ideology is a self-conscious, organized belief system; tradition encompasses entrenched beliefs that are taken for granted; common sense describes unselfconscious assumptions that are considered an 'undeniable part of the structure of the world'.[8] This trajectory elucidates how the (un)self-conscious interpretation of fashions to support dominant understandings leads incrementally to their blithe acceptance because they come to be perceived as 'natural, transparent', if they are perceived at all.[9] Cumulatively, these observations go some way to explain why contemporary fashions are often presumed to be constitutive of social values.[10] My argument can be refined by thinking about fashion's similarity to law.

The (de-)constitutive function of fashion (and law)

Fashion and law may seem an incongruous pairing but scholar Minh-Ha T. Pham has shown how both ratify and protect 'white cultural practices'.[11] An Italian rape case briefly alluded to in Chapter 8, which focused on a pair of tight blue jeans, demonstrates how the authority of both becomes manifest in similar ways.[12] Fashion and law are predicated on socialized beliefs that seem immutable, but their articulation and interpretation is contingent upon contemporary circumstances, and these are mutable. Moreover, in enshrining people's freedoms, law is also a project perpetually engaged with fantasies that facilitate human yearning and potential. Global responses to the US Supreme Court's decision to overturn *Roe vs. Wade* on 24 June 2022, which had affirmed a woman's right to abortion care during the first two trimesters of pregnancy, demonstrates how law is closely bound with personal and communal aspirations.[13] The connection between fashion and law can be explained by considering the Italian case further.

In 1999, the *Corte di Cassazione*, Italy's highest court of appeals, overturned the verdict of a lower court that had sentenced a 45-year-old man, a driving instructor, to prison for raping an 18-year-old girl, his student. The justices of the *Corte* argued that the girl must have been a complicit sex partner because her tight jeans could not have been removed without consent.[14] In her analysis of the 'ridiculous', 'shameful', 'sick', 'unreal' and 'scandalous decision', criminologist Kitty Calavita argues that law, which is conventionally thought to be constitutive of social values, can also be de-constitutive. If laws generally reflect and reinforce prevalent beliefs about good-ordered human conduct, Calavita suggests that occasions when their interpretation and enforcement appear out of step with popular thinking 'sabotage the very ideologies [they invoke]'.[15] The 'scandalous decision' was one of these occasions. By overturning the guilty verdict, the *Corte* appeared to be upholding a moral and ideological position that was not widely shared within Italy. Consequently, Calavita asserts:

> By referencing an ideological worldview – relating to assumptions about gender, consent, and rape – that has been largely superseded (at least by an important segment of the dominant culture), the *Corte di Cassazione*

has actually hastened the demise of that ideology. Far from shoring up the legitimacy of its ideological vision, this legal decision has exposed it to ridicule – an emblem of the foolishness of the normative order of yesteryear.[16]

The rarity of these missteps, coupled with people's unswerving belief in law's authoritative role, means that it survives 'such disappointments and signs of its fallibility virtually unscathed'. The law's authority might even be strengthened because exceptions substantiate a socialized rule that accepts its validity.[17] A fourth reason why people's belief in law is maintained when its application appears dubious is because these anomalies are prone to occur during unsettled times when social norms are in flux.[18] Calavita focuses on the legal implications of the *Corte*'s ruling, but as this hinged upon an interpretation of the connotation and function of an item of dress – a woman's tight blue jeans – her judgement is instructive when thinking about the meaning of (fashionable) clothing and appearance within the 'west'.

The episodes considered in previous chapters suggest that fashion operates in a similar way to law. The fashion industry is conventionally thought to be constitutive of the social values associated with the 'west'. However, many episodes demonstrate that specific fashions and fashion campaigns can be de-constitutive. Instead of upholding socialized values these anomalies, which cause physical or psychological harm to people, or appear unintelligible, contribute to their disavowal. De-constitutive episodes are typically sparked by a designer or brand pursuing a fantasy rooted in essentialist ideas. The garments and campaigns that manifest these thoughts appear out-of-step when they become public or are re-interpreted under changed circumstances at a later date. These occurrences typically happen during periods of personal or civic trauma when the meaning and roles of traditional attitudes are more likely to be questioned.[19] During these times, as 'competing ways of organizing action' are proposed to resolve the social crisis, the gap between fact and fantasy appears to be uncomfortably, untenably wide.[20] The 'chasm between myth and reality', which is how Whiteness manifests itself as a 'psychosis', according to sociologist Kehinde Andrews, is duly exposed.[21] Rational critique is therefore possible: the fantasy is considered risible and the values it manifests are rebuked. However, whilst people's opprobrium weakens the ideologies that fashionable garments and their linked campaigns espouse, change is seldom immediate. The fashion industry is often criticized for producing garments and campaigns that offend. It is admonished far more frequently than the law, particularly through social media, but its authority is rarely and decisively impugned. As Pham opines of debates about cultural misappropriation within fashion media:

> The popular chorus of *cultural appropriation! cultural appreciation!* quickly becomes a performance, in which neither side misses a cue nor forgets a

well-learned line.. . . . The debate around the event often gets more press and social-media attention than the event did itself, and nobody seems to change opinions for the next go-round.[22]

Ostensibly, fashion's authority and legitimacy are not seriously assailed by these damaging occurrences because of an entrenched belief that contemporary fashions do convey dominant understandings, at least from a 'western' perspective. These exceptions reinforce the rule that fashion is 'a powerful force in the construction of social meaning, identity, and everyday consciousness, as well as in the more material production of social ordering and relations of power to which these ideological props contribute'.[23] They also reinforce a 'western' axiom that clothing conveys character because these missteps are so odious, they damage the reputation of the people associated with them. This is possibly why fashion brands and designers typically respond to critiques with emotive rebuttals as though they have been subject to an *ad hominem* attack. The tenacity of the social values that limit the impact of de-constitutive occurrences, and reduce the likelihood of change, owes much to (anglophone) (fashion) journalism.

The role of fashion journalism

To understand how and why 'western'-centrism persists within the contemporary fashion industry, I have tried to shine a more critical light on the public negotiations that ensue when designs and campaigns become public. In so doing, I seek to supplement the burgeoning work that is being done to understand the place and contribution of fashion journalism within the industry. For most people, the latest fashions and their campaigns are experienced and understood via the mediation of (anglophone) fashion journalists. The verdicts of these opinion formers are consequently important in shaping dominant thinking about the meaning and role of contemporary fashions. However, their commentaries are rarely as straightforward as the colloquial tone, prose and place of publication imply. The reportage of many of the episodes considered in previous chapters has emphasized how much of the discourse about new fashions is ambivalent, sometimes cursory. If judgements are made, they are frequently declared and not demonstrated. If culturally freighted themes are scrutinized, humour is often deployed. Levity tends to result in the trivialization of the garment or campaign, which makes it risible and resistible as an outlier. In a similar way, theory sometimes appears to be used within academic discourse to neutralize problems posed by contemporary fashions and their presentation by placing them within an intelligible, safe frame.

This is not to dispute the 'discourse of intellectualisation' within fashion media that fashion scholar Aurélie Van de Peer has traced from the 1970s.[24]

But more analysis does not necessarily mean greater elucidation. Many of the media discussions referenced in this book are concerned to articulate fashion's purpose. At its simplest level, the enquiry is presented as a binary. Either fashion conveys prevalent social attitudes and acts like mirror, as fashion editor Tim Blanks opined in his discussion with artistic director Virgil Abloh, or it seeks to critique these attitudes.[25] A spectrum existing between these positions is more accurate based on the episodes considered, but as eager as fashion journalists are to situate new designs and campaigns, their judgements are rarely decisive. This is largely because authors seek to establish meaning by making connections with other near-contemporary examples. The corollary is that much of the analysis in fashion journalism becomes synchronic and focused on the present. Whilst designers' motives and influences are considered, along with the immediate implications of their work, writing tends to confirm socialized values more than challenge them.

Modernity's paradox

A focus on the present compounds the fashion industry's 'western'-centrism because it perpetuates the hegemony of modernity. If the binaries considered within this book were shaped by the classificatory imperatives of scientists, politicians and cultural commentators during the eighteenth and nineteenth centuries, one of the main reasons they endure is because they provide 'westerners' with an orientation and sense of structure to navigate and comment upon the condition of modernity. The point is easier to raise than refine. Philosopher Jürgen Habermas suggests people are more likely to experience the conditions of modernity than acknowledge the concept. Nonetheless, the episodes in this book evidence the spectre of modernity in two ways. First, through the fluidic interpretation of fashionable designs and campaigns. The public response to several episodes changed as shifting circumstances invested them with different meanings. Sometimes consumers and commentators developed diametrically opposed judgements within a period of several weeks. In other cases, older garments and campaigns were re-discovered and interpreted to align with current social and political concerns. The inclination to interpret fashions to buttress dominant contemporary preoccupations suggests people want, even expect, fashion to provide a social coherence and psychological salve. This may seem implausible given the frequency with which new designs are released, but the scale and speed of fashion launches mean consumers have an abundance of goods from which to construct personally meaningful and reassuring narratives. Paradoxically, a cause of bewilderment is simultaneously a source of stability.

Second, a desire for stability is evidenced by the persistence of social binaries. When established fashion magazines – like *Vogue* and *GQ* – and brands – like Burberry and Calvin Klein – question socialized values – about age, race, sexuality and shape, as previous chapters have discussed – consumers react with positivity and suspicion. They rarely go further and challenge the appropriateness of using binaries. At least two implications follow from this observation. First, the reductionist nature of a binary helps people who form part of the dominant culture (i.e. who accept 'western' values) to negotiate their self- and social identities. Second, the contemporary fashion industry is recognized as a contributor to the formation of dominant cultural and social understandings by explaining how essentialist binaries are maintained and mollified.

Binaries that bind

If binaries constitute the known-knowns, they help consumers as much as brands and designers probe unknown-unknowns, to borrow the torturous, but serviceable, terms used by former US secretary of defence Donald Rumsfeld. One example of this from the last chapter is the creation of Catty 8.1, which harnesses gender and sexuality binaries to probe the possibilities of what avatar design and fashionable appearances can look like in digital spaces. If this seems pessimistic, philosopher Slavoj Žižek raised a fourth category of knowing in response to Rumsfeld's public remarks: the known-unknowns. A known-unknown refers to something a person, perhaps even a culture, intentionally refuses to acknowledge that they know.[26] This category aptly describes fashions that appear de-constitutive. One of the main reasons the clothing and campaigns considered within this book cause such psychological hurt is because they confront people with experiences they would rather disavow, certainly in public. One positive of such discomfiture is that de-constitutive occurrences expose an 'outdated moral vision [that] appears as a caricature of an old normative order and a symbol of its folly'.[27] However, for this to lead to effective and enduring change within the fashion industry, a diachronic approach, which facilitates historical analysis and methods, is necessary.

De-constitutive occurrences may be more likely during unsettled periods, to use Ann Swidler's term, but Calavita rightly observes that 'all historical periods are no doubt to one degree or another "unsettled"'.[28] These are times when '[p]eople formulate, flesh out, and put into practice new habits of action'.[29] Consequently, Calavita suggests it may be possible 'to identify struggles between and among [competing] ideologies' over time to identify how dominant understandings are formed and challenged.[30] Where she proposes that law is 'one site of contestation for the construction of moral meaning', I contend that the same is true for fashion. Where the Italian decision indicates 'multiple moral meanings [exist] in a struggle for primacy [and that] *the law may undermine its own in that struggle*', episodes considered in this book suggest the same can be said of fashion.[31] Consequently, there is virtue in comparing the causes and circumstances in which fashionable designs and campaigns become contested over a wider chronological and cultural frame to more deeply comprehend fashion's constitutive role and to more readily critique its underlying 'western' bias.

Comments about 'western' bias emphasize the 'western' concerns that frame this book. The sources for this study are predominantly 'western', which inevitably heightens the perceived impact of 'western' actions in the past and present. I have tried to strike a balance by using social media and including the voices of people from around the world to suggest how centuries-old thinking continues to have a widespread influence beyond the 'west' and anglophone cultures. The immediate, emotive responses of people on social media need to be approached with caution, but they are instructive for showing the extent of antagonism towards the 'western'-centrism that is believed to reside within the contemporary fashion industry. As a British scholar, my contribution to discussions about fashion's 'western'-centrism is possibly clearer and more appropriate if approached from my perspectives and experiences. I also follow film scholar Peter Lehman, who asserts that only by centring something can we truly de-centre it. Fittingly, perhaps, Lehman made these remarks writing about the male body and the penis-phallus, which has long been symbolic of what Salami terms the world's Europatriarchalism.[32] Lehman suggests that 'when the penis-phallus is hidden from view in patriarchy . . . it is most centered'.[33] The same can be said for 'western'-centrism within the fashion industry. I acknowledge Kehinde Andrews's argument that whiteness, which is embedded within 'western'-centrism, is deeply entrenched, but I would stop short at calling it a 'psychosis' that it is 'beyond any rational engagement'.[34] Whilst I have been critical, I do think the negotiations documented in each chapter demonstrate attempts by white and 'western' people to grapple with their position and privilege, however falteringly and frustratingly.

As a historian I believe questions are very often more important than answers. Through this book I pose many questions, which require more work, and more people, to resolve. I sketch an approach that is diachronic, which purposefully considers how the past influences the present, that advocates for interdisciplinarity, the use of varied sources and the inclusion of diverse global voices. These also need expanding. In March 2020, Anna Wintour recognized that the fashion industry needed to re-orientate itself. Doubtless, what I outline is not the change she envisaged, but the task of confronting our denials and defensiveness about fashion's 'western'-centrism would certainly constitute 'a radical reset'.[35]

NOTES

Introduction

1. Quoted in Jessica Testa, Vanessa Friedman and Elizabeth Paton, 'Coronavirus Upends the Fashion Universe', *The New York Times International Edition* (7/8 March 2020), 16.
2. Alessandro Michele Instagram post, @alessandro_michele (24 March 2020). https://www.instagram.com/p/CAkszCYpBJV/?hl=en. Accessed: August 2022.
3. Ibid.
4. Business of Fashion, '#rewiringfashion', *The Financial Times* (23/24 May 2020), 7; Ellen MacArthur Foundation, 'A Solution to Build Back Better: The Circular Economy', *The Financial Times* (13/14 June 2020), 5.
5. Bob Usherwood and Margaret Usherwood, 'Culture Wars, Libraries and the BBC', *Library Management*, 45:4/5 (2021), 291–301; Samuel L. Perry, Andrew L. Whitehead and Joshua B. Grubbs, 'Culture Wars and COVID-19 Conduct: Christian Nationalism, Religiosity, and Americans' Behavior During the Coronavirus Pandemic', *Journal for the Scientific Study of Religion*, 59:3 (2020), 405–416.
6. Morwenna Ferrier, 'Anna Wintour Apologises for Not Giving Space to Black People at Vogue', *The Guardian* (10 June 2020). https://www.theguardian.com/fashion/2020/jun/10/anna-wintour-apologises-for-not-giving-space-to-black-people-at-vogue. Accessed: May 2022.
7. Edmund Lee, 'The White Issue: Has Anna Wintour's Diversity Push Come Too Late', *The New York Times* (24 October 2020). https://www.nytimes.com/2020/10/24/business/media/anna-wintour-vogue-race.html. Accessed: May 2022.
8. Ibid.
9. Angelo Flaccavento, 'Alessandro Michele: Quotations, the Past and Future of Fashion. Here's My Vision', Italian *Vogue*, 805 (September 2017), 191, translated by Antony Bowden. www.vogue.it/en/fashion/news/2017/09/01/alessandro-michele-quotations-past-future-fashion-interview-vogue-italia/. Accessed: December 2020; Angelo Flaccavento, 'Quotations: The Past and the Future of Fashion', *Time in Fashion*, ed. Caroline Evans and Alessandra Vaccari (London: Bloomsbury, 2020), 111–113.
10. Giorgia Sepe and Alessia Anzivino, 'Guccification: Redefining Luxury through Art—The Gucci Revolution', *The Artification of Luxury Fashion Brands*, eds. Marta Massi and Alex Turrini (London: Palgrave, 2020), 89–112.
11. Jean-Noël Kapferer, 'The Artification of Luxury: From Artisans to Artists', *Business Horizons*, 57 (2014), 371–380.

12. Paul Jobling, Philippa Nesbitt and Angelene Wong, *Fashion, Identity, Image* (London: Bloomsbury, 2022), 5.
13. Joanne Finkelstein, *The Fashioned Self* (Cambridge: Polity Press, 1991), 11.
14. Daniel Miller, 'The Little Black Dress is the Solution. But What's the Problem?' *Elusive Consumption*, eds. K. Ekstrom and H. Brembeck (Oxford: Berg, 2004), 113–127.
15. Ibid.; Daniel Miller, *Modernity: An Ethnographic Approach* (London: Routledge, 1994), 58–81.
16. Edward Said, *Orientalism* (London: Penguin, [1978] 2003), xvii.
17. Virgil Abloh, 'Tim's Take with Virgil Abloh', *The Business of Fashion* (4 February 2021). https://www.youtube.com/watch?v=Q4ipJM2xGUs. Accessed: May 2022, 00:27:49 to 00:27:57 minutes.
18. Ibid., 00:29:34 to 00:30:19 minutes.
19. Angela Buttolph et al., *The Fashion Book* (London: Phaidon, 1998); Giorgio Riello, *Back in Fashion: Western Fashion from the Middle Ages to the Present* (New Haven and London: Yale University Press, 2020).
20. 'Tim's Take', 00:18:56 to 00:18:57 minutes; 00:07:38 to 00:07:46 minutes.
21. André Leon Talley, *The Chiffon Trenches: A Memoir* (London: 4th Estate, 2020), 144.
22. Robert Ross, *Clothing: A Global History, Or, The Imperialists' New Clothes* (Cambridge: Polity, 2008), 1–4.
23. *The End of Fashion: Clothing and Dress in the Age of Globalization*, eds. Adam Geczy and Vicki Karaminas (London: Bloomsbury, 2019); Tim Blanks, 'The End of the (Fashion) World as We Know It', *Business of Fashion* (24 March 2020). https://www.businessoffashion.com/opinions/luxury/the-end-of-the-fashion-world-as-we-know-it?utm_campaign=1686245233687280&utm_medium=email&utm_source=daily-digest-newsletter&utm_term=11. Accessed: December 2020; Luca Solca, 'Is Fashion Ready for a Multicultural Minefield?' *Business of Fashion* (17 March 2020). https://www.businessoffashion.com/opinions/luxury/is-fashion-ready-for-a-multicultural-minefield?utm_campaign=1686406403908605&utm_medium=email&utm_source=daily-digest-newsletter&utm_term=11. Accessed: December 2020; Norimitsu Onishi and Constant Méheut, 'Heating Up Culture Wars, France to Scour Universities for Ideas That "Corrupt Society"', *The New York Times* (18 February 2020). https://www.nytimes.com/2021/02/18/world/europe/france-universities-culture-wars.html. Accessed: February 2020.
24. Fredric Jameson, *Postmodernism, Or The Cultural Logic of Late Capitalism* (London: Verso, 1991), ix.
25. David Andress, *Cultural Dementia: How the West has Lost its History, and Risks Losing Everything Else* (London: Head of Zeus, 2018).
26. Richard Ovenden, *Burning the Books: A History of Knowledge Under Attack* (London: John Murray, 2020), 4–5. 200–201.
27. Eric Alterman, 'The Decline of Historical Thinking', *The New Yorker* (4 February 2019). https://www.newyorker.com/news/news-desk/the-decline-of-historical-thinking. Accessed: May 2022. For the situation in Britain, and a debate about fluctuating numbers of history students at university, see Margot Finn and Jo Fox, 'The Economist and History: Economical with the Facts?', *Historical Transactions* (19 August 2019). https://blog.royalhistsoc.org/2019/08/19/rhs-ihr-letter-economist-and-history/. Accessed: May 2022.

NOTES

28 Alterman, 'The Decline of Historical Thinking'.

29 Ben Barry, 'How to Transform Fashion Education: A Manifesto for Equity, Inclusion and Decolonization', *International Journal of Fashion Studies*, 8:1 (2021), 125–126.

30 Orian Brook, Dave O'Brien and Mark Taylor, *Culture Is Bad for You: Inequality in the Cultural and Creative Industries* (Manchester: Manchester University Press, 2020), 1–2, 8–25.

31 Adam Geczy and Vicki Karaminas, *Critical Fashion Practice: From Westwood to Van Beirendonck* (London: Bloomsbury, 2017), 2.

32 Ann Swidler, 'Culture in Action: Symbols and Strategies', *American Sociological Review*, 51:2 (April, 1986), 273.

33 Ibid., 277.

34 Ibid., 274, 276.

35 Ibid., 280.

36 Ibid., 278–282.

37 Ibid., 281.

38 Ibid., 280.

39 Ibid., 278, 279.

40 Daniel Miller, 'Why Clothing is not Superficial', *Stuff* (Cambridge: Polity Press, 2010), 18.

41 Homi K. Bhabha, *The Location of Culture* (London: Routledge, 1994), 2.

42 Ibid., 2–3.

43 Ibid., 3, 37, 277.

44 Ibid., 51, 94.

45 Ibid., 10.

46 Ibid.

47 Audre Lorde, *The Master's Tools Will Never Dismantle the Master's House* (London: Penguin, 2018), 16–21.

48 Ibid., 16.

49 Susan B. Kaiser, *Fashion and Cultural Studies* (London: Bloomsbury, 2019), 2.

50 Ibid., 2.

51 Ibid., 2–3.

52 For a different response to Lorde's statement, see Sarah Cheang and Shehnaz Suterwalla, 'Decolonizing the Curriculum? Transformation, Emotion, and Positionality in Teaching', *Fashion Theory*, 24:6 (2020), 882.

53 Sandra Niessen, 'Defining Defashion: A Manifesto for Degrowth', *International Journal of Fashion Studies*, 9:2 (2022), 439.

54 Elizabeth Wilson, *Adorned in Dreams: Fashion and Modernity* (London: I.B. Tauris, [1985] 2003), 63.

55 Caroline Evans, *Fashion at the Edge: Spectacle, Modernity and Deathliness* (New Haven and London: Yale University Press, 2003), 7.

56 Ibid., 7–14.

57 Rolando Vázquez, *Vistas of Modernity: Decolonial Aesthesis and the End of the Contemporary* (Amsterdam: Mondriaan Fund, 2020).

58 Michael Pickering, 'Experience as Horizon: Koselleck, Expectation and Historical Time', *Cultural Studies*, 18:2–3 (2004), 282–287.

59 Jameson, *Postmodernism*, ix.

60 Jo Ellison, 'Lockdown Two has Unleashed the Selfish Gene', *The Financial Times: Life and Arts* (7/8 November 2020), 16; Nilanjana Roy, 'Is "Cancel Culture" a Failure of Kindness?', *The Financial Times* (17/18 April 2021), 10.

61 William Blake, 'London', *William Blake: Poems Selected by James Fenton* (London: Faber and Faber, 2010), 65.

62 Ken Kweku Nimo, *Africa Fashion: Luxury, Craft and Textile Heritage* (London: Laurence King, 2022), 13.

63 Evans, *Fashion at the Edge*, 7; Norbert Elias, *The Civilising Process: Sociogenetic and Psychogenetic Investigations*, trans. Edmund Jephcott. Revised Edition, eds. Eric Dunning, Johan Goudsblom and Stephen Menell (Oxford: Blackwell [1939] 1994), 406; Norbert Elias, *The Society of Individuals*, ed. Michael Schröter, translated by Edmund Jephcott (Oxford: Basil Blackwell [1987] 1991), 197–198. For a summary of Elias's thought, see Benjamin L. Wild, 'The Civilizing Process and Sartorial Studies', *Clothing Cultures*, 1:3 (2014), 214–217.

64 Richard Sennett, *The Fall of Public Man* (London: Penguin, 1974).

65 Jürgen Habermas, *The Philosophical Discourse of Modernity: Twelve Lectures* (Cambridge, MA: MIT Press, 1987), 18–20.

66 Elias, *The Society of Individuals*, 129. See also, Grant McCracken, 'The Making of Modern Consumption', *Culture and Consumption: New Approaches to the Symbolic Character of Consumer Goods and Activities* (Bloomington and Indianapolis: Indiana University Press, 1985), 3–30.

67 Ibid., 124.

68 Ibid., 123–124.

69 Noreena Hertz, *The Lonely Century: Coming Together in a World that's Pulling Apart* (London: Sceptre, 2020), 110.

70 Elias, *The Society of Individuals*, 180.

71 Ibid., 204–205.

72 Ibid., 129–130.

73 Fredric Jameson, 'Culture and Finance Capital', *Critical Inquiry*, 24:1 (1997), 246–265.

74 Ibid., 258–264.

75 Ibid., 264.

76 Ibid.

77 Georg Simmel, 'The Metropolis and Mental Life', *Georg Simmel on Individuality and Social Forms*, ed. Donald N. Levine (Chicago and London: The University of Chicago Press, [1903] 1971), 329–330.

78 Georg Simmel, 'Fashion', *Georg Simmel*, 294–323.

79 Rebecca Arnold, *Fashion, Desire and Anxiety: Image and Morality in the 20th Century* (London and New York: I.B. Tauris, 2001), 12.

NOTES

80 Gilles Lipovetsky, *The Empire of Fashion: Dressing Modern Democracy*, trans. Catherine Porter (Princeton and Oxford: Princeton University Press, [1987] 1994), 149.

81 Ibid., 195.

82 Ibid.

83 Ibid.

84 Ibid., 150.

85 Ibid., 120.

86 Linda Welters and Abby Lillethun, *Fashion History: A Global View* (London: Bloomsbury, 2018), 195.

87 Lipovetsky, *The Empire of Fashion*, 226.

88 Ibid., 18.

89 Jack Self, 'THE BIG FLAT NOW: Power, Flatness, and Nowness in the Third Millennium', *032c* (17 December 2018). https://032c.com/magazine/the-big-flat-now-power-flatness-and-nowness-in-the-third-millennium. Accessed: September 2022. Reference owed to Paddy Lonergan.

90 Ibid.

91 Caroline Evans and Alessandra Vaccari, 'Time in Fashion: An Introductory Essay', *Time in Fashion*, 3–40.

92 Charles Baudelaire, 'The Painter of Modern Life', *The Painter of Modern Life and Other Essays*, translated and edited by Jonathan Mayne (London: Phaidon Press Limited, [1863] 1964), 28.

93 Patricia Mears and G. Bruce Boyer, 'Introduction', *Elegance in an Age of Crisis: Fashions of the 1930s*, ed. Patricia Mears and G. Bruce Boyer (New Haven and London: Yale University Press, 2014), 4.

94 For example, McCracken, *Culture and Consumption*; Scott Lash and John Urry, *The End of Disorganized Capital* (Cambridge: Polity Press, 1987); Lipovetsky, *The Empire of Fashion* (1987); Fred Davis, *Fashion, Culture, and Identity* (Chicago and London: The University of Chicago Press, 1982); Wilson, *Adorned in Dreams*; Finkelstein, *The Fashioned Self*; Anthony Giddens, *Modernity and Self-Identity: Self and Society in the Late Modern Age* (Cambridge: Polity Press, 1991); Jennifer Craik, *The Face of Fashion: Cultural Studies in Fashion* (London: Routledge, 1993); Arjun Appadurai, *Modernity at Large: Cultural Dimensions of Globalization* (Minneapolis and London: University of Minnesota Press, 1996).

95 *Les noms d'epoque: De <<Restauration>> à <<années de plomb>>*, ed. Dominique Kalifa (Paris: Éditions Gallimard, 2019).

96 Andrew Bolton, 'Sixty Minutes of Fashion', *About Time: Fashion & Duration*, ed. Andrew Bolton (New Haven and London: Yales University Press, 2020), xiii.

97 Welters and Lillethun, *Fashion History*, 14.

98 Heike Jenss, 'Introduction: Locating Fashion/Studies: Research Methods, Sites and Practices', *Fashion Studies: Research Methods, Sites, and Practices*, ed. Heike Jenss (London: Bloomsbury, 2016), 3.

99 Yuniya Kawamura, *Fashion-ology: An Introduction to Fashion Studies* (Oxford: Berg, 2005), 1.

100 Craik, *The Face of Fashion*, xi.

101 Welters and Lillethun, *Fashion History*, 4.

102 Kehinde Andrews, 'The Psychosis of Whiteness: The Celluloid Hallucinations of Amazing Grace and Belle', *Journal of Black Studies*, 47:5 (2016), 436–437.

103 Ibid., 436.

104 Rosie Findlay and Johannes Reponen, 'Introduction', *Insights on Fashion Journalism,* eds. Rosie Findlay and Johannes Reponen (London: Routledege, 2022), 2–10; Katie Baker Jones, 'What a Difference a Page Makes: Contextualising Suzy Menkes' Fashion Criticism Within and Across Media Outlets', Ibid., 130.

105 Findlay and Reponen, 'Introduction', 1.

106 Josephine Collins, 'From the Typewriter to the Smartphone: How Changing Capture and Delivery Systems Have Influenced the Practice of Fashion Journalism', *Insights on Fashion Journalism*, 15.

107 Findlay and Reponen, 'Introduction', 6.

108 Aurélie Van Peer, 'The Politics of Fashion Criticism: How Newspaper Journalists' Evaluative Criteria for Fashion Changed Between 1949 and 2020', *Insights on Fashion Journalism*, 31.

109 Findlay and Reponen, 'Introduction', 4; Monique Mulholland, 'Sexy and Sovereign? Aboriginal Models Hit the "multicultural mainstream"', *Cultural Studies*, 33:2 (2019), 198–222. Reference owed to Rosie Findlay.

110 Agnès Rocamora, 'High Fashion and Pop Fashion: The Symbolic Production of Fashion in *Le Monde* and *The Guardian*', *Fashion Theory*, 5:2 (2001), 120.

111 For notable exceptions see, Geczy and Karaminas, *Critical Fashion Practice*; Jobling, Nesbitt and Wong, *Fashion, Identity, Image*.

112 See, Minh-Ha T. Pham, *Why We Can't Have Nice Things: Social Media's Influence on Fashion, Ethics, and Property* (Durham: Duke University Press, 2022); Minh-Ha T. Pham, *Asians Wear Clothes on the Internet: Race, Gender, and the Work of Personal Style Blogging* (Durham: Duke University Press, 2015).

113 See also Mike Thelwall, Olga Goriunova, Farida Vis, Simon Falkner, Anne Burns, Jim Aulich, Amalia Mas-Bleda, Emma Stuart and Francesco D'Orazio, 'Chatting Through Pictures? A Classification of Images Tweeted in One Week in the UK and USA', *Journal of the Association for Information Science and Technology*, 67:11 (2016), 2575.

114 Mike Thelwall and Farida Vis, 'Gender and Image Sharing on Facebook, Twitter, Instagram, Snapchat and WhatsApp in the UK: Hobbying Alone or Filtering for Friends?', *AJIM*, 69:6 (2017), 705, 710, 712–713.

115 Ibid., 704.

116 Emma Dabiri, *What White People Can Do Next: From Allyship to Coalition* (London: Penguin, 2021), 11.

117 Ibid., 66.

118 Michael Keevak, *Becoming Yellow: A Short History of Racial Thinking* (Princeton: Princeton University Press, 2011).

# Chapter 1

1. For example, Irvin G. Wyllie, 'Social Darwinism and the Businessman', *Proceedings of the American Philosophical Society*, 103:5 (1959), 629.
2. Mark Twain, *Mark Twain's Notebook by Mark Twain*, ed. Albert Bigelow Paine (New York: Harper & Brothers, 1897), 337.
3. Ernst van den Boogaart, 'De Brys' Africa', *Staging New Worlds: De Brys' Illustrated Travel Reports, 1590-1630*, ed. Susanna Burghartz (Basel: Schwabe, 2004), 97; Susanna Burghartz, 'The Fabric of Early Globalization: Skin, Fur and Cloth in de Bry's Travel Accounts, 1590-1630', *Dressing Global Bodies: The Political Power of Dress in World History*, ed. Beverly Lemire and Giorgio Riello (London: Routledge, 2020), 15–40.
4. Philip Carr-Gomm, *A Brief History of Nakedness* (London: Reaktion Books, 2010), 7–8.
5. John Berger, *The Art of Seeing* (London: Penguin, 1972), 54.
6. Anne Hollander, *Seeing Through Clothes* (Berkeley and Los Angeles: University of California Press, 1975), 84.
7. Kenneth Clark, *The Nude: A Study of Ideal Art* (London: Penguin Books, 1956), 1.
8. Ruth Barcan, *Nudity: A Cultural Anatomy* (London: Bloomsbury, 2004), where naked and nude are used interchangeably.
9. Sheena Wagstaff, 'Embodied Histories', *Like Life: Sculpture, Color, and the Body*, eds. Luke Syson, Sheena Wagstaff, Emerson Bower and Brinda Kumar (New Haven and London: Yale University Press, 2018), 2–13; John Monaghan and Peter Just, *Social and Cultural Anthropology: A Very Short Introduction* (Oxford: Oxford University Press, 2000), 17–18.
10. Misty L. Bastian, 'The Naked and the Nude: Historically Multiple Meanings of *Oto* (undress) in Southeastern Nigeria', *Dirt, Undress, and Difference: Critical Perspectives on the Body's Surface*, ed. Adeline Masquelier (Bloomington and Indianapolis: Indiana University Press, 2005), 35; Margaret Wiener, 'Breasts, (Un) Dress, and Modernist Desire in the Balinese-Tourist Encounter', *Dirt, Undress, and Difference*, 62; Katherine Frank, 'Body Talk: Revelations of Self and Body in Contemporary Strip Clubs', *Dirt, Undress, and Difference*, 98.
11. Ogden Goelet, 'Nudity in Ancient Egypt', *Notes in the History of Art*, 12:2 (1993), 21; Bastian, 'The Naked and the Nude', 40, 48; Cara Grace Tremain, 'The Varied Body', *The Adorned Body: Mapping Ancient Maya Dress*, eds. Nicholas Carter, Stephen D. Houston and Franco D. Rossi (Austin: University of Texas Press, 2020), 153.
12. Satsuki Kawano, 'Japanese Bodies and Western Ways of Seeing in the Late Nineteenth Century', *Dirt, Undress, and Difference*, 149–150; Nicholas Carter, Alyce de Carteret and Katharine Lukach, 'The Clothed Body', *The Adorned Body*, 27.

13. On the possibility of positive and negative readings see Wiener, 'Breasts, (Un)Dress, and Modernist Desire', 66.
14. Hollander, *Seeing Through Clothes*, 5, 64.
15. Kenneth J. Dover, *Greek Homosexuality* (London: Bloomsbury, [1978] 2016), 70.
16. Alexander Fury, 'Fashion in the Flesh: Real Shows Return to Milan', *The Financial Times* (24 June 2021). https://www.ft.com/content/6057f8cc-5ad5-4207-bdcc-fbe70951cbf4. Accessed: June 2022.
17. Helen Barrett, 'Brasher, Flasher and Raunchier – Why the Pelvic Cut-Out is Back', *Financial Times* (10 August 2021). https://www.ft.com/content/e36053eb-1f37-4632-b903-eaaf149b67ae. Accessed: June 2022.
18. Ana Murcho, 'São mamas, estúpido!' Portuguese *Vogue* (April 2021), 132–135.
19. Peter Lehman, *Running Scared: Masculinity and the Representation of the Male Body* (Philadelphia: Temple University Press, 1993), 164; Carol A. Stabile, 'Shooting the Mother: Fetal Photography and the Politics of Disappearance', *Camera Obscura*, 10:1 (1992), 191.
20. Anon., 'Designer Rick Owens Inspired by Old Sumbarine [sic.] Movies at Paris Men's Fashion Week', *AP Archive* (3 August 2015). https://www.youtube.com/watch?v=ANnyTNZyGE4., 00:01:06 to 00:01:08 minutes; 00:02:30 to 00:02:36 minutes. Accessed: April 2021.
21. Ibid., 00:02:24 to 00:02:26 minutes.
22. Ibid., 00:01:06 to 00:02:30 minutes.
23. Tim Blanks, 'Rick Owens: Fall 2015 Menswear', *Vogue* (22 January 2015). https://www.vogue.com/fashion-shows/fall-2015-menswear/rick-owens, Looks 11, 15, 17, 21, 22, 23. Accessed: August 2022.
24. Emma Akbarein, 'Rick Owens Puts Penises on Show At Paris Fashion Week Show', *The Independent* (23 January 2015). https://www.independent.co.uk/life-style/fashion/news/rick-owens-puts-penises-show-paris-fashion-week-show-9997472.html. Accessed: February 2021.
25. Hannah Marriott, 'Penises on the Fashion Catwalk – A Flesh Flash Too Far?' *The Guardian* (22 January 2015). https://www.theguardian.com/fashion/2015/jan/22/-sp-penis-flashing-at-rick-owens-menswear-show. Accessed: February 2021.
26. Susie Lau, '"Nudity is the most simple and primal gesture": The Designer Reflects on His Full-Frontal Fashion Statement', *Dazed Digital* (23 January 2015). https://www.dazeddigital.com/fashion/article/23285/1/rick-owens-aw15-livestream. Accessed: February 2021.
27. 'The models reveal everything, truly everything'. Anthony Vincent, '"Rick Owens Gate": les mannequins dévoilent tout, vraiment tout . . .', France *Grazia* (22 January 2015). https://www.grazia.fr/mode/rick-owens-gate-les-mannequins-devoilent-tout-vraiment-tout-734134. Accessed: April 2021.
28. Anon., 'Rick Owens Sends Models Down the Runway with Their Junk Out'. https://www.gq.com.au/style/news/rick-owens-sends-models-down-the-runway-with-their-junk-out/news-story/c419e795836aec6552526af6a3cd663d (23 January 2015). Accessed: April 2021.
29. Dazed Tweet, @Dazed (23 January 2015). https://twitter.com/dazed/status/558504477007683584?s=11. Accessed: August 2022.

NOTES

30. Zing Tsjeng, 'What Rick Owens' Full-Frontal Runway Show Says about Us', *Dazed Digital* (23 January 2015). https://www.dazeddigital.com/fashion/article/23353/1/what-rick-owens-full-frontal-runway-show-says-about-us. Accessed: April 2021.
31. Lau, 'Nudity'.
32. Marriott, 'Penises on the Fashion Catwalk'.
33. Adam Fletcher and I-D team, 'Rick Owens Spring/Summer 14', *i-D* (11 November 2013). https://i-d.vice.com/en_uk/article/8xnqav/rick-owens-springsummer-14. Accessed: April 2021.
34. Ibid.
35. Terry Jones, *Rick Owens* (Cologne: Taschen, 2013), 65–66.
36. Fletcher, 'Rick Owens'.
37. Vincent, 'Rick Owens Gate'.
38. Alison Bancroft, 'Masculinity, Masquerade and Display: Some thoughts on Rick Owens's Sphinx Collection and Men in Fashion', *Critical Studies in Fashion & Beauty*, 7:1 (2016), 21.
39. Ibid.
40. Ibid., 22.
41. Ibid., 24.
42. Ibid., 24–25.
43. Ibid., 23; Joan Rivière, 'Womanliness as Masquerade', *International Journal of Psychoanalysis*, 10 (1929), 305–306.
44. Ibid., 26.
45. Ibid.
46. Anon., 'RICK OWENS ABOUT FW15 SPHINX COLLECTION' (no date). https://journal.antonioli.eu/2015/01/rick-owens-about-fw15-sphinx-collection/. Accessed: February 2021.
47. Adam Geczy and Vicki Karaminas, *Critical Fashion Practice: From Westwood to Van Beirendonck* (London: Bloomsbury, 2017), 136.
48. Ibid., 128.
49. Lau, 'Nudity'.
50. Anja Aronowsky Cronberg, 'Interviews: Rick Owens', *Vestoj: On Masculinities*, 7 (2016), 233.
51. Fletcher, 'Rick Owens'.
52. Cronberg, 'Interviews', 233.
53. Ibid., 231.
54. Alexander Fury, 'The Alternatives: Designers Subverting Fashion's Status Quo', *The New York Times* (19 August 2015). https://www.nytimes.com/2015/08/19/t-magazine/vetements-matthew-adams-dolan-alyx-martine-rose.html. Accessed: April 2021.
55. Geczy and Karaminas, *Critical Fashion Practice*, 125.
56. Bancroft, 'Masculinity, Masquerade and Display', 20–21.

57   Lehman, *Running Scared*, 10.
58   Ibid., 5–9.
59   Tsjeng, 'Full-Frontal'.
60   Brian S. Mautz, Bob B. M. Wong, Richard A. Peters and Michael D. Jennions, 'Penis Size Interacts with Body Shape and Height to Influence Male Attractiveness', *Proceedings of the National Academy of Sciences of the United States of America*, 110:17 (2013), 6925–930.
61   Jo-Ann Furniss, quoted in Jones, *Rick Owens*, 81.
     MT Costello, autumn/winter 2015
62   Anon., 'Nude Male Model Causes Controversy with Fashion Week Orchestrators', *Cision PR Newswire* (27 February 2015). https://www.prnewswire.com/news-releases/nude-male-model-causes-controversy-with-fashion-week-orchestrators-300042911.html. Accessed: February 2021.
63   Ibid.
64   'ART HEARTS FASHION MERCEDES-BENZ FASHION WEEK FW 2015 COLLECTIONS'. *Australian Fashion Week* (4 March 2015). https://www.youtube.com/watch?v=XSS7SQoaY1g. 00:55.03 to 00:55:09 minutes; 01:04:15 to 01:04:23 minutes. Accessed: February 2021.
65   Siam Goorwich, 'Male Model Lets It All Hang Out on NYFW Catwalk Show', *METRO* (20 February 2015). https://metro.co.uk/2015/02/20/male-model-lets-it-all-hang-out-on-nyfw-catwalk-show-5071448/. Accessed: February 2021.
66   Cathy Donohue, 'Ballsy! Male Model Gives Onlookers an Eyeful at New York Fashion Week', *Her* (n.d.). https://www.her.ie/style/ballsy-male-model-gives-onlookers-an-eyeful-at-new-york-fashion-week-219710?cacheTtl=5&cacheKey=request-browser-httpswwwheriestyleballsy-male-model-gives-onlookers-an-eyeful-at-new-york-fashion-week219710. Accessed: March 2021.
67   Goorwich, 'Male Model'; Donohue, 'Male Model'.
68   Anon., 'Nude Male Model'.
69   'ART HEARTS FASHION', 00:52:43 to 00:52:51 minutes.
70   Anon., 'Nude Male Model'.
71   'ART HEARTS FASHION', 00:52:51 to 00:53:08 minutes.
72   'MT Costello at NYFW'. *Hollywood TV* (24 February 2015). https://www.youtube.com/watch?v=shYFcmTVcyA. 00:30:00 to 00:01:05 minutes. Accessed: February 2021.
73   The phrase is Bancroft's, 'Masculinity, Masquerade and Display', 20.
74   Clark, *The Nude*, 46.
75   'MT Costello at NYFW', 00:01:57 to 00:02:17 minutes.
76   Adam Tschorn, 'Stello, Formerly MT Costello, Mines the Darker Side of Hollywood in L.A. Fashion Week Debut', *The Los Angeles Times* (9 October 2015). www.latimes.com/fashion/alltherage/la-ar-stello-la-fashion-week-debut-20151008-story.html. Accessed: April 2021.
77   'ART HEARTS FASHION', 01:04:24 to 01:04:26 minutes.
78   Tsjeng, 'Full-Frontal'.

NOTES

79. Ingrid Silva Instagram post, *@ingridsilva* (13 November 2020). https://www.instagram.com/p/CHh_psajk_l/?igshid=10f9vc1rd4j1b. Instagram posts referred to in this section were. Accessed: 4 April 2021.
80. Brazilian *Vogue* Instagram post, *@voguebrasil* (13 November 2020). https://www.instagram.com/p/CHh7y3ulhVo/?utm_medium=copy_link.
81. Ibid.
82. Ibid.
83. Ibid.
84. Ibid. 'Lindíssima a capa, Ingrid maravilhosa, mas me pergunto se ninguém da direção da revista não pensou na representatividade por trás da camera. Um fofógrafo homem branco? MESMO?' In an adjoining comment, the author adds the names of four photographers, with the remark: 'apenas alguns nomes que facilmente poderiam ter feito essa capa. Bora repensar né @voguebrasil'.
85. Ingrid Silva Instagram post, *@ingridsilva*. 'Depois do escândalo da festa que a president desta revista protagonizou, é o mínimo que eles poderiam fazer: uma capa maravilhosa dessas, com uma enorme representatividade. Mas não me esqueço da festa não mesmo!'; Anna Jean Kaiser, 'Vogue Brazil Director Resigns over Birthday Photos Evoking Slavery', *The Guardian* (15 February 2019). https://www.theguardian.com/world/2019/feb/15/vogue-brazil-director-resigns-over-birthday-photos-evoking-slavery. Accessed: June 2021.
86. 'Cota batida com sucesso ✔ pensar que é da vontade de redação uma capa desta seria grande utopia para uma revista misógina.' Brazilian *Vogue* Instagram post, *@voguebrasil*.
87. Ingrid Silva Instagram post, *@ingridsilva*.
88. Imogen Tyler, 'Skin-Tight: Celebrity, Pregnancy and Subjectivity', *Transformations: Thinking Through Skin*, eds. Sara Ahmed and Jackie Stacey (London: Routledge, 2001), 69–83.
89. Ibid., 69.
90. Carol A. Stabile, *Feminism and the Technological Fix* (Manchester: Manchester University Press, 1994), 84.
91. Tyler, 'Skin-Tight', 75.
92. Ibid.
93. Ibid.
94. Matt Glazebrook, '10 Iconic Kate Moss Covers', *i-D* (19 February 2020). https://i-d.vice.com/en_uk/article/xgqvkw/10-iconic-kate-moss-magazine-covers. Accessed: June 2021. Glazebrook's comment is in reference to the portrait of Kate Moss that appeared on the cover of i-D's Name Issue, No. 258, September 2005; Colton Haynes Instagram post, @coltonlhaynes (31 March 2016), now removed.
95. Chioma Nnadi, 'Oh Baby! Rihanna's Plus One', *Vogue* (12 April 2022), https://www.vogue.com/article/rihanna-cover-may-2022. Accessed: May 2022.
96. Brazilian *Vogue* Instagram post, *@voguebrasil*.
97. Buzz Bissinger, 'Serena Williams's Love Match', *Vanity Fair* (27 June 2017). https://www.vanityfair.com/style/2017/06/serena-williams-cover-story. Accessed: June 2021.

98 Olivia Aylmer, 'Behind the Scenes of the Serena Williams Cover Shoot', *Vanity Fair* (27 June 2017). https://www.vanityfair.com/style/2017/06/serena-williams-cover-behind-the-scenes. Accessed: June 2021.
99 Ibid.
100 Tyler, 'Skin-Tight', 75.
101 Ibid., 74.
102 Ibid., 74, 75.
103 Aylmer, 'Behind the Scenes'.
104 Hollander, *Seeing Through Clothes*, 185.
105 Tyler, 'Skin-Tight', 75.
106 Ibid., 74.
107 Ibid.
108 Ibid.
109 Ibid.
110 Rosemary Betterton, 'Maternal Bodies in Visual Culture' (January 2009). https://www.researchgate.net/publication/237454497_Maternal_Bodies_in_Visual_Culture. Accessed: June 2021.
111 Julia Kristeva, 'Stabat Mater', *Poetics Today*, 6:1/2 (1985), 135.
112 Marques Travae, 'Ingrid Silva: First black Brazilian Ballerina Featured on the Cover of Vogue Brasil', *Black Brazil Today* (16 November 2020). https://blackbraziltoday.com/ingrid-silva-first-black-brazilian-ballerina-featured-on-the-cover-of-vogue-brasil/. Accessed: June 2021.
113 Ibid.
114 Luanda Vieira, 'Ingrid Silva: "Nada é mais poderoso do que lutar pela próxima geração e, agora, ser responsável por ela"', Brazilian *Vogue* (13 November 2020). https://vogue.globo.com/celebridade/noticia/2020/11/ingrid-silva-nada-e-mais-poderoso-do-que-lutar-pela-proxima-geracao-e-agora-ser-responsavel-por-ela.html. Accessed: June 2021.
115 Stabile, 'Shooting the Mother', 180.
116 Marques Travae, 'Palmitagem: The Discomfort in Thinking about Race and Relationships', *Black Brazil Today* (28 January 2020). https://blackbraziltoday.com/palmitagem-the-discomfort-in-thinking-about-race-and-relationships/. Accessed: June 2021.
117 Petrônio Domingues, 'A Visita de um Afro-Americano ao Paraíso Racial', *Revista de História*, 155 (2006), 161–181, 169.
118 Ibid., 168.
119 Ibid., 177.
120 Ibid., 179.
121 Ibid., 175.
122 Ibid., 173. 'A elite branca brasileira tinha sido educada desde o período colonial a ver os negros como inferiores. Tinha também aprendido a abrir exceções para alguns indivíduos negros ou mulatos. Assim, embora afirmando a superioridade

NOTES

dos brancos sobre os negros nas primeiras décadas do século XX, a elite aceitava "pessoas de cor" em seu meio. E tinha o desejo de eliminar o "problema" do negro no futuro, por intermédio da mestiçagem. Fomentando a miscigenação, a popu- lação tornar-se-ia cada vez mais branca.'

123 Fred Davis, *Fashion, Culture, and Identity* (Chicago: Chicago University Press, 1992). 'Ambiguous' and 'ambiguity' appear twenty-three times; 'Ambivalent' and 'ambivalence' appear fifty-eight times.

Chapter 2

1 See above, 21.

2 Aileen Ribeiro, 'Dress in Utopia', *Costume*, 21:1 (1987), 26–33.

3 Thomas More, *Utopia*, translated by Paul Turner (London: Penguin Books, 1965), 78.

4 Ibid., 75.

5 Ibid.

6 Ibid., 79, 87, 88.

7 Judith Butler, *Gender Trouble: Feminism and the Subversion of Identity* (London: Routledge, 1990).

8 Stephen O. Murray and Will Roscoe, 'Overview', Part II, West Africa, *Boy-Wives and Female Husbands: Studies in African Homosexualities*, eds. Stephen O. Murray and Will Roscoe (Albany: State University of New York Press, 1998), 92.

9 Kathleen Wilson, *The Island Race: Englishness, Empire and Gender in the Eighteenth Century* (London: Routledge, 2003), 195; Rudi C. Bleys, *The Geography of Perversion: Male-to-Male Sexual Behaviour Outside the West and the Ethnographic Imagination 1750-1918* (London: Cassell, 1996), 165; Jessica Hinchy, 'The Sexual Politics of Imperial Expansion: Eunuchs and Indirect Colonial Rule in Mid-Nineteenth-Century North India', *Gender, Imperialism and Global Exchanges*, eds. Stephan F. Miescher, Michelle Mitchell and Naoko Shibusawa (Chichester: John Wiley & Sons, 2015), 33.

10 More, *Utopia*, 75.

11 Londa Schiebinger, 'The Anatomy of Difference: Race and Sex in Eighteenth-Century Science', *Eighteenth-Century Studies*, 23:4 (1980), 388.

12 Ibid., 391–392; Bleys, *Geography of Perversion*, 157.

13 Schiebinger, 'The Anatomy of Difference', 392.

14 Wilson, *The Island Race*, 1–27.

15 Ibid., 12.

16 Bleys, *The Geography of Perversion*, 85; Patrick Mauriès, *Androgyne: Fashion and Gender* (London: Thames and Hudson, 2017), 18–19; Nancy Leys Stepan, 'Race, Gender, Science and Citizenship', *Cultures of Empire: Colonizers in Britain and the Empire in the Nineteenth and Twentieth Centuries*, ed. Catherine Hall (Manchester: Manchester University Press, 2000), 77–8.

17 Ariel Beaujot, 'Gender and Sexuality', *A Cultural History of Dress and Fashion in the Age of Empire*, vol. 5, ed. Denise Amy Baxter (London: Bloomsbury, 2017), 99.

18 Nancy Leys Stepan, 'Race and Gender: The Role of Analogy in Science', *Isis*, 77:2 (1986), 266.

19 Hinchy, 'Sexual Politics', 28, 31.

20 Ben Barker-Benfield, 'The Spermatic Economy: A Nineteenth Century View of Sexuality', *Feminist Studies*, 1:1 (1957), 57.

21 Jack Hartnell, *Medieval Bodies: Life, Death and Art in the Middle Ages* (London: Profile Books, 2018), 44.

22 Stepan, 'Race, Gender, Science and Citizenship', 63.

23 Wilson, *The Island Race*, 6.

24 Schiebinger, 'The Anatomy of Difference', 389.

25 Stepan, 'Race and Gender', 264.

26 Hinchy, 'Sexual Politics', 37.

27 Bleys, *The Geography of Perversion*, 83.

28 Judith Butler, 'Why is the Idea of "gender" Provoking Backlash the World Over?' *The Guardian* (23 October 2021). https://www.theguardian.com/us-news/commentisfree/2021/oct/23/judith-butler-gender-ideology-backlash. Accessed: June 2022.

29 Anon., 'My Self, My Avatar, My Identity: Diversity and Inclusivity within Virtual Worlds' (Institute of Digital Fashion, 2021). https://docsend.com/view/wem8e7ppe7gr4mrk. Accessed: June 2022, 15; See below, 178–179.

30 See above, 8–9.

31 Anon., 'Céline Spring 2019 Ready-to-Wear', *Vogue.com* (no date). https://www.vogue.com/fashion-shows/spring-2019-ready-to-wear/celine/slideshow/collection#1. Accessed: June 2021.

32 Anon., 'Pre-fall 2018 Celine', *Vogue.com* (no date). https://www.vogue.com/fashion-shows/pre-fall-2018/celine/slideshow/collection#1. Accessed: June 2021.

33 Leanne Delap, 'Toxic Masculinity at Paris Fashion Week: Why Hedi Slimane's Celine Debut was so Egregiously Tone-Deaf', *The Kit* (1 October 2018). https://thekit.ca/style/hedi-slimane-celine-debut-misogynist/. Accessed: April 2021.

34 Vanessa Friedman, 'Hedi Slimane's Celine: Mamma Mia! Here We Go Again', *The New York Times* (29 September 2018). https://www.nytimes.com/2018/09/29/fashion/celine-hedi-slimane-paris-fashion-week.html. Accessed: May 2021.

35 Ibid.

36 Tim Blanks, 'A Dark New Dawn at Celine', *Business of Fashion* (29 September 2018). https://www.businessoffashion.com/reviews/fashion-week/a-dark-new-dawn-at-celine. Accessed: April 2021.

37 Delap, 'Toxic Masculinity at Paris Fashion Week'.

38 Booth Moore, 'Is Hedi Slimane the Donald Trump of Fashion?', *The Hollywood Reporter* (30 September 2018). https://www.hollywoodreporter.com/lifestyle/style/is-hedi-slimane-donald-trump-fashion-1148087/. Accessed: July 2021.

NOTES

39 Anon., 'The Most Savage Reviews of Hedi Slimane's Celine Debut', *Fashionista* (1 October 2018). https://fashionista.com/2018/10/hedi-slimane-celine-debut-bad-reviews. Accessed: April 2021.

40 Sarah Mower, 'Celine: Pre-Fall 2018', *Vogue.com* (2 May 2018). https://www.vogue.com/fashion-shows/pre-fall-2018/celine. Accessed: June 2021.

41 Zoe Ruffner, '5 Céline Beauty Rules to Get You through Phoebe Philo's Absence Today in Paris', *Vogue.com* (4 March 2018). https://www.vogue.com/article/celine-phoebe-philo-beauty-minimalist-makeup-dick-page-paris-fashion-week. Accessed: June 2021.

42 Delap, 'Toxic Masculinity at Paris Fashion Week'.

43 Friedman, 'Hedi Slimane's Celine'.

44 AFP-Relaxnews, 'Hedi Slimane Reveals Iconic Venue for His Debut Celine Show in Paris', *Fashion Network* (21 September 2018). https://www.fashionnetwork.com/news/Hedi-slimane-reveals-iconic-venue-for-his-debut-celine-show-in-paris,1016466.html. Accessed: June 2021.

45 Friedman, 'Hedi Slimane's Celine'.

46 Anne Hollander, *Sex and Suits: The Evolution of Modern Dress* (New York: Alfred A. Knopf, 1994), 3; Christopher Breward, *The Suit: Form, Function and Style* (London: Reaktion Books, 2016), 7.

47 Laurence Benaïm, 'Hedi Slimane's First Celine Interview', *Business of Fashion* (25 September 2018). https://www.businessoffashion.com/articles/news-analysis/hedi-slimane-interview-celine. Accessed: April 2021.

48 Ibid.

49 Ibid.

50 Ibid.

51 Ibid.

52 Ibid.

53 Ibid.

54 Ibid.

55 Joanna de Groot, '"Sex" and "race": The Construction of Language and Image in the Nineteenth Century', *Cultures of Empire*, 42c45.

56 Benaïm, 'Celine Interview'.

57 Ibid.

58 Ibid.

59 de Groot, '"Sex" and "race"', 47.

60 Ibid., 50–51.

61 Friedman, 'Hedi Slimane's Celine'.

62 John Berger, *Ways of Seeing* (London: Penguin, 1972), 41.

63 Laura Mulvey, 'Visual Pleasure in Narrative Cinema', *Screen*, 16:3 (1975), 7, 11.

64 For context, see Benjamin William Vincent, 'Studying Trans: Recommendations for Ethical Recruitment and Collaboration with Transgender Participants in Academic Research', *Psychology & Sexuality*, 9:2 (2018), 102–116.

65 Mulvey, 'Visual Pleasure', 7.

66 Benaïm, 'Celine Interview'.

67 Anabel Maldonado, 'In Defense of Hedi Slimane', *Business of Fashion* (16 October 2018). https://www.businessoffashion.com/opinions/news-analysis/defense-of-hedi-slimane-celine. Accessed: April 2021.

68 Delap, 'Toxic Masculinity at Paris Fashion Week'.

69 Moore, 'The Donald Trump of Fashion?'.

70 Maldonado, 'In Defense of Hedi Slimane'.

71 Luce Irigaray, *This Sex Which Is Not One*, trans. Catherine Porter (Ithaca: Cornell University Press, [1977] 1985), 124.

72 Paul Jobling, Philippa Nesbitt and Angelene Wong, *Fashion, Identity, Image* (London: Bloomsbury, 2022), 10.

73 'Shimmer in the Dark: Jimmy Choo CR18 Featuring Cara Delevingne', *Jimmy Choo YouTube* (9 November 2017). https://www.youtube.com/watch?v=DPrRRgagQg8. Accessed: May 2021.

74 Ibid., 00:00:36 minutes to 00:00:39 minutes.

75 Ibid., 00:00:40 minutes to 00:00:44 minutes.

76 Ibid., 00:00:45 minutes to 00:00:52 minutes.

77 Ibid., 00:01:08 minutes to 00:01:25 minutes.

78 Ibid., 00:01:33 minutes to 00:01:35 minutes.

79 Ibid., 00:00:58 minutes to 00:01:03 minutes.

80 Hannah Van-De-Peer, 'Jimmy Choo Winter Ad 2017: A Problematic Portrayal of Sexism in Our Society', *Affinity* (23 December 2017). http://culture.affinitymagazine.us/jimmy-choo-winter-ad-2017-a-problematic-portrayal-of-sexism-in-our-society/. Accessed: May 2021.

81 Hayley Petersen, 'Jimmy Choo Comes under Fire for "sexist" Ad Depicting Men Cat-Calling a Woman on the Street', *Business Insider* (19 December 2017). https://www.businessinsider.com/jimmy-choo-comes-under-fire-for-ad-depicting-cat-calling-2017-12?r=US&IR=T. Accessed: May 2021.

82 Lee Moran, 'Jimmy Choo's "Tone Deaf" Ad Goes Viral for All the Wrong Reasons', *Huffington Post* (22 December 2017). https://www.huffingtonpost.co.uk/entry/jimmy-choo-ad-sexist_n_5a3cd44ae4b0b0e5a7a1499d?ri18n=true. Accessed: May 2021.

83 Hannah Ongley, 'Jimmy Choo's Cara Delevingne Catcalling Ad is "Tone Deaf", Says Twitter', *i-D* (20 December 2017). https://i-d.vice.com/en_uk/article/kznwex/jimmy-choos-cara-delevingne-catcalling-ad-is-tone-deaf-says-twitter. Accessed: June 2021.

84 Miranda Larbi, 'Everyone Thinks Cara Delevingne's New Jimmy Choo Ad is Sexist – Do You?', *Metro* (24 December 2017). https://metro.co.uk/2017/12/24/everyone-thinks-cara-delevingnes-new-jimmy-choo-ad-sexist-7183143/. Accessed: May 2021.

85 William Hunt, 'Jimmy Choo: Simmer in the Dark: The Brand Taps Cara Delevingne for Cruise 18', *Wonderland* (9 November 2017). https://www.wonderlandmagazine.com/2017/11/09/jimmy-choo-cruise-18/. Accessed: May 2021.

NOTES

86 Cassia Carter, 'Cara Delevingne: À La Fois Féminine Et Androgyne Pour Jimmy Choo', *Grazia Fr.* (10 November 2017). https://www.grazia.fr/mode/cara-delevingne-a-la-fois-feminine-et-androgyne-pour-jimmy-choo-873013. Accessed: May 2021.

87 Ibid.

88 Ibid.

89 Jobling, Nesbitt and Wong, *Fashion, Identity, Image*, 10.

90 Jodi Kantor and Megan Twohey, 'Harvey Weinstein Paid Off Sexual Harassment Accusers for Decades', *The New York Times* (5 October 2017). https://www.nytimes.com/2017/10/05/us/harvey-weinstein-harassment-allegations.html. Accessed: June 2021.

91 Instagram post @caradelevingne (11 October 2017). https://www.instagram.com/p/BaHc485FRVx/?taken-by=caradelevingne. Accessed: June 2021.

92 Anon., 'Harvey Weinstein Timeline: How the Scandal Unfolded', *BBC News* (7 April 2021), https://www.bbc.co.uk/news/entertainment-arts-41594672. Accessed: June 2021.

93 Dara Plant, 'Must Read: Cara Delevingne's Catcalling Jimmy Choo Ad Prompts Twitter Outrage, Valentino May Sell a Quarter of the Company', *Fashionista* (21 December 2017). https://fashionista.com/2017/12/jimmy-choo-cara-delevingne-ad-controversy. Accessed: June 2021.

94 N. Phelps, '"We're Nobody's Third Love, We're Their First Love"—The Architects of the Victoria's Secret Fashion Show Are Still Banking on Bombshells', *Vogue* (8 November 2018). https://www.vogue.com/article/victorias-secret-ed-razek-monica-mitro-interview. Accessed: May 2021.

95 Emma Hope Allwood, 'Trans Activists Aren't Buying Victoria's Secret's Apology', *DazedDigital* (11 November 2018). https://www.dazeddigital.com/fashion/article/42179/1/victoria-s-secret-backpeddles-over-transphobia-ed-razek-comments-trans-models. Accessed: May 2021.

96 Phelps, '"We're Nobody's Third Love".

97 Tweet quoted in Allwood, 'Trans Activists Aren't Buying Victoria's Secret's Apology'.

98 Emma Elizabeth Davidson, 'The 2018 Victoria's Secret Show had Its Lowest TV Ratings Ever', *DazedDigital* (4 December 2018). https://www.dazeddigital.com/fashion/article/42469/1/victorias-secret-lowest-tv-ratings-ever-halsey-lgbtq-plus-size-ed-razek. Accessed: July 2021.

99 Emma Elizabeth Davidson, 'Victoria's Secret just Hired Its First Ever Trans Model', *DazedDigital* (5 August 2019). https://www.dazeddigital.com/fashion/article/45499/1/victorias-secret-angel-transgender-model-valentina-sampaio-underwear-label. Accessed: May 2021; Christine Hauser, 'Victoria's Secret Casts First Openly Transgender Woman as a Model', *The New York Times* (5 August 2019), https://www.nytimes.com/2019/08/05/business/victoria-secret-transgender-model.html. Accessed: May 2021.

100 Tiffany Hsu and Emily Steel, 'Victoria's Secret Executive Leaves as Company Distances Itself from Epstein', *The New York Times* (5 August 2019). https://www.nytimes.com/2019/08/05/business/victorias-secret-ed-razek.html. Accessed:

July 2021; Ellie Violet Bramley, 'Marketing Boss Quits Victoria's Secret after First Trans Model Hired', *The Guardian* (6 August 2019). https://www.theguardian.com/fashion/2019/aug/06/marketing-boss-quits-victorias-secret-first-trans-model-hired. Accessed: May 2021.

101 Kyle Munzenrider, 'Victoria's Secret Exec Explains Why They Don't Use Trans or Plus-Size Models', *W Magazine* (9 November 2018). https://www.wmagazine.com/story/victorias-secret-fashion-show-ed-razek-comments-trans-plus-size-models. Accessed: July 2021.

102 Jobling, Nesbitt and Wong, *Fashion, Identity, Image*, 79.

103 Jada Yuan and Aaron Wong, 'The First Black Trans Model Had Her Face on a Box of Clairol', *The Cut* (15 December 2015). https://www.thecut.com/2015/12/tracey-africa-transgender-model-c-v-r.html. Accessed: June 2022.

104 Phelps, '"We're Nobody's Third Love".

105 Ibid.

106 Tarana Burke, '#MeToo Founder Tarana Burke on the Rigorous Work That Still Lies Ahead', *Variety* (25 September 2018). https://variety.com/2018/biz/features/tarana-burke-metoo-one-year-later-1202954797/. Accessed: June 2022.

107 Phelps, '"We're Nobody's Third Love".

108 Munzenrieder, 'Victoria's Secret'.

109 Phelps, '"We're Nobody's Third Love".

110 Allwood, 'Trans Activists Aren't Buying Victoria's Secret's Apology'.

111 Jobling, Nesbitt and Wong, *Fashion, Identity, Image*, 79.

112 Ibid.

113 Michel Foucault, trans. Jay Miskowiec, 'Of Other Spaces: Utopias and Heterotopias', *Architecture /Mouvement/ Continuité* (October 1984), 3–4.

114 Jobling, Nesbitt and Wong, *Fashion, Identity, Image*, 81.

115 Cynthia Silva, 'Ariel Nicholson is U.S. Vogue's First Transgender Cover Model', *NBC News* (9 August 2021). https://www.nbcnews.com/nbc-out/out-life-and-style/ariel-nicholson-us-vogues-first-transgender-cover-model-rcna1630. Accessed: August 2022.

116 Jobling, Nesbitt and Wong, *Fashion, Identity, Image*, 67.

117 Ibid., 101.

118 Michel Foucault, *The Order of Things: An Archaeology of the Human Sciences* (London: Routledge, [1966] 1970), cxviii.

119 See below, 125–127.

Chapter 3

1 Plato, *The Republic*, translated by A. D. Lindsay (London: Random House, [1935] 1976), IX, 280–281.

2 Antonio Gramsci, *Selections from Cultural Writings*, eds. David Forgas and Geoffrey Nowell-Smith, translated by William Boelhower (London: Lawrence and Wishart, 1985), 349.

NOTES

3. Sarah Cheang, 'Ethnicity', *A Cultural History of Dress and Fashion in the Age of Empire*, vol. 5, ed. Denise Amy Baxter (London: Bloomsbury, 2017), 141.

4. Jess Cartner-Morley, 'Kanye West Stirs Controversy in "White Lives Matter" T-shirt at Paris Fashion Week', *The Guardian* (4 October 2022). https://www.theguardian.com/music/2022/oct/04/kanye-west-white-lives-matter-t-shirt-paris-fashion-week. Accessed: January 2023.

5. Edward Said, *Orientalism* (London: Penguin, [1978] 2013), 1; Joanne P. Sharp, *Geographies of Postcolonialism: Spaces of Power and Representation* (London: Sage, 2009), 16.

6. Said, *Orientalism*, 3, 4.

7. Ibid., 6.

8. Ibid., 206.

9. Londa Schiebinger, *Nature's Body: Gender in the Making of Modern Science* (New Brunswick: Rutgers University Press, 1993), 143.

10. Ibid., 144.

11. Ibid., 144–145.

12. Arthur de Gobineau, *Essai sur l'inégalité des races humaines*, 4 vols (Paris: Librairie de Firmin Didot, 1853-1855), i, 81.

13. David Graeber and David Wengrove, *The Dawn of Everything: A New History of Humanity* (London: Penguin, 2021), 92–93.

14. Stuart Hall, 'Race, Articulation, and Societies Structured in Dominance', *Black British Cultural Studies: A Reader*, eds. Houston A. Baker, Jr., Manthia Diawara and Ruth H. Lindeborg (Chicago and London: The University of Chicago Press, [1980] 1996), 56.

15. Sharp, *Geographies of Postcolonialism*, 32.

16. Hall, 'Race', 57.

17. Cheang, 'Ethnicity', 148.

18. Ibid.

19. Ibid., 148–163.

20. Emma Dabiri, *What White People Can Do Next: From Allyship to Coalition* (London: Penguin, 2021), 51.

21. Emma Dabiri, 'The Speakeasier with Emma Dabiri: When was race & ethnicity invented? The *Unmistakables* (20 May 2021). https://www.theunmistakables.com/post/the-speakeasier-with-emma-dabiri. Accessed: August 2021.

22. Dabiri, *What White People Can Do Next*, 45. Original emphasis.

23. Hall, 'Race', 53.

24. Ibid.

25. Ibid., 51.

26. Roland Betancourt, *Byzantine Intersectionality: Sexuality, Gender & Race in the Middle Ages* (Princeton and Oxford: Princeton University Press, 2020), 176.

27. Ibid., 182.

28 Rictor Norton, *The Myth of the Modern Homosexual: Queer History and the Search for Cultural Unity* (London and Washington: Cassell, 1997), 99.

29 Chinyere Ezie Facebook post (14 December 2019). https://www.facebook.com/300322/posts/10102198924210054/. Accessed: August 2021.

30 Ibid.

31 Marc Bain, 'Prada has Pulled Its Red-Lipped Monkey Dolls, which Echoed Racist "Sambo" Imagery', *Quartz* (14 December 2018). https://qz.com/quartzy/1496189/prada-pulls-sambo-esque-monkey-dolls-after-blackface-criticism/. Accessed: August 2021.

32 Asri Jasman, 'Meet Prada's New Pradamalia Collectibles', *Esquire* (12 October 2018). https://www.esquiresg.com/prada-accessories-new-pradamalia-collectibles/. Accessed: August 2021.

33 Ibid.

34 Ibid.

35 Ibid.

36 Jake Offenhartz, 'Soho Prada Pulls "Extremely Racist" Products with "Blackface Imagery" From Window Display', *Gothamist* (14 December 2018). https://gothamist.com/news/soho-prada-pulls-extremely-racist-products-with-blackface-imagery-from-window-display. Accessed: August 2021.

37 Julia Gonzales, 'Prada Scrambles To Remove Monkey Collection Amid Racist Backlash', *UWIRE Text* (16 December 2018). https://go.gale.com/ps/i.do?p=AONE&u=mmucal5&id=GALE|A566009545&v=2.1&it=r&sid=bookmark-AONE&asid=5d75f4d9. Accessed: August 2021.

38 Amanda Coletta, 'Prada Pulls Products after Blackface Imagery Accusations', *CTV News* (16 December 2018). https://www.ctvnews.ca/business/prada-pulls-products-after-blackface-imagery-accusations-1.4220256. Accessed: August 2021. Quotation from embedded video at 00:00:42 to 00:00:47 minutes.

39 Prada Tweet, @prada (14 December 2018). https://twitter.com/Prada/status/1073614897207017481?ref_src=twsrc%5Etfw%7Ctwcamp%5Etweetembed%7Ctwterm%5E1073614897207017481%7Ctwgr%5E%7Ctwcon%5Es1_&ref_url=https%3A%2F%2Fwww.ctvnews.ca%2Fbusiness%2Fprada-pulls-products-after-blackface-imagery-accusations-1.4220256. Accessed: August 2021.

40 Ibid.

41 Offenhartz, 'Soho Prada Pulls "Extremely Racist" Products'.

42 Press release, *The New York City Commission on Human Rights* (5 February 2020). https://www1.nyc.gov/assets/cchr/downloads/pdf/press-releases/Prada_Settlement_Press_Release.pdf. Accessed: August 2021.

43 Ibid.

44 Jasman, 'Meet Prada's New Pradamalia Collectibles'.

45 Jen Chung, 'After Blackface Scandal, Prada Agrees To "Landmark" Restorative Justice Settlement with NYC', https://doodle.com/meeting/participate/id/eZzqkQwe (5 February 2021). https://gothamist.com/arts-entertainment/after-blackface-scandal-prada-agrees-landmark-restorative-justice-settlement-nyc. Accessed: August 2021.

46 Ayanna Thompson, *Blackface* (London: Bloomsbury 2021), 6.

47. Ibid., 5–6.
48. Ibid., 12–18; 53–73.
49. Ibid., 40.
50. Ibid.
51. Minh-Ha T. Pham, 'Racial Plagiarism', *QED*, 4:3 (2017), 74.
52. Thompson, *Blackface*, 34.
53. Robin Bernstein, *Racial Innocence: Performing American Childhood from Slavery to Civil Rights* (New York: New York University Press, 2011), 16.
54. Ibid., 67, and see Plate 3.
55. Ibid., 66.
56. Ibid., 149, 157–165, 171–178, 219–222.
57. Schiebinger, *Nature's Body*, 78, 98.
58. Ibid., 94–95.
59. Bernstein, *Racial Innocence*, 181.
60. Jennifer C. Mueller, Danielle Dirks and Leslie Houts Picca, 'Unmasking Racism: Halloween Costuming and Engagement of the Racial Other', *Qualitative Sociology*, 30 (April 2007), 331.
61. Benjamin L. Wild, 'Critical Reflections on Cultural Appropriation, Race and the Role of Fancy Dress Costume', *Critical Studies in Fashion and Beauty*, 11:2 (2020), 157–160.
62. Ibid., 161.
63. Morwenna Ferrier, 'Gucci Withdraws $890 Jumper after Blackface Blacklash', *The Guardian* (7 February 2019). https://www.theguardian.com/fashion/2019/feb/07/gucci-withdraws-jumper-blackface-balaclava. Accessed: August 2021.
64. Gucci Twitter (7 February 2019). https://twitter.com/gucci/status/1093345744080306176/photo/1. Accessed: August 2021.
65. Dapper Dan Instagram @dapperdanharlem (10 February 2019). https://www.instagram.com/p/BttpJA7gCIy/?utm_source=ig_web_copy_link. Accessed: August 2021.
66. Ibid.
67. Ibid.
68. Dapper Dan Instagram @dapperdanharlem (15 February 2019). https://www.instagram.com/p/Bt6Y5pYg3ny/?utm_source=ig_web_copy_link. Accessed: August 2021.
69. Luisa Zargani, 'Gucci Launches Initiatives to Foster Cultural Diversity and Awareness', *WWD* (15 February 2021). https://wwd.com/fashion-news/designer-luxury/gucci-launches-initiatives-to-foster-cultural-diversity-and-awareness-1203028610/. Accessed: August 2021.
70. Luisa Zargani, 'EXCLUSIVE: Gucci's Marco Bizzarri on Learning Amid Blackface Accusations', *WWD* (12 February 2019). https://wwd.com/fashion-news/designer-luxury/gucci-blackface-response-marco-bizzarri-alessandro-michele-1203020161/. Accessed: August 2021; Alyssa Vingan Klein, 'Internal Memo

from Gucci CEO Shows He's Taking The Blackface Scandal Very, Very Seriously', *Fashionista* (11 February 2019). https://fashionista.com/2019/02/gucci-blackface-sweater-ceo-marco-bizzarri-statement. Accessed: August 2021.

71 Anon., 'Alessando Michele Breaks His Silence about Gucci's Blackface Scandal', *Fashionista* (12 February 2019). https://fashionista.com/2019/02/gucci-blackface-sweater-alessandro-michele-statement. Accessed: August 2021.

72 Lauren Alexis Fisher, 'Things Got Weird At Gucci's Fall 2018 Show', *Harper's Bazaar* (21 February 2018). https://www.harpersbazaar.com/fashion/fashion-week/a18564887/gucci-fall-2018-show/. Accessed: August 2021.

73 Tyler McCall, 'Gucci Out-Guccis Itself for Fall 2018', *Fashionista* (21 February 2018). https://fashionista.com/2018/02/gucci-fall-2018-review. Accessed: August 2021.

74 Sarah Mower, 'Gucci: Fall 2018 Ready-to-Wear', *Vogue* (21 February 2021). https://www.vogue.com/fashion-shows/fall-2018-ready-to-wear/gucci. Accessed: August 2021.

75 Ibid.

76 Ibid.

77 Fisher, 'Things Got Weird'.

78 Tahmina Begum, 'Gucci Criticised for Cultural Appropriation on a Global Scale', *The Huffington Post* (22 February 2018). https://www.huffingtonpost.co.uk/entry/gucci-autumn-winter-2018-show_uk_5a8e996be4b0161d4318dfdc. Accessed: August 2021.

79 For example, looks 8, 12, 20, 36, 41, 63, Mower, 'Gucci: Fall 2018 Ready-to-Wear'.

80 Amy Held, 'Gucci Apologizes and Removes Sweater Following "Blackface" Backlash', *NPR* (7 February 2019). https://www.npr.org/2019/02/07/692314950/gucci-apologizes-and-removes-sweater-following-blackface-backlash?t=1629114462933&t=1629197197660. Accessed: August 2021.

81 Ibid.

82 Thompson, *Blackface*, 10–15.

83 Caroline Evans and Alessandra Vaccari, 'Time in Fashion: An Introductory Essay', *Time in Fashion: Industrial, Antilinear and Uchronic Temporalities*, eds. Caroline Evans and Alessandra Vaccari (London: Bloomsbury, 2020), 4.

84 Angelo Flaccavento, 'Alessandro Michele: Quotations, the Past and Future of Fashion. Here's My Vision', Italian *Vogue*, 805 (September 2017), 191, translated by Antony Bowden. www.vogue.it/en/fashion/news/2017/09/01/alessandro-michele-quotations-past-future-fashion-interview-vogue-italia/. Accessed: December 2020; Angelo Flaccavento, 'Quotations: The Past and the Future of Fashion', *Time in Fashion*, 111–113.

85 Giorgia Sepe and Alessia Anzivino, 'Guccification: Redefining Luxury through Art—The Gucci Revolution', *The Artification of Luxury Fashion Brands*, eds. Marta Massi and Alex Turrini (London: Palgrave, 2020), 89–112.

86 Jean-Noël Kapferer, 'The Artification of Luxury: From Artisans to Artists', *Business Horizons*, 57 (2014), 371–380.

87 https://www.instagram.com/p/CAkszCYpBJV/. Accessed: January 2021.
88 Anon., 'Sponsor's Statement', *Camp: Notes on Fashion*, ed. Andrew Bolton (New Haven and London: Yale University Press, 2019), 1/6.
89 See above, 4–5.
90 Adam Geczy and Vicki Karaminas, *Critical Fashion Practice: From Westwood to Van Beirendonck* (London: Bloomsbury, 2017), 3–4.
91 Ibid., 4.
92 Anna Wintour, 'Can Fashion Keep Up with 21st-Century Trends', *The Economist* (18 July 2019). https://www.economist.com/podcasts/2019/07/18/can-fashion-keep-up-with-21st-century-trends. Accessed: June 2022.
93 Paul Jobling, Philippa Nesbitt and Angelene Wong, *Fashion, Identity, Image* (London: Bloomsbury, 2022), 115–136.
94 Ibid., 135.
95 Ibid., 124.
96 Ibid., 128.
97 Ibid., 136.
98 Ibid., 116, 125.
99 Benjamin L. Wild, *Carnival to Catwalk: Global Reflections on Fancy Dress Costume* (London: Bloomsbury, 2020), 148–149.
100 Patrice Peck, 'J. Crew Just Apologized for a Black Model's Seriously Controversial Hairstyle', *Buzzfeed* (11 November 2017). https://www.buzzfeed.com/patricepeck/this-black-models-hair-is-causing-a-debate-and-people-are. Accessed: August 2021.
101 J. Crew tweet, @jcrew (10 November 2017). https://twitter.com/jcrew/status/929021088796958720?ref_src=twsrc%5Etfw%7Ctwcamp%5Etweetembed%7Ctwterm%5E929021088796958720%7Ctwgr%5E%7Ctwcon%5Es1_&ref_url=https%3A%2F%2Fwww.cosmopolitan.com%2Fstyle-beauty%2Ffashion%2Fa13524555%2Fthe-internet-is-mad-at-j-crew-over-this-black-models-hairstyle%2F. Accessed: August 2021.
102 https://theshaderoom.com/who-are-we/. Accessed: September 2021.
103 The Shade Room @theshaderoom Instagram post (11 November 2017). https://www.instagram.com/p/BbWHD4mlWFq/?utm_source=ig_web_copy_link. Accessed: August 2021.
104 The Editors, 'The Internet Is Mad at J. Crew Over This Black Model's Hairstyle', *Cosmopolitan* (12 November 2017). https://www.cosmopolitan.com/style-beauty/fashion/a13524555/the-internet-is-mad-at-j-crew-over-this-black-models-hairstyle/. Accessed: August 2021.
105 Essence Gant, 'This Model Said Stylists Would Be Fired If They Couldn't Do White Models' Hair, and She's Right', *Buzzfeed* (5 October 2017). https://www.buzzfeed.com/essencegant/this-model-blasted-industry-after-fashion-wk-stylists?utm_term=.sh5zm4da2V#.paYZ4jaKRp. Accessed: August 2021.
106 Daniel Boan, 'Lupita Nyong'o Called Out a Magazine for Photoshopping Her Natural Hair on the Cover', *Insider* (10 November 2017). https://www.insider

107 Ibid.

108 Victoria Sanusi, 'Solange Responded to the Evening Standard After It Photoshopped Her Braid Out of its Cover', *Buzzfeed* (20 October 2017). https://www.buzzfeed.com/victoriasanusi/solange-responded-to-the-evening-standard-after-they?utm_term=.rlNalXjDB#.jnbK1XQG6. Accessed: August 2021.

109 Emma Dabiri, *Don't Touch My Hair* (London: Penguin, 2019), 6.

110 Ibid., 29.

111 Ibid., 15.

112 Ibid., 10.

113 Ibid., 93.

114 Ibid., 39, 87; Emma Tarlo, *Entanglement: The Secret Lives of Hair* (London: Bloomsbury, 2016), 142–153.

115 Peck, 'J. Crew Just Apologized'.

116 Ayana Lage, 'Everyone is Pissed at Madewell for This Black Model's Hair, But There May Be More to the Story', *Bustle* (13 November 2017). https://www.bustle.com/p/everyone-is-pissed-at-madewell-for-this-black-models-hair-but-there-may-be-more-to-the-story-3909817. Accessed: September 2021.

117 Chaédria Labouvier, 'This Black Model's "Messy" Hair Sparked Debate on Social Media', *Allure* (10 November 2017). https://www.allure.com/story/madewell-model-messy-hair-debate. Accessed: September 2021.

118 Jobling, Nesbitt and Wong, *Fashion, Identity, Image*, 121.

119 Minh-Ha T. Pham, 'Fashion's Cultural-Appropriation Debate: Pointless', *The Atlantic* (15 May 2014). www.theatlantic.com/entertainment/archive/2014/05/cultural-appropriation-in-fashion-stop-talking-about-it/370826. Accessed: November 2019.

120 Dal Chodha, 'In Defence of Fashion's Limits – And Its Infinite Possibilities', *i-D*, 368 (2022), 209.

121 Ibid.

Chapter 4

1 Joanne Finkelstein, *The Fashioned Self* (Cambridge: Polity Press, 1991), 1.

2 Ruth Barcan, *Nudity: A Cultural Anatomy* (London: Bloomsbury, 2004), 11.

3 Virginia Wolff, *Orlando: A Biography* (London: Vintage Books, [1928] 1992), 121.

4 Ibid.

5 Ann L. Stoler, 'Making Empire Respectable: The Politics of Race and Sexual Morality in 20th-Century Colonial Cultures', *American Ethnologist*, 16:4 (1989), 645.

NOTES 215

6. Jayne Elizabeth Lewis, *Mary Queen of Scots: Romance and Nation* (London: Routledge, 1998), 78.
7. Ibid., 207.
8. Richard Ovenden, *Burning the Books: A History of Knowledge Under Attack* (London: John Murray, 2020), 4.
9. Edward W. Said, *Orientalism* (London: Penguin, [1978] 2003), 6, 207.
10. Stoler, 'Making Empire Respectable, 637.
11. Ibid., 641.
12. Matt Smith, *Losing Venus* (Oxford: Pitt Rivers Museum, 2020), 6–17.
13. Stoler, 'Making Empire Respectable', 636, 646.
14. Rudi C. Bleys, *The Geography of Perversion: Male-to-male Sexual Behaviour outside the West and the Ethnographic Imagination 1750-1918* (London: Cassell, 1996), 89–91; Robert Aldrich, *Colonialism and Homosexuality* (London: Routledge, 2003).
15. Bleys, *The Geography of Perversion*, 70.
16. Stoler, 'Making Empire Respectable', 635.
17. Gayle S. Rubin, 'Thinking Sex: Notes for a Radical Theory of the Politics of Sexuality', *Culture, Society and Sexuality: A Reader*, second edn, eds. Richard Parker and Peter Aggleton (London: Routledge, [1984] 1999), 150.
18. Bleys, *The Geography of Perversion*, 49.
19. See above 39, 40.
20. Kenneth James Dover, *Greek Homosexuality* (London: Bloomsbury, [1978] 2016), 16.
21. Ibid., 20.
22. Ibid., 59.
23. Charles Hupperts, 'Homosexuality in Greece and Rome', *Gay Life and Culture: A World History*, ed. Robert Aldrich (London: Thames and Hudson, 2006), 41.
24. Ibid.
25. Ibid., 52–53.
26. *Boy-Wives and Female Husbands: Studies in African Homosexualities*, eds. Stephen O. Murray and Will Roscoe (Albany: State University of New York Press, 1998), part 1, 230–231.
27. Ibid., part 3, 258.
28. Ibid., part 3, 294–296.
29. Adrian Carton, 'Desire and Same Sex Intimacies in Asia', *Gay Life and Culture*, 323.
30. Londa Schiebinger, 'The Anatomy of Difference: Race and Sex in Eighteenth-Century Science', *Eighteenth-Century Studies*, 23:4 (1980), 389. Schiebinger limits her remark to the eighteenth century, but it is no less applicable to the nineteenth.
31. Bleys, *The Geography of Perversion*, 65.
32. Ibid., 157.

33 Ibid., 157–160.
34 Rictor Norton, *The Myth of the Modern Homosexual: Queer History and the Search for Cultural Unity* (London: Cassell, 1997), 67.
35 Ibid.
36 Ibid.
37 Bleys, *The Geography of Perversion*, 145.
38 Stoler, 'Making Empire Respectable', 635.
39 Ibid., 636.
40 Bleys, *The Geography of Perversion*, 145.
41 Rubin, 'Thinking Sex', 150.
42 Rebecca Ratcliffe, 'Singapore to Repeal Law that Criminalises Sex between Men', *The Guardian* (21 August 2022). https://www.theguardian.com/world/2022/aug/21/singapore-to-repeal-law-that-criminalises-sex-between-men. Accessed: August 2022.
43 Bleys, *The Geography of Perversion*, 1.
44 Ibid.
45 Norton, *Modern Homosexual*, 50.
46 Bleys, *The Geography of Perversion*, 1.
47 Mark Gevisser, *The Pink Line: The World's Queer Frontiers* (London: Profile Books, 2020), xi.
48 Ibid.
49 Ibid., xii.
50 'What Does Demisexual Mean?', *Gay Times* Instagram post (23 August 2021). https://www.instagram.com/p/CS6c9brjJtV/. Accessed: June 2022; 'What Does Abrosexual Mean?', *Gay Times* Instagram post (30 August 2021). https://www.instagram.com/p/CTMthuijp_h/. Accessed: June 2022.
51 'Love is Love', Dolce & Gabbana, https://www.youtube.com/watch?v=s13RrPD7DnE (12 February 2021). Accessed: July 2021.
52 Reuters, 'Russian Prosecutor Seeks to Ban Dolce & Gabbana Same-Sex Kiss Ads', *Fashion Network* (25 May 2021). https://ww.fashionnetwork.com/news/Russian-prosecutor-seeks-to-ban-dolce-gabbana-same-sex-kiss-ads,1305049.html. Accessed: July 2021.
53 Gevisser, *The Pink Line*, 22, 192.
54 TFL, 'Dolce & Gabbana "Love is Love" Ads Allegedly Run Afoul of Russian Anti-Propaganda Law', *TheFashionLaw* (24 May 2021). https://www.thefashionlaw.com/dolce-gabbana-love-is-love-ads-allegedly-run-afoul-of-russian-anti-propaganda-law/. Accessed: July 2021; Alistair James, 'Russian Prosecuteors Want to Ban Dolce & Gabbana Same-Sex Kiss Adverts', *Attitude* (27 May 2021). https://attitude.co.uk/article/russian-prosecutors-want-to-ban-dolce-gabbana-same-sex-kiss-adverts/25073/. Accessed: July 2021.
55 Online content cited in this chapter was last accessed on 25 July 2021.
56 Dolce & Gabbana Instagram post (12 February 2021). https://www.instagram.com/reel/CLNGt48j28X/?utm_medium=copy_link. Accessed: July 2021; Dolce

NOTES

& Gabbana Instagram post (13 February 2021). https://www.instagram.com/reel/CLPrbWmKOhO/?utm_source=ig_web_copy_link. Accessed: July 2021.

57 'А я устал от пропаганды гетеросексуальных отношений! Вот они везде прям блевать тянет фу. Вы любите друг друга просто не на публику'. Dolce & Gabbana Instagram post (12 February 2021). Emphasis added.

58 Dolce & Gabbana Instagram post (12 February 2021); 'Love is Love', Dolce & Gabbana, YouTube video (12 February 2021).

59 'يستطع، فبقلبه وذلك أضعف الإيمان) حسبي الله وكفى فيكم وفي براندكم وعيالنا وبناتنا يشترون منهم ويدعمونه، قاطعوهم إجعلوا لكم موقف ومكانة ومهابة انصروا', Dolce & Gabbana Instagram post (12 February 2021).

60 'جميع الاديان المثلية الجنسية محرمة لأنها خلاف الفطرة ، أنا ضد المثلية الجنسية ، أنا مسلم وأفتخر'. Ibid.

61 'Totalmente desagradables, tienen que prohibir está clase de publicadades y multaros con un alto precio'. Dolce & Gabbana Instagram post (12 February 2021).

62 Ibid.

63 Ibid.

64 Ibid.

65 Dolce & Gabbana Instagram post (13 February 2021).

66 Ibid.

67 Ibid.

68 Dolce & Gabbana Instagram post (13 February 2021). https://www.instagram.com/reel/CLO1zugqARD/?utm_source=ig_web_copy_link. Accessed: July 2021.

69 Ibid.

70 Gevisser, *The Pink Line*, 12.

71 Andrew Foxall, 'From Evropa to Gayropa: A Critical Geopolitics of the European Union as Seen from Russia', *Geopolitics*, 24:1 (2019), 177, 186.

72 Joseph A. Massad, 'Re-Orienting Desire: The Gay International and the Arab World', *Public Culture*, 14:2 (2002), 363.

73 Joseph A. Massad, *Desiring Arabs* (Chicago and London: University of Chicago Press, 2007), 175.

74 Gevisser, *The Pink Line*, 79–80.

75 Emmanuel Akinwotu, 'Ghana: Anti-Gay Bill Proposing 10-year Prison Sentences Sparks Outrage', *The Guardian* (23 July 2021). https://www.theguardian.com/global-development/2021/jul/23/ghana-anti-gay-bill-proposing-10-year-prison-sentences-sparks-outrage. Accessed: August 2021.

76 Vladimir Putin, 'Meeting of the Valdai International Discussion Club' (19 September 2013), *Kremlin website*, http://en.kremlin.ru/events/president/news/19243. Accessed: August 2021.

77 Ibid.

78 Ibid.

79 Vladimir Putin, 'Presidential Address to the Federal Assembly' (12 December 2013), *Kremlin website*, http://en.kremlin.ru/events/president/news/19825. Accessed: August 2021.

80 Gevisser, *The Pink Line*, 21.

81 Will Stroude, 'Tom Daley Hits Back after Russian State TV's Homophobic Slurs against LGBTQ Olympians', *Attitude* (9 August 2021), https://attitude.co.uk/article/tom-daley-hits-back-after-russian-state-tvs-homophobic-slurs-against-lgbtq-olympians/25564/. Accessed: August 2021.

82 John d'Emilio, 'Capitalism and Gay Identity', *Culture, Society and Sexuality* [1983], 251.

83 Michel Foucault, *The History of Sexuality, Volume 1: An Introduction*, translated by Robert Hurley (New York: Pantheon Books, 1978), 36.

84 Norton, *Modern Homosexual*, 62.

85 Ben Barker-Benfield, 'The Spermatic Economy: A Nineteenth Century View of Sexuality', *Feminist Studies*, 1:1 (1972), 47–48.

86 Norton, *Modern Homosexual*, 6–11, 25.

87 *Gay Life and Culture: A World History*, ed. Robert Aldrich (London: Thames & Hudson, 2006).

88 Rubin, 'Thinking Sex', 150.

89 Tom Boellstorff, 'The Emergence of Political Homophobia in Indonesia: Masculinity and National Belonging', *Ethnos*, 69:4 (2004), 469.

90 Ibid., 469, 480–481. For the defence minister's remark, see Gevisser, *The Pink Line*, 32.

91 Homi K. Bhabha, *The Location of Culture* (London: Routledge, 1992), 2.

92 Ibid., 175–198, 232–235.

93 Sarah Mower, 'Burberry: Fall 2018 Ready-To-Wear', *Vogue* (17 February 2018). https://www.vogue.com/fashion-shows/fall-2018-ready-to-wear/burberry-prorsum#gallery-atmosphere. Accessed: July 2021.

94 Amanda Arnold, 'Scenes from Christopher Bailey's Emotional Final Burberry Show', *The Cut* (no date). https://www.thecut.com/2018/02/scenes-from-christopher-baileys-final-burberry-show.html. Accessed: June 2021.

95 Ibid.

96 Mower, 'Burberry'.

97 Massad, 'Re-Orienting Desire', 363.

98 Cordelia Tai, 'Diversity Report: The Fall 2018 Runways Were the Most Race and Transgender-Inclusive Ever; Not So Much for Age and Size Diversity', *TheFashionSpot* (22 March 2018). https://www.thefashionspot.com/runway-news/786015-runway-diversity-report-fall-2018/. Accessed: June 2021.

99 See above, 49–50.

100 Ellie Abraham, 'Cara Delevingne Says Her Sexuality is "like a pendulum swinging"', *Independent* (22 June 2020). https://www.independent.co.uk/life-style/dating/cara-delevingne-sexuality-bisexual-pansexual-b1870363.html. Accessed: August 2021.

101 Georgina Evans, 'Show Report: Burberry A/W 18', *SHOWStudio* (19 February 2018). https://showstudio.com/collections/autumn-winter-2018/burberry_london_a_w_18/georgina_evans_reports_on_the_burberry_show. Accessed: June 2021.

NOTES **219**

102 Show Studio, 'Panel Discussion: Burberry A/W 18', *SHOWstudio* (18 February 2018). https://showstudio.com/collections/autumn-winter-2018/burberry_london_a_w_18. Accessed: June 2021.

103 Evans, 'Show Report'.

104 Bandana Tewari, 'Burberry's LGBTQ+ Statement Was More Than Marketing', *Business of Fashion* (23 February 2018). https://www.businessoffashion.com/opinions/news-analysis/burberrys-lgbtq-statement-was-more-than-marketing. Accessed: June 2021.

105 Ibid.

106 Gevisser, *The Pink Line*, 12.

107 Ibid., 127–128.

108 Tewari, 'Burberry's LGBTQ+ Statement'.

109 Caroline Evans and Alessandra Vaccari, 'Time in Fashion: An Introductory Essay', *Time in Fashion: Industrial, Antilinear and Uchronic Temporalities*, ed. Caroline Evans and Alessandra Vaccari (London; Bloomsbury, 2020), 12.

110 Ibid., 13.

111 Burberry Instagram (4 July 2018). https://www.instagram.com/p/Bk0ORdrHCEl/?utm_source=ig_web_copy_link, https://www.instagram.com/p/Bk0UNyjH7Jz/?utm_source=ig_web_copy_link, https://www.instagram.com/p/Bk0aehwHnUv/?utm_source=ig_web_copy_link. Accessed: August 2021.

112 Burberry Instagram (4 July 2018). https://www.instagram.com/p/Bk0aehwHnUv/?utm_source=ig_web_copy_link.

113 Ibid.

114 Burberry Instagram (4 July 2018). https://www.instagram.com/p/Bk0ORdrHCEl/?utm_source=ig_web_copy_link.

115 'Thom Browne, Spring Summer 2019 Full Fashion Show, Menswear', *FF Channel* (10 July 2018). https://www.youtube.com/watch?v=mrynQuppGyY. Accessed: July 2021.

116 Ibid., 00:00:18 minutes.

117 Ibid., 00:00:01 to 00:00:16 minutes.

118 Ibid., 00:00:21 to 00:00:34 minutes.

119 Ibid., 00:00:34 to 00:00:44 minutes.

120 Luke Leitch, 'Thom Browne: Spring 2019 Menswear', *Vogue* (23 June 2018). https://www.vogue.com/fashion-shows/spring-2019-menswear/thom-browne. Accessed: July 2021.

121 Ibid.

122 Ibid.

123 Ibid.

124 'Thom Browne', 00:13:56 to 00:14:44 minutes.

125 Samantha Conti, 'Thom Browne Men's Spring 2019', *WWD* (23 June 2018). https://wwd.com/runway/mens-spring-collections-2019/paris/thom-browne/review/. Accessed: July 2021; Leitch, 'Thom Browne'; Anon., 'Paris Fashion Week Men's S/S 2019 Editor's Picks', *Wallpaper* (June 23 2018). https://www.wallpaper.com/fashion/paris-fashion-week-mens-ss-2020-editors-picks. Accessed March 2019.

126 Leitch, 'Thom Browne'.

127 Tim Blanks, 'A Play on Proportion at Thom Browne', *Business of Fashion* (24 June 2018). https://www.businessoffashion.com/reviews/fashion-week/a-play-on-proportion-at-thom-browne. Accessed: July 2021.

128 Quoted by Leitch, 'Thom Browne'.

129 Conti, 'Thom Browne Men's Spring 2019'.

130 Charlie Porter, 'Hermès, Thom Browne SS19 Men's Review: Paris Gets Idealistic', *The Financial Times* (24 June 2018). https://www.ft.com/content/8c71525c-77b5-11e8-bc55-50daf11b720d. Accessed: July 2021.

131 Ibid.

132 Thom Browne Instagram post (23 June 2018). https://www.instagram.com/p/BkYHnccH-9C/?utm_source=ig_web_copy_link. Accessed: August 2021.

133 Thom Browne Instagram post (27 June 2018). https://www.instagram.com/p/BkinfmcHc6I/?utm_source=ig_web_copy_link. Accessed: August 2021.

134 Ibid.

135 Ibid.

136 Ibid.

137 Thom Browne Instagram post (27 June 2020). https://www.instagram.com/p/CB8M9vUF_gy/?utm_source=ig_web_copy_link. Accessed: August 2021.

138 Ibid.

139 Benjamin L. Wild, 'We Need to Talk About Fancy Dress Costume: Connections (and Complications) Between the Catwalk and Fancy Dress Costume', *Fashion Theory*, 26:1 (2019), 101–103; Benjamin L. Wild, *Carnival to Catwalk: Global Reflections on Fancy Dress Costume* (London: Bloomsbury, 2020), 147.

140 The Editorial Board, 'Trump's Heartless Transgender Military Ban Gets a Second Shot', *The New York Times* (28 March 2018). https://www.nytimes.com/2018/03/28/opinion/trump-transgender-military-ban.html. Accessed: August 2021.

141 Gevisser, *The Pink Line*, 33; Javier C. Hernández and Zoe Mou, 'I Am Gay, Not a Pervert'L Furor in China as Sina Weibo Bans Gay Content', *The New York Times* (15 April 2018). https://www.nytimes.com/2018/04/15/world/asia/china-gay-ban-sina-weibo-.html. Accessed: August 2021.

142 Gevisser, *The Pink Line*, 319.

143 Ibid., 258–259.

144 Caroline Evans, *Fashion At The Edge: Spectacle, Modernity and Deathliness* (London and New Haven: Yale University Press, 2003); Rebecca Arnold, *Fashion, Desire and Anxiety: Image and Morality in the 20th Century* (London and New York: I.B. Tauris, 2001); Francesca Granata, *Experimental Fashion: Performance Art, Carnival and the Grotesque Body* (London and New York: I.B. Tauris, 2017); Adam Geczy and Vicki Karaminas, *Critical Fashion Practice: From Westwood to Van Beirendonck* (London: Bloomsbury, 2017).

145 Benjamin L. Wild, 'Critical Reflections on Cultural Appropriation, Race and the Role of Fancy Dress Costume', *Critical Studies in Fashion and Beauty*, 11:2 (2020), 161.

146 Martin Duberman, *Has The Gay Movement Failed?* (Oakland: University of California Press, 2018), 20.

147 Ibid.

148 Gevisser, *The Pink Line*, 309.

Chapter 5

1. John E. Morley, 'A Brief History of Geriatrics', *Journal of Gerontology*, 59A:11 (2004), 1132.

2. William Shakespeare, *As You Like It*, *William Shakespeare: Complete Works*, eds. Jonathan Bate and Eric Rasmussen (Basingstoke: Macmillan, 2007), 3:1, lines 142–159, 496–497.

3. Ovid, *The Art of Love with The Cures of Love and Treatments for the Feminine Fate*, trans. Tom Payne (London: Vintage Books, 2012), 49.

4. Giacomo Leopardi, *Dialogue between Fashion and Death*, trans. Giovanni Cecchetti (London: Penguin, 2020), 9.

5. Beverly Gordon, *The Saturated World: Aesthetic Meaning, Intimate Objects, Women's Lives, 1890-1940* (Knoxville: University of Tennessee Press, 2006), 2–5, 14.

6. Daniel Thomas Cook, *The Commodification of Childhood: The Children's Clothing Industry and the Rise of the Child Consumer* (Durham and London: Duke University Press, 2004), 28–30.

7. Ibid., 99.

8. Ibid., 36–40.

9. Caroline Evans and Alessandra Vaccari, 'Time in Fashion: An Introductory Essay', *Time in Fashion: Industrial, Antilinear and Uchronic*, eds. Caroline Evans and Alessandra Vaccari (London: Bloomsbury, 2020), 13.

10. M. J. Denham, 'The History of Geriatric Medicine and Hospital Care of the Elderly in England between 1929 and the 1970s' (Unpublished PhD thesis, University College, London, 2004), 14.

11. Morley, 'Geriatrics', 1136.

12. Joseph F. Coughlan, 'How "old age" was Invented – and Why It Needs to be Reinvented', *MIT Technology Review*, 122:5 (September/October 2019), 35.

13. Kathleen Wilson, *The Island Race: Englishness, Empire and Gender in the Eighteenth Century* (London: Routledge, 2003), 6–11, 77–80.

14. Eric Hobsbawm, 'Mass-Producing Traditions: Europe, 1870-1914', *The Invention of Tradition*, ed. Eric Hobsbawm and Terence Ranger (Cambridge: Cambridge University Press, 1983), 263–308. In the same volume, see David Cannadine, 'The Context, Performance and Meaning of Ritual: The British Monarchy and the "Invention of Tradition", *c.*1820-1977', 101–164. Also see Ronald Hutton, *The Stations of the Sun: A History of the Ritual Year in Britain* (Oxford: Oxford University Press, 1996).

15. Wilson, *The Island Race*, 9.

16. Morley, 'Geriatrics', 1134.

17 Coughlan, 'How "old age" was Invented', 35.

18 Amy J. Cuddy, Michael I. Norton and Susan T. Fiske, 'This Old Stereotype: The Pervasiveness and Persistence of the Elderly Stereotype', *Journal of Social Issues*, 61:2 (2005), 273.

19 For a more balanced picture, see Carole Haber and Brian Gratton, *Old Age and the Search for Security: An American Social History* (Bloomington and Indianapolis: Indiana University Press, 1994), 3–19.

20 Camilla Cavendish, 'We Are Prioritising the Old and will have to Make It Up to the Young', *The Financial Times* (28/29 March 2020), 14; Anjana Ahuja, 'Should the Old or Young be Vaccinated First?', *The Financial Times* (14/15 November 2020), 13.

21 Harm-Peer Zimmermann, 'Alienation and Alterity: Age in the Existentialist Discourse on Others', *Journal of Aging Studies*, 39 (2016), 83, 93.

22 Ibid.

23 David Rotman, 'Don't Fear the Gray Tsunami', *MIT Technology Review*, 122:5 (September/October 2019), 10.

24 Zimmermann, 'Alienation and Alterity', 93.

25 Mélanie Huynh et al., 'Cadeaux', Parisian *Vogue* (Paris: Condé Nast, December 2010/January 2011), 61–102.

26 Ibid., 88.

27 Frédérique Verley and Théodora Aspart, '*Quel maquillage à quel âge*', Parisian *Vogue*, 157.

28 Ibid., 158.

29 Ibid.

30 Ibid.

31 Ibid.

32 Ibid., 159.

33 Ibid.

34 Ibid.

35 A.-H. Cayley, 'Ten-Year-Old Thylane Blondeau Models for French Vogue', *Pedestrian* (11 May 2017). https://www.pedestrian.tv/style/ten-year-old-thylane-blondeau-models-for-french-vogue/. Accessed: December 2021.

36 Katie Moisse, '10-Year-Old Model's Grown-Up Look: High Fashion or High Risk?', *ABC News* (3 August 2011). https://abcnews.go.com/Health/w_MindBodyResource/10-year-models-grown-high-fashion-high-risk/story?id=14221160. Accessed: December 2021.

37 Vivian Dang, 'Ten-year-old as Sex Symbol: Thylane Blondeau and the Troubling Choices of Vogue Enfant', *Vancouver Observer* (29 August 2011). https://www.vancouverobserver.com/politics/commentary/2011/08/29/ten-year-old-sex-symbol-thylane-blondeau-and-troubling-choices-vogue. Accessed: December 2021.

38 Eddie, 'Petits CADEAUX', *Noir Addict* (5 August 2011). https://fashionfatty.wordpress.com/tag/vogue-paris-christmas-issue-december-2010january-2011/. Accessed: December 2011.

NOTES   **223**

39 Mail Foreign Service, 'Far Too Much, Far Too Young: Outrage over Shocking Images of the 10-YEAR-OLD Model Who has Graced the Pages of Vogue', *The Daily Mail* (10 August 2011). https://www.dailymail.co.uk/femail/article-2022305/Thylane-Lena-Rose-Blondeau-Shocking-images-10-YEAR-OLD-Vogue-model.html. Accessed: December 2021.

40 Meredith Clark, 'Balenciaga Apologises after "disgusting" Ads of Children Holding "bondage" Teddy Bears Spark Backlash', *The Independent* (23 November 2022). https://www.independent.co.uk/life-style/fashion/balenciaga-plush-bear-bag-holiday-campaign-b2231068.html. Accessed: January 2023.

41 Mark E., 'The 5 Most Controversial Vogue Images Ever Published', *The Fashion Spot* (29 August 2014). https://www.thefashionspot.com/runway-news/450991-controversial-vogue-images-ever-published/5/. Accessed: July 2022.

42 Eddie, 'Petits CADEAUX'.

43 Sadie Whitelocks and Daisy Dumas, '10-Year-Old Vogue Model's Mother Shuts Down Facebook Fan Site in Response to Outrage over Daughter's Career', *The Daily Mail* (10 August 2011). https://www.dailymail.co.uk/femail/article-2022979/10-year-old-Vogue-models-mother-shuts-Facebook-fan-site-response-outrage-daughters-career.html. Accessed: December 2021.

44 Belinda White, 'Mother of 10-Year-Old Vogue Model Speaks Out', *The Daily Telegraph* (9 August 2011). http://fashion.telegraph.co.uk/news-features/TMG8690624/Mother-of-10-year-old-Vogue-model-speaks-out.html. Accessed: December 2021.

45 Anon., 'This 10-Year-Old French Model Has a Tumblr Dedicated to Her', *BlackBook* (28 July 2011). https://blackbookmag.com/fashion-style/fashioneer/this-10-year-old-french-model-has-a-tumblr-dedicated-to-her/. Accessed: December 2021.

46 Anon., '10-Year-Old Model Thylane Blondeau's Mother Speaks, Closes Her Daughter's Facebook Group', *BlackBook* (5 August 2011). https://blackbookmag.com/fashion-style/fashioneer/10-year-old-model-thylane-blondeaus-mother-speaks-closes-her-daughters-facebook-group/. Accessed: December 2021.

47 Anon., 'Vogue's Disturbing "fashion" Images of Girl Aged Ten', *The Christian Institute* (12 August 2011). https://www.christian.org.uk/news/vogues-disturbing-fashion-images-of-girl-aged-ten/. Accessed: December 2021; Suzy O'Connor, 'Cameron Moves To Protect Child Models and Children', *Talent Management Blog* (20 October 2011). https://www.talentmanagement.com/blog/2011/10/3772/. Accessed: December 2021; Damien Pearse, 'Sexualised Advertising to Children Faces New Rules in Cameron Crackdown', *The Guardian* (24 December 2011). https://www.theguardian.com/media/2011/dec/24/sexualised-advertising-children-cameron-crackdown. Accessed: December 2021.

48 Moisse, '10-Year-Old Model's Grown-Up Look'.

49 Mark E., 'The 5 Most Controversial Vogue Images Ever Published'.

50 Amy Verner, 'Guo Pei: Spring 2017 Couture', *Vogue* (27 January 2017). https://www.vogue.com/fashion-shows/spring-2017-couture/guo-pei. Accessed: December 2021.

51 Ibid.

52 Anon., 'Guo Pei S/S 2017 Couture Collection: Legends', *Guo Pei*, https://www.youtube.com/watch?v=dZE2OXlx2Jo (13 March 2017). Accessed: January 2022. 00:09:11 to 00:09:57 minutes.

53 Ibid., 00:11:12 to 00:11:16 minutes.

54 Nick Verreos, 'RUNWAY REPORT . . . Paris Haute Couture Fashion Week: Guo Pei Couture Spring 2017', *Nick Verreos* (no date). http://nickverreos.blogspot.com/2017/01/runway-reportparis-haute-couture_27.html. Accessed: January 2022.

55 Erica Gonzales, 'Carmen Dell'Orefice, 85 Years Young, Closed a Couture Show', *Harper's Bazaar* (27 January 2017). https://www.harpersbazaar.com/fashion/models/news/a20233/carmen-dell-orefice-guo-pei-couture/. Accessed: December 2021.

56 Ibid..

57 Véronique Hyland, '85-Year-Old Model Carmen Dell'Orefice Closed a Couture Show', *The Cut* (26 January 2017). https://www.thecut.com/2017/01/carmen-dellorefeice-guo-pei-spring-2017-couture.html. Accessed: December 2021.

58 Kendrick, 'Guo Pei is a Legend, not because She Named Her Fashion Show "Legend", but for Her Art', *Benude* (1 September 2019). https://medium.com/@luci_38260/guo-pei-is-a-legend-not-because-she-named-her-fashion-show-legend-but-for-her-art-a874d4423c87. Accessed: December 2021.

59 Daisy Murray, 'Let's All Hope We Will Be As Fabulous As Carmen Dell'Orefice When We Are 85', *Elle* (30 January 2017). https://www.elle.com/uk/fashion/trends/articles/a33668/lets-all-hope-we-will-be-as-fabulous-as/. Accessed: January 2022.

60 Verner, 'Guo Pei'.

61 Francesca Fearon, 'China's Renowned Couturier Guo Pei has a Cosmetics Fridge, a Collection of Kaleidoscopes and a Studio Full of Dolls', *The Financial Times: How To Spend It* (30 October 2020). https://www.ft.com/content/e5c870cc-d9a0-4d69-8ca7-33e13d6b01bd. Accessed: January 2022.

62 Anon., 'Population Ageing in China: Crisis or Opportunity?', *The Lancet*, 400:10366 (2022), 1821.

63 Cathy Horyn, 'Year of Couturière', *The New York Times* (1 December 2010). https://archive.nytimes.com/tmagazine.blogs.nytimes.com/2010/12/01/year-of-the-couturiere/?_r=2. Accessed: July 2022.

64 Ibid.

65 Murray, 'Carmen Dell'Orefice'.

66 Gonzales, 'Carmen Dell'Orefice'.

67 Verner, 'Guo Pei'.

68 Gonzales, 'Carmen Dell'Orefice'.

69 Murray, 'Carmen Dell'Orefice'.

70 Paul Jobling, Philippa Nesbitt and Angelene Wong, *Fashion, Identity, Image* (London: Bloomsbury, 2022), 40.

71 Horyn, 'Year of Couturière'.

NOTES

72 Adrien Goetz, *Marie-Antoinette* (New York: Assouline, 2005), 4.

73 Rolf Fjelde, 'Peer Gynt, Naturalism, and The Dissolving Self', *The Drama Review*, 13:2 (1968), 28–43; Kurt Taroff, 'Home is Where the Self Is: Monodrama, Journey Plat Structure, and the Modernist Fairy Tale', *Marvels & Tales*, 28:2 (2014), 325–345.

74 Caroline Weber, *Queen of Fashion: What Marie Antoinette Wore to the Revolution* (London: Aurum, 2006), 286-288.

75 Anon., 'Sofia Coppola Directs Calvin Klein Or Nothing At All', *DNA Magazine* (19 April 2017). https://www.dnamag.co/home/sofia-coppola-calvin-klein. Accessed: January 2022.

76 Steff Yotka, 'Calvin Klein's New Campaign Proves There's No Age Limit to Being an Underwear Model', *Vogue* (18 April 2017). https://www.vogue.com/article/calvin-klein-lauren-hutton-underwear-ads. Accessed: January 2022.

77 Hannah Ongley and i-D staff, 'Sofia Coppola Explores First Kisses and Crushes for Calvin Klein's New Underwear Campaign', *i-D* (18 April 2017). https://i-d.vice.com/en_uk/article/nenvd7/sofia-coppola-explores-first-kisses-and-crushes-for-calvin-kleins-new-underwear-campaign. Accessed: January 2022.

78 Lauren Alexis Fisher, 'Lauren Hutton, 73, Stars in Calvin Klein's New Underwear Campaign', *Harper's Bazaar* (18 April 2017). https://www.harpersbazaar.com/fashion/designers/news/a22061/calvin-klein-womens-underwear-campaign-spring-2017/. Accessed: January 2022.

79 Ongley and i-D staff, 'Sofia Coppola'.

80 Yotka, 'New Campaign'.

81 Danielle Fowler, 'Calvin Klein's Latest Campaign Celebrates Women of All Ages', *Grazia* (20 April 2017). https://graziadaily.co.uk/fashion/news/calvin-klein-spring-summer-campaign/. Accessed: January 2022.

82 Yotka, 'New Campaign'.

83 Ongley and i-D staff, 'Sofia Coppola'.

84 Fisher, 'Lauren Hutton'.

85 Yotka, 'New Campaign'.

86 Fowler, 'Lauren Hutton'.

87 Anon., 'Lauren Hutton, 73, Models Underwear for Calvin Klein', *BBC News* (20 April 2017). https://www.bbc.co.uk/news/entertainment-arts-39652171. Accessed: January 2022; Fisher, 'Lauren Hutton'; Fowler, 'Lauren Hutton'.

88 Anon., 'Lauren Hutton is in this Calvin Klein ad for about Two Seconds', *stuff* (20 April 2017). https://www.stuff.co.nz/life-style/fashion/91733573/lauren-hutton-is-in-this-calvin-klein-ad-for-about-two-seconds. Accessed: January 2022.

89 Anon., 'Lauren Hutton Poses Nude at 61', *ABC News* (21 October 2005). https://abcnews.go.com/GMA/BeautySecrets/story?id=1236581&page=1. Accessed: July 2022.

90 Ibid.

91 Jobling, Nesbitt and Wong, *Fashion, Identity, Image*, 37.

92 Kate Dingwall, 'Calvin Klein Taps Cast of Moonlight for Campaign Following the Oscars', *Fashion Network* (28 February 2017), https://uk.fashionnetwork.com

/news/calvin-klein-taps-cast-of-moonlight-for-campaign-following-the-oscars,798542.html. Accessed: July 2022.

93 John Berger, *Ways of Seeing* (London: Penguin, 1972), 41.

94 Susan Sontag, 'The Double Standard of Ageing', *An Ageing Population: A Reader and Sourcebook*, eds. Vida Carver and Penny Liddiard (New York: Holmes and Meir, [1972] 1979), 72–80.

95 Verley and Aspart, '*Quel maquillage à quel âge*', 158.

96 Anon., 'Why Is No One Outraged by Calvin Kleinâs Latest Underwear Ad?', *Data & Marketing Association* (17 November 2017). https://dma.org.uk/article/why-is-no-one-outraged-by-calvin-kleins-latest-underwear-ad. Accessed: January 2022.

97 Anon., 'About the DMA', https://dma.org.uk/about-the-dma. Accessed: July 2022.

98 Anon., 'Why Is No One Outraged'.

99 Ibid.

100 Ibid.

Chapter 6

1 Daniel Miller, 'Materiality: An Introduction', *Materiality*, ed. Daniel Miller (Durham and London: Duke University Press, 2005), 1.

2 Aileen Ribeiro, *Dress and Morality* (London: Berg, 2003), 13.

3 *Walter of Henley and Other Treaties on Estate Management*, ed. Dorothea Oschinsky (Oxford: Clarendon Press, 1971), 387–407.

4 Carolos M. Eire, *Reformations: The Early Modern World, 1450-1650* (New Haven and London: Yale University Press, 2016), 39, 116–117.

5 Hannah Rochell, 'Let the Devil wear Prada – the Man in the Vatican was Dressed by Christ', *The Times* (12 February 2013), 6.

6 Ibid., 7.

7 James F. McCue, 'The Doctrine of Transubstantiation from Berengar through Trent: The Point at Issue', *The Harvard Theological Review*, 61:3 (1968), 385–430.

8 Max Weber, *The Protestant Work Ethic and the "Spirit" of Capitalism*, edited and translated by Peter Baehr and Gordon C. Wells (London: Penguin Books, [1905] 2002), 7.

9 Ibid., 1.

10 *The Protestant Work Ethic Debate: Max Weber's Replies to His Critics, 1907-1910*, eds. David Chalcraft and Austin Harrington (Liverpool: Liverpool University Press, 2001); Felix Kersting, Iris Wohnsiedler and Nikolaus Wolf, 'Weber Revisited: The Protestant Ethic and Spirit of Nationalism', *The Journal of Economic History*, 80:3 (2020), 710–745; Liana Giorgi and Catherine Marsh, 'The Protestant Work Ethic as a Cultural Phenomenon', *European Journal of Social Psychology*, 20:6 (1990), 499–517.

11 Bill Ashcroft, Gareth Griffiths and Helen Tiffin, 'The Sacred', *The Post-Colonial Studies Reader*, eds. Bill Ashcroft, Gareth Griffiths and Helen Tiffin, second edn (London: Routledge, 2006), 517.

NOTES 227

12. Laura E. Donaldson, 'God, Gold, and Gender', *The Post-Colonial Studies Reader*, 522.
13. Catherine Hall, 'Introduction: Thinking the Postcolonial, Thinking the Empire', *Cultures of Empire: Colonizers in Britain and the Empire in the Nineteenth and Twentieth Centuries. A Reader*, ed. Catherine Hall (Manchester: Manchester University Press, 2000), 7.
14. Eire, *Reformations*, viii.
15. William Baldridge, 'Reclaiming Our Histories', *The Post-Colonial Studies Reader*, 528.
16. Robert Ross, *Clothing: A Global History, Or, The Imperialists' New Clothes* (Cambridge: Polity, 2008), 88.
17. Ibid., 89.
18. Laura Cappelle, 'When the Only in Town is Church', *The New York Times International Edition* (12/13 December 2020), 19.
19. Eire, *Reformations*, viii.
20. Ari Lisner, 'Prayers Up: How God Became the Hottest Thing in Fashion', *GQ* (31 August 2021). https://www.gq.com/story/god-is-trending. Accessed: July 2022.
21. Ibid.
22. Thomas P. Campbell, 'Foreword', Hamish Bowles, *Vogue & The Metropolitan Museum of Art Costume Institute: Parties, Exhibitions, People* (New York: Abrams, 2014), 7.
23. Andrew Bolton, 'Introduction', *Heavenly Bodies: Fashion and the Catholic Imagination*, 2 vols. (New Haven and London: Yale University Press), i, 95.
24. Anon., 'Oh Good Lord, did they Really Wear that?', *The Daily Telegraph* (9 May 2018), 20–21.
25. Hilary Rose, 'Lord! What Happened at the Met Ball, Fashion's High Altar' *Times 2* (9 May 2021), 2–3.
26. Piers Morgan, 'If the Met Gala was Islam or Jewish-Themed, All Hell would Break Loose – So Why was It OK for a Bunch of Flesh-Flashing Celebrities to Disrespect MY Religion?' *The Daily Mail* (9 May 2018). https://www.dailymail.co.uk/news/article-5703953/PIERS-MORGAN-Met-Islam-Jewish-themed-hell-break-loose-disrespect-religion.html. Accessed: September 2021.
27. Marisa Tom, 'Somebody Douse Us in Holy Water Because Sarah Jessica Parker Just Took Us to Church', *Pop Sugar* (8 May 2021). https://www.popsugar.co.uk/fashion/Sarah-Jessica-Parker-Met-Gala-Dress-2018-44820684. Accessed: September 2021.
28. Ibid., 3.
29. Morgan, 'Met Gala'.
30. Rose, 'Lord!', 2.
31. Jess Rutherford, 'The MetGala: Heavenly Bodies', *The Oxford Student* (20 May 2018). https://www.oxfordstudent.com/2018/05/20/the-metgala-heavenly-bodies/. Accessed: September 2018.
32. The Catholic Channel, 'Cardinal Dolan Talks about the Met Gala 2018', *SiriusXM News & Issues* (9 May 2018). https://soundcloud.com/siriusxm-news-issues/

cardinal-dolan-talks-about-the-met-gala-2018. 00:00:09 to 00:00:15 minutes; 00:01:18 minutes. Accessed: September 2021

33 Ibid., 00:05:55 to 00:06:00 minutes.
34 Ibid., 00:06:05 to 00:06:13 minutes.
35 Ibid., 00:05:01 to 00:05:20 minutes.
36 Daniella Greenbaum, '"Pope Rihanna" and the Met Gala Expose the Double Standard of What People will Consider Cultural Appropriation', *Business Insider* (8 May 2018). https://www.businessinsider.com/rihanna-pope-met-gala-double-standard-cultural-appropriation-2018-5?r=US&IR=T. Accessed: September 2021
37 Osman Ahmed, 'Divine Inspiration: How Met Gala Guests Tackled the "Heavenly Bodies" Theme', *Vogue* (8 May 2021). https://www.vogue.co.uk/article/how-met-gala-guests-tackled-heavenly-bodies-theme. Accessed: September 2021.
38 Ibid.
39 The Catholic Channel, 'Cardinal Dolan', 00:04:26 to 00:04:33 minutes.
40 Ibid., 00:07:36 to 00:08:02 minutes.
41 00:11:03 to 00:11:15 minutes.
42 00:00:48 to 00:01:16 minutes.
43 The Catholic Channel, 'Cardinal Dolan'.
44 Greenbaum, '"Pope Rihanna"'.
45 Adrienne Keene (@NativeApprops) Twitter post (9 May 2018). https://twitter.com/NativeApprops/status/994203349632217088?ref_src=twsrc%5Etfw%7Ctwcamp%5Etweetembed%7Ctwterm%5E994203349632217088%7Ctwgr%5E%7Ctwcon%5Es1_&ref_url=https%3A%2F%2Fwww.buzzfeednews.com%2Farticle%2Fmichaelblackmon%2Fmet-gala-catholic-cardinal-dolan-rihanna. Accessed: September 2021; Michael Blackmon, 'Cardinal Timothy Dolan Joked He Lent Rihanna His Headdress for The Met Gala', *Buzzfeed* (9 May 2021). https://www.buzzfeednews.com/article/michaelblackmon/met-gala-catholic-cardinal-dolan-rihanna. Accessed: September 2021.
46 Roopa (@RadRoopa) Twitter post (8 May 2018). https://twitter.com/RadRoopa/status/993805957908971520?ref_src=twsrc%5Etfw%7Ctwcamp%5Etweetembed%7Ctwterm%5E993805957908971520%7Ctwgr%5E%7Ctwcon%5Es1_&ref_url=https%3A%2F%2Fwww.buzzfeednews.com%2Farticle%2Fmichaelblackmon%2Fmet-gala-catholic-cardinal-dolan-rihanna. Accessed: September 2021; Blackmon, 'Cardinal Timothy Dolan'.
47 Greenbaum, '"Pope Rihanna"'.
48 Rutherford, 'The MetGala: Heavenly Bodies'.
49 Nathalie Bondil, 'The Stylings of a Humanist Couturier', *The Fashion World of Jean Paul Gaultier: From Sidewalk to Catwalk*, ed. Thierry-Maxime Loriot (New York: Abrams, 2011), 18.
50 Amy Spinder, 'Patterns', *The New York Times* (16 March 1993), Section B, 8. https://www.nytimes.com/1993/03/16/news/patterns-082793.html?src=pm. Accessed: September 2021.

NOTES **229**

51. Ibid.
52. Stylerunner7, 'Jean Paul Gaultier Rabbi Chic Fall Winter 1993, Part 1' (29 August 2008). https://www.youtube.com/watch?v=7WrgRjNEXcQ. 00:00:15 to 00:00:30 minutes.
53. Spinder, 'Patterns'.
54. Jean Paul Gaultier, *Fashion World*, 316.
55. Ibid.
56. 'Jean Paul Gaultier Fall Winter 1993 – Report', *Stylerunner7* (4 September 2008). https://www.youtube.com/watch?v=sWHmcmYNejg. 00:03:05 to 00:03:20 minutes. Accessed: October 2021.
57. Douglas Keeve, *UnZipped* (Miramax, 1995), 00:34:57 to 00:34:58 minutes. Accessed: September 2021.
58. Ibid., 00:034:58 to 00:35:36 minutes.
59. Quoted in Degan Pener, 'Fantasy or Affront?' *The New York Times* (1 August 1993), Section 9, 4.
60. Bernadine Morris, 'Fall Winter 1993 – Report', 00:01:23 to 00:01:25 minutes.
61. Gaultier, *Fashion World*, 316.
62. Ibid.
63. Richard Buckley, 'Jean Paul Gaultier Fall Winter 1993 – Report', 00:01:20 to 00:01:08 minutes.
64. Ibid.
65. Bernadine Morris, 'Fall Winter 1993 – Report', 00:02:04 to 00:02:32 minutes.
66. Ben Kiernan, *Blood and Soil: A World History of Genocide and Extermination from Sparta to Darfur* (New Haven: Yale University Press, 2007); *The Holocaust and North Africa*, ed. Aomar Boum and Sarah Abrevaya Stein (Stanford: Stanford University Press, 2018).
67. See above, 63–64.
68. Suzy Menkes, 'The Power of the Show', *Fashion World*, 22.
69. Katie Baker Jones, 'What a Difference a Page Makes: Contextualizing Suzy Menkes' Fashion Criticism Within and Across Media Outlets', *Insights On Fashion Journalism*, eds. Rosie Findlay and Johannes Reponen (London: Routledge, 2022), 128.
70. See above, 44–45.
71. See below, 138–139.
72. Ana Alacovska and Dan Kärreman, 'Tormented Selves: The Social Imaginary of the Tortured Artist and the Identity Work of Creative Workers', *Organization Studies* (2022), 3; Doris Ruth Eikof and Axel Haunschild, 'Lifestyle Meets Market: Bohemian Entrepreneurs in Creative Industries', *Creative and Innovation Management*, 15:3 (2006), 235–237.
73. Bondil, 'The Sayings of a Humanist Curator', *Fashion World*, 16.
74. Ibid.
75. Ibid., 18.

76　Sophie Mellor, '"I can say anti-Semitic things, and Adidas can't drop me. Now what?" As Kanye West Taunts Adidas, Calls Grow for German Sportswear Giant to Cut Ties', *Fortune* (24 October 2022). https://fortune.com/2022/10/24/i-can-say-anti-semitic-things-and-adidas-cant-drop-me-now-what-as-kanye-west-taunts-adidas-calls-grow-for-german-sportswear-giant-to-cut-ties/. Accessed: January 2023; Marissa Dellatto and Carlie Porterfield, 'Kanye West's Antisemitic, Troubling Behavior—Here's Everything He's Said in Recent Weeks', *Fortune* (2 December 2022). https://www.forbes.com/sites/marisadellatto/2022/12/02/kanye-wests-anti-semitic-troubling-behavior-heres-everything-hes-said-in-recent weeks/?sh=6903f6286de3. Accessed: January 2023.

77　Edward Helmore, 'Adidas to Investigate Claims Kanye West Showed Pornography to Staff', *The Guardian* (24 November 2022). https://www.theguardian.com/music/2022/nov/24/adidas-kanye-west-investigation. Accessed: January 2023.

78　Kate Bethune, 'Encyclopedia of Collections', *Alexander McQueen*, ed. Claire Wilcox (London: V&A Publishing, 2015), 308.

79　Ibid.

80　Ibid.

81　Anon., 'Alexander McQueen S/S 2000 Eye', *Scroobily* (16 June 2017). https://www.youtube.com/watch?v=GbSl5B3XXaw. 00:05:20 to 00:05:38 minutes. Accessed: October 2021.

82　Ibid., 00:09:38 to 00:10:26 minutes; 00:12:08 to 00:12:19 minutes.

83　Anon., 'Alexander McQueen: Spring 2000 Ready-to-Wear', *Vogue* (3 October 2015). https://www.vogue.com/fashion-shows/spring-2000-ready-to-wear/alexander-mcqueen#review. Accessed: October 2021.

84　Ekaterina Lysenko, 'Alexander McQueen: Eye SS 2000', *Vernite potselui* (23 March 2000). https://vernitepotselui.ru/2020/03/23/alexander-mcqueen-eye-ss-2000/. Accessed: October 2021.

85　Ana Finel Honigman, *What Alexander McQueen Can Teach You About Fashion* (London: Frances Lincoln Publishing, 2021), 20, 23.

86　Bethune, *Alexander McQueen*, 308.

87　Dana Thomas, *Gods and Kings: The Rise and Fall of Alexander McQueen and John Galliano* (London: Allen Lane, 2015), 300.

88　Fred Davis, *Fashion, Culture, and Identity* (Chicago and London: The University of Chicago Press, 1992), 17.

89　Anon., 'Costliest U.S. Tropical Cyclones Tables Updated' (Miami: National Hurricane Center, 26 January 2018), https://www.nhc.noaa.gov/news/UpdatedCostliest.pdf. Accessed: November 2021.

90　Anon., 'Alexander McQueen SS2000: "*Eye*"', *Long Live McQueen* (no date). https://the-widows-of-culloden.tumblr.com/post/61599254756/alexander-mcqueen-ss2000-eye-spring-2000-was. Accessed: October 2021.

91　Lysenko, 'Alexander McQueen'.

92　Ibid.

93　Anon., 'Alexander McQueen'.

94 Ibid.

95 Alford T. Welch, *Studies in Qur'an and Tafsir* (Riga: Scholars Press, 1980/2008), 756.

96 Alma Hernández Briseño, 'La Poupee and Voss: Alexander McQueen's Heterotopias', *The Fashion Studies Journal* (17 May 2020). www.fashionstudiesjournal.org/longform/2020/5/17/alexander-mcqueen. Accessed: November 2021.

97 Ibid.

98 Michel Foucault, translated by Jay Miskowiec, 'Of Other Spaces: Utopias and Heterotopias', *Architecture /Mouvement/ Continuité* (October 1984). https://web.mit.edu/allanmc/www/foucault1.pdf, 4.

99 Ibid.

100 Angharad E. Beckett, Paul Bagguley and Tom Campbell, 'Foucault, Social Movements and Heterotopic Horizons: Rupturing the Order of Things', *Social Movement Studies*, 16:2 (2017), 170–171, 172.

101 Michel Foucault, *The Order of Things: An Archaeology of the Human Sciences* (London: Routledge, [1966] 1970), xviii.

102 Julia Emberley, 'The Fashion Apparatus and the Deconstruction of Postmodern Subjectivity', *Canadian Journal of Political and Social Theory/Revue Canadienne de théorie politique et sociale*, XI, 1–2 (1987), 45.

103 Ibid.

104 Beckett, Bagguley and Campbell, 'Heterotopic Horizons', 174.

105 See above, 90–91.

Chapter 7

1 Benjamin Linley Wild, 'Imitation in Fashion: Further Reflections of the Work of Thorstein Veblen and Georg Simmel', *Fashion, Style & Popular Culture*, 3:1 (2016), 271–94.

2 *The Fashion Reader*, eds. Linda Welters and Abby Lillethun, third edition (London: Bloomsbury, 2022), 2, 72, 117–118; *The Anthropology of Dress and Fashion: A Reader*, eds. Brent Luvaas and Joanne B. Eicher (London: Bloomsbury, 2019), 100, 210–211, 230, 240; *Fashion Studies: Research Methods, Sites, and Practices*, ed. Heike Jenss (London: Bloomsbury, 2016), 4; Susan B. Kaiser, *Fashion and Cultural Studies* (London: Bloomsbury, 2012), 8, 116.

3 Thorstein Veblen, *The Theory of the Leisure Class*, ed. Martha Banta (Oxford: Oxford University Press, [1899] 2007), 112.

4 For context see Peter Frankopan, *The New Silk Roads: The Present and Future of the World* (London: Bloomsbury, 2018).

5 Susie Heller, 'People Are Pretending to Fall Out of Cars and Posing Amid Strewn Luxury Goods for the Viral "flaunt your wealth" Challenge on Instagram', *Insider* (24 October 2018), https://www.insider.com/viral-flaunt-your-wealth-challenge-weibo-instagram-2018-10. Accessed: July 2022.

6. William Shakespeare, *Hamlet*, *William Shakespeare: Complete Works*, eds. Jonathan Bate and Eric Rasmussen (Basingstoke: Macmillan, 2007), 1.3, line 75, 1935.

7. Colin Morris, *The Discovery of the Individual 1050-1200* (Toronto: University of Toronto Press, 1987), 2.

8. Larry Siedentop, *Inventing the Individual: The Origins of Western Liberalism* (London: Penguin, 2014), 42.

9. Morris, *The Discovery of the Individual*, 11.

10. Ibid.

11. Ibid.

12. Mark J. Brandt and Christine Reyna, 'The Chain of Being: A Hierarchy of Morality', *Perspectives on Psychological Science*, 6:5 (2011), 428–446.

13. Simon Schama, *The Embarrassment of Riches: An Interpretation of Dutch Culture in the Golden Age* (London: Fontana Press, 1987), 338.

14. Fredric Jameson, 'Culture and Finance Capital', *Critical Inquiry*, 24:1 (1997), 254.

15. Ulinka Rublack and Giorgio Riello, 'Introduction', *The Right to Dress: Sumptuary Laws in Global Perspective, c.1200-1800* (Cambridge: Cambridge University Press, 2019), 24.

16. Rachel Worth, *Fashion and Class* (London: Bloomsbury, 2020), 6–7.

17. Ibid., 7.

18. John Harvey, 'From Black in Spain to Black in Shakespeare', *The Men's Fashion Reader*, eds. Peter McNeil and Vicki Karaminas (London: Berg, 2009), 19–43.

19. Anne McClintock, *Imperial Leather: Race, Gender and Sexuality in the Colonial Contest* (London: Routledge, 1995), 208.

20. Ibid., 207–208.

21. Ibid., 208.

22. Worth, *Fashion and Class*, 17.

23. Ibid., 16.

24. Rublack and Riello, 'Introduction', 9.

25. For example, see Sophie White, 'Dressing Enslaved Africans in Colonial Louisiana', *Dressing Global Bodies: The Political Power of Dress in World History*, eds. Beverly Gordon and Giorgio Riello (London: Routledge, 2020), 85–103.

26. Worth, *Fashion and Class*, 155.

27. Matthew Schneier, 'Karl Lagerfeld on Fur (Yea), Selfies (Nay) and Keeping Busy', *The New York Times* (3 March 2015). https://www.nytimes.com/2015/03/05/fashion/karl-lagerfeld-on-fur-yea-selfies-nay-and-keeping-busy.html?_r=3. Accessed: November 2021.

28. Katie Ramsingh and Marina Nelson, 'Milan Fashion Week AW13/14: Day Two', *Global Blue* (21 February 2013). https://www.globalblue.com/destinations/italy/milan-fashion-week-aw13-14-day-two/. Accessed: November 2021.

29. Gunjan Nanda, 'Karl Lagerfeld's Fur Controversy with PETA', *I Knock Fashion* (14 July 2019). https://www.iknockfashion.com/karl-lagerfelds-fur-controversy-with-peta. Accessed: November 2021.

NOTES

30 Jonathan Faiers, *Fur: A Sensitive History* (New Haven and London: Yale University Press, 2020), 226.
31 Rosemary Barrow, 'From Praxiteles to De Chirico: Art and Reception', *International Journal of the Classical Tradition*, 11:3 (2005), 345–348.
32 Tim Blanks, 'Fendi Fall 2015 Couture', *Vogue* (8 July 2015). https://www.vogue.com/fashion-shows/fall-2015-couture/fendi. Accessed: November 2021.
33 Karen Dacre, 'Fendi Couture: Karl Lagerfeld Courts Controversy with a Catwalk Collection Dedicated to Fur', *The Evening Standard* (9 July 2015). https://www.standard.co.uk/insider/fashion/fendi-couture-karl-lagerfeld-courts-controversy-with-a-catwalk-collection-dedicated-to-fur-10377918.html. Accessed: November 2021; Blanks, 'Fendi Fall 2015 Couture'.
34 Faiers, *Fur*, 94.
35 Ibid., 141, 148, 225.
36 Ibid., 119–120.
37 Ibid., 120.
38 Ibid., 1, 120.
39 Tim Blanks, 'Fendi Fall 2014 Ready-to-Wear', *Vogue* (19 February 2014). https://www.vogue.com/fashion-shows/fall-2014-ready-to-wear/fendi. Accessed: December 2021.
40 See above, 54–55.
41 Blanks, 'Fendi Fall 2015 Couture'.
42 Faiers, *Fur*, 44, 147.
43 Dacre, 'Fendi Couture'.
44 Linda Sharkey, 'Karl Lagerfeld Fights Back Against PETA and Defends Use of Fur in Fashion, Saying "A Butcher Shop Is Worse"', *The Independent* (5 March 2015). https://www.independent.co.uk/life-style/fashion/news/a-butcher-shop-is-worse-karl-lagerfeld-fights-back-against-peta-and-defends-use-of-fur-in-fashion-10087884.html. Accessed: November 2021.
45 Blanks, 'Fendi Fall 2015 Couture'.
46 Ted Stansfield, 'Fendi Brings Its Fur-Only Couture Show to Paris', *Dazed* (9 July 2015). https://www.dazeddigital.com/fashion/article/25421/1/fendi-brings-its-fur-only-couture-show-to-paris. Accessed: November 2021.
47 Alex Williams, 'Fur Is Back in Fashion and Debate', *The New York Times* (3 July 2015). https://www.nytimes.com/2015/07/05/fashion/fur-is-back-in-fashion-and-debate.html. Accessed: November 2021.
48 Wyanet Vaz, 'Fendi Haute Fourrure 2015-2016 Show Decoded', *Verve* (15 July 2015). https://www.vervemagazine.in/fashion-and-beauty/fendi-haute-fourrure-2015-2016-show-decoded. Accessed: November 2021.
49 Jessica Michault, 'Fendi Couture Fall Winter 2015 Paris', *NowFashion* (no date). https://nowfashion.com/fendi-couture-fall-winter-2015-paris-15076. Accessed: November 2021.
50 Crash redaction, 'Fendi Haute Fourrure Fall-Winter 1015-16 by Frank Perrin', *Crash* (No date). https://www.crash.fr/fendi-haute-fourrure-fall-winter-2015-16-by-frank-perrin/. Accessed: November 2021.

51. Faiers, *Fur*, 55.
52. Julia V. Emberley, *The Cultural Politics of Fur* (Ithaca and London: Cornell University Press, 1997), 4, 76.
53. Worth, *Fashion and Class*, 2, 153. Discussion of fur focuses on sumptuary legislation. There is acknowledgement that '[f]or centuries . . . fur [was] in the main the preserve of the elite', 32–34.
54. Veblen, *The Theory of the Leisure Class*, 118.

    Dior *haute couture* spring 2000, Les Clochards
55. Alexander Fury, *Dior Catwalk: The Complete Collections* (London: Thames and Hudson, 2017), 318.
56. Court Williams, 'Art Imitates Life: Dior's "Homeless" Couture', *WWD* (14 April 2010). https://wwd.com/fashion-news/fashion-features/art-imitates-life-diors-homeless-couture-3036220/. Accessed: November 2021; Fury, *Dior Catwalk*, 319–323.
57. Fury, *Dior Catwalk*, 318.
58. Emma Izek, 'Haute Homeless is a Faulted Fad' (7 June 2019). https://medium.com/@eizek/about. Accessed: November 2021.
59. Bridget Foley, 'Moment 87: Homeless by Dior', *WWD* (1 November 2010). https://wwd.com/fashion-news/fashion-features/moment-87-homeless-by-dior-3346959/. Accessed: November 2021.
60. Ibid.
61. Suzie Menkes, 'Galliano's Hobo Couture Takes On the Old Masters: DECONSTRUCTING DIOR', *The New York Times* (18 January 2000). https://www.nytimes.com/2000/01/18/style/IHT-gallianos-hobo-couture-takes-on-the-old-masters-deconstructing-dior.html. Accessed: November 2000.
62. Pierre Marcelle, 'le coup du SDF, par Dior', *Libération* (20 January 2000). https://www.liberation.fr/tribune/2000/01/20/le-coup-du-sdf-par-dior_313901/. Accessed: November 2021.
63. Maureen Dowd, 'Liberties; Haute Homeless', *The New York Times* (23 January 2000). https://www.nytimes.com/2000/01/23/opinion/liberties-haute-homeless.html. Accessed: November 2021.
64. Ibid.
65. Dana Thomas, *Gods and Kings: The Rise and Fall of Alexander McQueen and John Galliano* (London: Allen Lane, 2015), 305.
66. Ibid., 306.
67. Vicente Benavent, 'Los "clochards" de Galliano: mendigos vestidoes de Dior', *Harpers Bazaar* (13 May 2015). https://www.harpersbazaar.com/es/moda/noticias-moda/a179665/galliano-dior-clochards-homeless-2000/. Accessed: November 2021.
68. Ibid.
69. Laird Borrelli-Persson, 'Nice Day for a White Wedding? Flashback to Dior Couture's Transgressive Fall 2000 Collection', *Vogue* (3 July 2006). https://www.vogue.com/article/christian-dior-haute-couture-fall-2000-john-galliano. Accessed: November 2021.

70. Virginie Mouzat, 'Galliano s'en va', *Madame Figaro* (2 March 2011). https://madame.lefigaro.fr/style/galliano-sen-020311-139146. Accessed: November 2021.
71. Thomas, *Gods and Kings*, 305.
72. Ibid., 306.
73. Anne-Laure Quilleriet, 'John Galliano raconte 60 ans de Dior', *L'Express* (12 January 2007). https://www.lexpress.fr/styles/mode/john-galliano-raconte-60-ans-de-dior_478779.html. Accessed: November 2021.
74. Thomas, *Gods and Kings*, 305.
75. Anon., 'Christian Dior Haute Couture 2000 Spring Summer (Full)', *Bilitum* (31 August 2013). https://www.youtube.com/watch?v=Y-9mCi58gvM. Accessed: November 2021. 00:15:54 to 00:16:02 minutes; 00:16:24 to 00:16:30 minutes.
76. Thomas, *Gods and Kings*, 28; Stacy Thompson, *Punk Productions: Unfinished Business* (Albany: State University of New York Press, 2004), 19.
77. Thompson, *Punk Productions*, 20.
78. Shaun Cole, 'New Styles, New Sounds: Clubbing, Music and Fashion in 1980s London', *80s Fashion: From Club to Catwalk*, ed. Sonnet Stanfill (London: V&A Publishing, 2013), 39.
79. Thompson, *Punk Productions*, 29.
80. Ibid.
81. Thomas, *Gods and Kings*, 23.
82. Alexander Fury, *Vivienne Westwood Catwalk: The Complete Collections* (London: Thames and Hudson, 2021), 9.
83. Thomas, *Gods and Kings*, 23.
84. Richard Sennett, 'Foreward', Gilles Lipovetsky, *The Empire of Things: Dressing Modern Democracy*, translated by Catherine Porter (Princeton: Princeton University Press, 1994), vii.
85. Lipovetsky, *The Empire of Things*, 103.
86. Ibid., 103, 105.
87. Ibid., 104.
88. Ibid., 104, 105.
89. Ibid., 120.
90. Anon., 'Vivienne Westwood Controversial Milan Menswear Runway', *Trendhunter* (no date). https://www.trendhunter.com/trends/gypsies-westwood-milan. Accessed: November 2021.
91. Anon., 'Milan Spring Summer 2009: Vivienne Westwood', *DScene* (24 June 2008). https://www.designscene.net/2008/06/milan-spring-summer-2009-vivienne.html. Accessed: November 2021; David Graham, 'Roma Hit the Runway', *Toronto Star* (26 June 2008). https://www.thestar.com/life/2008/06/26/roma_hit_the_runway.html. Accessed: November 2021; Jessica Michault, 'Vivienne Westwood: Gypsy on the Road', *The New York Times* (23 June 2008). https://www.nytimes.com/2008/06/23/style/23iht-rwest.1.13911862.html. Accessed: November 2021.

92. Anon., 'VIVIENNE WESTWOOD Spring Summer 2009 Menswear', *Fashion Channel* (1 March 2019). https://www.youtube.com/watch?v=aT7-j6M2duU. Accessed: November 2021, 00:02:04 to 00:02:05 minutes; 00:03:20 to 00:03:20 to 00:03:22 minutes; 00:04:32 to 00:04:34 minutes.
93. Ibid., 00:04:52 to 00:04:54 minutes; 00:05:03 to 00:05:05 minutes.
94. Ibid., 00:07:50 to 00:08:07 minutes.
95. Ibid., 00:07:07 to 00:07:19 minutes.
96. Graham, 'Roma Hit the Runway'.
97. Francelia Butler, 'The Poetry of Rope-Skipping', *The New York Times* (16 December 1973), 356.
98. User comment posted on 22 June 2005, *The Fashion Spot*. https://forums.thefashionspot.com/threads/vivienne-westwood-mens-s-s-09-milan.138443/. Accessed: November 2021.
99. Ibid.
100. User comment posted on 23 June 2005, *The Fashion Spot*. https://forums.thefashionspot.com/threads/vivienne-westwood-mens-s-s-09-milan.138443/page-3. Accessed: November 2021.
101. User comment posted on 27 June 2005, *The Fashion Spot*. https://forums.thefashionspot.com/threads/vivienne-westwood-mens-s-s-09-milan.138443/page-4. Accessed: November 2021.
102. User comment posted on 24 June 2005, *The Fashion Spot*. https://forums.thefashionspot.com/threads/vivienne-westwood-mens-s-s-09-milan.138443/page-3. Accessed: November 2021.
103. Tom Kington, 'Rebuff for Westwood', *The Guardian* (24 June 2005). https://www.theguardian.com/lifeandstyle/2008/jun/24/fashion.italy. Accessed: November 2021.
104. Anon., 'Vivienne Westwood'.
105. Thompson, *Punk Productions*, 29.
106. Ibid., 30.
107. Guy Debord, *Society of Spectacle* (Detroit: Black & Red, 1983), ¶1 and ¶6.
108. See above, 13.
109. Debord, *Society of Spectacle*, ¶9.

Chapter 8

1. Alison Matthews David, *Fashion Victims: The Dangers of Dress Past and Present* (London: Bloomsbury, 2015), 4.
2. Ibid.
3. Yuniya Kawamura, *Fashion-ology: An Introduction to Fashion* Studies (London: Berg, 2005), 1.
4. Ibid., 1–2.

NOTES **237**

5   Frank Trentmann, *Empire of Things: How We Became a World of Consumers, from the Fifteenth Century to the Twenty-First* (London: Allen Lane, 2016), 194.

6   David, *Fashion Victims*, 18–19.

7   Aileen Ribeiro, *Dress and Morality* (London: Berg, 2003), 119–120.

8   Giacomo Leopardi, *Dialogue between Fashion and Death*, trans. Giovanni Cecchetti (London: Penguin, [1827] 2010), 7–8.

9   Valerie Steele, *The Corset: A Cultural History* (New Haven and London: Yale University Press, 2003); Joanne Entwistle, *The Fashioned Body: Fashion, Dress and Modern Social Theory* (Cambridge: Polity Press, 2000), 20, 24, 54, 162–163, 195–200.
    Elizabeth Wilson, *Adorned in Dreams: Fashion and Modernity* (London: I.B. Tauris, [1985] 2013), 97–99.

10 Anaïs Orieul, '"Il faut souffrir pour être belle": 8 tendances beauté très douloureuses qui ont marqué l'histoire', *The Huffington Post* (1 January 2016). https://www.huffingtonpost.fr/2016/01/01/souffrir-pour-etre-belle-8-tendances-beaute-douloureuses_n_8889156.html. Accessed: July 2022.

11 Helen Perrson, 'Objects of Desire: The Cult of Shoes', *Shoes: Pleasure & Pain*, ed. Helen Perrson (London: V&A Publishing, 2015), 12.

12 Hilary Davidson, 'Shoes as Magical Objects', *Shoes: Pleasure & Pain*, 26–28.

13 Perrson, 'Objects of Desire', 17–18.

14 J. C. Flügel, *The Psychology of Clothes* (London: Hogarth Press, 1930), 43; Lawrence Langner, *The Importance of Wearing Clothes* (Los Angeles: Elysium Growth Press, 1991), 53; Perrson, 'Objects of Desire', 17.

15 Flügel, *The Psychology of Clothes*, 43.

16 Perrson, 'Objects of Desire', 17.

17 Colin McDowell, *The Anatomy of Fashion: Why We Dress The Way We Do* (London: Phaidon, 2013), 103.

18 Ibid., 142.

19 Perrson, 'Objects of Desire', 17.

20 Anon., 'DOLCE & GABBANA Fashion Show Spring Summer 2007 Milan by Fashion Channel', *Fashion Channel* (15 December 2015). https://www.youtube.com/watch?v=1ANpVGecozE. Accessed: April 2022.

21 John Berger, *Ways of Seeing* (London: Penguin, 1972), 41.

22 Fashionattheedge, 'Dolce & Gabbana Spring/Summer 2007', *The Edge* (24 May 2007). http://fashionontheedge.blogspot.com/2007/05/dolce-gabbana-springsummer-2007.html. Accessed: April 2022.

23 Ibid.

24 Ibid.

25 Ibid.

26 Anon., 'Dolce & Gabbana Bow to Criticism and Pull Ad', *Reuters* (6 March 2007). https://www.reuters.com/article/us-italy-dolcegabbana-advert-idUSL0631454820070306. Accessed: April 2022.

27 Ibid.
28 Tim Nudd, 'Stefano Gabbana: Really, We Love Women!', *Adweek* (7 March 2007). https://www.adweek.com/creativity/stefano-gabbana-really-we-love-women-17647/. Accessed: April 2022.
29 Anon. 'Dolce & Gabbana pondrán a los hombres de rodillas en su próxima campaña publicitaria', *ABC Cultura* (13 January 2009). https://www.abc.es/cultura/abci-dolce-yamp-gabbana-pondran-hombres-rodillas-proxima-campana-publicitaria-200901130300-912418418049_noticia.html. Accessed: April 2022.
30 Victoria Burnett, 'Fashion Ads Touch a Nerve in Gender-Conscious Spain', *The New York Times* (25 March 2007). https://www.nytimes.com/2007/03/25/business/worldbusiness/25iht-fashion26.1.5014898.html. Accessed: April 2022.
31 Ibid.
32 Ibid.
33 Ibid.
34 DeSwiss, '"Gang Rape" Dolce and Gabbana Advert Banned', forum post 'Fashion Designers Dolce and Gabbana's "Gang Rape" Ad Banned', *Democratic Underground* (7 March 2007). https://www.democraticunderground.com/discuss/duboard.php?az=view_all&address=389x358015. Accessed: April 2022.
35 Amy Duncan, 'Dolce & Gabbana in Hot Water again after "gang rape" advert Resurfaces just Days after IVF Furore', *Metro* (18 March 2015). https://metro.co.uk/2015/03/18/dolce-gabbana-in-hot-water-again-after-gang-rape-ad-campaign-resurfaces-just-days-after-ivf-furore-5108624/. Accessed: March 2022.
36 Kitty Calavita, 'Blue Jeans, Rape, and the "De-Constitutive" Power of Law', *Law & Society Review*, 35:1 (2001), 93.
37 Ibid., 96.
38 Morwenna Ferrier, 'Dolenico Dolce Apologies for Remarks about IVF and Gay Families', *The Guardian* (17 August 2015). https://www.theguardian.com/fashion/2015/aug/17/domenico-dolce-apologises-for-remarks-about-ivf-and-gay-families. Accessed: July 2022.
39 Duncan, 'Dolce & Gabbana'.
40 Elton John Instagram post (15 March 2015). https://www.instagram.com/p/0PJUURgGUI/?utm_source=ig_embed&ig_rid=4e457673-8708-43b6-9068-dc26efdf979f. Accessed: April 2022.
41 Ibid.
42 Ibid.
43 Anon., 'Dolce & Gabbana under Fire over "gang rape" Ad', *India Today* (18 March 2015). https://www.indiatoday.in/world/story/dolce-and-gabbana-under-fire-over-gang-rape-ad-244792-2015-03-18. Accessed: April 2022; Rachel Moss, '"Gang Rape" Dolce & Gabbana Advert Brings Yet More Controversy for Brand after "Synthetic" IVF Comments', *The Huffington Post* (18 March 2015). https://www.huffingtonpost.co.uk/2015/03/18/dolce-and-gabbana0gang-rape-advert_n_6893044.html. Accessed: April 2022; Chris Spargo, 'Dolce & Gabbana under Fire AGAIN just Days after Referring to Children Born through IVF as "synthetic" as Critics Discover Ad that Depicts "woman being gang raped"', *The Daily Mail* (17

NOTES 239

March 2015). https://www.dailymail.co.uk/news/article-2999045/Dolce-Gabbana-fire-just-days-referring-children-born-IVF-synthetic-critics-discover-ad-depicts-woman-gang-raped.html. Accessed: April 2022.

44 Annalisa Merelli, 'When Fashion Shoots Try to Make Social Commentary, the Result is Often Ugly', *Quartz* (6 August 2014). https://qz.com/245343/when-fashion-shoots-try-to-make-social-commentary-the-result-is-often-ugly/. Accessed: April 2022; Spargo, 'Dolce & Gabbana under fire AGAIN'.

45 Anon., 'Dolce & Gabbana – Advertising too Explicit and Sexual?', *Sex in Fashion Advertising Campaigns* (no date). http://sexinfashionadvertising.blogspot.com/2016/11/dolce-gabbana-gang-rape-okay.html. Accessed: April 2022.

46 Women's Aid, Marianne Hester, Sarah-Jane Walker and Emma Williamson, 'Gendered Experiences of Justice and Domestic Abuse: Evidence for Policy and Practice' (Bristol: Women's Aid, 2021). https://www.womensaid.org.uk/wp-content/uploads/2021/07/FINAL-Gendered-experiences-WA-UoB-July-2021.pdf. Accessed: July 2022.

47 Lori Heise, Mary Ellsberg and M. Gottmoeller, 'A Global Overview of Gender-Based Violence', *International Journal of Gynecology and Obstetrics*, 78, Supplement 1 (2002), 5.

48 Tommy J. Curry, 'Reconstituting the Object: Black Male Studies and the Problem of Studying Black Men and Boys within Patriarchal Gender Theory', *The Palgrave Handbook of Critical Race and Gender*, ed. S. A. Tate and E. Gutiérrez Rodríguez (Basingstoke: Palgrave Macmillan, 2022), 525–544.

49 Heise, Ellsberg and Gottmoeller, 'Gender-Based Violence', 8.

50 Emma Hope Allwood, 'Fashion v Censorship: A History of Banned Ads', *Dazed Digital* (13 May 2015). https://www.dazeddigital.com/fashion/article/24720/1/fashion-v-censorship-a-history-of-banned-ads-miu-miu-tom-ford. Accessed: April 2022.

51 Ibid.

52 Miu Miu (2); Gucci (2), Sisley (3) Tom Ford (3) United Colors of Benetton (4), Yves Saint Laurent (2).

53 Lorella Pagnucco Salvemini, *United Colors: The Benetton Campaigns* (London: Scriptum Editions, 2002), 90–91.

54 Ibid., 88–89.

55 'Unhate', *United Colors of Benetton* (no date). https://www.benettongroup.com/en/media-press/image-gallery/institutional-communication/other-campaigns/unhate/. Accessed: April 2022.

56 Allwood, 'Fashion v Censorship'.

57 Jess McCabe, 'Benetton Uses Domestic Violence to Sell Clothes?' *The f word* (27 May 2007). https://thefword.org.uk/2007/05/benetton_uses_d/. Accessed: April 2022.

58 Anon., 'United Colors of Benetton: Colors of Domestic Violence', *DrPrem* (no date). https://drprem.com/business/united-colors-of-benetton-colors-of-domestic-violence. Accessed: April 2022.

59 Sara, 'Benetton – Campaign on Domestic Violence', *in deep existential crisis . . .* (30 May 2007). https://nuttyorbcreepysara.wordpress.com/2007/05/30/benetton-campaign-on-domestic-violence/. Accessed: April 2022.

60 Ibid.

61 Jill Miller Zimon, 'Roots News: Colors of Domestic Violence=fake, not Benetton ad, Salon says Feministing "punked"', *Writes like she talks* (30 May 2007). https://writeslikeshetalks.blogspot.com/2007/05/colors-of-domestic-violencefake-not.html. Accessed: April 2022.

62 Ibid.

63 Steve Hall, 'United Colors of Benetton Returns From Dead with New Campaign', *AdRants* (30 May 2007). https://www.adrants.com/2007/05/united-colors-of-benetton-returns-from.php. Accessed: April 2022.

64 Ibid.

65 Ibid.

66 Sarah Mower, 'Burberry Fall 2019 Ready-to-Wear', *Vogue* (17 February 2019). https://www.vogue.com/fashion-shows/fall-2019-ready-to-wear/burberry-prorsum. Accessed: April 2022.

67 Ibid.

68 'Burberry | Fall Winter 2019/2020 Full Fashion Show | Exclusive', *FF Channel* (no date). https://www.youtube.com/watch?v=PtcreYr03Lo/. Accessed: April 2022.

69 Liz Kennedy Instagram post, *@liz.kennedy_* (17 February 2019). https://www.instagram.com/p/Bt_e9OpgGG3/. Accessed: April 2022.

70 Associated press, '"It was insensitive": Burberry Apologises for "noose" Hoodie after Model Complains', *The Guardian* (20 February 2019). https://www.theguardian.com/fashion/2019/feb/20/it-was-insensitive-burberry-apologises-for-noose-hoodie-after-model-complains. Accessed: April 2022.

71 Ibid.

72 Rob Picheta, '"Suicide isn't fashion": Burberry Apologizes for Hoodie with Noose around the Neck', *CNN Style* (19 February 2019). https://edition.cnn.com/style/article/burberry-noose-hoodie-scli-gbr-intl/index.html. Accessed: April 2022.

73 Alaina Demopoulos, 'The "Burberry Noose" Is Just the Latest Controversy. Why Can't Fashion Houses Do Better?', *The Daily Beast* (20 February 2019), https://www.thedailybeast.com/the-burberry-noose-is-just-the-latest-controversy-why-cant-fashion-houses-do-better. Accessed: April 2022.

74 Anon., 'Burberry Takes Suicide Hoodie off Shelves, Apologises after Social Media Rips Brand Apart', *India Today* (21 February 2019). https://www.indiatoday.in/trending-news/story/burberry-takes-suicide-hoodie-off-shelves-apologises-after-social-media-rips-brand-apart-1461752-2019-02-21. Accessed: April 2022; Picheta, '"Suicide isn't Fashion"'.

75 Natasha Hinde, 'Burberry Apologises and Removes "Noose" Hoodie After Model's Complaints', *HuffPost* (19 February 2019). https://www.huffingtonpost.co.uk/entry/burberry-apologises-for-noose-hoodie-model-complaints_uk_5c6bd76ae4b01cea6b88fff7. Accessed: April 2022.

76 Anon., 'Burberry Sorry for "suicide" Hoodie with Noose around Neck', *BBC News* (20 February 2019). https://www.bbc.co.uk/news/newsbeat-47302587. Accessed: April 2022; Associated press, ''It was insensitive''.

77 Saaed Jones tweet, @theferocity (19 February 2019). https://twitter.com/theferocity/status/1097894728236974081. Accessed: April 2022.
78 Ibid.
79 See above, 63–64.
80 Nancy MacLean, *Behind the Mask of Chivalry: The Making of the Second Ku Klux Klan* (Oxford: Oxford University Press, 1994), 125–126, 149–152, 171–173; Elaine Frantz-Parsons, *Ku-Klux Klan: The Birth of the Klan during Reconstruction* (Chapel Hill: The University of North Carolina Press, 2015), 111–126.
81 Hinde, 'Burberry Apologises'; Chelsea Ritschel, 'Burberry Apologies over Jumper with "noose" on Neck after London Fashion Week Anger', *The Independent* (19 February 2019). https://www.independent.co.uk/life-style/fashion/burberry-noose-jumper-hoodie-sweater-suicide-apology-controversy-a8787006.html. Accessed: April 2022.
82 David Lester, 'Culture and Suicide', *Suicide: A Global Perspective* (Bentham Science Publishers, 2012), 26.
83 Ibid., 12.
84 Ibid., 17.
85 Émile Durkheim, *Suicide: A Study in Sociology*, trans. John A. Spaulding and George Simpson (London: Routledge, [1897] 1952), xlv–xlvi.
86 Mower, 'Burberry Fall 2019 Ready-to-Wear'.
87 Katie Baker Jones, 'What a Difference a Page Makes: Contextualising Suzy Menkes' Fashion Criticism Within and Across Media Outlets', *Insights On Fashion Journalism*, eds. Rosie Findlay and Johannes Reponen (London: Routledge, 2022), 127.
88 Aurélie Van de Peer, 'The Politics of Fashion Criticism: How Newspaper Journalists' Evaluative Criteria for Fashion Changed Between 1949 and 2010', *Insights On Fashion Journalism*, 28.

Chapter 9

1 *The First Book of Fashion: The Books of Clothes of Matthäus & Veit Konrad Schwarz of Augsburg*, eds. Ulinka Rublack and Maria Hayward (London: Bloomsbury, 2015).
2 Ulinka Rublack, *Dressing Up: Cultural Identity in Renaissance Europe* (Oxford: Oxford University Press, 2010), 39–78.
3 *The First Book of Fashion*, 128–129, 288–289.
4 See above, 21–22.
5 Rublack, *Dressing Up*, 37.
6 Ibid., 33.
7 Norbert Wolf, *Dürer* (Köln: Taschen, 2016), 95.
8 Rublack, *Dressing Up*, 36.

9. Oliver J. T. Harris, Jessica Hughes, Robin Osborne, John Robb and Simon Stoddart, 'The Body and Politics', *The Body in History: Europe from the Paleolithic to the Future* (Oxford: Oxford University Press, 2013), 98–128.

10. Joav Merrick, Ariel Tenenbaum, Mohammed Morad and Eli Carmeli, 'A Short History of Disability Aspects from Israel', *The Routledge History of Disability*, eds. Roy Hanes, Ivan Brown and Nancy E. Hansen (London: Routledge, 2018), 95; Paul M. Ajuwon, 'Disabilities and Disability Services in Nigeria: Past, Present and Future', *History of Disability*, 134–135; Karen K. H. Ngai, Simon W. K. Wu and Joanna L. P. Chung, 'A Journey of Change – History of Disability in Hong Kong 1841-2014', *History of Disability*, 164–165.

11. Edward Enninful, 'Editor's Letter', British *Vogue* (May 2023), 34.

12. Tim Stainton, 'Reason, Value and Persons: The Construction of Intellectual Disability in Western Thought from Antiquity to the Romantic Age', *History of Disability*, 11.

13. Ibid., 12.

14. Luigi Croce, Federica Di Cosimo and Marco Lombardi, 'A Short History of Disability in Italy', *History of Disability*, 71.

15. See above, 130.

16. Stainton, 'Reason, Value and Persons', 13.

17. Lennard J. Davis, 'Bodies of Difference: Politics, Disability, and Representation', *Disability Studies: Enabling the Humanities*, eds. Brenda Jo Brueggemann, Sharron L. Snyder and Rosemarie Garland-Thomson (New York: Modern Language Association, 2002), 101.

18. See above, 41, 75.

19. Andrea Zittlau, 'The Freak Show Act: Science and Spectacle in the Nineteenth Century', *History of Disability*, 381.

20. Ibid., 381, 391.

21. Joanne Finkelstein, *The Fashioned Self* (Oxford: Polity Press, 1991), 59–64.

22. Croce, Di Cosimo and Lombardi, 'Disability in Italy', 71.

23. Pieter Verstraete, Evelyne Verhaegen and Marc Depaepe, 'One Difference is Enough: Towards a History of Disability in the Belgian Congo, 1908-1960', *History of Disability*, 231–232.

24. Shaun Grech, 'Decolonising Eurocentric Disability Studies: Why Colonialism Matters in the Disability and Global South Debate', *Journal for the Study of Race, Nation and Culture*, 21:1 (2015), 12.

25. Stainton, 'Reason, Value and Persons', 28–29.

26. David L. Braddock and Susan L. Parish, 'An Institutional History of Disability', *Handbook of Disability Studies*, eds. Gary L. Albrecht, Katherine D. Seelman and Michael Bury (London: Sage Publications, 2001), 23–24, 28–31, 39.

27. Mualla Erkilic, 'Developments in Disability Issues During the Late Ottoman Period of Turkish History from 1876 to 1909', *History of Disability*, 61.

28. Peter N. Stearns, *Fat History: Bodies and Beauty in the Modern West* (New York: New York University Press, 1997), viii, 3–24.

NOTES

29 Ibid., 27.
30 Ibid., 17–21, 32–38.
31 Conor Ashleigh, 'Controlling the Global Obesity Epidemic', *World Health Organization* (no date). https://www.who.int/activities/controlling-the-global-obesity-epidemic. Accessed: January 2023.
32 Ibid.
33 John Offer, 'From "natural selection" to "survival of the fittest": On the Significance of Spencer's Refashioning of Darwin in the 1860s', *Journal of Classical Sociology*, 14:2 (2014), 156.
34 Zittlau, 'The Freak Show Act', 387.
35 Armand Marie Leroi, *Mutants: On the form, Varieties and Errors of the Human Body* (London: HarperCollins, 2003), 349.
36 Ibid., 351; Winfried Menninghaus, 'Caprices of Fashion in Culture and Biology: Charles Darwin's Aesthetics of "Ornament"', *Philosophical Perspectives on Fashion*, eds. Giovanni Matteucci and Stefano Marino (London: Bloomsbury, 2017), 137–138.
37 Roy Hanes, 'Introduction', *History of Disability*, 2.
38 Jia Tolentino, 'The Age of Instagram Face', *The New Yorker* (12 December 2019), https://www.newyorker.com/culture/decade-in-review/the-age-of-instagram-face. Accessed: August 2022.
39 Ibid.
40 Finkelstein, *The Fashioned Self*, 183.
41 Ibid., 187.
42 Juliana Ferraz, 'Corpo positivo: Preta Gil, Duda Beat e Rita Carreira estrelam a Vogue de novembro', Brazilian *Vogue* (3 November 2020). https://vogue.globo.com/moda/noticia/2020/11/corpo-positivo-preta-gil-duda-beat-e-rita-carreira-estrelam-vogue-de-novembro.html. Accessed: April 2021.
43 Anon., 'Duda Beat encarna Madonna e declara: "vamos celebrar nossos corpos livres!"', Brazilian *Vogue* (3 November 2020). https://vogue.globo.com/celebridade/noticia/2020/11/duda-beat-encarna-madonna-e-declara-vamos-celebrar-nossos-corpos-livres.html. Accessed: April 2021.
44 Anon., 'Preta Gil: "Se tem alguma coisa da qual me arrependo é de ter mutilado meu corpo com cirurgias, de ter o escondido por vergonha"', Brazilian *Vogue* (3 November 2020), https://vogue.globo.com/celebridade/noticia/2020/11/preta-gil-se-tem-alguma-coisa-da-qual-me-arrependo-e-de-ter-mutilado-meu-corpo-com-cirurgias-de-ter-o-escondido-por-vergonha.html. Accessed: April 2021.
45 Luanda Vieira, 'Rita Carreira: "Nunca precisei de terapia para me aceitar, porque em casa não me deixaram cair na ilusão de que a felicidade só estava no padrão"', Brazilian *Vogue* (14 November 2020). https://vogue.globo.com/moda/noticia/2020/11/rita-carreira-nunca-precisei-de-terapia-para-me-aceitar-porque-em-casa-nao-me-deixaram-cair-na-ilusao-de-que-felicidade-so-estava-no-padrao.html. Accessed: April 2021.
46 Ibid.

47 Natália Eiras, 'Negra, gorda e estrela da SPFW: "Não tive em quem me espelhar", conta Rita', *Universa* (16 October 2019). https://www.uol.com.br/universa/noticias/redacao/2019/10/16/negra-gorda-e-estrela-da-spfw-nao-tive-em-quem-me-espelhar-conta-rita.htm. Accessed: April 2021.

48 Brasilian *Vogue* Instagram post (3 November 2020). https://www.instagram.com/p/CHILncxFrmN/. Accessed: May 2022.

49 Ibid.

50 Ibid.

51 Ibid.

52 Brazilian *Vogue* Instagram post (3 November 2020). https://www.instagram.com/p/CHIPDWIFokD/. Accessed: May 2022.

53 Ibid.

54 Ibid.

55 Andrew Ballantyne, *Architecture: A Very Short Introduction* (Oxford: Oxford University Press, 2002), 121.

56 Sheena Wagstaff, 'Embodied Histories', *Like Life: Sculpture, Color, and the Body* (New Haven and London: Yale University Press, 2018), 2.

57 Ibid.

58 Ibid., 3–4.

59 Aileen Ribeiro, *Dress and Morality* (London: Berg, 2003), 19.

60 Anon., 'Duda Beat encarna Madonna'.

61 See above, 36.

62 *Brazsilian Vogue* Instagram post (3 November 2020). https://www.instagram.com/p/CHISgqflmef/. Accessed: May 2022.

63 Brazilian *Vogue* Instagram post (3 November 2020). https://www.instagram.com/p/CHIPDWIFokD/. Accessed: May 2022.

64 Djurda Bartlett, 'Political Fashion, Fashionable Politics', *Fashion and Politics*, ed. Djurda Bartlett (New Haven and London: Yale University Press, 2019), 39.

65 Paul Jobling, Philippa Nesbitt and Angelene Wong, *Fashion, Identity Image* (London: Bloomsbury, 2022), X.

66 Olivier Lalanne, 'Édito', France *GQ* (March 2021), 13.

67 Ibid.

68 Hugo Compain, '<<Je suis en paix avec mon corps>>', France *GQ* (March 2021), 77.

69 Lalanne, 'Édito', 13.

70 Ibid.

71 Compain, '<<Je suis en paix avec mon corps>>', 70.

72 Héloïse Rambert, 'Grossophobie: Les hommes aussi', France *GQ* (March 2021), 80–85.

73 France *GQ* Instagram post (1 March 2021). https://www.instagram.com/p/CL4uWc4sny-/. Accessed: May 2022.

74 Ibid.

75 'GQ France March 2021: Grant Douglas by James Brodribb', forum discussion, *The Fashion Spot* (3 March 2021). https://forums.thefashionspot.com/threads/gq-france-march-2021-grant-douglas-by-james-brodribb.402816/. Accessed: May 2021.

76 Ibid.

77 Ibid.

78 Ben Barry, 'Fabulous Masculinities: Refashioning the Fat and Disabled Male Body', *Fashion Theory*, 23:2 (2019), 294–295.

79 *The Fashion Spot*.

80 Stearns, *Fat History*, 167.

81 Ibid., 189–191.

82 *The Fashion Spot*.

83 Communications team, 'Condé Nast Unveils New Global Content Strategy', *Condé Nast* (15 December 2020). https://www.condenast.com/news/new-global-content-strategy-conde-nast. Accessed: August 2022.

84 *The Fashion Spot*.

85 Barry, 'Fabulous Masculinities', 278.

86 Ibid., 282.

87 Madison Moore, *Fabulous: The Rise of the Beautiful Eccentric* (New Haven and London: Yale University Press, 2018), 14.

88 Barry, 'Fabulous Masculinities', 282.

89 Moore, *Fabulous*, 7–8.

90 Anon., 'My Self, My Avatar, My Identity: Diversity and Inclusivity within Virtual Worlds' (Institute of Digital Fashion: 2021). https://docsend.com/view/wem8e7ppe7gr4mrk. Accessed: August 2022, 10; Anon., 'Daz 3d and Institute of Digital Fashion Link Up for Pride', *ShowStudio* (29 June 2021). https://www.showstudio.com/news/daz-3d-and-institute-of-digital-fashion-link-up-for-pride. Accessed: August 2022.

91 'Catty 8.1', *Daz3D*, https://www.daz3d.com/catty-81. Accessed: August 2022.

92 Institute of Digital Fashion Instagram posts (28 June 2021), https://www.instagram.com/p/CQq58qCAVH8/ (28 June 2021). https://www.instagram.com/p/CQtH5KotRB1/; https://www.instagram.com/p/CQv1HWlNFTa/. Accessed: August 2022.

93 Ibid., https://www.instagram.com/p/CQq58qCAVH8/.

94 Ibid., https://www.instagram.com/p/CQtH5KotRB1/.

95 Ibid., https://www.instagram.com/p/CQv1HWlNFTa/.

96 Daz 3d Instagram post (28 June 2011). https://www.instagram.com/p/CQrQDIglBnZ/. Accessed: August 2022.

97 Anon., 'Link Up for Pride'.

98 Ibid.

99 Anon., 'Daz 3d and the Institute of Digital Fashion Launch Digital Double for Pride', *Daz3d* (no date). https://blog.daz3d.com/daz-3d-and-the-institute-of-digital-fashion-launch-digital-double-for-pride/. Accessed: August 2022.

100 Anon., 'My Self, My Avatar, My Identity', 13, 22–23.

101 Ibid., 15.
102 Ibid., 7.
103 Ibid., 27.
104 Ibid., 25.
105 Ibid., 46.
106 *The First Book of Fashion*, 128–129.
107 Anon., 'My Self, My Avatar, My Identity', 35.
108 Ibid.
109 Juyeon Park and Jennifer Paff Ogle, 'How Virtual Avatar Experience Interplays with Self-concepts: The Use of Anthropometric 3D Body Models in the Visual Stimulation Process', *Fashion and Textiles*, 8:28 (2021), 2.
110 'Catty 8.1'.
111 See above, 23, 33–35.
112 Richard A. Spears, 'On the Etymology of *Dike*', *American Speech*, 60:4 (1985), 318.
113 John Ortved, 'The Mustache Is Thriving. But What Does It Mean?', *Esquire* (9 July 2020). https://www.esquire.com/style/grooming/a32947149/mustache-trend-history/. Accessed: August 2022.
114 https://www.instagram.com/p/CQv1HWINFTa/.
115 https://www.instagram.com/p/CQq58qCAVH8/.
116 Ibid.
117 Ibid.
118 Ibid.
119 https://www.instagram.com/p/CQtH5KotRB1/.
120 Ibid.
121 Park and Ogle, 'Virtual Avatar Experience', 2.
122 Ibid., 14.
123 Ibid., 16.
124 Ibid., 17.
125 Ibid., 19.
126 Ibid., 6.
127 Ibid., 11.

Conclusion

1 David Graeber and David Wengrove, *The Dawn of Everything: A New History of Humanity* (London: Penguin, 2021), 405.

NOTES

2   Nicholas Carter, Alyce de Carteret and Katharine Lukach, 'The Clothed Body', *The Adorned Body: Mapping Ancient Maya Dress*, eds. Nicholas Carter, Stephen D. Houston and Franco D. Rossi (Austin: University of Texas Press, 2020), 12–13, 25.

3   Minna Salami, *Sensuous Knowledge: A Black Feminist Approach for Everyone* (London: Zed Books, 2020), 37.

4   Philip T. Hoffman, *Why Did Europe Conquer the World?* (Princeton: Princeton University Press, 2015), 2–3.

5   Graeber and Wengrove, *The Dawn of Everything*, 495.

6   Robert Ross, *Clothing: A Global History, Or, The Imperialists' New Clothes* (Cambridge: Polity, 2008), 10.

7   Yuniya Kawamura, *Fashion-ology: An Introduction to Fashion Studies* (Oxford: Berg, 2005), 1–2.

8   Ann Swidler, 'Culture in Action: Symbols and Strategies', *American Sociological Review*, 51:2 (April, 1986), 278–279.

9   Ibid., 279.

10 Susan F. Hirsch and Mindie Lazarus-Black, 'Introduction/Performance and Paradox: Exploring Law's Role in Hegemony and Resistance', *Contested States: Law, Hegemony, and Resistance*, ed. Mindie Lazarus-Black and Susan F. Hirsch (London: Routledge, 1994), 20.

11 Minh-Ha T. Pham, *Why We Can't Have Nice Things: Social Media's Influence on Fashion, Ethics, and Property* (Durham: Duke University Press, 2022), 41–52.

12 See above, 152–153.

13 Terry McGovern, Harriet and Robert H. Heilbrunn, 'Overturning Roe v Wade Has Had an Immediate and Chilling Effect on Reproductive Healthcare', *thebmj* (30 June 2022). https://www.bmj.com/content/377/bmj.o1622. Accessed: September 2022.

14 Kitty Calavita, 'Blue Jeans, Rape, and the "De-Constitutive" Power of Law', *Law and Society Review*, 35:1 (2001), 93.

15 Ibid., 89.

16 Ibid., 106.

17 Ibid., 108.

18 Ibid., 107.

19 See above, 8–9.

20 Swidler, 'Culture in Action', 279.

21 Kehinde Andrews, 'The Psychosis of Whiteness: The Celluloid Hallucinations of Amazing Grace and Belle', *Journal of Black Studies*, 47:5 (2016), 439–440.

22 Minh-Ha T. Pham, 'Fashion's Cultural-Appropriation Debate: Pointless', *The Atlantic* (15 May 2014). https://www.theatlantic.com/entertainment/archive/2014/05/cultural-appropriation-in-fashion-stop-talking-about-it/370826/. Accessed: September 2022.

23 Calavita, 'Blue Jeans', 101.

24 Aurélie Van de Peer, 'The Politics of Fashion Criticism: How Newspaper Journalists' Evaluative Criteria for Fashion has Changed between 1949 and 2010', *Insights on Fashion Journalism*, eds. Rosie Findlay and Johannes Reponen (London: Bloomsbury, 2022), 31.

25 See above, 5.

26 Slavoj Žižek, 'What Donald Rumsfeld Doesn't Know That He Knows About Abu Ghraib' (21 May 2004). https://www.lacan.com/zizekrumsfeld.htm. Accessed: September 2022.

27 Calavita, 'Blue Jeans', 108.

28 Ibid., 107.

29 Ibid.

30 Swidler, 'Culture in Action', 279; Calavita, 'Blue Jeans', 107.

31 Calavita, 'Blue Jeans', 107.

32 Salami, *Sensuous Knowledge*, 2.

33 Peter Lehman, *Running Scared: Masculinity and the Representation of the Male Body* (Philadelphia: Temple University Press, 1993), 5.

34 Andrews, 'The Psychosis of Whiteness', 436.

35 Quoted in Jessica Testa, Vanessa Friedman and Elizabeth Paton, 'Coronavirus Upends the Fashion Universe', *The New York Times International Edition* (7/8 March 2020), 16.

BIBLIOGRAPHY

Abloh, Virgil, 'Tim's Take with Virgil Abloh', *Business of Fashion* (4 February 2021), https://www.youtube.com/watch?v=Q4ipJM2xGUs.
Abraham, Ellie, 'Cara Delevingne Says Her Sexuality is "like a pendulum swinging"', *Independent* (22 June 2020), https://www.independent.co.uk/life-style/dating/cara-delevingne-sexuality-bisexual-pansexual-b1870363.html.
AFP-Relaxnews, 'Hedi Slimane Reveals Iconic Venue for His Debut Celine Show in Paris', *Fashion Network* (21 September 2018), https://ww.fashionnetwork.com/news/Hedi-slimane-reveals-iconic-venue-for-his-debut-celine-show-in-paris,1016466.html.
Ahmed, Osman, 'Divine Inspiration: How Met Gala Guests Tackled the "Heavenly Bodies" Theme', *Vogue* (8 May 2021), https://www.vogue.co.uk/article/how-met-gala-guests-tackled-heavenly-bodies-theme.
Ahuja, Anjana, 'Should the Old or Young be Vaccinated First?', *The Financial Times* (14/15 November 2020), 13.
Ajuwon, Paul M., 'Disabilities and Disability Services in Nigeria: Past, Present and Future', *The Routledge History of Disability*, eds. Roy Hanes, Ivan Brown and Nancy E. Hansen (London: Routledge, 2018), 133–150.
Akbarein, Emma, 'Rick Owens Puts Penises on Show at Paris Fashion Week Show', *The Independent* (23 January 2015), https://www.independent.co.uk/life-style/fashion/news/rick-owens-puts-penises-show-paris-fashion-week-show-9997472.html.
Akinwotu, Emmanuel, 'Ghana: Anti-gay Bill Proposing 10-Year Prison Sentences Sparks Outrage', *The Guardian* (23 July 2021), https://www.theguardian.com/global-development/2021/jul/23/ghana-anti-gay-bill-proposing-10-year-prison-sentences-sparks-outrage.
Alacovska, Ana and Kärreman, Dan, 'Tormented Selves: The Social Imaginary of the Tortured Artist and the Identity Work of Creative Workers', *Organization Studies* (2022), https://doi.org/10.1177/01708406221089594.
Aldrich, Robert, *Colonialism and Homosexuality* (London: Routledge, 2003).
Aldrich, Robert, ed., *Gay Life and Culture: A World History* (London: Thames & Hudson, 2006).
Allwood, Emma Hope, 'Fashion v Censorship: A History of Banned Ads', *Dazed Digital* (13 May 2015), https://www.dazeddigital.com/fashion/article/24720/1/fashion-v-censorship-a-history-of-banned-ads-miu-miu-tom-ford.
Allwood, Emma Hope, 'Trans Activists Aren't Buying Victoria's Secret's Apology', *DazedDigital* (11 November 2018), https://www.dazeddigital.com/fashion/article/42179/1/victoria-s-secret-backpeddles-over-transphobia-ed-razek-comments-trans-models.
Alterman, Eric, 'The Decline of Historical Thinking', *The New Yorker* (4 February 2019), https://www.newyorker.com/news/news-desk/the-decline-of-historical-thinking.

Andress, David, *Cultural Dementia: How the West has Lost Its History, and Risks Losing Everything Else* (London: Head of Zeus, 2018).

Andrews, Kehinde, 'The Psychosis of Whiteness: The Celluloid Hallucinations of Amazing Grace and Belle', *Journal of Black Studies*, 47:5 (2016), 435–453.

Anon., '10-Year-Old Model Thylane Blondeau's Mother Speaks, Closes Her Daughter's Facebook Group', *BlackBook* (5 August 2011), https://blackbookmag.com/fashion-style/fashioneer/10-year-old-model-thylane-blondeaus-mother-speaks-closes-her-daughters-facebook-group/.

Anon., 'Alessandro Michele Breaks His Silence about Gucci's Blackface Scandal', *Fashionista* (12 February 2019), https://fashionista.com/2019/02/gucci-blackface-sweater-alessandro-michele-statement.

Anon., 'Alexander McQueen: Spring 2000 Ready-to-Wear', *Vogue* (3 October 2015), https://www.vogue.com/fashion-shows/spring-2000-ready-to-wear/alexander-mcqueen#review.

Anon., 'Alexander McQueen SS2000: "*Eye*"', *Long Live McQueen* (no date), https://the-widows-of-culloden.tumblr.com/post/61599254756/alexander-mcqueen-ss2000-eye-spring-2000-was.

Anon., 'Burberry Sorry for "suicide" Hoodie with Noose around Neck', *BBC News* (20 February 2019), https://www.bbc.co.uk/news/newsbeat-47302587.

Anon., 'Burberry Takes Suicide Hoodie off Shelves, Apologises after Social Media Rips Brand Apart', *India Today* (21 February 2019), https://www.indiatoday.in/trending-news/story/burberry-takes-suicide-hoodie-off-shelves-apologises-after-social-media-rips-brand-apart-1461752-2019-02-21.

Anon., 'Céline Spring 2019 Ready-to-Wear', *Vogue.com* (no date), https://www.vogue.com/fashion-shows/spring-2019-ready-to-wear/celine/slideshow/collection#1.

Anon., 'Costliest U.S. Tropical Cyclones Tables Updated' (Miami: National Hurricane Center, 26 January 2018), https://www.nhc.noaa.gov/news/UpdatedCostliest.pdf.

Anon., 'Daz 3d and the Institute of Digital Fashion Launch Digital Double for Pride', *Daz3d* (no date), https://blog.daz3d.com/daz-3d-and-the-institute-of-digital-fashion-launch-digital-double-for-pride/.

Anon., 'Daz 3d and Institute of Digital Fashion Link Up for Pride', *ShowStudio* (29 June 2021), https://www.showstudio.com/news/daz-3d-and-institute-of-digital-fashion-link-up-for-pride.

Anon., 'Designer Rick Owens Inspired by Old Sumbarine [sic.] Movies at Paris Men's Fashion Week', *AP Archive* (3 August 2015), https://www.youtube.com/watch?v=ANnyTNZyGE4.

Anon., 'Dolce & Gabbana – Advertising Too Explicit and Sexual?', *Sex in Fashion Advertising Campaigns* (no date), http://sexinfashionadvertising.blogspot.com/2016/11/dolce-gabbana-gang-rape-okay.html.

Anon., 'Dolce & Gabbana Bow to Criticism and Pull Ad', *Reuters* (6 March 2007), https://www.reuters.com/article/us-italy-dolcegabbana-advert-idUSL0631454820070306.

Anon., 'Dolce & Gabbana pondrán a los hombres de rodillas en su próxima campaña publicitaria', *ABC Cultura* (13 January 2009), https://www.abc.es/cultura/abci-dolce-yamp-gabbana-pondran-hombres-rodillas-proxima-campana-publicitaria-200901130300-912418418049_noticia.html.

Anon., 'Dolce & Gabbana under Fire Over "gang rape" Ad', *India Today* (18 March 2015), https://www.indiatoday.in/world/story/dolce-and-gabbana-under-fire-over-gang-rape-ad-244792-2015-03-18.

BIBLIOGRAPHY 251

Anon., 'Duda Beat encarna Madonna e declara: "vamos celebrar nossos corpos livres!"' (3 November 2020), https://vogue.globo.com/celebridade/noticia/2020/11/duda-beat-encarna-madonna-e-declara-vamos-celebrar-nossos-corpos-livres.html.

Anon., 'Harvey Weinstein Timeline: How the Scandal Unfolded', *BBC News* (7 April 2021), https://www.bbc.co.uk/news/entertainment-arts-41594672.

Anon., 'Lauren Hutton, 73, Models Underwear for Calvin Klein', *BBC News* (20 April 2017), https://www.bbc.co.uk/news/entertainment-arts-39652171.

Anon., 'Lauren Hutton is in this Calvin Klein ad for about Two Seconds', *stuff* (20 April 2017), https://www.stuff.co.nz/life-style/fashion/91733573/lauren-hutton-is-in-this-calvin-klein-ad-for-about-two-seconds.

Anon., 'Milan Spring Summer 2009: Vivienne Westwood', *DScene* (24 June 2008), https://www.designscene.net/2008/06/milan-spring-summer-2009-vivienne.html.

Anon., 'The Most Savage Reviews of Hedi Slimane's Celine Debut', *Fashionista* (1 October 2018), https://fashionista.com/2018/10/hedi-slimane-celine-debut-bad-reviews.

Anon., 'My Self, My Avatar, My Identity: Diversity and Inclusivity within Virtual Worlds' (Institute of Digital Fashion, 2021), https://docsend.com/view/wem8e7ppe7gr4mrk.

Anon., 'Nude Male Model Causes Controversy with Fashion Week Orchestrators', *Cision PR Newswire* (27 February 2015), https://www.prnewswire.com/news-releases/nude-male-model-causes-controversy-with-fashion-week-orchestrators-300042911.html.

Anon., 'Oh Good Lord, Did They Really Wear That?', *The Daily Telegraph* (9 May 2018), 20–21.

Anon., 'Paris Fashion Week Men's S/S 2019 Editor's Picks', *Wallpaper* (23 June 2018), https://www.wallpaper.com/fashion/paris-fashion-week-mens-ss-2020-editors-picks.

Anon., 'Population Ageing in China: Crisis or Opportunity?', *The Lancet*, 400:10366 (2022), 1821.

Anon., 'Pre-fall 2018 Celine', *Vogue.com* (no date), https://www.vogue.com/fashion-shows/pre-fall-2018/celine/slideshow/collection#1.

Anon., 'Preta Gil: "Se tem alguma coisa da qual me arrependo é de ter mutilado meu corpo com cirurgias, de ter o escondido por vergonha"', *Brasilian Vogue* (3 November 2020), https://vogue.globo.com/celebridade/noticia/2020/11/preta-gil-se-tem-alguma-coisa-da-qual-me-arrependo-e-de-ter-mutilado-meu-corpo-com-cirurgias-de-ter-o-escondido-por-vergonha.html.

Anon., 'RICK OWENS ABOUT FW15 SPHINX COLLECTION' (no date), https://journal.antonioli.eu/2015/01/rick-owens-about-fw15-sphinx-collection/.

Anon., 'Rick Owens Sends Models down the Runway with Their Junk Out, '*GQ* Australia (23 January 2015), https://www.gq.com.au/style/news/rick-owens-sends-models-down-the-runway-with-their-junk-out-news-story/c419e795836aec6552526af6a3cd663d.

Anon., 'Sofia Coppola Directs Calvin Klein or Nothing At All', *DNA Magazine* (19 April 2017), https://www.dnamag.co/home/sofia-coppola-calvin-klein.

Anon., 'Sponsor's Statement', *Camp: Notes on Fashion*, ed. Andrew Bolton (New Haven and London: Yale University Press, 2019), i, 6.

Anon., 'This 10-Year-Old French Model Has a Tumblr Dedicated to Her', *BlackBook* (28 July 2011), https://blackbookmag.com/fashion-style/fashioneer/this-10-year-old-french-model-has-a-tumblr-dedicated-to-her/.

Anon., 'United Colors of Benetton: Colors of Domestic Violence', *DrPrem* (no date), https://drprem.com/business/united-colors-of-benetton-colors-of-domestic-violence.

Anon., 'Vivienne Westwood Controversial Milan Menswear Runway', *Trendhunter* (no date), https://www.trendhunter.com/trends/gypsies-westwood-milan.

Anon., 'Vogue's Disturbing "fashion" Images of Girl Aged Ten', *The Christian Institute* (12 August 2011), https://www.christian.org.uk/news/vogues-disturbing-fashion-images-of-girl-aged-ten/.

Anon., 'Why is No One Outraged by Calvin Kleinâs Latest Underwear Ad?', *Data & Marketing Association* (17 November 2017), https://dma.org.uk/article/why-is-no-one-outraged-by-calvin-kleins-latest-underwear-ad.

Arnold, Amanda, 'Scenes from Christopher Bailey's Emotional Final Burberry Show', *The Cut* (no date), https://www.thecut.com/2018/02/scenes-from-christopher-baileys-final-burberry-show.html.

Appadurai, Arjun, *Modernity at Large: Cultural Dimensions of Globalization* (Minneapolis and London: University of Minnesota Press, 1996).

Arnold, Rebecca, *Fashion, Desire and Anxiety: Image and Morality in the 20th Century* (London and New York: I.B. Tauris, 2001).

Ashcroft, Bill, Griffiths, Gareth and Tiffin, Helen, 'The Sacred', *The Post-Colonial Studies Reader*, eds. Bill Ashcroft, Gareth Griffiths and Helen Tiffin (London: Routledge, second edition, 2006), 517–518.

Ashleigh, Conor, 'Controlling the Global Obesity Epidemic', *World Health Organization* (no date), https://www.who.int/activities/controlling-the-global-obesity-epidemic.

Associated Press, '"It was insensitive": Burberry Apologises for "noose" Hoodie after Model Complains', *The Guardian* (20 February 2019), https://www.theguardian.com/fashion/2019/feb/20/it-was-insensitive-burberry-apologises-for-noose-hoodie-after-model-complains.

Bain, Marc, 'Prada has Pulled Its Red-Lipped Monkey Dolls, which Echoed Racist "Sambo" Imagery', *Quartz* (14 December 2018), https://qz.com/quartzy/1496189/prada-pulls-sambo-esque-monkey-dolls-after-blackface-criticism/.

Baker Jones, Katie, 'What a Difference a Page Makes: Contextualising Suzy Menkes' Fashion Criticism Within and Across Media Outlets', *Insights on Fashion Journalism*, eds. Rosie Findlay and Johannes Reponen (London: Routledge, 2022), 127–139.

Baldridge, William, 'Reclaiming Our Histories', *The Post-Colonial Studies Reader*, eds. Bill Ashcroft, Gareth Griffiths and Helen Tiffin (London: Routledge, second edition, 2006), 528–530.

Ballantyne, Andrew, *Architecture: A Very Short Introduction* (Oxford: Oxford University Press, 2002).

Bancroft, Alison, 'Masculinity, Masquerade and Display: Some thoughts on Rick Owens's Sphinx Collection and Men in Fashion', *Critical Studies in Fashion & Beauty*, 7:1 (2016), 19–29.

Barcan, Ruth, *Nudity: A Cultural Anatomy* (London: Bloomsbury, 2004).

Barker-Benfield, Ben, 'The Spermatic Economy: A Nineteenth Century View of Sexuality', *Feminist Studies*, 1:1 (1957), 45–74.

Barrett, Helen, 'Brasher, Flasher and Raunchier – Why the Pelvic Cut-Out Is Back', *The Financial Times* (10 August 2021), https://www.ft.com/content/e36053eb-1f37-4632-b903-eaaf149b67ae.

Barrow, Rosemary, 'From Praxiteles to De Chirico: Art and Reception', *International Journal of the Classical Tradition*, 11:3 (2005), 344–368.

Barry, Ben, 'Fabulous Masculinities: Refashioning the Fat and Disabled Male Body', *Fashion Theory*, 23:2 (2019), 275–307.

Barry, Ben, 'How to Transform Fashion Education: A Manifesto for Equity, Inclusion and Decolonization', *International Journal of Fashion Studies*, 8:1 (2021), 123–130.

Bartlett, Djurda, 'Can Fashion Be Defended?', *Fashion and Politics*, ed. Djurda Bartlett (New Haven and London: Yale University Press, 2019), 17–57.

Bastian, Misty L., 'The Naked and the Nude: Historically Multiple Meanings of *Oto* (undress) in Southeastern Nigeria', *Dirt, Undress, and Difference: Critical Perspectives on the Body's Surface*, ed. Adeline Masquelier (Bloomington and Indianapolis: Indiana University Press, 2005), 34–60.

Baudelaire, Charles, 'The Painter of Modern Life', *The Painter of Modern Life and Other Essays*, translated and edited by Jonathan Mayne (London: Phaidon Press Limited, [1863] 1964), 1–41.

Beaujot, Ariel, 'Gender and Sexuality', *A Cultural History of Dress and Fashion in the Age of Empire*, 5, ed. Denise Amy Baxter (London: Bloomsbury, 2017), 99–120.

Beckett, Angharad E., Bagguley, Paul and Campbell, Tom, 'Foucault, Social Movements and Heterotopic Horizons: Rupturing the Order of Things', *Social Movement Studies*, 16:2 (2017), 169–181.

Begum, Tahmina, 'Gucci Criticised for Cultural Appropriation on a Global Scale', *HuffPost* (22 February 2018), https://www.huffingtonpost.co.uk/entry/gucci-autumn-winter-2018-show_uk_5a8e996be4b0161d4318dfdc.

Benaïm, Laurence, 'Hedi Slimane's First Celine Interview', *Business of Fashion* (25 September 2018), https://www.businessoffashion.com/articles/news-analysis/hedi-slimane-interview-celine.

Benavent, Vicente, 'Los "clochards" de Galliano: Mendigos vestidoes de Dior', *Harpers Bazaar* (13 May 2015), https://www.harpersbazaar.com/es/moda/noticias-moda/a179665/galliano-dior-clochards-homeless-2000/.

Berger, John, *The Art of Seeing* (London: Penguin, 1972).

Bernstein, Robin, *Racial Innocence: Performing American Childhood from Slavery to Civil Rights* (New York: New York University Press, 2011).

Betancourt, Roland, *Byzantine Intersectionality: Sexuality, Gender & Race in the Middle Ages* (Princeton and Oxford: Princeton University Press, 2020).

Bethune, Kate, 'Encyclopedia of Collections', *Alexander McQueen*, ed. Claire Wilcox (London: V&A Publishing, 2015), 311.

Betterton, Rosemary, 'Maternal Bodies in Visual Culture' (January 2009), https://www.researchgate.net/publication/237454497_Maternal_Bodies_in_Visual_Culture.

Bhabha, Homi K., *The Location of Culture* (London: Routledge, 1994).

Bissinger, Buzz, 'Serena Williams's Love Match', *Vanity Fair* (27 June 2017), https://www.vanityfair.com/style/2017/06/serena-williams-cover-story.

Blackmon, Michael, 'Cardinal Timothy Dolan Joked He Lent Rihanna His Headdress for the Met Gala', *Buzzfeed* (9 May 2021), https://www.buzzfeednews.com/article/michaelblackmon/met-gala-catholic-cardinal-dolan-rihanna.

Blake, William, *William Blake: Poems Selected by James Fenton* (London: Faber and Faber, 2010).

Blanks, Tim, 'A Dark New Dawn at Celine', *BoF* (29 September 2018), https://www.businessoffashion.com/reviews/fashion-week/a-dark-new-dawn-at-celine.

Blanks, Tim, 'The End of the (Fashion) World as We Know It', *Business of Fashion* (24 March 2020), https://www.businessoffashion.com/opinions/luxury/the-end-of-the-fashion-world-as-we-know-it?utm_campaign=1686245233687280&utm_medium=email&utm_source=daily-digest-newsletter&utm_term=11.

Blanks, Tim, 'Fendi Fall 2014 Ready-to-Wear', *Vogue* (19 February 2014), https://www.vogue.com/fashion-shows/fall-2014-ready-to-wear/fendi.

Blanks, Tim, 'Fendi Fall 2015 Couture', *Vogue* (8 July 2015), https://www.vogue.com/fashion-shows/fall-2015-couture/fendi.

Blanks, Tim, 'A Play on Proportion at Thom Browne', *Business of Fashion* (24 June 2018), https://www.businessoffashion.com/reviews/fashion-week/a-play-on-proportion-at-thom-browne.

Blanks, Tim, 'Rick Owens: Fall 2015 Menswear', *Vogue* (22 January 2015), https://www.vogue.com/fashion-shows/fall-2015-menswear/rick-owens.

Bleys, Rudi C., *The Geography of Perversion: Male-to-Male Sexual Behaviour outside the West and the Ethnographic Imagination 1750–1918* (London: Cassell, 1996).

Boan, Daniel, 'Lupita Nyong'o Called Out a Magazine for Photoshopping Her Natural Hair on the Cover', *Insider* (10 November 2017), https://www.insider.com/lupita-nyongo-is-disappointed-in-grazia-daily-for-altering-her-hair-2017-11.

Boellstorff, Tom, 'The Emergence of Political Homophobia in Indonesia: Masculinity and National Belonging', *Ethnos*, 69:4 (2004), 465–486.

Bolton, Andrew, 'Introduction', *Heavenly Bodies: Fashion and the Catholic Imagination*, 2 vols. (New Haven and London: Yale University Press), ii, 95–96.

Bolton, Andrew, 'Sixty Minutes of Fashion', *About Time: Fashion & Duration*, ed. Andrew Bolton (New Haven and London: Yales University Press, 2020), x–xv.

Bondil, Nathalie, 'The Stylings of a Humanist Couturier', *The World of Jean Paul Gaultier: From Sidewalk to Catwalk*, ed. Thierry-Maxime Loriot (New York: Abrams, 2011).

Borrelli-Persson, Laird, 'Nice Day for a White Wedding? Flashback to Dior Couture's Transgressive Fall 2000 Collection', *Vogue* (3 July 2006), https://www.vogue.com/article/christian-dior-haute-couture-fall-2000-john-galliano.

Boum, Aomar and Abrevaya Stein, Sarah, eds., *The Holocaust and North Africa* (Stanford: Stanford University Press, 2018).

Braddock, David L. and Parish, Susan L., 'An Institutional History of Disability', *Handbook of Disability Studies*, eds. Gary L. Albrecht, Katherine D. Seelman and Michael Bury (London: Sage Publications, 2001), 11–68.

Bramley, Ellie Violet, 'Marketing Boss Quits Victoria's Secret after First Trans Model Hired', *The Guardian* (6 August 2019), https://www.theguardian.com/fashion/2019/aug/06/marketing-boss-quits-victorias-secret-first-trans-model-hired.

Brandt, Mark J. and Reyna, Christine, 'The Chain of Being: A Hierarchy of Morality', *Perspectives on Psychological Science*, 6:5 (2011), 428–446.

Breward, Christopher, *The Suit: Form, Function and Style* (London: Reaktion Books, 2016).

Briseño, Alma Hernández, 'La Poupee and Voss: Alexander McQueen's Heterotopias', *The Fashion Studies Journal* (17 May 2020), www.fashionstudiesjournal.org/longform/2020/5/17/alexander-mcqueen.

Brook, Orian, O'Brien, Dave and Taylor, Mark, *Culture is Bad for You: Inequality in the Cultural and Creative Industries* (Manchester: Manchester University Press, 2020).

Burghartz, Susanna, 'The Fabric of Early Globalization: Skin, fur and cloth in de Bry's travel accounts, 1590–1630', *Dressing Global Bodies: The Political Power of Dress in World History*, eds. Beverly Lemire and Giorgio Riello (London: Routledge), 15–40.

Burke, Tarana, '#MeToo Founder Tarana Burke on the Rigorous Work That Still Lies Ahead', *Variety* (25 September 2018), https://variety.com/2018/biz/features/tarana-burke-metoo-one-year-later-1202954797/.

Burnett, Victoria, 'Fashion Ads Touch a Nerve in Gender-Conscious Spain', *The New York Times* (25 March 2007), https://www.nytimes.com/2007/03/25/business/worldbusiness/25iht-fashion26.1.5014898.html.

Butler, Francelia, 'The Poetry of Rope-Skipping', *The New York Times* (16 December 1973), 356.
Butler, Judith, *Gender Trouble: Feminism and the Subversion of Identity* (London: Routledge, 1990).
Butler, Judith, 'Why is the Idea of "gender" Provoking Backlash the World Over?' *The Guardian* (23 October 2021), https://www.theguardian.com/us-news/commentisfree/2021/oct/23/judith-butler-gender-ideology-backlash.
Buttolph, Angela et al., *The Fashion Book* (London: Phaidon, 1998).
Calavita, Kitty, 'Blue Jeans, Rape, and the "De-Constitutive" Power of Law', *Law & Society Review*, 35:1 (2001), 89–116.
Campbell, Thomas P., 'Foreword', Hamish Bowles, *Vogue & The Metropolitan Museum of Art Costume Institute: Parties, Exhibitions, People* (New York: Abrams, 2014), 7.
Cannadine, David, 'The Context, Performance and Meaning of Ritual: The British Monarchy and the "Invention of Tradition", *c.*1820–1977', *The Invention of Tradition*, eds. Eric Hobsbawm and Terence Ranger (Cambridge: Cambridge University Press, 1983), 101–164.
Cappelle, Laura, 'When the only in Town is Church', *The New York Times International Edition* (12/13 December 2020), 19.
Carr-Gomm, Philip, *A Brief History of Nakedness* (London: Reaktion Books, 2010).
Carter, Cassia, 'Cara Delevingne: À La Fois Féminine Et Androgyne Pour Jimmy Choo', *Grazia Fr.* (10 November 2017), https://www.grazia.fr/mode/cara-delevingne-a-la-fois-feminine-et-androgyne-pour-jimmy-choo-873013.
Carter, Nicholas, Carteret, Alyce de and Lukach, Katharine, 'The Clothed Body', *The Adorned Body: Mapping Ancient Maya Dress*, eds. Nicholas Carter, Stephen D. Houston, Franco D. Rossi (Austin: University of Texas Press, 2020), 9–31.
Cartner-Morley, Jess, 'Kanye West Stirs Controversy in "White Lives Matter" T-shirt at Paris Fashion Week', *The Guardian* (4 October 2022), https://www.theguardian.com/music/2022/oct/04/kanye-west-white-lives-matter-t-shirt-paris-fashion-week.
Carton, Adrian, 'Desire and Same Sex Intimacies in Asia', *Gay Life and Culture: A World History*, ed. Robert Aldrich (London: Thames & Hudson, 2006), 303–332.
Cavendish, Camilla, 'We Are Prioritising the Old and will have to Make It up to the Young', *The Financial Times* (28/29 March 2020), 14.
Cayley, A.-H., 'Ten-Year-Old Thylane Blondeau Models for French Vogue', *Pedestrian* (11 May 2017), https://www.pedestrian.tv/style/ten-year-old-thylane-blondeau-models-for-french-vogue/.
Chalcraft, David and Harrington, Austin, ed., *The Protestant Work Ethic Debate: Max Weber's Replies to His Critics, 1907–1910* (Liverpool: Liverpool University Press, 2001).
Cheang, Sarah, 'Ethnicity', *A Cultural History of Dress and Fashion in the Age of Empire*, vol. 5, ed. Denise Amy Baxter (London: Bloomsbury, 2017), 141–164.
Cheang, Sarah and Suterwalla, Shehnaz, 'Decolonizing the Curriculum? Transformation, Emotion, and Positionality in Teaching', *Fashion Theory*, 24:6 (2020), 879–900.
Chodha, Dal, 'In Defence of Fashion's Limits – and Its Infinite Possibilities', *i-D*, 368 (2022), 208–209.
Chung, Jen, 'After Blackface Scandal, Prada Agrees to "Landmark" Restorative Justice Settlement with NYC', *The Gothamist* (5 February 2021), https://gothamist.com/arts-entertainment/after-blackface-scandal-prada-agrees-landmark-restorative-justice-settlement-nyc.
Clark, Kenneth, *The Nude: A Study of Ideal Art* (London: Penguin Books, 1956).
Clark, Meredith, 'Balenciaga Apologises after "disgusting" Ads of Children Holding "bondage" Teddy Bears Spark Backlash', *The Independent* (23 November 2022),

https://www.independent.co.uk/life-style/fashion/balenciaga-plush-bear-bag-holiday-campaign-b2231068.html.

Cole, Shaun, 'New Styles, New Sounds: Clubbing, Music and Fashion in 1980s London', *80s Fashion: From Club to Catwalk*, ed. Sonnet Stanfill (London: V&A Publishing, 2013), 32–47.

Coletta, Amanda, 'Prada Pulls Products after Blackface Imagery Accusations', *CTV News* (16 December 2018), https://www.ctvnews.ca/business/prada-pulls-products-after-blackface-imagery-accusations-1.4220256.

Collins, Josephine, 'From the Typewriter to the Smartphone: How Changing Capture and Delivery Systems Have Influenced the Practice of Fashion Journalism', *Insights on Fashion Journalism*, ed. Rosie Findlay and Johannes Reponen (London: Routledge, 2022), 15–19.

Communications team, 'Condé Nast unveils New Global Content Strategy', *Condé Nast* (15 December 2020), https://www.condenast.com/news/new-global-content-strategy-conde-nast.

Compain, Hugo, '<<Je suis en paix avec mon corps>>', *France GQ* (March 2021), 70–79.

Conti, Samantha, 'Thom Browne Men's Spring 2019', *WWD* (23 June 2018), https://wwd.com/runway/mens-spring-collections-2019/paris/thom-browne/review/.

Cook, Daniel Thomas, *The Commodification of Childhood: The Children's Clothing Industry and the Rise of the Child Consumer* (Durham and London: Duke University Press, 2004).

Coughlan, Joseph F., 'How "old age" was Invented – And Why It needs to be Reinvented', *MIT Technology Review*, 122:5 (September/October 2019), 33–37.

Craik, Jennifer, *The Face of Fashion: Cultural Studies in Fashion* (London and New York: Routledge, 1993).

Crash redaction, 'Fendi Haute Fourrure Fall-Winter 1015–16 by Frank Perrin', *Crash* (no date), https://www.crash.fr/fendi-haute-fourrure-fall-winter-2015-16-by-frank-perrin/.

Croce, Luigi, Cosimo, Federica Di and Lombardi, Marco, 'A Short History of Disability in Italy', *The Routledge History of Disability*, eds. Roy Hanes, Ivan Brown and Nancy E. Hansen (London: Routledge, 2018), 70–93.

Cronberg, Anja Aronowsky, 'Inteviews: Rick Owens', *Vestoj: On Masculinities*, 7 (2016), 230–233.

Cuddy, Amy J., Norton, Michael I. and Fiske, Susan T., 'This Old Stereotype: The Pervasiveness and Persistence of the Elderly Stereotype', *Journal of Social Issues*, 61:2 (2005), 267–285.

Curry, Tommy J., 'Reconstituting the Object: Black Male Studies and the Problem of Studying Black Men and Boys within Patriarchal Gender Theory', *The Palgrave Handbook of Critical Race and Gender*, eds. S.A. Tate and E. Gutiérrez Rodríguez (Basingstoke: Palgrave Macmillan, 2022), 525–544.

Dabiri, Emma, *Don't Touch My Hair* (London: Penguin, 2019).

Dabiri, Emma, 'The Speakeasier with Emma Dabiri: When was Race & Ethnicity Invented?' *The Unmistakables* (20 May 2021), https://www.theunmistakables.com/post/the-speakeasier-with-emma-dabiri.

Dabiri, Emma, *What White People Can Do Next: From Allyship to Coalition* (London: Penguin, 2021).

Dacre, Karen, 'Fendi Couture: Karl Lagerfeld Courts Controversy with a Catwalk Collection Dedicated to Fur', *The Evening Standard* (9 July 2015), https://www.standard.co.uk/insider/fashion/fendi-couture-karl-lagerfeld-courts-controversy-with-a-catwalk-collection-dedicated-to-fur-10377918.html.

Dang, Vivian, 'Ten-Year-Old as Sex Symbol: Thylane Blondeau and the Troubling Choices of Vogue Enfant', *Vancouver Observer* (29 August 2011), https://www.vancouverobserver.com/politics/commentary/2011/08/29/ten-year-old-sex-symbol-thylane-blondeau-and-troubling-choices-vogue.

David, Alison Matthews, *Fashion Victims: The Dangers of Dress Past and Present* (London: Bloomsbury, 2015).

Davidson, Emma Elizabeth, 'The 2018 Victoria's Secret Show had Its Lowest TV Ratings Ever', *DazedDigital* (4 December 2018), https://www.dazeddigital.com/fashion/article/42469/1/victorias-secret-lowest-tv-ratings-ever-halsey-lgbtq-plus-size-ed-razek.

Davidson, Emma Elizabeth, 'Victoria's Secret just Hired Its First Ever Trans Model', *DazedDigital* (5 August 2019), https://www.dazeddigital.com/fashion/article/45499/1/victorias-secret-angel-transgender-model-valentina-sampaio-underwear-label.

Davidson, Hilary, 'Shoes as Magical Objects', *Shoes: Pleasure & Pain*, ed. Helen Persson (London: V&A Publishing, 2015), 24–35.

Davis, Fred, *Fashion, Culture, and Identity* (Chicago and London: The University of Chicago Press, 1982).

Davis, Lennard J., 'Bodies of Difference: Politics, Disability, and Representation', *Disability Studies: Enabling the Humanities*, eds. Brenda Jo Brueggemann, Sharron L. Snyder and Rosemarie Garland-Thomson (New York: Modern Language Association, 2002), 100–106.

Debord, Guy, *Society of Spectacle* (Detroit: Black & Red, 1983).

de Gobineau, Arthur, *Essai sur l'inégalité des races humaines*, 4 vols. (Paris: Librairie de Firmin Didot, 1853–1855).

de Groot, Joanna, '"Sex" and "race": The Construction of Language and Image in the Nineteenth Century', *Cultures of Empire: Colonizers in Britain and the Empire in the Nineteenth and Twentieth Centuries. A Reader*, ed. Catherine Hall (Manchester: Manchester University Press, 2000), 37–60.

Delap, Leanne, 'Toxic Masculinity at Paris Fashion Week: Why Hedi Slimane's Celine Debut was so Egregiously Tone-Deaf', *The Kit* (1 October 2018), https://thekit.ca/style/hedi-slimane-celine-debut-misogynist/.

Dellatto, Marissa and Porterfield, Carlie, 'Kanye West's Antisemitic, Troubling Behavior—Here's Everything He's Said in Recent Weeks', *Fortune* (2 December 2022), https://www.forbes.com/sites/marisadellatto/2022/12/02/kanye-wests-anti-semitic-troubling-behavior-heres-everything-hes-said-in-recent-weeks/?sh=6903f6286de3.

d'Emilio, John, 'Capitalism and Gay Identity', *Culture, Society and Sexuality: A Reader*, eds. Richard Parker and Peter Aggleton (London: Routledge, [1983] 2007, second edition), 150–258.

Demopoulos, Alaina, 'The "Burberry Noose" Is Just the Latest Controversy. Why Can't Fashion Houses Do Better?' *The Daily Beast* (20 February 2019), https://www.thedailybeast.com/the-burberry-noose-is-just-the-latest-controversy-why-cant-fashion-houses-do-better.

Denham, M. J., 'The History of Geriatric Medicine and Hospital Care of the Elderly in England between 1929 and the 1970s' (Unpublished PhD thesis, University College, London, 2004).

DeSwiss, '"Gang Rape" Dolce and Gabbana Advert Banned', forum post 'Fashion Designers Dolce and Gabbana's "Gang Rape" Ad Banned', *Democratic Underground* (7 March 2007), https://www.democraticunderground.com/discuss/duboard.php?az=view_all&address=389x358015.

Dingwall, Kate, 'Calvin Klein Taps Cast of Moonlight for Campaign Following the Oscars', *Fashion Network* (28 February 2017), https://uk.fashionnetwork.com/news/calvin-klein-taps-cast-of-moonlight-for-campaign-following-the-oscars,798542.html.

Domingues, Petrônio, 'A Visita de um Afro-Americano ao Paraíso Racial', *Revista de História*, 155 (2006), 161–181.

Donaldson, Laura E., 'God, Gold, and Gender', *The Post-Colonial Studies Reader*, eds. Bill Ashcroft, Gareth Griffiths and Helen Tiffin (London: Routledge, second edition, 2006), 522–527.

Donohue, Cathy, 'Ballsy! Male Model Gives Onlookers an Eyeful at New York Fashion Week', *Her* (no date), https://www.her.ie/style/ballsy-male-model-gives-onlookers-an-eyeful-at-new-york-fashion-week-219710?cacheTtl=5&cacheKey=request-browser-httpswwwheriestyleballsy-male-model-gives-onlookers-an-eyeful-at-new-york-fashion-week219710.

Dover, Kenneth J., *Greek Homosexuality* (London: Bloomsbury, [1978] 2016).

Dowd, Maureen, 'Liberties; Haute Homeless', *The New York Times* (23 January 2000), https://www.nytimes.com/2000/01/23/opinion/liberties-haute-homeless.html.

Duberman, Martin, *Has The Gay Movement Failed?* (Oakland: University of California Press, 2018).

Duncan, Amy, 'Dolce & Gabbana in Hot Water again after "gang rape" Advert Resurfaces just Days after IVF Furore', *Metro* (18 March 2015), https://metro.co.uk/2015/03/18/dolce-gabbana-in-hot-water-again-after-gang-rape-ad-campaign-resurfaces-just-days-after-ivf-furore-5108624/.

Durkheim, Émile, *Suicide: A Study in Sociology*, translated by John A. Spaulding and George Simpson (London: Routledge, [1897] 1952).

E., Mark, 'The 5 Most Controversial Vogue Images Ever Published', *The Fashion Spot* (29 August 2014), https://www.thefashionspot.com/runway-news/450991-controversial-vogue-images-ever-published/5/.

Eddie, 'Petits CADEAUX', *Noir Addict* (5 August 2011), https://fashionfatty.wordpress.com/tag/vogue-paris-christmas-issue-december-2010january-2011/.

The Editorial Board, 'Trump's Heartless Transgender Military Ban Gets a Second Shot', *The New York Times* (28 March 2018), https://www.nytimes.com/2018/03/28/opinion/trump-transgender-military-ban.html.

The Editors, 'The Internet Is Mad at J. Crew over This Black Model's Hairstyle', *Cosmopolitan* (12 November 2017), https://www.cosmopolitan.com/style-beauty/fashion/a13524555/the-internet-is-mad-at-j-crew-over-this-black-models-hairstyle/.

Eikof, Doris Ruth and Haunschild, Axel, 'Lifestyle Meets Market: Bohemian Entrepreneurs in Creative Industries', *Creative and Innovation Management*, 15:3 (2006), 234–241.

Eiras, Natália, 'Negra, gorda e estrela da SPFW: "Não tive em quem me espelhar", conta Rita', *Universa* (16 October 2019), https://www.uol.com.br/universa/noticias/redacao/2019/10/16/negra-gorda-e-estrela-da-spfw-nao-tive-em-quem-me-espelhar-conta-rita.htm.

Eire, Carlos M., *Reformations: The Early Modern World, 1450–1650* (New Haven and London: Yale University Press, 2016).

Elias, Norbert, *The Civilising Process: Sociogenetic and Psychogenetic Investigations*, translated by Edmund Jephcott. Revised Edition, eds. Eric Dunning, Johan Goudsblom and Stephen Menell (Oxford: Blackwell, [1939] 1994).

Elias, Norbert, *The Society of Individuals*, ed., Michael Schröter, translated by Edmund Jephcott (Oxford: Basil Blackwell, [Elias, Norbert, 1987] 1991).

Ellison, Jo, 'Lockdown Two has Unleashed the Selfish Gene', *The Financial Times: Life and Arts* (7/8 November 2020), 16.

Emberley, Julia, *The Cultural Politics of Fur* (Ithaca and London: Cornell University Press, 1997).

Emberley, Julia, 'The Fashion Apparatus and the Deconstruction of Postmodern Subjectivity', *Canadian Journal of Political and Social Theory/Revue Canadienne de théorie politique et sociale*, XI:1–2 (1987), 39–50.

Enninful, Edward, 'Editor's Letter', British *Vogue* (May 2023), 31–4.

Entwistle, Joanne, *The Fashioned Body: Fashion, Dress and Modern Social Theory* (Cambridge: Polity Press, 2000).

Erkilic, Mualla, 'Developments in Disability Issues During the Late Ottoman Period of Turkish History from 1876 to 1909', *The Routledge History of Disability*, eds. Roy Hanes, Ivan Brown and Nancy E. Hansen (London: Routledge, 2018), 56–69.

Evans, Caroline, *Fashion at the Edge: Spectacle, Modernity and Deathliness* (New Haven and London: Yale University Press, 2003).

Evans, Caroline and Vaccari, Alessandra, 'Time in Fashion: An Introductory Essay', *Time in Fashion*, eds. Caroline Evans and Alessandra Vaccari (London: Bloomsbury, 2020), 3–40.

Evans, Georgina, 'Show Report: Burberry A/W 18', *SHOWStudio* (19 February 2018), https://showstudio.com/collections/autumn-winter-2018/burberry_london_a_w_18/georgina_evans_reports_on_the_burberry_show.

Faiers, Jonathan, *Fur: A Sensitive History* (New Haven and London: Yale University Press, 2020).

Fashionattheedge, 'Dolce & Gabbana Spring/Summer 2007', *The Edge* (24 May 2007), http://fashionontheedge.blogspot.com/2007/05/dolce-gabbana-springsummer-2007.html.

Fearon, Francesca, 'China's Renowned Couturier Guo Pei has a Cosmetics Fridge, a Collection of Kaleidoscopes and a Studio Full of Dolls', *The Financial Times: How To Spend It* (30 October 2020), https://www.ft.com/content/e5c870cc-d9a0-4d69-8ca7-33e13d6b01bd.

Ferraz, Juliana, 'Corpo positivo: Preta Gil, Duda Beat e Rita Carreira estrelam a Vogue de novembro', Brazilian *Vogue* (3 November 2020), https://vogue.globo.com/moda/noticia/2020/11/corpo-positivo-preta-gil-duda-beat-e-rita-carreira-estrelam-vogue-de-novembro.html.

Ferrier, Morwenna, 'Anna Wintour Apologises for not Giving Space to Black People at Vogue', *The Guardian* (10 June 2020), https://www.theguardian.com/fashion/2020/jun/10/anna-wintour-apologises-for-not-giving-space-to-black-people-at-vogue.

Ferrier, Morwenna, 'Domenico Dolce Apologies for Remarks about IVF and Gay Families', *The Guardian* (17 August 2015), https://www.theguardian.com/fashion/2015/aug/17/domenico-dolce-apologises-for-remarks-about-ivf-and-gay-families.

Ferrier, Morwenna, 'Gucci Withdraws $890 Jumper after Blackface Blacklash', *The Guardian* (7 February 2019), https://www.theguardian.com/fashion/2019/feb/07/gucci-withdraws-jumper-blackface-balaclava.

Findlay, Rosie and Reponen, Johannes, 'Introduction', *Insights on Fashion Journalism*, eds. Rosie Findlay and Johannes Reponen (London: Routledge, 2022), 1–11.

Finkelstein, Joanne, *The Fashioned Self* (Cambridge: Polity Press, 1991).

Finn, Margot and Fox, Jo, 'The Economist and History: Economical with the Facts?', *Historical Transactions* (19 August 2019), https://blog.royalhistsoc.org/2019/08/19/rhs-ihr-letter-economist-and-history/.

Fisher, Lauren Alexis, 'Lauren Hutton, 73, Stars in Calvin Klein's New Underwear Campaign', *Harper's Bazaar* (18 April 2017), https://www.harpersbazaar.com/fashion/designers/news/a22061/calvin-klein-womens-underwear-campaign-spring-2017/.

Fisher, Lauren Alexis, 'Things Got Weird at Gucci's Fall 2018 Show', *Harper's Bazaar* (21 February 2018), https://www.harpersbazaar.com/fashion/fashion-week/a18564887/gucci-fall-2018-show/.

Fjelde, Rolf, 'Peer Gynt, Naturalism, and The Dissolving Self', *The Drama Review*, 13:2 (1968), 28–43.

Flaccavento, Angelo, 'Alessandro Michele: Quotations, the Past and Future of Fashion. Here's My Vision', trans. Antony Bowden, Italian *Vogue*, 805 (September 2017), 191–194.

Fletcher, Adam and I-D team, 'Rick Owens Spring/Summer 14', *i-D* (11 November 2013), https://i-d.vice.com/en_uk/article/8xnqav/rick-owens-springsummer-14.

Flügel, J. C., *The Psychology of Clothes* (London: Hogarth Press, 1930).

Foley, Bridget, 'Moment 87: Homeless by Dior', *WWD* (1 November 2010), https://wwd.com/fashion-news/fashion-features/moment-87-homeless-by-dior-3346959/.

Foucault, Michel, translated by Jay Miskowiec, 'Of Other Spaces: Utopias and Heterotopias', *Architecture /Mouvement/ Continuité* (October 1984), https://web.mit.edu/allanmc/www/foucault1.pdf.

Foucault, Michel, *The History of Sexuality, Volume 1: An Introduction*, translated by Robert Hurley (New York: Pantheon Books, 1978).

Foucault, Michel, *The Order of Things: An Archaeology of the Human Sciences* (London: Routledge, [1966] 1970).

Fowler, Danielle, 'Calvin Klein's Latest Campaign Celebrates Women of All Ages', *Grazia* (20 April 2017), https://graziadaily.co.uk/fashion/news/calvin-klein-spring-summer-campaign/.

Foxall, Andrew, 'From Evropa to Gayropa: A Critical Geopolitics of the European Union as Seen from Russia', *Geopolitics*, 24:1 (2019), 174–193.

Frank, Katherine, 'Body Talk: Revelations of Self and Body in Contemporary Strip Clubs', *Dirt, Undress, and Difference: Critical Perspectives on the Body's Surface*, ed. Adeline Masquelier (Bloomington and Indianapolis: Indiana University Press, 2005), 96–121.

Frankopan, Peter, *The New Silk Roads: The Present and Future of the World* (London: Bloomsbury, 2018).

Frantz-Parsons, Elaine, *Ku-Klux Klan: The Birth of the Klan during Reconstruction* (Chapel Hill: The University of North Carolina Press, 2015).

Friedman, Vanessa, 'Hedi Slimane's Celine: Mamma Mia! Here We Go Again', *The New York Times* (29 September 2018), https://www.nytimes.com/2018/09/29/fashion/celine-hedi-slimane-paris-fashion-week.html.

Fury, Alexander, 'The Alternatives: Designers Subverting Fashion's Status Quo', *The New York Times* (19 August 2015), https://www.nytimes.com/2015/08/19/t-magazine/vetements-matthew-adams-dolan-alyx-martine-rose.html.

Fury, Alexander, *Dior Catwalk: The Complete Collections* (London: Thames and Hudson, 2017).

Fury, Alexander, 'Fashion in the Flesh: Real Shows Return to Milan', *The Financial Times* (24 June 2021), https://www.ft.com/content/6057f8cc-5ad5-4207-bdcc-fbe70951cbf4.

Fury, Alexander, *Vivienne Westwood Catwalk: The Complete Collections* (London: Thames and Hudson, 2021).

BIBLIOGRAPHY

Gant, Essence, 'This Model Said Stylists Would Be Fired If They Couldn't Do White Models' Hair, And She's Right', *Buzzfeed* (5 October 2017), https://www.buzzfeed.com/essencegant/this-model-blasted-industry-after-fashion-wk-stylists?utm_term=.sh5zm4da2V#.paYZ4jaKRp.

Geczy, Adam and Karaminas, Vicki, *Critical Fashion Practice: From Westwood to Van Beirendonck* (London: Bloomsbury, 2017).

Geczy, Adam and Karaminas, Vicki, eds, *The End of Fashion: Clothing and Dress in the Age of Globalization* (London: Bloomsbury, 2019).

Gevisser, Mark, *The Pink Line: The World's Queer Frontiers* (London: Profile Books, 2020).

Giddens, Anthony, *Modernity and Self-Identity: Self and Society in the Late Modern Age* (Cambridge: Polity Press, 1991).

Giorgi, Liana and Marsh, Catherine, 'The Protestant Work Ethic as a Cultural Phenomenon', *European Journal of Social Psychology*, 20:6 (1990), 499–517.

Glazebrook, Matt, '10 Iconic Kate Moss Covers', *i-D* (19 February 2020), https://i-d.vice.com/en_uk/article/xgqvkw/10-iconic-kate-moss-magazine-covers.

Goelet, Ogden, 'Nudity in Ancient Egypt', *Notes in the History of Art*, 12:2 (1993), 20–31.

Goetz, Adrien, *Marie-Antoinette* (New York: Assouline, 2005).

Gonzales, Erica, 'Carmen Dell'Orefice, 85 Years Young, Closed a Couture Show', *Harper's Bazaar* (27 January 2017), https://www.harpersbazaar.com/fashion/models/news/a20233/carmen-dell-orefice-guo-pei-couture/.

Gonzales, Julia, 'Prada Scrambles To Remove Monkey Collection Amid Racist Backlash', *UWIRE Text* (16 December 2018), https://go.gale.com/ps/i.do?p=AONE&u=mmucal5&id=GALE|A566009545&v=2.1&it=r&sid=bookmark-AONE&asid=5d75f4d9.

Goorwich, Siam, 'Male Model Lets it All Hang Out on NYFW Catwalk Show', *METRO* (20 February 2015), https://metro.co.uk/2015/02/20/male-model-lets-it-all-hang-out-on-nyfw-catwalk-show-5071448/.

Gordon, Beverly, *The Saturated World: Aesthetic Meaning, Intimate Objects, Women's Lives, 1890–1940* (Knoxville: University of Tennessee Press, 2006).

Graeber, David and Wengrove, David, *The Dawn of Everything: A New History of Humanity* (London: Penguin, 2021).

Graham, David, 'Roma Hit the Runway', *Toronto Star* (26 June 2008), https://www.thestar.com/life/2008/06/26/roma_hit_the_runway.html.

Gramsci, Antonio, *Selections from Cultural Writings*, eds. David Forgas and Geoffrey Nowell-Smith, trans. William Boelhower (London: Lawrence and Wishart, 1985).

Granata, Francesca, *Experimental Fashion: Performance Art, Carnival and the Grotesque Body* (London and New York: I.B. Tauris, 2017).

Grech, Shaun, 'Decolonising Eurocentric Disability Studies: Why Colonialism Matters in the Disability and Global South Debate', *Journal for the Study of Race, Nation and Culture*, 21:1 (2015), 6–21.

Greenbaum, Daniella, '"Pope Rihanna" and the Met Gala Expose the Double Standard of What People Will Consider Cultural Appropriation', *Business Insider* (8 May 2018), https://www.businessinsider.com/rihanna-pope-met-gala-double-standard-cultural-appropriation-2018-5?r=US&IR=T.

Haber, Carole and Gratton, Brian, *Old Age and the Search for Security: An American Social History* (Bloomington and Indianapolis: Indiana University Press, 1994).

Habermas, Jürgen, *The Philosophical Discourse of Modernity: Twelve Lectures* (Cambridge, MA: MIT Press, 1987).

Hall, Catherine, 'Introduction: Thinking the Postcolonial, Thinking the Empire', *Cultures of Empire: Colonizers in Britain and the Empire in the Nineteenth and Twentieth Centuries. A Reader*, ed. Catherine Hall (Manchester: Manchester University Press, 2000), 1–33.

Hall, Steve, 'United Colors of Benetton Returns From Dead with New Campaign', *AdRants* (30 May 2007), https://www.adrants.com/2007/05/united-colors-of-benetton-returns-from.php.

Hall, Stuart, 'Race, Articulation, and Societies Structured in Dominance', *Black British Cultural Studies: A Reader*, eds. Houston A. Baker, Jr., Manthia Diawara and Ruth H. Lindeborg (Chicago and London: The University of Chicago Press, [1980] 1996), 305–345.

Harris, Oliver J. T., Hughes, Jessica, Osborne, Robin, Robb, John and Stoddart, Simon, 'The Body and Politics', *The Body in History: Europe from the Paleolithic to the Future* (Oxford: Oxford University Press, 2013), 98–128.

Hartnell, Jack, *Medieval Bodies: Life, Death and Art in the Middle Ages* (London: Profile Books, 2018).

Harvey, John, 'From Black in Spain to Black in Shakespeare', *The Men's Fashion Reader*, eds. Peter McNeil and Vicki Karaminas (London: Berg, 2009), 19–43.

Heise, Lori, Ellsberg, Mary and Gottmoeller, M., 'A Global Overview of Gender-Based Violence', *International Journal of Gynecology and Obstetrics*, 78:Supplement 1 (2002), 5–14.

Held, Amy, 'Gucci Apologizes and Removes Sweater Following "Blackface" Backlash', *NPR* (7 February 2019), https://www.npr.org/2019/02/07/692314950/gucci-apologizes-and-removes-sweater-following-blackface-backlash?t=1629114462933&t=1629197197660.

Heller, Susie, 'People Are Pretending to Fall Out of Cars and Posing Amid Strewn Luxury Goods for the Viral "flaunt your wealth" Challenge on Instagram', *Insider* (24 October 2018), https://www.insider.com/viral-flaunt-your-wealth-challenge-weibo-instagram-2018-10.

Helmore, Edward, 'Adidas to Investigate Claims Kanye West Showed Pornography to Staff', *The Guardian* (24 November 2022), https://www.theguardian.com/music/2022/nov/24/adidas-kanye-west-investigation.

Hernández, Javier C. and Mou, Zoe, '"I Am Gay, Not a Pervert" Furor in China as Sina Weibo Bans Gay Content', *The New York Times* (15 April 2018), https://www.nytimes.com/2018/04/15/world/asia/china-gay-ban-sina-weibo-.html.

Hertz, Noreena, *The Lonely Century: Coming Together in a World that's Pulling Apart* (London: Sceptre, 2020).

Hinchy, Jessica, 'The Sexual Politics of Imperial Expansion: Eunuchs and Indirect Colonial Rule in Mid-Nineteenth-Century North India', *Gender, Imperialism and Global Exchanges*, eds. Stephan F. Miescher, Michelle Mitchell and Naoko Shibusawa (Chichester: John Wiley & Sons, 2015), 25–48.

Hinde, Natasha, 'Burberry Apologises and Removes "Noose" Hoodie after Model's Complaints', *The Huffington Post* (19 February 2019), https://www.huffingtonpost.co.uk/entry/burberry-apologises-for-noose-hoodie-model-complaints_uk_5c6bd76ae4b01cea6b88fff7.

Hirsch, Susan F. and Lazarus-Black, Mindie, 'Introduction/Performance and Paradox: Exploring Law's Role in Hegemony and Resistance', *Contested States: Law, Hegemony, and Resistance*, eds. Mindie Lazarus-Black and Susan F. Hirsch (London: Routledge, 1994), 1–34.

BIBLIOGRAPHY

Hobsbawm, Eric, 'Mass-Producing Traditions: Europe, 1870–1914', *The Invention of Tradition*, eds. Eric Hobsbawm and Terence Ranger (Cambridge: Cambridge University Press, 1983), 263–308.

Hoffman, Philip T., *Why Did Europe Conquer the World?* (Princeton: Princeton University Press, 2015).

Hollander, Anne, *Seeing Through Clothes* (Berkeley and Los Angeles: University of California Press, 1975).

Hollander, Anne, *Sex and Suits: The Evolution of Modern Dress* (New York: Alfred A. Knopf, 1994).

Honigman, Ana Finel, *What Alexander McQueen Can Teach You About Fashion* (London: Frances Lincoln Publishing, 2021).

Horyn, Cathy, 'Year of Couturière', *The New York Times* (1 December 2010), https://archive.nytimes.com/tmagazine.blogs.nytimes.com/2010/12/01/year-of-the-couturiere/?_r=2.

Hsu, Tiffany and Steel, Emily, 'Victoria's Secret Executive Leaves as Company Distances Itself from Epstein', *The New York Times* (5 August 2019), https://www.nytimes.com/2019/08/05/business/victorias-secret-ed-razek.html.

Hunt, William, 'Jimmy Choo: Simmer in the Dark: The Brand Taps Cara Delevingne for Cruise 18', *Wonderland* (9 November 2017), https://www.wonderlandmagazine.com/2017/11/09/jimmy-choo-cruise-18/.

Hupperts, Charles, 'Homosexuality in Greece and Rome', *Gay Life and Culture: A World History*, ed. Robert Aldrich (London: Thames and Hudson, 2006), 29–56.

Hutton, Ronald, *The Stations of the Sun: A History of the Ritual Year in Britain* (Oxford: Oxford University Press, 1996)

Huynh, Mélanie et al., 'Cadeaux', Parisian *Vogue* (Paris: Condé Nast, December 2010/January 2011), 61–102.

Hyland, Véronique, '85-Year-Old Model Carmen Dell'Orefice Closed a Couture Show', *The Cut* (26 January 2017), https://www.thecut.com/2017/01/carmen-dellorefeice-guo-pei-spring-2017-couture.html.

Irigaray, Luce, *This Sex Which Is Not One*, translated by Catherine Porter (Ithaca: Cornell University Press, [1977] 1985).

Izek, Emma, 'Haute Homeless is a Faulted Fad' (7 June 2019), https://medium.com/@eizek/about.

James, Alistair, 'Russian Prosecutors Want to Ban Dolce & Gabbana Same-Sex Kiss Adverts', *Attitude* (27 May 2021), https://attitude.co.uk/article/russian-prosecutors-want-to-ban-dolce-gabbana-same-sex-kiss-adverts/25073/.

Jameson, Fredric, 'Culture and Finance Capital', *Critical Inquiry*, 24:1 (1997), 246–265.

Jameson, Fredric, *Postmodernism, Or The Cultural Logic of Late Capitalism* (London: Verso, 1991).

Jasman, Asri, 'Meet Prada's New Pradamalia Collectibles', *Esquire* (12 October 2018), https://www.esquiresg.com/prada-accessories-new-pradamalia-collectibles/.

Jenss, Heike, 'Introduction: Locating Fashion/Studies: Research Methods, Sites and Practices', *Fashion Studies: Research Methods, Sites, and Practices*, ed. Heike Jenss (London: Bloomsbury, 2016), 1–18.

Jobling, Paul, Nesbitt, Philippa and Wong, Angelene, *Fashion, Identity, Image* (London: Bloomsbury, 2022).

Jones, Terry, *Rick Owens* (Cologne: Taschen, 2013).

Kaiser, Susan B., *Fashion and Cultural Studies* (London: Bloomsbury, 2019).

Kalifa, Dominique, ed., *Les noms d'epoque: De <<Restauration>> à <<années de plomb>>* (Paris: Éditions Gallimard, 2019).

Kantor, Jodi and Twohey, Megan, 'Harvey Weinstein Paid Off Sexual Harassment Accusers for Decades', *The New York Times* (5 October 2017), https://www.nytimes.com/2017/10/05/us/harvey-weinstein-harassment-allegations.html.

Kapferer, Jean-Noël, 'The Artification of Luxury: From Artisans to Artists', *Business Horizons*, 57 (2014), 371–380.

Kawamura, Yuniya, *Fashion-ology: An Introduction to Fashion Studies* (Oxford: Berg, 2005).

Kawano, Satsuki, 'Japanese Bodies and Western Ways of Seeing in the Late Nineteenth Century', *Dirt, Undress, and Difference: Critical Perspectives on the Body's Surface*, ed. Adeline Masquelier (Bloomington and Indianapolis: Indiana University Press, 2005), 149–167.

Keevak, Michael, *Becoming Yellow: A Short History of Racial Thinking* (Princeton: Princeton University Press, 2011).

Kendrick, 'Guo Pei is a Legend, not because She Named Her Fashion Show "Legend", but for Her Art', *Benude* (1 September 2019), https://medium.com/@luci_38260/guo-pei-is-a-legend-not-because-she-named-her-fashion-show-legend-but-for-her-art-a874d4423c87.

Kersting, Felix, Wohnsiedler, Iris and Wolf, Nikolaus, 'Weber Revisited: The Protestant Ethic and Spirit of Nationalism', *The Journal of Economic History*, 80:3 (2020), 710–745.

Kiernan, Ben, *Blood and Soil: A World History of Genocide and Extermination from Sparta to Darfur* (New Haven: Yale University Press, 2007).

Kington, Tom, 'Rebuff for Westwood', *The Guardian* (24 June 2005), https://www.theguardian.com/lifeandstyle/2008/jun/24/fashion.italy.

Klein, Alyssa Vingan, 'Internal Memo From Gucci CEO Shows He's Taking The Blackface Scandal Very, Very Seriously', *Fashionista* (11 February 2019), https://fashionista.com/2019/02/gucci-blackface-sweater-ceo-marco-bizzarri-statement.

Kristeva, Julia, 'Stabat Mater', *Poetics Today*, 6:1/2 (1985), 133–152.

Kweku Nimo, Ken, *Africa Fashion: Luxury, Craft and Textile Heritage* (London: Laurence King, 2022).

Labouvier, Chaédria, 'This Black Model's "Messy" Hair Sparked Debate on Social Media', *Allure* (10 November 2017), https://www.allure.com/story/madewell-model-messy-hair-debate.

Lage, Ayana, 'Everyone Is Pissed At Madewell For This Black Model's Hair, But There May Be More To The Story', *Bustle* (13 November 2017), https://www.bustle.com/p/everyone-is-pissed-at-madewell-for-this-black-models-hair-but-there-may-be-more-to-the-story-3909817.

Lalanne, Olivier, 'Édito', France *GQ* (March 2021), 13.

Langner, Lawrence, *The Importance of Wearing Clothes* (Los Angeles: Elysium Growth Press, 1991).

Larbi, Miranda, 'Everyone Thinks Cara Delevingne's New Jimmy Choo ad is Sexist – Do You?', *Metro* (24 December 2017), https://metro.co.uk/2017/12/24/everyone-thinks-cara-delevingnes-new-jimmy-choo-ad-sexist-7183143/.

Lash, Scott and Urry, John, *The End of Disorganized Capital* (Cambridge: Polity Press, 1987).

Lau, Susie, '"Nudity is the most simple and primal gesture": The Designer Reflects on His Full-Frontal Fashion Statement', *Dazed Digital*, 23 January 2015, https://www.dazeddigital.com/fashion/article/23285/1/rick-owens-aw15-livestream.

Lee, Edmund, 'The White Issue: Has Anna Wintour's Diversity Push Come Too Late', *The New York Times* (24 October 2020), https://www.nytimes.com/2020/10/24/business/media/anna-wintour-vogue-race.html.

Lehman, Peter, *Running Scared: Masculinity and the Representation of the Male Body* (Philadelphia: Temple University Press, 1993).
Leitch, Luke, 'Thom Browne: Spring 2019 Menswear', *Vogue* (23 June 2018), https://www.vogue.com/fashion-shows/spring-2019-menswear/thom-browne.
Leopardi, Giacomo, *Dialogue between Fashion and Death*, translated by Giovanni Cecchetti (London: Penguin, 2020).
Leroi, Armand Marie, *Mutants: On the Form, Varieties and Errors of the Human Body* (London: HarperCollins, 2003).
Lester, David, 'Culture and Suicide', *Suicide: A Global Perspective*, ed. Maurizio Pompili (Bentham Science Publishers, 2012), 9–29.
Lewis, Jayne Elizabeth, *Mary Queen of Scots: Romance and Nation* (London: Routledge, 1998).
Lipovetsky, Gilles, *The Empire of Fashion: Dressing Modern Democracy*, translated by Catherine Porter (Princeton and Oxford: Princeton University Press, [1987] 1994).
Lisner, Ari, 'Prayers Up: How God Became the Hottest Thing in Fashion', *GQ* (31 August 2021), https://www.gq.com/story/god-is-trending.
Lorde, Audre, *The Master's Tools Will Never Dismantle The Master's House* (London: Penguin, 2018).
Luvaas, Brent and Eicher, Joanne B., eds., *The Anthropology of Dress and Fashion: A Reader* (London: Bloomsbury, 2019).
Lysenko, Ekaterina, 'Alexander McQueen: Eye SS 2000', *Vernite potselui* (23 March 2000), https://vernitepotselui.ru/2020/03/23/alexander-mcqueen-eye-ss-2000/.
MacLean, Nancy, *Behind the Mask of Chivalry: The Making of the Second Ku Klux Klan* (Oxford: Oxford University Press, 1994).
Mail Foreign Service, 'Far Too Much, Far Too Young: Outrage over Shocking Images of the 10-YEAR-OLD Model Who has Graced the Pages of Vogue', *The Daily Mail* (10 August 2011), https://www.dailymail.co.uk/femail/article-2022305/Thylane-Lena-Rose-Blondeau-Shocking-images-10-YEAR-OLD-Vogue-model.html.
Maldonado, Anabel, 'In Defense of Hedi Slimane', *Business of Fashion* (16 October 2018), https://www.businessoffashion.com/opinions/news-analysis/defense-of-hedi-slimane-celine (accessed April 2021).
Marcelle, Pierre, 'le coup du SDF, par Dior', *Libération* (20 January 2000), https://www.liberation.fr/tribune/2000/01/20/le-coup-du-sdf-par-dior_313901/.
Marriott, Hannah, 'Penises on the Fashion Catwalk – A Flesh Flash Too Far?' *The Guardian* (22 January 2015), https://www.theguardian.com/fashion/2015/jan/22/-sp-penis-flashing-at-rick-owens-menswear-show.
Massad, Joseph A., *Desiring Arabs* (Chicago and London: University of Chicago Press, 2007).
Massad, Joseph A., 'Re-Orienting Desire: The Gay International and the Arab World', *Public Culture*, 14:2 (2002), 361–385.
Mauriès, Patrick, *Androgyne: Fashion and Gender* (London: Thames and Hudson, 2017).
Mautz, Brian S., Wong, Bob B. M., Peters, Richard A. and Jennions, Michael D., 'Penis Size Interacts with Body Shape and Height to Influence Male Attractiveness', *Proceedings of the National Academy of Sciences of the United States of America*, 110:17 (2013), 6925–6930.
McCabe, Jess, 'Benetton uses Domestic Violence to Sell Clothes?' *The f word* (27 May 2007), https://thefword.org.uk/2007/05/benetton_uses_d/.
McCall, Tyler, 'Gucci Out-Guccis Itself for Fall 2018', *Fashionista* (21 February 2018), https://fashionista.com/2018/02/gucci-fall-2018-review.

McClintock, Anne, *Imperial Leather: Race, Gender and Sexuality in the Colonial Contest* (London: Routledge, 1995).

McCracken, Grant, 'The Making of Modern Consumption', *Culture and Consumption: New Approaches to the Symbolic Character of Consumer Goods and Activities* (Bloomington and Indianapolis: Indiana University Press, 1985).

McCue, James F., 'The Doctrine of Transubstantiation from Berengar through Trent: The Point at Issue', *The Harvard Theological Review*, 61:3 (1968), 385–430.

McDowell, Colin, *The Anatomy of Fashion: Why We Dress The Way We Do* (London: Phaidon, 2013).

McGovern, Terry, Heilbrunn, Harriet and Robert, H., 'Overturning Row v Wade has had an Immediate and Chilling Effet on Reproductive Healthcare', *The BMJ* (30 June 2022), https://www.bmj.com/content/377/bmj.o1622.

Mears, Patricia and Bruce Boyer, G., 'Introduction', *Elegance in an Age of Crisis: Fashions of the 1930s*, eds. Patricia Mears and G. Bruce Boyer (New Haven and London: Yale University Press, 2014), 1–16.

Mellor, Sophie, '"I can say anti-Semitic things, and Adidas can't drop me. Now what?" As Kanye West Taunts Adidas, Calls Grow for German Sportswear Giant to Cut Ties', *Fortune* (24 October 2022), https://fortune.com/2022/10/24/i-can-say-anti-semitic-things-and-adidas-cant-drop-me-now-what-as-kanye-west-taunts-adidas-calls-grow-for-german-sportswear-giant-to-cut-ties/.

Menkes, Suzy, 'Galliano's Hobo Couture Takes on the Old Masters: DECONSTRUCTING DIOR', *The New York Times* (18 January 2000), https://www.nytimes.com/2000/01/18/style/IHT-gallianos-hobo-couture-takes-on-the-old-masters-deconstructing-dior.html.

Menkes, Suzy, 'The Power of the Show', *The World of Jean Paul Gaultier: From Sidewalk to Catwalk*, ed. Thierry-Maxime Loriot (New York: Abrams, 2011), 20–23.

Menninghaus, Winfried, 'Caprices of Fashion in Culture and Biology: Charles Darwin's Aesthetics of "Ornament"', *Philosophical Perspectives on Fashion*, eds. Giovanni Matteucci and Stefano Marino (London: Bloomsbury, 2017), 137–150.

Merelli, Annalisa, 'When Fashion Shoots Try to make Social Commentary, the Result is Often Ugly', *Quartz* (6 August 2014), https://qz.com/245343/when-fashion-shoots-try-to-make-social-commentary-the-result-is-often-ugly/.

Merrick, Joav, Tenenbaum, Ariel, Morad, Mohammed and Carmeli, Eli, 'A Short History of Disability Aspects from Israel', *The Routledge History of Disability*, eds. Roy Hanes, Ivan Brown and Nancy E. Hansen (London: Routledge, 2018), 94–114.

Michault, Jessica, 'Fendi Couture Fall Winter 2015 Paris', *NowFashion* (no date), https://nowfashion.com/fendi-couture-fall-winter-2015-paris-15076.

Michault, Jessica, 'Vivienne Westwood: Gypsy on the Road', *The New York Times* (23 June 2008), https://www.nytimes.com/2008/06/23/style/23iht-rwest.1.13911862.html.

Miller, Daniel, 'The Little Black Dress is the Solution. But What's the Problem?' *Elusive Consumption*, eds. K. Ekstrom and H. Brembeck (Oxford: Berg, 2004), 113–127.

Miller, Daniel, 'Materiality: An Introduction', *Materiality*, ed. Daniel Miller (Durham and London: Duke University Press, 2005), 1–50.

Miller, Daniel, *Modernity: An Ethnographic Approach* (London: Routledge, 1994).

Miller, Daniel, 'Why Clothing is not Superficial', *Stuff* (Cambridge: Polity Press, 2010), 11–23.

Moisse, Katie, '10-Year-Old Model's Grown-Up Look: High Fashion or High Risk?', *ABC News* (3 August 2011), https://abcnews.go.com/Health/w_MindBodyResource/10-year-models-grown-high-fashion-high-risk/story?id=14221160.

Monaghan, John and Just, Peter, *Social and Cultural Anthropology: A Very Short Introduction* (Oxford: Oxford University Press, 2000).
Moore, Booth, 'Is Hedi Slimane the Donald Trump of Fashion?', *The Hollywood Reporter* (30 September 2018), https://www.hollywoodreporter.com/lifestyle/style/is-hedi-slimane-donald-trump-fashion-1148087/.
Moore, Madison, *Fabulous: The Rise of the Beautiful Eccentric* (New Haven and London: Yale University Press, 2018).
Moran, Lee, 'Jimmy Choo's "Tone Deaf" Ad Goes Viral For All The Wrong Reasons', *The Huffington Post* (22 December 2017), https://www.huffingtonpost.co.uk/entry/jimmy-choo-ad-sexist_n_5a3cd44ae4b0b0e5a7a1499d?ri18n=true.
More, Thomas, *Utopia*, translated by Paul Turner (London: Penguin Books, 1965).
Morgan, Piers, 'If the Met Gala was Islam or Jewish-themed, all Hell would Break Loose – So Why Was It OK for a Bunch of Flesh-Flashing Celebrities to Disrespect MY Religion?' *The Daily Mail* (9 May 2018), https://www.dailymail.co.uk/news/article-5703953/PIERS-MORGAN-Met-Islam-Jewish-themed-hell-break-loose-disrespect-religion.html.
Morley, John E., 'A Brief History of Geriatrics', *Journal of Gerontology*, 59A:11 (2004), 1132–1152.
Morris, Colin, *The Discovery of the Individual 1050–1200* (Toronto: University of Toronto Press, 1987).
Moss, Rachel, '"Gang Rape" Dolce & Gabbana Advert Brings Yet More Controversy For Brand After "Synthetic" IVF Comments', *The Huffington Post* (18 March 2015), https://www.huffingtonpost.co.uk/2015/03/18/dolce-and-gabbana0gang-rape-advert_n_6893044.html.
Mouzat, Virginie, 'Galliano s'en va', *Madame Figaro* (2 March 2011), https://madame.lefigaro.fr/style/galliano-sen-020311-139146.
Mower, Sarah, 'Burberry: Fall 2018 Ready-to-Wear', *Vogue* (17 February 2018), https://www.vogue.com/fashion-shows/fall-2018-ready-to-wear/burberry-prorsum#gallery-atmosphere.
Mower, Sarah, 'Burberry Fall 2019 Ready-to-Wear', *Vogue* (17 February 2019), https://www.vogue.com/fashion-shows/fall-2019-ready-to-wear/burberry-prorsum.
Mower, Sarah, 'Celine: Pre-Fall 2018', *Vogue.com* (2 May 2018), https://www.vogue.com/fashion-shows/pre-fall-2018/celine.
Mower, Sarah, 'Gucci: Fall 2018 Ready-to-Wear', *Vogue* (21 February 2021), https://www.vogue.com/fashion-shows/fall-2018-ready-to-wear/gucci.
Mueller, Jennifer C., Dirks, Danielle and Picca, Leslie Houts, 'Unmasking Racism: Halloween Costuming and Engagement of the Racial Other', *Qualitative Sociology*, 30 (April 2007), 315–335.
Mulholland, Monique, 'Sexy and Sovereign? Aboriginal Models Hit the "multicultural mainstream"', *Cultural Studies*, 33:2 (2019), 198–222.
Mulvey, Laura, 'Visual Pleasure in Narrative Cinema', *Screen*, 16:3 (1975), 6–18.
Munzenrider, Kyle, 'Victoria's Secret Exec Explains Why They Don't Use Trans or Plus-Size Models', *W Magazine* (9 November 2018), https://www.wmagazine.com/story/victorias-secret-fashion-show-ed-razek-comments-trans-plus-size-models.
Murcho, Ana, '*São mamas, estúpido!*' *Vogue Portugal* (April 2021), 132–135.
Murray, Daisy, 'Let's All Hope We Will Be as Fabulous as Carmen Dell'Orefice When We Are 85', *Elle* (30 January 2017), https://www.elle.com/uk/fashion/trends/articles/a33668/lets-all-hope-we-will-be-as-fabulous-as/.
Murray, Stephen O. and Roscoe, Will, 'Overview', Part II, West Africa, *Boy-Wives and Female Husbands: Studies in African Homosexualities*, eds. Stephen O. Murray and Will Roscoe (Albany: State University of New York Press, 1998), 182–212.

Nanda, Gunjan, 'Karl Lagerfeld's Fur Controversy with PETA', *I Knock Fashion* (14 July 2019), https://www.iknockfashion.com/karl-lagerfelds-fur-controversy-with-peta.

Niessen, Sandra, 'Defining Defashion: A Manifesto for Degrowth', *International Journal of Fashion Studies*, 9:2 (2022), 439–444.

Nnadi, Chioma, 'Oh Baby! Rihanna's Plus One', *Vogue* (12 April 2022), https://www.vogue.com/article/rihanna-cover-may-2022.

Norton, Rictor, *The Myth of the Modern Homosexual: Queer History and the Search for Cultural Unity* (London and Washington: Cassell, 1997).

Nudd, Tim, 'Stefano Gabbana: Really, We Love Women!', *Adweek* (7 March 2007), https://www.adweek.com/creativity/stefano-gabbana-really-we-love-women-17647/.

O'Connor, Suzy, 'Cameron Moves To Protect Child Models and Children', *Talent Management Blog* (20 October 2011), https://www.talentmanagement.com/blog/2011/10/3772/.

Offenhartz, Jake, 'Soho Prada Pulls "Extremely Racist" Products with "Blackface Imagery" From Window Display', *Gothamist* (14 December 2018), https://gothamist.com/news/soho-prada-pulls-extremely-racist-products-with-blackface-imagery-from-window-display.

Offer, John, 'From "natural selection" to "survival of the fittest": On the Significance of Spencer's Refashioning of Darwin in the 1860s', *Journal of Classical Sociology*, 14:2 (2014), 156–177.

Ongley, Hannah, 'Jimmy Choo's Cara Delevingne Catcalling Ad is "Tone Deaf", Says Twitter', *i-D* (20 December 2017), https://i-d.vice.com/en_uk/article/kznwex/jimmy-choos-cara-delevingne-catcalling-ad-is-tone-deaf-says-twitter.

Ongley, Hannah and i-D staff, 'Sofia Coppola Explores First Kisses and Crushes for Calvin Klein's New Underwear Campaign', *i-D* (18 April 2017), https://i-d.vice.com/en_uk/article/nenvd7/sofia-coppola-explores-first-kisses-and-crushes-for-calvin-kleins-new-underwear-campaign.

Onishi, Norimitsu and Méheut, Constant, 'Heating Up Culture Wars, France to Scour Universities for Ideas That "Corrupt Society"', *The New York Times* (18 February 2020), https://www.nytimes.com/2021/02/18/world/europe/france-universities-culture-wars.html.

Orieul, Anaïs, '"Il faut souffrir pour être belle": 8 tendances beauté très douloureuses qui ont marqué l'histoire', *The Huffington Post* (1 January 2016), https://www.huffingtonpost.fr/2016/01/01/souffrir-pour-etre-belle-8-tendances-beaute-douloureuses_n_8889156.html.

Ortved, John, 'The Mustache Is Thriving. But What Does It Mean?', *Esquire* (9 July 2020), https://www.esquire.com/style/grooming/a32947149/mustache-trend-history/.

Oschinsky, Dorothea, ed., *Walter of Henley and Other Treaties on Estate Management* (Oxford: Clarendon Press, 1971).

Ovenden, Richard, *Burning the Books: A History of Knowledge Under Attack* (London: John Murray, 2020).

Ovid, *The Art of Love with The Cures of Love and Treatments for the Feminine Fate*, translated by Tom Payne (London: Vintage Books, 2012).

Park, Juyeon and Paff Ogle, Jennifer, 'How Virtual Avatar Experience Interplays with Self-concepts: The Use of Anthropometric 3D Body Models in the Visual Stimulation Process', *Fashion and Textiles*, 8:28 (2021), https://doi.org/10.1186/s40691-021-00257-6.

Pearse, Damien, 'Sexualised Advertising to Children Faces New Rules in Cameron Crackdown', *The Guardian* (24 December 2011), https://www.theguardian.com/media/2011/dec/24/sexualised-advertising-children-cameron-crackdown.

Peck, Patrice, 'J. Crew Just Apologized for a Black Model's Seriously Controversial Hairstyle', *Buzzfeed* (11 November 2017), https://www.buzzfeed.com/patricepeck/this-black-models-hair-is-causing-a-debate-and-people-are.

Perrson, Helen, 'Objects of Desire: The Cult of Shoes', *Shoes: Pleasure & Pain*, ed. Helen Persson (London: V&A Publishing, 2015), 10–21.

Perry, Samuel L., Whitehead, Andrew L., Grubbs, Joshua B., 'Culture Wars and COVID-19 Conduct: Christian Nationalism, Religiosity, and Americans' Behavior during the Coronavirus Pandemic', *Journal for the Scientific Study of Religion*, 59:3 (2020), 405–416.

Petersen, Hayley, 'Jimmy Choo Comes under Fire for "sexist" Ad Depicting Men Cat-Calling a Woman on the Street', *Business Insider* (19 December 2017), https://www.businessinsider.com/jimmy-choo-comes-under-fire-for-ad-depicting-cat-calling-2017-12?r=US&IR=T.

Pham, Minh-Ha T., 'Fashion's Cultural-Appropriation Debate: Pointless', *The Atlantic* (15 May 2014), www.theatlantic.com/entertainment/archive/2014/05/cultural-appropriation-in-fashion-stop-talking-about-it/370826.

Pham, Minh-Ha T., *Asians Wear Clothes on the Internet: Race, Gender, and the Work of Personal Style Blogging* (Durham: Duke University Press, 2015).

Pham, Minh-Ha T., 'Racial Plagiarism and Fashion', *QED*, 4:3 (2017), 67–80.

Pham, Minh-Ha T., *Why We Can't Have Nice Things: Social Media's Influence on Fashion, Ethics, and Property* (Durham: Duke University Press, 2022).

Phelps, N., '"We're Nobody's Third Love, We're Their First Love"—The Architects of the Victoria's Secret Fashion Show Are Still Banking on Bombshells', *Vogue* (8 November 2018), https://www.vogue.com/article/victorias-secret-ed-razek-monica-mitro-interview.

Picheta, Rob, '"Suicide isn't fashion": Burberry Apologizes for Hoodie with Noose around the Neck', *CNN Style* (19 February 2019), https://edition.cnn.com/style/article/burberry-noose-hoodie-scli-gbr-intl/index.html.

Pickering, Michae, 'Experience as Horizon: Koselleck, Expectation and Historical Time', *Cultural Studies*, 18:2–3 (2004), 271–289.

Plant, Dara, 'Must Read: Cara Delevingne's Catcalling Jimmy Choo Ad Prompts Twitter Outrage, Valentino May Sell a Quarter of the Company', *Fashionista* (21 December 2017), https://fashionista.com/2017/12/jimmy-choo-cara-delevingne-ad-controversy.

Plato, *The Republic*, translated by A. D. Lindsay (London: Random House, [1935] 1976).

Porter, Charlie, 'Hermès, Thom Browne SS19 Men's Review: Paris Gets Idealistic', *The Financial Times* (24 June 2018), https://www.ft.com/content/8c71525c-77b5-11e8-bc55-50daf11b720d.

Putin, Vladimir, 'Meeting of the Valdai International Discussion Club', *Kremlin Website* (19 September 2013), http://en.kremlin.ru/events/president/news/19243.

Putin, Vladimir, 'Presidential Address to the Federal Assembly', *Kremlin Website* (12 December 2013), http://en.kremlin.ru/events/president/news/19825.

Quilleriet, Anne-Laure, 'John Galliano raconte 60 ans de Dior', *L'Express* (12 January 2007), https://www.lexpress.fr/styles/mode/john-galliano-raconte-60-ans-de-dior_478779.html.

Rambert, Héloïse, 'Grossophobie: Les hommes aussi', *France GQ* (March 2021), 80–85.

Ramsingh, Katie and Nelson, Marina, 'Milan Fashion Week AW13/14: Day Two', *Global Blue* (21 February 2013), https://www.globalblue.com/destinations/italy/milan-fashion-week-aw13-14-day-two/.

Ratcliffe, Rebecca, 'Singapore to Repeal Law that Criminalises Sex between Men', *The Guardian* (21 August 2022), https://www.theguardian.com/world/2022/aug/21/singapore-to-repeal-law-that-criminalises-sex-between-men.

Reuters, 'Russian Prosecutor Seeks to Ban Dolce & Gabbana Same-Sex Kiss Ads', *Fashion Network* (25 May 2021), https://ww.fashionnetwork.com/news/Russian-prosecutor-seeks-to-ban-dolce-gabbana-same-sex-kiss-ads,1305049.html.

Ribeiro, Aileen, *Dress and Morality* (London: Berg, 2003).

Ribeiro, Aileen, 'Dress in Utopia', *Costume*, 21:1 (1987), 26–33.

Riello, Giorgio, *Back in Fashion: Western Fashion from the Middle Ages to the Present* (New Haven and London: Yale University Press, 2020).

Ritschel, Chelsea, 'Burberry Apologies over Jumper with "noose" on Neck after London Fashion Week Anger', *The Independent* (19 February 2019), https://www.independent.co.uk/life-style/fashion/burberry-noose-jumper-hoodie-sweater-suicide-apology-controversy-a8787006.html.

Rivière, Joan, 'Womanliness as Masquerade', *International Journal of Psychoanalysis*, 10 (1929), 303–313.

Rocamora, Agnès, 'High Fashion and Pop Fashion: The Symbolic Production of Fashion in *Le Monde* and *The Guardian*', *Fashion Theory*, 5:2 (2001), 123–142.

Rochell, Hannah, 'Let the Devil Wear Prada – The Man in the Vatican was Dressed by Christ', *The Times* (12 February 2013), 6–7.

Rose, Hilary, 'Lord! What happened at the Met Ball, Fashion's High Altar', *Times* 2 (9 May 2021), 2–3.

Ross, Robert, *Clothing: A Global History, Or, The Imperialists' New Clothes* (Cambridge: Polity, 2008).

Rotman, David, 'Don't Fear the Gray Tsunami', *MIT Technology Review*, 122: 5 (September/October 2019), 8–11.

Roy, Nilanjana, 'Is "Cancel Culture" a Failure of Kindness?', *The Financial Times* (17/18 April 2021), 10.

Rubin, Gayle S., 'Thinking Sex: Notes for a Radical Theory of the Politics of Sexuality', *Culture, Society and Sexuality: A Reader*, eds. Richard Parker and Peter Aggleton (London: Routledge, [1984] 1999, second edition), 150–187.

Rublack, Ulinka and Riello, Giorgio, 'Introduction', *The Right to Dress: Sumptuary Laws in Global Perspective, c.1200-1800* (Cambridge: Cambridge University Press, 2019), 1–33.

Rublack, Ulinka and Hayward, Maria, eds., *The First Book of Fashion: The Books of Clothes of Matthäus & Veit Konrad Schwarz of Augsburg* (London: Bloomsbury, 2015).

Ruffner, Zoe, '5 Céline Beauty Rules to Get You through Phoebe Philo's Absence Today in Paris', *Vogue.com* (4 March 2018), https://www.vogue.com/article/celine-phoebe-philo-beauty-minimalist-makeup-dick-page-paris-fashion-week.

Rutherford, Jess, 'The MetGala: Heavenly Bodies', *The Oxford Student* (20 May 2018), https://www.oxfordstudent.com/2018/05/20/the-metgala-heavenly-bodies/.

Said, Edward, *Orientalism* (London: Penguin, [1978] 2003).

Salami, Minna, *Sensuous Knowledge: A Black Feminist Approach for Everyone* (London: Zed Books, 2020).

Sanusi, Victoria, 'Solange Responded to the Evening Standard after it Photoshopped Her Braid Out of its Cover', *Buzzfeed* (20 October 2017), https://www.buzzfeed.com

/victoriasanusi/solange-responded-to-the-evening-standard-after-they?utm_term=.rlNalXjDB#.jnbK1XQG6.

Sara, 'Benetton – Campaign on Domestic Violence', *in deep existential crisis . . .* (30 May 2007), https://nuttyorbcreepysara.wordpress.com/2007/05/30/benetton-campaign-on-domestic-violence/.

Schama, Simon, *The Embarrassment of Riches: An Interpretation of Dutch Culture in the Golden Age* (London: Fontana Press, 1987).

Schiebinger, Londa, 'The Anatomy of Difference: Race and Sex in Eighteenth-Century Science', *Eighteenth-Century Studies*, 23:4 (1980), 387–405.

Schiebinger, Londa, *Nature's Body: Gender in the Making of Modern Science* (New Brunswick: Rutgers University Press, 1993).

Schneier, Matthew, 'Karl Lagerfeld on Fur (Yea), Selfies (Nay) and Keeping Busy', *The New York Times* (3 March 2015), https://www.nytimes.com/2015/03/05/fashion/karl-lagerfeld-on-fur-yea-selfies-nay-and-keeping-busy.html?_r=3.

Self, Jack, 'THE BIG FLAT NOW: Power, Flatness, and Nowness in the Third Millennium', *032c* (17 December 2018), https://032c.com/magazine/the-big-flat-now-power-flatness-and-nowness-in-the-third-millennium.

Sennett, Richard, *The Fall of Public Man* (London: Penguin, 1974).

Sennett, Richard, 'Foreward', Gilles Lipovetsky, *The Empire of Things: Dressing Modern Democracy*, translated by Catherine Porter (Princeton: Princeton University Press, 1994),

Sepe, Giorgia and Anzivino, Alessia, 'Guccification: Redefining Luxury Through Art—The Gucci Revolution', *The Artification of Luxury Fashion Brands*, eds. Marta Massi and Alex Turrini (London: Palgrave, 2020), 89–112.

Shakespeare, William, *William Shakespeare: Complete Works*, eds. Jonathan Bate and Eric Rasmussen (Basingstoke: Macmillan, 2007).

Sharkey, Linda, 'Karl Lagerfeld Fights Back against PETA and Defends Use of Fur in Fashion, Saying "A Butcher Shop Is Worse"', *The Independent* (5 March 2015), https://www.independent.co.uk/life-style/fashion/news/a-butcher-shop-is-worse-karl-lagerfeld-fights-back-against-peta-and-defends-use-of-fur-in-fashion-10087884.html.

Sharp, Joanne P., *Geographies of Postcolonialism: Spaces of Power and Representation* (London: Sage, 2009).

Siedentop, Larry, *Inventing the Individual: The Origins of Western Liberalism* (London: Penguin, 2014).

Silva, Cynthia, 'Ariel Nicholson is U.S. Vogue's First Transgender Cover Model', *NBC News* (9 August 2021), https://www.nbcnews.com/nbc-out/out-life-and-style/ariel-nicholson-us-vogues-first-transgender-cover-model-rcna1630.

Simmel, Georg, 'The Metropolis and Mental Life', *Georg Simmel on Individuality and Social Forms*, ed. Donald N. Levine (Chicago and London: The University of Chicago Press, [1903] 1971), 324–339.

Smith, Matt, *Losing Venus* (Oxford: Pitt Rivers Museum, 2020).

Solca, Luca, 'Is Fashion Ready for a Multicultural Minefield?', *Business of Fashion* (17 March 2020), https://www.businessoffashion.com/opinions/luxury/is-fashion-ready-for-a-multicultural-minefield?utm_campaign=1686406403908605&utm_medium=email&utm_source=daily-digest-newsletter&utm_term=11.

Sontag, Susan, 'The Double Standard of Ageing', *An Ageing Population: A Reader and Sourcebook*, eds. Vida Carver and Penny Liddiard (New York: Holmes and Meir, [1972] 1979), 72–80.

Spargo, Chris, 'Dolce & Gabbana under fire AGAIN just Days after Referring to Children Born through IVF as "synthetic" as Critics Discover ad that Depicts "woman being gang raped"', *The Daily Mail* (17 March 2015), https://www.dailymail.co.uk/news/article-2999045/Dolce-Gabbana-fire-just-days-referring-children-born-IVF-synthetic-critics-discover-ad-depicts-woman-gang-raped.html.

Spears, Richard A., 'On the Etymology of *Dike*', *American Speech*, 60:4 (1985), 318–327.

Spinder, Amy, 'Patterns', *The New York Times* (16 March 1993), Section B, 8, https://www.nytimes.com/1993/03/16/news/patterns-082793.html?src=pm.

Stabile, Carol A., *Feminism and the Technological Fix* (Manchester: Manchester University Press, 1994).

Stabile, Carol A., 'Shooting the Mother: Fetal Photography and the Politics of Disappearance', *Camera Obscura*, 10:1 (1992), 178–205.

Stainton, Tim, 'Reason, Value and Persons: The Construction of Intellectual Disability in Western Thought from Antiquity to the Romantic Age', *The Routledge History of Disability*, eds. Roy Hanes, Ivan Brown and Nancy E. Hansen (London: Routledge, 2018), 11–34.

Stansfield, Ted, 'Fendi Brings Its Fur-Only Couture Show to Paris', *Dazed* (9 July 2015), https://www.dazeddigital.com/fashion/article/25421/1/fendi-brings-its-fur-only-couture-show-to-paris.

Stearns, Peter N., *Fat History: Bodies and Beauty in the Modern West* (New York: New York University Press, 1997).

Steele, Valerie, *The Corset: A Cultural History* (New Haven and London: Yale University Press, 2003).

Stepan, Nancy Leys, 'Race and Gender: The Role of Analogy in Science', *Isis*, 77:2 (1986), 261–277.

Stepan, Nancy Leys, 'Race, Gender, Science and Citizenship', *Cultures of Empire: Colonizers in Britain and the Empire in the Nineteenth and Twentieth Centuries. A Reader*, ed. Catherine Hall (Manchester: Manchester University Press, 2000), 61–86.

Stoler, Ann L., 'Making Empire Respectable: The Politics of Race and Sexual Morality in 20th-Century Colonial Cultures', *American Ethnologist*, 16:4 (1989), 634–660.

Stroude, Will, 'Tom Daley Hits Back after Russian State TV's Homophobic Slurs against LGBTQ Olympians', *Attitude* (9 August 2021), https://attitude.co.uk/article/tom-daley-hits-back-after-russian-state-tvs-homophobic-slurs-against-lgbtq-olympians/25564/.

Swidler, Ann, 'Culture in Action: Symbols and Strategies', *American Sociological Review*, 51:2 (April 1986), 273–286.

Tai, Cordelia, 'Diversity Report: The Fall 2018 Runways Were the Most Race and Transgender-Inclusive Ever; Not So Much for Age and Size Diversity', *TheFashionSpot* (22 March 2018), https://www.thefashionspot.com/runway-news/786015-runway-diversity-report-fall-2018/.

Talley, André Leon, *The Chiffon Trenches: A Memoir* (London: 4th Estate, 2020).

Tarlo, Emma, *Entanglement: The Secret Lives of Hair* (London: Bloomsbury, 2016).

Taroff, Kurt, 'Home is Where the Self Is: Monodrama, Journey Plat Structure, and the Modernist Fairy Tale', *Marvels & Tales*, 28:2 (2014), 325–345.

Testa, Jessica, Friedman, Vanessa and Paton, Elizabeth, 'Coronavirus Upends the Fashion Universe', *The New York Times International Edition* (7/8 March 2020), 16.

Tewari, Bandana, 'Burberry's LGBTQ+ Statement Was More Than Marketing', *Business of Fashion* (23 February 2018), https://www.businessoffashion.com/opinions/news-analysis/burberrys-lgbtq-statement-was-more-than-marketing.

TFL, 'Dolce & Gabbana "Love is Love" Ads Allegedly Run Afoul of Russian Anti-Propaganda Law', *TheFashionLaw* (24 May 2021), https://www.thefashionlaw.com/dolce-gabbana-love-is-love-ads-allegedly-run-afoul-of-russian-anti-propaganda-law/.

Thelwall, Mike and Vis, Farida, 'Gender and Image Sharing on Facebook, Twitter, Instagram, Snapchat and WhatsApp in the UK: Hobbying Alone or Filtering for Friends?', *AJIM*, 69:6 (2017), 2050–3806.

Thelwall, Mike, Goriunova, Olga, Vis, Farida, Falkner, Simon, Burns, Anne, Aulich, Jim, Mas-Bleda, Amalia, Stuart, Emma, and D'Orazio, Francesco, 'Chatting Through Pictures? A Classification of Images Tweeted in One Week in the UK and USA', *Journal of the Association for Information Science and Technology*, 67:11 (2016), 2575–2586.

Thomas, Dana, *Gods and Kings: The Rise and Fall of Alexander McQueen and John Galliano* (London: Allen Lane, 2015).

Thompson, Ayanna, *Blackface* (London: Bloomsbury, 2021).

Thompson, Stacy, *Punk Productions: Unfinished Business* (Albany: State University of New York Press, 2004).

Tolentino, Jia, 'The Age of Instagram Face', *The New Yorker* (12 December 2019), https://www.newyorker.com/culture/decade-in-review/the-age-of-instagram-face.

Tom, Marisa, 'Somebody Douse Us in Holy Water Because Sarah Jessica Parker Just Took Us to Church', *Pop Sugar* (8 May 2021), https://www.popsugar.co.uk/fashion/Sarah-Jessica-Parker-Met-Gala-Dress-2018-44820684.

Travae, Marques, 'Ingrid Silva: First Black Brazilian Ballerina Featured on the cover of Vogue Brasil', *Black Brazil Today* (16 November 2020), https://blackbraziltoday.com/ingrid-silva-first-black-brazilian-ballerina-featured-on-the-cover-of-vogue-brasil/.

Travae, Marques, 'Palmitagem: The Discomfort in Thinking about Race and Relationships', *Black Brazil Today* (28 January 2020), https://blackbraziltoday.com/palmitagem-the-discomfort-in-thinking-about-race-and-relationships/.

Tremain, Cara Grace, 'The Varied Body', *The Adorned Body: Mapping Ancient Maya Dress*, ed. Nicholas Carter, Stephen D. Houston and Franco D. Rossi (Austin: University of Texas Press, 2020), 153–165.

Trentmann, Frank, *Empire of Things: How We Became a World of Consumers, from the Fifteenth Century to the Twenty-First* (London: Allen Lane, 2016).

Tschorn, Adam, 'Stello, Formerly MT Costello, Mines the Darker Side of Hollywood in L.A. Fashion Week Debut', *The Los Angeles Times* (9 October 2015), www.latimes.com/fashion/alltherage/la-ar-stello-la-fashion-week-debut-20151008-story.html.

Tsjeng, Zing, 'What Rick Owens' Full-Frontal Runway Show Says about Us', *Dazed Digital* (23 January 2015), https://www.dazeddigital.com/fashion/article/23353/1/what-rick-owens-full-frontal-runway-show-says-about-us.

Twain, Mark, *Mark Twain's Notebook by Mark Twain*, ed. Albert Bigelow Paine (New York: Harper & Brothers, 1897).

Tyler, Imogen, 'Skin-Tight: Celebrity, Pregnancy and Subjectivity', *Transformations: Thinking Through Skin*, eds. Sara Ahmed and Jackie Stacey (London: Routledge, 2001), 69–83.

Usherwood, Bob and Usherwood, Margaret, 'Culture Wars, Libraries and the BBC', *Library Management*, 45:4/5 (2021), 291–301.

Van-De-Peer, Hannah, 'Jimmy Choo Winter Ad 2017: A Problematic Portrayal of Sexism in our Society', *Affinity* (23 December 2017), http://culture.affinitymagazine.us/jimmy-choo-winter-ad-2017-a-problematic-portrayal-of-sexism-in-our-society/.

van den Boogaart, Ernst, 'De Brys' Africa', *Staging New Worlds: De Brys' Illustrated Travel Reports, 1590–1630*, ed. Susanna Burghartz (Basel: Schwabe, 2004), 95–149.

Van Peer, Aurélie, 'The Politics of Fashion Criticism: How Newspaper Journalists' Evaluative Criteria for Fashion Changed Between 1949 and 2020', *Insights on Fashion Journalism*, eds. Rosie Findlay and Johannes Reponen (London: Routledge, 2022), 20–36.

Vaz, Wyanet, 'Fendi Haute Fourrure 2015–2016 Show Decoded', *Verve* (15 July 2015), https://www.vervemagazine.in/fashion-and-beauty/fendi-haute-fourrure-2015-2016-show-decoded.

Vázquez, Rolando, *Vistas of Modernity: Decolonial Aesthesis and the End of the Contemporary* (Amsterdam: Mondriaan Fund, 2020).

Veblen, Thorstein, *The Theory of the Leisure Class*, ed. Martha Banta (Oxford: Oxford University Press, [1899] 2007).

Verley, Frédérique and Aspart, Théodora, '*Quel maquillage à quel âge*', Parisian *Vogue* (Paris: Condé Nast, December 2010/January 2011), 157.

Verner, Amy, 'Guo Pei: Spring 2017 Couture', *Vogue* (27 January 2017), https://www.vogue.com/fashion-shows/spring-2017-couture/guo-pei.

Verreos, Nick, 'RUNWAY REPORT . . . Paris Haute Couture Fashion Week: Guo Pei Couture Spring 2017', *Nick Verreos* (no date), http://nickverreos.blogspot.com/2017/01/runway-reportparis-haute-couture_27.html.

Verstraete, Pieter, Verhaegen, Evelyne and Depaepe, Marc, 'One Difference is Enough: Towards a History of Disability in the Belgian Congo, 1908–1960', *The Routledge History of Disability*, ed. Roy Hanes, Ivan Brown and Nancy E. Hansen (London: Routledge, 2018), 231–242.

Vieira, Luanda, 'Ingrid Silva: "Nada é mais poderoso do que lutar pela próxima geração e, agora, ser responsável por ela"', Vogue *Brazil* (13 November 2020), https://vogue.globo.com/celebridade/noticia/2020/11/ingrid-silva-nada-e-mais-poderoso-do-que-lutar-pela-proxima-geracao-e-agora-ser-responsavel-por-ela.html.

Vieira, Luanda, 'Rita Carreira: "Nunca precisei de terapia para me aceitar, porque em casa não me deixaram cair na ilusão de que a felicidade só estava no padrão"', Brazilian *Vogue* (14 November 2020), https://vogue.globo.com/moda/noticia/2020/11/rita-carreira-nunca-precisei-de-terapia-para-me-aceitar-porque-em-casa-nao-me-deixaram-cair-na-ilusao-de-que-felicidade-so-estava-no-padrao.html.

Vincent, Anthony, '"Rick Owens Gate": les mannequins dévoilent tout, vraiment tout...', France *Grazia* (22 January 2015), https://www.grazia.fr/mode/rick-owens-gate-les-mannequins-devoilent-tout-vraiment-tout-734134.

Vincent, Benjamin William, 'Studying Trans: Recommendations for Ethical Recruitment and Collaboration with Transgender Participants in Academic Research', *Psychology & Sexuality*, 9:2 (2018), 102–116.

Wagstaff, Sheena, 'Embodied Histories', *Like Life: Sculpture, Color, and the Body*, eds. Luke Syson, Sheena Wagstaff, Emerson Bower and Brinda Kumar (New Haven and London: Yale University Press, 2018), 2–13.

Weber, Caroline, *Queen of Fashion: What Marie Antoinette Wore to the Revolution* (London: Aurum, 2006).

Weber, Max, *The Protestant Work Ethic and the "Spirit" of Capitalism*, edited and translated by Peter Baehr and Gordon C. Wells (London: Penguin Books, [1905] 2002).

Welch, Alford T., *Studies in Qur'an and Tafsir* (Riga: Scholars Press, 1980/2008).

Welters, Linda and Lillethun, Abby, *Fashion History: A Global View* (London: Bloomsbury, 2018).

Welters, Linda and Lillethun, Abby, eds., *The Fashion Reader* (London: Bloomsbury, third edition, 2022).
White, Belinda, 'Mother of 10-Year-Old Vogue Model Speaks Out', *The Daily Telegraph* (9 August 2011), http://fashion.telegraph.co.uk/news-features/TMG8690624/Mother-of-10-year-old-Vogue-model-speaks-out.html.
White, Sophie, 'Dressing Enslaved Africans in Colonial Louisiana', *Dressing Global Bodies: The Political Power of Dress in World History*, eds. Beverly Gordon and Giorgio Riello (London: Routledge, 2020), 85–103.
Whitelocks, Sadie and Dumas, Daisy, '10-Year-Old Vogue Model's Mother Shuts Down Facebook Fan Site in Response to Outrage over Daughter's Career', *The Daily Mail* (10 August 2011), https://www.dailymail.co.uk/femail/article-2022979/10-year-old-Vogue-models-mother-shuts-Facebook-fan-site-response-outrage-daughters-career.html.
Wiener, Margaret, 'Breasts, (Un)Dress, and Modernist Desire in the Balinese-Tourist Encounter', *Dirt, Undress, and Difference: Critical Perspectives on the Body's Surface*, ed. Adeline Masquelier (Bloomington and Indianapolis: Indiana University Press, 2005), 61–95.
Wild, Benjamin Linley, *Carnival to Catwalk: Global Reflections on Fancy Dress Costume* (London: Bloomsbury, 2020).
Wild, Benjamin Linley, 'The Civilizing Process and Sartorial Studies', *Clothing Cultures*, 1:3 (2014), 213–224.
Wild, Benjamin Linley, 'Critical Reflections on Cultural Appropriation, Race and the Role of Fancy Dress Costume', *Critical Studies in Fashion and Beauty*, 11:2 (2020), 153–173.
Wild, Benjamin Linley, 'Imitation in Fashion: Further Reflections of the Work of Thorstein Veblen and Georg Simmel', *Fashion, Style & Popular Culture*, 3:1 (2016), 271–294.
Wild, Benjamin Linley, 'We Need to Talk About Fancy Dress Costume: Connections (and Complications) Between the Catwalk and Fancy Dress Costume', *Fashion Theory*, 26:1 (2019), 91–114.
Williams, Alex, 'Fur Is Back in Fashion and Debate', *The New York Times* (3 July 2015), https://www.nytimes.com/2015/07/05/fashion/fur-is-back-in-fashion-and-debate.html.
Williams, Court, 'Art Imitates Life: Dior's "Homeless" Couture', *WWD* (14 April 2010), https://wwd.com/fashion-news/fashion-features/art-imitates-life-diors-homeless-couture-3036220/.
Wilson, Elizabeth, *Adorned in Dreams: Fashion and Modernity* (London: I.B. Tauris, [1985] 2003).
Wilson, Kathleen, *The Island Race: Englishness, Empire and Gender in the Eighteenth Century* (London: Routledge, 2003).
Wintour, Anna, 'Can Fashion Keep Up with 21st-Century Trends', *The Economist* (18 July 2019), https://www.economist.com/podcasts/2019/07/18/can-fashion-keep-up-with-21st-century-trends.
Wolf, Norbert, *Dürer* (Köln: Taschen, 2016).
Wolff, Virginia, *Orlando: A Biography* (London: Vintage Books, [1928] 1992).
Women's Aid, Hester, Marianne, Walker, Sarah-Jane, and Williamson, Emma, *Gendered Experiences of Justice and Domestic Abuse: Evidence for Policy and Practice* (Bristol: Women's Aid, 2021), https://www.womensaid.org.uk/wp-content/uploads/2021/07/FINAL-Gendered-experiences-WA-UoB-July-2021.pdf.
Worth, Rachel, *Fashion and Class* (London: Bloomsbury, 2020).

Wu, Simon W. K. and Chung, Joanna L. P., 'A Journey of Change – History of Disability in Hong Kong 1841–2014', *The Routledge History of Disability*, eds. Roy Hanes, Ivan Brown and Nancy E. Hansen (London: Routledge, 2018), 163–203.

Wyllie, Irvin G., 'Social Darwinism and the Businessman', *Proceedings of the American Philosophical Society*, 103:5 (1959), 629–635.

Yotka, Steff, 'Calvin Klein's New Campaign Proves There's No Age Limit to Being an Underwear Model', *Vogue* (18 April 2017), https://www.vogue.com/article/calvin-klein-lauren-hutton-underwear-ads.

Yuan, Jada and Wong, Aaron, 'The First Black Trans Model Had Her Face on a Box of Clairol', *The Cut* (15 December 2015), https://www.thecut.com/2015/12/tracey-africa-transgender-model-c-v-r.html.

Zargani, Luisa, 'EXCLUSIVE: Gucci's Marco Bizzarri on Learning Amid Blackface Accusations', *WWD* (12 February 2019), https://wwd.com/fashion-news/designer-luxury/gucci-blackface-response-marco-bizzarri-alessandro-michele-1203020161/.

Zargani, Luisa, 'Gucci Launches Initiatives to Foster Cultural Diversity and Awareness', *WWD* (15 February 2021), https://wwd.com/fashion-news/designer-luxury/gucci-launches-initiatives-to-foster-cultural-diversity-and-awareness-1203028610/.

Zimmermann, Harm-Peer, 'Alienation and Alterity: Age in the Existentialist Discourse on Others', *Journal of Aging Studies*, 39 (2016), 83–95.

Zimon, Jill Miller, 'Roots News: Colors of Domestic Violence=fake, *not* Benetton ad, Salon says Feministing "punked"', *Writes Like She Talks* (30 May 2007), https://writeslikeshetalks.blogspot.com/2007/05/colors-of-domestic-violencefake-not.html.

Zittlau, Andrea, 'The Freak Show Act: Science and Spectacle in the Nineteenth Century', *The Routledge History of Disability*, eds. Roy Hanes, Ivan Brown and Nancy E. Hansen (London: Routledge, 2018), 381–393.

Žižek, Slavoj, 'What Donald Rumsfeld Doesn't Know that He Knows about Abu Ghraib' (21 May 2004), https://www.lacan.com/zizekrumsfeld.htm.

INDEX

Abloh, Virgil   4–5, 70, 88
Adorno, Theodor   8
ageing   51, 53, 77, 95–9, 101, 102, 104–5, 107–8
   gendered   100, 108
Andrews, Kehinde   17, 186
appropriation, concept of   68, 118, 123, 126, 128, 186–7
Arbus, Diane   136
Arnault, Bernard   138
Arnold, Rebecca   13, 92
Askill, Lorin   48, 49

Bailey, Christopher   85–7. *See also* Burberry
Balenciaga   101
Bancroft, Alison   25–7
Barry, Ben   176
Barthes, Roland   12
Bartlett, Durdja   172
Baudelaire, Charles   14
Baudrillard, Jean   167
Beat, Duda   167, 168, 171
Beauvoir, Simone de   98
Benedict XVI. *See* religion
Berger, John   21–2, 46, 108, 151. *See also* gender
Bhabha, Homi   8–10, 85, 89. *See also* culture
Bible. *See* religion
blackface. *See* racism

Blanks, Tim   4–5, 70, 90, 135, 188, *See also* Business of Fashion
Bleys, Rudi   76, 78, 79
Blondeau, Thylane Loubry   99, 101, 102, 104, 105, 108
body. *See also* ageing; undress, concept of; violence
   disability   164, 179
   weight   163, 166, 168, 170, 173, 175, 177
Boellstorff, Tom   84–5, 88–94
Bolton, Andrew   15, 114, 116–17
Bonaparte, Napoleon   44
Bowery, Leigh   67
Brodribb, James   173
Browne, Thom   79, 89–94, 127
Burberry   79, 85–9, 91, 149–50, 158–61, 189. *See also* Bailey, Christopher; Tisci, Ricardo
Burckhardt, Jacob   171
Business of Fashion   1, 4, 5, 47, 87, 90. *See also* Blanks, Tim
Butler, Judith   26, 39, 42. *See also* gender

Calavita, Kitty   152, 185–6, 189
Calvin Klein   99, 106–9, 155, 189
Cameron, David   93, 102
Carreira, Rita   167–70
Catty 8.1   167, 177, 181, 189

Celine 42–8. *See also* Slimane, Hedi; Philo, Phoebe
Chodha, Dal 74
civilization 40, 97, 132, 165, 183
Clark, Hazel 27
class, concept of 131–3, 145
Cole, Shuan 140
colonialism 11–12, 36–7, 41, 42, 59, 112, 132, 160, 165
   neocolonialism 85
Condé Nast 176. *See also* Vogue; Wintour, Anna
Confucianism. *See* religion
Coppola, Sofia 106, 107
Covid-19 1, 6, 9, 11, 15, 16, 23, 70, 98, 113, 179
culture, concept of 2–6, 8–15, 22, 33, 39, 47, 54, 63, 67, 70, 77, 78, 83, 85, 95, 97–9, 107, 116–18, 120, 121, 124, 128, 129, 131, 141, 142, 158, 160, 164, 171, 184, 185, 189, 190. *See also* appropriation; Bhabha, Homi; Swidler, Ann
  culture wars 2, 15
  jamming 65, 93
  material 111
    of youth 12, 108
  popular 23, 54, 57, 86, 113, 180
  subcultures 140 (*see also* Punk)

Dabiri, Emma 19, 60, 73
Dan, Dapper 66
Darwin, Charles 59, 166, 167
Davis, Fred 66
Debord, Guy 145, 148, 167
decentralization, concept of 4, 14, 15
Delevingne, Cara 48–51, 86, 88
Dell'Orefice, Carmen 99, 102–7
Dior 47, 133, 136–41, 168

disability. *See* body
Dolce, Domenico. *See* Dolce & Gabbana
Dolce & Gabbana 79–85, 91, 115, 149–55, 161
  Dolce, Domenico 151–3
  Gabbana, Stefano 151–3
Douglas, Grant 167, 173–7
Duberman, Martin 93
Dürer, Albrecht 163
Durkheim, Émile 160

Elias, Norbert 12
Emberley, Julia 126, 127, 136
Engels, Friedrich 132
enlightenment 11, 41, 42, 88, 100
Enninful, Edward 164
Eurocentrism 2, 9, 112, 121
Evans, Caroline 11, 88, 92
Ezie, Chinyere 61–5

Faiers, Jonathan 134–6
Fanon, Frantz 98
fashion
  fantasy of 47, 54–5, 63, 64, 74, 75, 146, 164, 184 (*see also* orientalism)
  journalism 17–18, 37–8, 161, 187–8
feminism. *See* gender
Fendi 23, 133–6. *See also* Lagerfeld, Karl
Finkelstein, Joanne 3, 75, 167
Ford, Tom 99, 155
Foucault, Michel 54, 55, 66, 83, 84, 125–6
  Heterotopia 54–5, 66, 125–7
Friedman, Vanessa 44, 191, 204, 247
fur 133–5, 141
  PETA 133, 135
Fury, Alexander 23

INDEX

Gabbana, Stefano. *See* Dolce & Gabbana
Galliano, John   121, 126, 136–41, 144–6. *See also* Dior; Maison Margiela
Gandhi, Mahatma   87
Gaultier, Jean Paul   102, 113–14, 118–22
Geczy, Adam   8, 70, 71, 92
gender   39–43, 108, 136. *See also* Butler, Judith; Lea T; Nef, Hari; Norman, Tracey; Pejic, Andrea; Sampaio, Valentina
  androgyny   50
  feminism   25–6, 49, 96, 105
  male gaze   44, 46, 48, 108, 150–1
  masculinities   25, 43, 150, 152
    fabulousness   176–7
  #MeToo movement   53
  non-binary   46, 167, 177–81
  transgender   51–2, 54
Gendre, Henrique   32, 33, 35, 37
Gevisser, Mark   79, 81–3, 87
Gibbon, Edward   76
Gil, Preta   167, 168
Giuliani, Rudy   138
Givenchy   52
globalization. *See* modernity
GQ
  British   113
  France   167, 172–7
Graeber, David   59, 183
Gramsci, Antonio   57
Grazia Churi, Maria   47
Grieg, Edvard   103, 105
Groeneveld, Daphne   99
Gucci   13, 61, 66–71, 73, 74, 155, 159, 161. *See also* Michele, Alessandro

Guo Pei   99, 102–6
Gypsy   138, 139. *See also* Romani

Habermas, Jürgen   3–4, 12, 189. *See also* modernity
Hamza, Sharif   99, 102
Harari, Yuval Noah   59
Harper's Bazaar   103, 104, 126
  Arabia   103
  Spain   138
heterotopia. *See* Foucault, Michel
history, concept of   4, 6, 7, 75–6
Hollander, Anne   35
Hutton, Lauren   99, 100, 106–8

Ibsen, Henrik   103, 105
i-D   25, 34
Islam. *See* religion

Jameson, Fredric   6, 12, 13, 130
Jimmy Choo   42, 48–51, 55, 99, 100
Jones, Stephen   90
Judaism. *See* religion

Kaiser, Susan   10
Karaminas, Vicki   8, 70, 71, 92
Karamura, Yuniya   17, 55, 147
Kawakubo, Rei   137
Klein, Steve   149–54, 158
Kristeva, Julia   35–6
Kronthaler, Andreas   142, 144, 145

Lacan, Jacques   25
Lady Gaga   178
Lagerfeld, Karl   133–5, 141, 146, 160. *See also* Fendi
Laver, James   23
Lea T   52. *See also* gender
Lefebvre, Henri   134
Lehman, Peter   27, 190

Leibovitz, Annie   33–5
Leopardi, Giacomo   96, 148
Lipovetsky, Gilles   13, 14, 141
Locke, John   96
Lorde, Audre   9–10

McClaren, Malcolm   140. *See also* Westwood, Vivienne
McQueen, Alexander   55, 114, 122–8, 178
Madewell   61, 71–4
Madonna   136, 168, 171, 172
Maison Margiela   115. *See also* Margiela, Martin
Marchand, Charles Laurent   28–31
Margiela, Martin   137
Marx, Karl   132
masculinities. *See* gender
Massad, Joseph   32
May, Theresa   92
Menkes, Suzie   137
#MeToo movement. *See* Gender
Michele, Alessandro   1, 3, 7, 15, 67, 68. *See also* Gucci
Miller, Daniel   3, 9
modernity   3–4, 146, 160, 188–9. *See also* Habermas, Jürgen; Jameson, Fredric
　globalization   4, 6, 11, 14, 16, 17, 36, 40, 52, 60, 68, 81, 83–9, 98, 167
　time, concept of   10–15, 88, 97
Moore, Demi   33–6
Moore, Madison   176–7
More, Thomas   39, 40, 77
Mower, Sarah   67, 86, 158, 161
MT Costello   23, 28–31, 38
Mulvey, Laura   46. *See also* gender

Nef, Hari   52. *See also* Gender
Norman, Tracey   52. *See also* gender
Norton, Rictor   61, 78, 79

orientalism. *See* Said, Edward
Ovid   95, 109
Owens, Rick   23–9, 31

Parker, Sarah Jessica   155
Pasible, Marihenny   61, 71–3
Pejic, Andrea   52. *See also* gender
PETA. *See* Fur
Pham, Minh-Ha T.   64, 74, 185–7
Philo, Phoebe   43, 44, 47. *See also* Celine
Plato   57, 164
Porter, Charlie   91, 93
postmodernism. *See* modernity
Prada   23, 61–6, 79
Punk   139, 140, 144. *See also* Thompson, Stacy; Westwood, Vivienne
Putin, Vladimir   81–3

race   2, 32–6, 76, 171
　hair   71–3
　whiteness   35, 59, 60, 186, 190
　whitening   33, 35, 171
racism   59, 61, 62, 64
　antisemitism   120, 122
　blackface   61, 63–4, 66–8, 159, 160
　Holocaust   120, 121
　lynching   159, 160
　slavery   33, 37, 60, 61, 64
Raf Simons   107
Razek, Ed   51–4. *See also* Victoria's Secret
religion
　Catholicism   111–18, 125, 127–30, 163, 164, 166
　　Benedict XVI   111–12
　　Bible   22, 30, 111, 164
　　Vatican   111
　Confucianism   164

INDEX

Islam   80, 114, 122–8, 164
Judaism   114, 116, 118–22, 127–8
Protestantism   8, 89, 112, 130
Rihanna   115–18
Rivière, Joan   25
Rocamora, Agnès   18
Romani   142–4. *See also* Gypsy
Rousseau, Jean Jacques   96
Rubin, Gayle   76, 78, 84

Said, Edward   4, 58, 68, 76
  Orientalism   58, 68, 76
Salami, Minna   183, 190,
Sampaio, Valentina   52. *See also* gender
Sartre, Jean-Paul   98
Schiaparelli, Elsa   137
Schiebinger, Londa   40–1, 64
Self, Jack   14
Sennett, Richard   141
sexuality   49, 76, 78, 79, 94. *See also* Stonewall (riots)
  bisexuality   49, 86
  heterosexuality   78, 183
  homosexuality   29, 78, 80, 81, 83, 84, 180, 183, 189
Shakespeare, William   64, 95, 98, 129
SHOWstudio   86, 178
Silva, Ingrid   23, 32–7
Simmel, Georg   13, 145
slavery. *See* racism
Slimane, Hedi   42–8. *See also* Celine
social media   6, 18–19, 24, 48, 52, 61–3, 66, 69, 71–2, 79–81, 91, 92, 101, 102, 118, 153, 158–9, 169, 170, 172, 177–80
Sontag, Susan   108
Spencer, Herbert   166

Stonewall (riots)   177
Stravinsky, Igor   134–5
suicide   158–60
Swidler, Ann   8–10, 42–3, 47, 102, 184–5, 189. *See also* culture

Talley, André Leon   5–6
Thomas, Dana   124
Thompson, Ayanna   63–63, 121
Thompson, Stacy   140, 143–4. *See also* Punk
time, concept of. *See* modernity
Tisci, Ricardo   159. *See also* Burberry
Tomaz, Fernando   168
Toscani, Oliviero   155
transgender. *See* gender
Trump, Donald   43, 47, 76, 92
Turlington, Christy   119
Twain, Mark   21, 23, 39, 184
Tyler, Imogen   33–5

undress, concept of
  Hebriac   21–2, 30
  Hellenic   22–3, 28, 30
  human body
    breasts   23, 32, 178
    penis   23–8, 31, 190
United Colors of Benetton   149, 155–8

Vaccari, Alessandra   88
Vanderperre, Willy   106, 108
Vanity Fair   33–4
Vatican. *See* religion
Veblen, Thorstein   129, 136, 147
Victoria's Secret   42, 51–5. *See also* Razek, Ed
violence   147–50
  domestic abuse   155, 156
  rape   150–4, 185
  'relaxed hair'   73

Vogue 188
   America 2, 42, 54, 107, 116, 117, 125, 138, 158 (*see also* Wintour, Anna)
   Brazil 23, 32–7, 167–72, 174, 181
   British 89, 164 (*see also* Enninful, Edward)
   India 87
   Italy 68, 69
   Paris 99–102, 104
   Portugal 23

Weber, Max 112
Weinstein, Harvey 50–1
Wengrove, David 59, 183
West, Kanye 57–8, 113
Westwood, Vivienne 133, 140, 142–5. *See also* McClaren, Malcolm; Punk
Williams, Serena 34, 36
Wilson, Elizabeth 10–11
Wintour, Anna 1, 3, 7, 15, 70–1, 117, 120, 190. *See also* Vogue
Wolff, Virginia 75
Worth, Rachel 131, 145

youth. *See* ageing; culture

Žižek, Slavoj 189